SUCCESS IN

MANAGING PEOPLE

PENNY HACKETT, MA, PhD, FIPD

JOHN MURRAY

© Penny Hackett 1979, 1985, 1987, 1989, 1990, 1996

First published as Success in Management: Personnel 1979
Reprinted 1985
Second edition 1985
Reprinted (revised) 1987
Third edition 1989
Reprinted (revised) 1990, 1992, 1994
New edition, as Success in Managing People, 1996
Reprinted 1998

Typeset by Colset Pte Ltd, Singapore
Printed and bound in Great Britain by
Biddles Ltd, Guildford and King's Lynn
A CIP catalogue record for this book is available from the
British Library

ISBN 0–7195–7203–7

Contents

Foreword

There is only one boss: the customer. He can fire everybody in the company simply by spending his money somewhere else.

Sam Walton

Public and private sector organisations, providers of services as well as producers of goods, are increasingly recognising the truth of this. As customers' expectations become ever greater, only those who are able continuously to improve the quality, value and service they offer have any real future. Yet the extent to which organisations **succeed** in getting and keeping customers depends, in very large measure, on the people they employ.

Being able to get the right people, in the right place, at the right time, willing and able to do the right things well, and at a cost the organisation can afford has always been fundamental for managers. Today, being able to respond quickly and at minimum cost demands a highly flexible, totally committed team, working together to make sure every necessary element of the process of creating, meeting and exceeding customer expectations is in place and working as efficiently and as effectively as possible.

Success in Managing People aims to help. It is based on *Success in Management: Personnel* but has been thoroughly revised and extended to take account of the latest management thinking and practices, as well as the latest legal requirements. It covers all the essential elements of attracting, recruiting and retaining employees to help build 'world-class' organisations. In particular, new sections on employee development, coaching, team working and empowerment reflect current trends and the likely direction for the future.

The change in title is itself a response to the changing nature of employment. As **staff** management gave way to **personnel** management and then **human resource** management, as a specialist function within management, we were, perhaps, in danger of losing sight of the **people**. In today's flatter, decentralised organisations where traditional demarcation between workers is less clear-cut, we no longer have need of fancy titles. This book is about managing people.

It offers a self-contained course in all aspects of the employment process. It is designed for practising and aspiring managers in commerce, industry and the public service, in the UK and overseas. It is especially appropriate for business and management students whose studies include personnel, the management of human resources, employee relations or employee resourcing, on courses such as the Professional Management Foundation Programme, the certificate and diploma in Management Studies, BTEC Higher national diplomas and certificates and Business Studies degrees.

Each unit is followed by a number of questions. Many of these can be tackled as either written assignments or for oral presentation and class debate. Some also invite students to research the approach taken in their own organisations or to suggest how the ideas might be applied there. Suggestions for further reading are provided at the end of the book.

The ideas presented here are not intended as a prescription, but rather as a guide to the range of approaches and techniques available. Even if your own role does not at present include all the elements covered, I hope you will be able to see how they could apply, to yourself or your colleagues, now or in the future. By taking responsibility for your own learning and, where necessary, coaching your boss or others more senior than yourself, you may well be able to help your organisation move forward.

While every effort has been made to ensure the text is up to date, some parts of it will inevitably be out of date before long. This is particularly true of the sections on employment law which generally feature towards the end of relevant units. Students in countries outside the UK must also recognise that their own legislation differs from that referred to in the book. Please take careful note of changes. This can be done through the parliamentary pages of leading national newspapers and, in the UK, through a legal updating service such as *Croner's Reference Book for Employers* (see 'Suggested Further Reading', page 325).

Although managing people is a serious and important subject, it should also be enjoyable. It has its lighter side too. We have tried to reflect this by using case studies and examples, and by illustrating the text with cartoons by well-known artists.

I have tried to feature both men and women in the examples used, but to help keep the text simple, and for no other reason, I have used the male pronoun where references to the third person are needed. No discrimination is implied and, unless specifically indicated to the contrary, the text applies equally to men and women.

P.J.H.

Acknowledgements

I would like to thank my former colleagues at Kingston University for their help and advice when this book was first written, everyone at C & J Clark International Ltd who has helped me learn so much since and John Whitmore and David Hemery whose approach to developing performance has been a particularly significant influence on my thinking. I am grateful, too, for the guidance I have received from my father, Tom Duncan, and for the unfailing support given by my husband.

Cartoons were kindly provided by the following: Punch Library (pages 92, 132, 159, 179, 214), Ali Press Agency (page 7), *Management in Action* (page 236), Alex Noel Watson (pages 66, 226, 293), Cor Hoekstra (page 248), *Shell News* USA (page 39), Mirror Group Newspapers (pages 107, 311) and *News and Views for Young Workers* (page 203). Special thanks are due to Mrs Cheryl Dowler of Shell International for her help in tracing the sources of these cartoons.

Figure 1.1 (page 2) is based on a graph in *Employment Gazette* (November 1989) with the permission of the Controller of Her Majesty's Stationery Office.

P.J.H.

UNIT 1

People and Profitability

1.1 Introduction

How many people do you need to run a successful business? Taken at face value, this question appears to be as impossible to answer as 'How long is a piece of string?' When we examine it more closely, however, it does raise a number of issues which deserve careful consideration.

The question presupposes that we do need people in order to run businesses. Current unemployment statistics for parts of Great Britain may seem to indicate that we need fewer people to run them than previously, and the type of work which people do may be changing as mechanisation and the demands of society dictate (see Fig. 1.1), but no business can exist entirely without people. (Even computer-automated factories require a few – though a conventional plant with similar capacity might require several hundred.)

The second point raised by the question concerns the nature of successful businesses. Whatever the size and type of business, it exists for a purpose, which may be any of those listed below:

(*a*) To provide an income for the proprietor and his family.

(*b*) To maximise profits to meet the dividend expectations of the shareholders.

(*c*) To provide goods or services essential to the community while meeting government-imposed financial targets (as is the case with nationalised industries).

(*d*) To perform charitable acts on a break-even basis.

In recent years many senior management teams have worked to define clearly just what the aims of their particular business actually are. The most far-sighted have tried to share these with other employees. Their **vision** of what they are trying to create and the **values** which will guide their conduct may be communicated formally in words – or implied in their deeds. We will discuss some examples in Unit 19.3.

Many have also set out explicit **goals** for the business: such as: '£*x* million turnover and a *y* per cent return on capital employed', and tried to explain their true **mission**. This might be 'to become best in class at attracting and retaining loyal customers, profitably.' Although visions and missions may be dismissed as the sort of 'flavour of the month' propounded by management consultants,

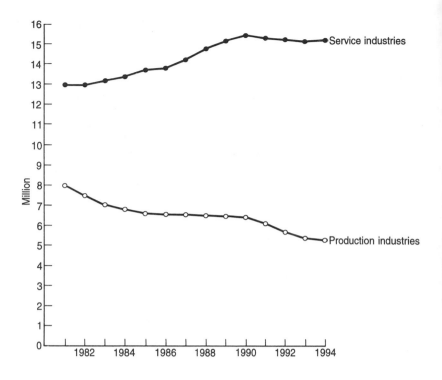

Fig. 1.1   Employees in employment in Great Britain seasonally adjusted 1981–94

they **can** play a valuable role in focusing the attention of both employees and shareholders on the direction in which the organisation must travel.

But for the purposes of answering our original question, we need to think of success in terms of the fulfilment of the main purposes of most types of organisation. And this success is likely to be measured in financial terms.

To make a profit, a business needs to maximise its revenue and minimise its costs. The short answer to our question 'How many people do you need to run a successful business?' might therefore seem to be: 'As few as you can get away with and still get the job done.'

This, however, is not really a satisfactory answer for four reasons:

(*a*) You may be able to cope with your present turnover with a staff of three. If they are already fully stretched, it will be difficult to handle any more business in the future. Although an additional employee will increase your costs, the additional business he can generate should, in the longer term, more than compensate for this. When revenue increases faster than costs, profits rise.

(*b*) In some circumstances you may be able to use machines instead of people, thereby keeping employee numbers to a minimum. In order to determine which is the best investment you will need to consider the capital outlay and the running costs for each. If you invest in machines you must cost in depreciation. If you invest in people you may find that they appreciate in value as they gain experience of your business.

(c) Quality as well as quantity is an important factor. When output per worker is high, fewer workers will be needed to generate any given amount of turnover. Although with people, as with any other expense item, you do to some extent get what you pay for, what you pay does not have to be considered purely in cash terms. The most highly paid employees are not always the most highly motivated. We will be considering this further in Unit 13.

(d) It is not necessarily the **number** of people you employ, but the hours for which you employ them, that adds to your costs. About 28 per cent of the UK workforce is part-time. By matching the hours worked carefully to the requirements of your customers, you can keep your wage bill down and your head count up.

A more acceptable answer to our question might therefore be: 'It depends on whether you want your profit to grow or stand still, on the costs of the alternatives, on the calibre of those employed and the number of hours they work.'

The decision regarding profit growth will depend upon the wishes of the stakeholders and cannot be prescribed. The costs of alternative courses of action can be calculated, but an eye should be kept on the benefits, too. Fig. 1.2 gives an indication of how employee costs are built up. This is something that we will consider more fully in Units 14 and 15. In this unit, we will look at the general question of employee calibre. We will examine the benefits of a stable workforce and then, by way of contrast, we will consider the consequences, in cash and in kind, of labour turnover. This will lead to a discussion of the factors which determine whether your employees will contribute effectively to your business, and of the ways in which personnel management techniques may be able to help.

1.2 Benefits of a Stable Workforce

Perhaps the benefits of having employees who have worked for a business for long enough to 'know the ropes' can best be demonstrated by a brief case study.

Case Study

T. E. Cupps and Co. make crockery, most of which it sells direct to the catering trade. The firm employs about 800 people and its sales force is twelve strong.

Mike Jugg has worked for the company for eight years, starting when he left school. He has now been promoted to the sales team and looks after a group of counties in the south of England.

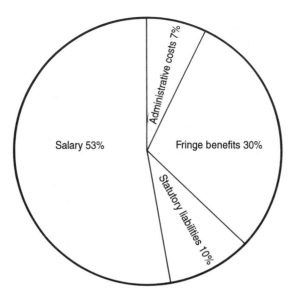

Fig. 1.2   Employee costs

During a recent visit to a valued client, the proprietor of the Bayview Hotel in Westmouth, the hotelier confided to Mike: 'I really don't know where to turn. We've got an important conference here next week, everyone in town will be fully stretched, and three of my silver service waitresses have just been poached by the Majestic. If we fall down on the conference this year, the VIPs will all go and stay at the Seascape next time, and we'll be left with the hangers-on.' Mike made suitably sympathetic noises, turned the conversation to a happier topic, and left with an order for replacement crockery.

Having been with T. E. Cupps and Co. long enough to know that it believed in 'doing whatever it takes to exceed customer expectations', Mike gave the hotelier's problem some thought on his way back to base. On his arrival, he went straight to the canteen kitchen to see Doris, the cook.

Doris didn't mix much with other employees, but Mike had fostered her acquaintance over the years that they had both been with the company. Now he sought her advice. In the course of a ten-minute chat, Mike learned two things. He discovered that Doris had a sister, recently widowed, who was looking for a job in the area. She had spent many years as a waitress in a top London hotel. He also found out that the waitress in the Directors' Dining Room of the large factory down the road from T. E. Cupps was saving up to visit her son in Australia. While the factory was closed down for its early summer break the following week, she would be glad of the chance to earn some extra money.

Continuing his calls, Mike went to see a client in Eastmouth, who he knew had quite a different problem. The client had recruited an extra waitress in anticipation of the opening of additional restaurant space, but had been let down by the contractor and the building work was unfinished. The new waitress would therefore be something of an embarrassment to him.

As a result of his contacts inside and outside T. E. Cupps and Co., Mike was able to put the Bayview proprietor in touch with two permanent and one temporary silver service waitresses, none of whom would have been aware of the opportunity if it had not been for his intervention.

When Mike modestly recounted this saga to a recently recruited sales representative in the pub a few days later, he was greeted with open-mouthed astonishment, followed by a torrent of questions. 'How did you know who to talk to? That old girl in the kitchen never has a polite word for anyone. And how did you find out about the waitress in Eastmouth? I've been here three months, but I wouldn't know where to start. Anyway, what makes you think it was worth the effort?' Mike answered: 'It's not much of an effort when you know the right people, and when you've been around as long as I have, you know when it's worth it.'

Six months later, the Bayview opened a sister hotel with one hundred bedrooms further down the coast. Mike was given the order to equip the restaurant.

When we analyse this case, several points emerge:

(a) Mike had been with T. E. Cupps and Co. long enough to make the acquaintance of many of its employees.

(b) He had been a sales representative long enough to know his customers, their problems and their plans.

(c) He had been with the company long enough to understand and become committed to its policy of 'doing whatever it takes to exceed customer expectations'.

Perhaps we should also add that Mike was clearly a dedicated salesman, with an eye to maximising business wherever he found it. But however keen he was, to resolve this situation he needed experience, and specifically experience with T. E. Cupps.

The stability of your workforce can, then, have a significant bearing on how well your employees can contribute to the success of your business.

You can calculate your **stability index** using the following formula:

$$\frac{\text{Number of employees with more than one year's service now}}{\text{Total employed one year ago}} \times 100$$

In a company like T. E. Cupps, for instance, employing about 800 people in what appears to be a fairly slow-changing environment, it seems likely that the stability rate would be at least 95 per cent:

$$\frac{760 \text{ employees with more than one year's service now}}{800 \text{ total employees one year ago}} \times 100$$

This would show that only 40 out of the 800 jobs in the organisation underwent a change of occupant in the last year. If, for some reason, more longer-serving employees began to leave the company, the stability rate would go down.

Calculating your stability index will enable you to determine whether the organisation does have at least a nucleus of experienced workers – experienced in the ways of the company as well as in their jobs. If you measure this annually you will be able to monitor the trend. In the next section we will look at how it can be used in conjunction with your labour turnover percentage to give you a clearer picture.

Because in management there are usually at least two sides to every question, we cannot leave this section without pointing out that, for real effectiveness, what is needed is stability without stagnation. When taken to extremes, complete lack of movement into and out of the workforce can drag the business into a deeper and deeper rut. A controlled influx of new employees with fresh ideas, and initiatives, may provide the best of both worlds.

1.3 Consequences of Labour Turnover

If stability brings certain benefits to an organisation, the loss and replacement process can bring with it a daunting list of disadvantages. These accrue under two main headings:

(a) The Departing Employee

All employees are an investment: some bring a good return, others are less worthwhile. Either way, their departure means that the opportunity to obtain any return in the future is forfeit.

(i) **Training costs.** The departing employee may have received training which will not now be used. If he has attended a course outside the company, you may have paid up to a month's salary for a one-week course. If he has been trained in-company, there will be the costs of the trainer's time and of any equipment or materials used. In either case, if he has been away from his job for training, whatever he would have produced at work in the way of output – tangible or intangible – will be lost to the business. When he leaves, his skills may only be replaceable after a repetition of the training process. Worse still, if the departing employee takes these hard-won skills to a competitor, your loss will be compounded.

(ii) Lost opportunities. We must also consider what the leaver might have achieved for you had he stayed. Take the case of the research chemist who is nearing a breakthrough in developing a new drug for a pharmaceutical company. If he leaves before his research is completed, the breakthrough may never happen. If the pharmaceutical company does not know that success is imminent, his departure might be taken as an excuse to abandon the project. His successor may lack the expertise to bring it to a speedy conclusion, or the process of handover may delay the act of discovery. If the work lies unfinished for a while, for any reason, a competitor may achieve the breakthrough first.

(iii) Direct cash costs. A resignation may give rise to unforeseen payments, perhaps causing cash flow problems for the small firm. In some circumstances – for instance, where the departing employee has access to cash or company secrets – pay in lieu of notice is considered appropriate (though this must be allowed for in the contract of employment). In others, payment in lieu of holidays or other entitlements will have to be made. Where the termination is at the employer's instigation, cash costs in terms of redundancy payments or compensation for unfair dismissal may arise, as will be explained in Units 20 and 21.

(iv) Illicit gains. Even the most honourable of employees has been known to find parting with his company-issue pocket calculator when he leaves just too much of a wrench. Where specific items of uniform have been issued, it may be impracticable to re-use them, so their value, too, will be lost to the organisation.

'I assure you that I am sorry to see you go. You have been for me like a son; lazy, presumptuous, generally useless and expensive.'

(b) The Replacement

Depending upon the length of notice served by the departing incumbent, the state of the labour market, and the efficacy of your recruitment procedures, there may be a hiatus during which the position remains vacant.

(i) Lost output. Until a replacement has been found and trained, output is almost bound to suffer. Other employees may be able to cover on a temporary basis, but, unless your business is grossly over-staffed, somewhere along the line there will be a failure to produce, or to control, or to contribute in some other way, to the long-term profitability of the enterprise.

We will be examining the steps involved in recruiting in Unit 3 and in selecting employees in Unit 4. All these steps take time if they are to be carried out properly. (If they are not carried out properly, a new recruit either will not be found or will not stay very long.)

(ii) Recruitment and selection costs. The costs of replacing staff soon mount up. A 30 per cent annual labour turnover on a wage bill of two million pounds could add an extra £120,000 to labour costs (6 per cent). Other estimates put the cost even higher.

An advertisement in your local paper for a junior clerical or manual position could cost you several days' pay – depending on the size of the ad. An advertisement in a major national paper for a managerial or professional appointment could cost over a month's salary for a 10 cm double-column space. Recruitment agencies will generally charge between 12 and 15 per cent of the first year's pay; consultancies will ask for around 25 per cent, but will save you time by doing some preliminary screening.

Postage, stationery, travelling costs and the cost of refreshments for interviews all mount up before a new recruit joins the company – although the precise level of expenditure will depend upon the nature of the position.

(iii) Induction costs. When the new recruit does start, there will be training costs to induct him into the company, and perhaps to improve his job skills. We have already indicated how these costs can build up.

Depending upon the nature of the job and the skills of the newcomer, it can take from days to years before he is fully effective and can contribute as much as his predecessor. When this **lead time** has expired – or even earlier – he too may leave the company unless the shortcomings of the job which led to the original resignation have been rectified.

The new recruit may turn out to be a very much better contributor than the previous job-holder. But he will have to contribute considerably to offset all the costs that his employer has incurred in recruiting and training him. One large company employing specialist sales staff found that the average time in a post before a new recruit could generate enough business even to pay his own salary and training costs was nine months.

The benefits of having a stable workforce and the costs of labour turnover are two very powerful arguments in favour of keeping a watchful eye on movement out of your business. You can calculate **labour turnover** using this formula:

$$\frac{\text{Number of leavers during the year}}{\text{Average number employed during year}} \times 100$$

You should note, however, that the average number of employees is found by adding together the numbers in post at the end of each month and dividing by twelve. Otherwise seasonal fluctuations through the employment of temporary staff may distort the figures.

If you are in fact trying to reduce your workforce, the simple labour turnover figure that this formula will give you may be misleading. In this case,

$$\frac{\text{Total replacements during the year}}{\text{Average number employed during year}} \times 100$$

may provide a better yardstick.

Once you have calculated your labour turnover, you can use it in three ways:

(*a*) You can compare it with other companies to try and establish the general level of your particular industry. (The Department for Education and Employment publishes statistics which can help you here.)

(*b*) You can compare it with your own standard of what is acceptable.

(*c*) You can compare it with figures from previous years to determine the trend.

Your labour turnover figure will provide an indicator of the morale of your workforce. But bear in mind the stability index that we discussed in Unit 1.2. A high labour turnover rate may co-exist with a high stability rate if there are just a few jobs in the organisation which people seem to pass rapidly in and out of.

Thus in the case of T. E. Cupps, whose stability rate we have suggested might be around 95 per cent, there might have been sixty leavers in the course of the last year. This would give a labour turnover figure of 7.5 per cent:

$$\frac{60 \text{ leavers during the year}}{800 \text{ average number employed during the year}} \times 100$$

When we look at this in conjunction with the stability rate, we can see that some of the 5 per cent of jobs which underwent a change of occupant must, in fact, have changed hands more than once in the course of the year.

By looking at both indices and then, if necessary, refining them down to department/section level, you will begin to identify the problem area. If you make it a practice to interview all leavers you will soon build up a picture of what is going wrong and can then weigh up the consequences of doing something to put it right. Although at first the costs of remedial action may seem to outweigh the benefits, labour turnover has a 'snowball' effect. Nothing undermines an employee's morale as quickly as watching his colleagues leave the sinking ship, one by one, especially as every new departure is likely to add, either directly or indirectly, to his own workload.

In the next section we shall be looking at the factors which help to determine employee stability. (In Units 9, 10 and 11 we will consider how we can make them not only stable, but effective as well.)

1.4 Getting the Best from Employees

There are many reasons why people work: money, social relationships, feelings of self-respect, a sense of achievement or self-fulfilment. In recent years much research has been done in this area and we will examine this in more detail in Unit 13. In this section we will consider, in more general terms, the kind of managerial policies and behaviour which have a bearing on whether employees will become stable members of the workforce.

(a) Organisation Climate

Organisations divide into two broad categories, although many fall somewhere in between – including those which are attempting to change from the first to the second.

(i) Mechanistic organisations. These correspond to the popular image of a bureaucracy, where there are set procedures and channels of communication for every activity. Each employee has a clearly identified and restricted area of authority. Career paths are well mapped out, with promotion tending to be on the basis of length of service rather than merit.

(ii) Organic organisations. This form of organisation is far less tightly structured than its mechanistic counterpart. Decisions may be made lower down in the hierarchy and jobs are likely to be more amorphous, adapting more readily to meet the changing needs of the business. The chain of command and channels of communication are more fluid. People will come together as project groups and task forces to solve particular problems without concerning themselves unduly about the relative status of those involved.

Some individuals fit more easily into one of these types of organisation than the other. If you are an entrepreneurial type and like to get results in your own way, rather than by rigid adherence to prescribed procedures, you would probably find a full-blooded bureaucracy frustrating. On the other hand, if you have been used to the security and neatly ordered existence of a mechanistic type of organisation, a move to the apparent free-for-all of an organisation at the organic end of the spectrum could be an uncomfortable experience.

Unless the organisation represents one extreme or the other (which few do), such a change in culture is, alone, perhaps unlikely to cause you to resign. But you will certainly find your first few weeks in your new environment difficult. And it is during the first three or four months of employment, known as **the induction crisis**, that the highest proportion of resignations occur.

(b) Management Style

The overall 'feel' of a company may be determined by its organisation climate, but even closer to home, especially for the new recruit, is the management style of his particular boss. Many attempts have been made to categorise different managerial approaches. Douglas McGregor, an American industrial psychologist, propounded the existence of the **Theory X** manager (who thinks that work does not come naturally to employees so they must be bribed and cajoled into contributing) and the **Theory Y** manager (who believes that all employees have a contribution to make and that they will make it, provided the manager gives them the opportunity). Others have examined the picture in terms of the manager's concern for people in relation to his concern for production. Blake and Mouton, two American consultants, have, in fact, designed a system by which managers can measure their own position on a managerial grid constructed along these two dimensions. This is discussed in their book, *The Managerial Grid* (1964).

From the point of view of the new recruit, however, the style of his manager is likely to strike him in one of four main ways:

(i) Autocratic. This approach requires complete obedience on the part of the subordinate and affords little opportunity for him to put forward his own ideas. It corresponds to McGregor's Theory X.

(ii) *Laissez-faire*. A manager who adopts this style takes little interest in how his subordinates do their work, but leaves them to carry on with their jobs however they see fit. He exercises little control over their actions and may appear uninterested in their activities.

(iii) Democratic. This approach calls for participation by employees in deciding how the work is to be done and how problems are to be tackled. It allows the individual to contribute his own ideas rather than become subservient to the will of his boss. This relates to McGregor's Theory Y.

(iv) Empowering. There are some managers who genuinely believe that there is 'a spark of greatness' in everyone. They see it as their job as a manager to help bring that out, to the mutual benefit of the individual and the organisation. A number of management experts now advocate unleashing the potential of the workforce by abandoning traditional hierarchies and fostering personal creativity and learning. Tom Peters in his book *Liberation Management* provides many examples of where this has been done to good effect. In Units 9 and 11 we will explore in more detail how such an approach may be put into practice.

It is not our purpose to comment on the appropriateness or effectiveness of any particular managerial style or organisation climate. The search for a panacea continues among behavioural scientists, but its existence is by no means certain.

What is important here is the effect that the adoption of a particular management style may have on an employee who has been used to something different. This applies just as much to the person who suddenly finds that he is expected to participate in decision-making after being accustomed to obeying orders passively, as it does to the one who finds that he is expected to obey orders to the letter when he has been used to a *laissez-faire* approach. He may or may not adapt to the change and, in time, find it acceptable.

(c) Conditions of Employment

So far we have talked about intangibles, things which we may feel on joining a new organisation, but which we may tend to dismiss as just part of being new. When we move into the area of pay and conditions of employment, we are dealing with more overt causes of unrest. Regardless of an employee's length of service, management policy in this area can affect future loyalty.

(i) Pay and benefits. In Units 14 and 15 we will consider the intricacies of determining pay and fringe benefits. At this stage it is the overall remuneration policy which concerns us (although individual rates of pay are clearly important).

Any organisation which has been a 'market leader' in terms of pay and benefits may find employee stability threatened if it ceases to lead the field. The converse is also more true than is often realised. In some subtle way, the organisation's remuneration package sets the tone for the kind of employees who will be happy working for it. If the firm suddenly starts to offer a more attractive package, it may find itself attracting a different kind of recruit, causing adaptation and integration problems for both old and new employees.

Specific aspects of the package may make a positive contribution to employee retention. A company pension scheme, for instance, is still seen by many as a strong argument for staying put in their later years, notwithstanding recent developments in personal pensions and inter-company transferability. An even more powerful retainer for the younger element is the provision of loans and mortgages at preferential rates. Whether these strong financial arguments against moving on are altogether a good thing where commitment to the job and the company is dwindling must be open to debate. They have been dubbed 'golden handcuffs' by some caught in the trap.

(ii) Physical conditions. The kind of working conditions offered must be considered in relation to the type of work involved. As with the other aspects that we have discussed, it is changes rather than the situation remaining the same which may affect employee loyalty. If you have been used to a private office with a carpet on the floor and a rubber plant in the corner you will not be happy with bare boards in a draughty open-plan office. On its own, again, it is possibly not enough to provoke a resignation; it is just another contributory factor to a feeling of being under-valued by the organisation.

(d) Promotion and Development Prospects

If you have selected employees who are thinking in terms of a career, rather than just a job, you will need to think carefully about the kind of career development opportunities that are open to them in your business. If they find that the opportunities for enhanced responsibility/status/pay which they seek are not, after all, available, they will leave you in favour of greener pastures. Encouraging and fulfilling their aspirations by the adoption of a policy of promotion from within has certain advantages.

(i) Employees will perhaps be encouraged to work hard if they see that this is likely to be rewarded by the organisation.

(ii) You may attract employees of a higher calibre if they see that they have a future in the business.

(iii) It may be easier to identify potential in an employee whose behaviour you can observe on a day-to-day basis than in external applicants whom you see only for a brief period during selection (when they are probably on their best behaviour anyway). This can lead to better selection decisions being made.

(iv) The internal candidate for promotion should require less induction into the organisation and will already be familiar with its management style and climate. This should mean less expense and a shorter lead time before he is fully effective.

(v) The promotee is presumably already committed to the organisation and is therefore less likely to leave after a short time.

Nevertheless, internal promotion also has its drawbacks.

(i) There may be a tendency for the **Peter Principle** – devised by L. J. Peter and described in his book of the same name – to prevail. People may be promoted to the next job up the ladder on the basis of their performance in their present job, notwithstanding the fact that completely different skills may be called for. If they do not perform well in their new job they will not be promoted further. Thus everyone is promoted to his level of incompetence.

(ii) Where an employee is promoted within the same section or department, there may be an element of what is called **role conflict**. The promotee is used to being 'one of the gang', but suddenly he finds he is expected to adopt another stance as their boss.

(iii) Because the promotee is familiar with the organisation, there may be a tendency for all concerned to assume that he is also more familiar with the content of his new job than he actually is. This could mean that he fails to receive necessary training, with a consequent adverse effect on job performance.

(iv) Taken to its natural conclusions, a policy of promotion from within will have a snowball effect. In one organisation two new middle-management positions were created and filled internally, and the vacancies thus created were also filled by promotion. This brought about more vacancies – again filled internally – and so it went on. The last ripple finally died down about twelve months later, after substantial training and relocation costs had been met.

(v) The criteria for selection for promotion are often unclear or misunderstood, so the singling out of one employee from his fellows may give rise to ill-feeling, loss of morale and labour turnover. If promotion is perceived to be on the basis of length of service, this may encourage a time-serving mentality among employees and lead to the departure of ambitious younger people, who see ahead of them little prospect of rapid movement inside the firm.

(vi) If the flow of promotion opportunities is stemmed through lack of either growth or movement out of the organisation, employees will become more frustrated than if they had never expected the opportunities to be there in the first place.

Most of these disadvantages can be overcome. In Unit 12 we will consider how such a policy might operate.

(e) The Job Itself

If an employee finds that the job he is doing is different from that which he was led to expect when he was recruited, he is likely to feel cheated. Even when he has been employed for some time, if the job ceases to meet his expectations, whatever these may be, he will become dissatisfied. In either case, if another opportunity occurs elsewhere, he will be tempted to move on. It is only by ensuring the best possible match between job and employee that this can be eliminated. It is not sufficient just to select the right person initially. Regular appraisal of the situation will be required to ensure that the demands of the employer and the aspirations of the employee remain in harmony. We will be discussing how this can be done in Unit 9.

In this section we have looked at the range of factors which can influence an employee's length of stay in and positive contribution to an organisation. (We must not, however, lose sight of the fact that, unless he knows what his job is, has the skills to perform it to the required standard and the will to use those skills, he will never be 100 per cent effective.)

There is, unfortunately, no standardised procedure which will guarantee success in all situations. What you as a manager can do is to examine all the factors we have discussed within your own business, and then make a decision. You can try to change your organisation and the jobs within it to meet the needs of potential recruits. Or you can look for recruits who will be content with the organisation as it is. A knowledge of the techniques of personnel management can help in both areas.

1.5   Contribution of Personnel Management Techniques

There are two ways of running a business. You can operate by trial and error and learn from your own mistakes or you can take advantage of other people's mistakes by building on accumulated knowledge and experience.

Throughout the twentieth century a great deal of thought and research has been devoted to finding ways of selecting and retaining employees who will make the best possible contribution to an organisation. The expertise of behavioural scientists was first harnessed during World War I to investigate problems, like fatigue, which prevented maximum output. Subsequently psychologists, particularly, have contributed in many ways to the identification of suitable candidates for employment, to the development of training techniques and to our understanding of why people work. Industrial sociologists have examined the ways in which organisations are structured, and with what effect, and the behaviour of groups of people within their work environment.

It is upon this expertise that many personnel management techniques are based. If some of them closely resemble common sense, it is because they are just that.

Some of the techniques which have been developed are listed below.

(*a*) Methods of matching people to jobs in the most cost-effective way, through the use of systematic recruitment and selection procedures.

(*b*) Methods of appraising performance to identify training needs and areas for development.

(c) Methods of training and developing employees to enable them to master the most effective ways of doing their jobs.

(d) Methods of rewarding employees through pay and other means, and of motivating them to make their best contribution.

(e) Methods of dealing with employee relations effectively, fairly and legally.

(f) Methods of forecasting the availability of employees to meet the future needs of the business.

We will be considering each of these techniques, their use and effectiveness, starting with the forecasting of human resources, in Unit 2.

1.6 Work, Law, Society and Business

There are three major and intertwining factors which influence employment practice:

(a) The Right to Work

In the years following World War II the right to work became a driving force in British political and economic life. The trade unions fought hard to uphold this right, particularly during the 1970s. Change that might lead to job losses was resisted and there was continuous upward pressure on terms and conditions of employment. Security for those in work was enhanced by a series of statutes including the Redundancy Payments Act 1965, the Trade Union and Labour Relations Act 1974, the Employment Protection Act 1975 and the Employment Protection (Consolidation) Act 1978.

Such legislation protected the rights of those already working and made it more time-consuming and/or costly for employers to terminate employment. Other measures, including the Rehabilitation of Offenders Act 1974, the Sex Discrimination Acts 1975 and 1986 and the Race Relations Act 1976, upheld the rights of potentially disadvantaged sections of the population not to be discriminated against in getting or keeping work. Like much legislation, these acts were the offspring, not the begetters, of public opinion and social values.

Persistently high levels of joblessness during the 1980s gave rise to a series of government measures designed to alleviate unemployment. Some, like the Jobshare Scheme and its predecessors, the Job Splitting Scheme and the Job Release Scheme, sought to encourage employers to recruit from the ranks of the unemployed instead of or in addition to those already in work. Others, like the Work Experience Programme, the Youth Opportunities Programme, the Youth Training Scheme and Employment Training, aimed to involve employers in the training of particular groups and to increase the likelihood that those taking part would find permanent work.

In subsequent units we will be dealing with the law as it affects particular aspects of employment today. Here we are interested in the legal backing that has been given to the idea of the right to work. During the 1990s more people are having to come to terms with the fact that a full-time, fifty-year, one-career working life is ever more unlikely in the light of technological and social changes. Even so, the level of unemployment remains a key indicator of the economic health of the nation – for government and electorate alike.

(b) The Quality of Life

A stream of thought running parallel with this preoccupation with the right to work is a concern for the quality of life. The quality of working life is one aspect of this and is reflected in debates on participation (see Unit 18.9) in the kind of job enrichment and empowerment programmes that we will be discussing in Unit 13 and in the Health and Safety at Work Act, which will be dealt with in Unit 17.

Beyond this, however, there is a concern for the quality of life in general. Protection – for consumers, of the environment, of the health and safety of the population – is greater now than at any time in our history. Despite differences in emphasis and expression between those of different political persuasions, society as a whole places high value on good standards of housing, education, health care, law and order, leisure facilities, the eradication of hunger and poverty and the provision of a safe and healthy environment. This is unlikely to change in the near future.

(c) The Need for Efficiency

Alongside both these concerns runs the quest for efficient industry capable of competing in world markets. Many organisations have embarked on programmes of Total Quality Management (TQM) and/or Business Process Re-engineering. Their aim is to provide unsurpassed quality to their customers – from a cost-base lower than that of their competitors. We will discuss this in more detail in Unit 11.

This is not incompatible with concern for the quality of life, or in fact the right to work. Indeed for companies like Rover, now several years into such a programme, team work, enhanced educational opportunities and security of employment, albeit for a reduced workforce, are an integral part of the new approach.

In subsequent units we will be delving more deeply into the problems and complexities of modern employment. We are not going to delude ourselves that they can all be resolved easily and painlessly, or that all conflict can be avoided. Some conflict, both inside and outside the business, is healthy and productive. What we are going to do is to see how each part of the employment process can be handled constructively, to obtain the best possible levels of efficiency, but not at the expense of either the right to work or the quality of life.

Questions

1. In what ways might a business suffer if its rate of labour turnover became too high?
2. What are the arguments for and against a policy of promotion from within an organisation?
3. What are the main factors which determine staff stability? Why is this important?
4. How can a knowledge of personnel management techniques assist a manager?

UNIT 2

Human Resource Planning

2.1 Introduction

Before we embark upon our study of how you can set about attracting and retaining the employees you need to help your business be successful, we will pause to consider the nature and importance of the planning process. Similarly, before you rush headlong into recruitment, selection and training, you must stop to plan ahead.

Effective planning will enable you to identify the areas where a shortage or excess of human resources is likely to occur in the future, or where there is inefficient use of people. Armed with this information, you can take steps to deal with the situation before it becomes a crisis. Some of the major uses of human resource planning are listed below:

(a) to help determine recruitment levels, thus avoiding expensive and unsatisfactory panic measures when you suddenly realise that you are short-staffed, or the frustration of losing business through lack of trained staff to handle it;

(b) to anticipate redundancies and, if possible, find ways of preventing them and their attendant human and financial costs (see Unit 20);

(c) to monitor the ratio of employment to other costs, in order to assist decisions regarding the best use of financial resources (see Unit 1);

(d) to provide a basis for training and development programmes geared to meet the needs of the business and related to company succession plans (see Unit 11);

(e) to identify future accommodation requirements in the form of working space, canteen or recreational facilities (see Unit 16).

The basic principles of human resource planning can be applied both to the organisation as a whole and to individual sections of it. In order to derive maximum benefit from the process you must:

(i) identify your future demand for people;
(ii) identify what internal resources you will have to meet that demand;
(iii) compare (i) and (ii);
(iv) take steps to reduce a surplus, or to assess the state of the labour market on which you will depend for future recruits. Your choice between these two will depend on the outcome of (iii);

(v) cope with a number of problems which tend to make the planning of a resource as unpredictable as people difficult but not impossible.

We will deal with each of these aspects in turn.

2.2 Assessing Demand

Your future requirements will be determined both by the direction that you plan that your business should take in the future and by the use that you are making of your people now. The second of these is referred to as **employee utilisation**. The first brings you into the area of **corporate/business planning**.

(a) Corporate/Business Planning

This means devising a picture of how the organisation will look in three or five years' time, and of how it can reach that state over the next three or five years. Common items for consideration include: anticipated financial situation (turnover, gross and net profit, return on investment); intended product markets and market share; desired output and productivity; changes in location and the opening of new plants or outlets; employee numbers.

Most organisations engage in some form of planning, although not all would recognise it as such. Every small trader who has sat down and decided that he will open a new shop and double his turnover, improve his return on investment and increase his market share has engaged in corporate planning. In its more sophisticated guise, the plan will involve a team of experts working closely with the senior management of a large company, applying a range of advanced modelling techniques to the consideration of future probabilities. Successful corporate planning is heavily dependent upon accurate information. It requires constant testing of the feasibility of proposals and constant input from managers at all levels in the organisation.

Business plans and human resource plans must be mutually inter-dependent. This has two main facets:

(i) Corporate policy shaping human resource plans. If business policy determines that the company is to expand and diversify, additional recruits and new skills will probably be needed to make this possible. Different parts of the business, different functions and different geographical locations will be dealt with separately in the plan, and should also be considered separately when you are examining their implications. This will help to prevent the regrettably all too frequent occurrence where one part of the business is declaring redundancies, while in another a desperate recruitment drive is afoot. If such situations are identified in time, corrective action can be taken – through retraining and redeployment – to avoid the worst consequences of both.

(ii) Human resource plans influencing business policy. Human resources can act as a very real constraint upon the feasibility of specific company goals. One large company recently decided to start operations in a location which, research indicated, would provide appropriate supply and distribution channels for its products. As the kind of staff required were not highly skilled, little attention was paid to the question of their availability. In fact, most of the residential accommodation in the area was in a price bracket attainable only by those in the higher socio-economic groups. Recruits were not forthcoming, and an expensive white elephant resulted. This could certainly have been prevented by a closer analysis of the local labour market, along the lines described in Unit 2.4.

Conversely, the existence of competence in a particular field is a useful starting point for future company developments. Faced with a choice between competing in the French market and the Italian market, the language skills of the marketing team may be one relevant factor, at least in the short term.

(b) Employee Utilisation

Whatever goods or services it produces, your organisation transforms **inputs** into **outputs**, using a number of **processes**. The inputs may include ideas, information, skill, cash and tangible materials. The outputs could be anything from appealing and reliable vehicles – if you are a motor manufacturer – to attractive and safe public gardens – if you are a local authority parks department – to above average exam results and job placements – if you are a college. The sequence of steps through which you convert inputs into outputs are the processes running through the organisation. They are the channels along which information, materials and other resources flow.

Some of these processes may operate efficiently and effectively, with minimum waste of time and effort, and without any in-built delays or the need for inspection and re-work – none of which adds any value for the customer. Others may be more cumbersome. Processes which have been partially automated without being completely redesigned are particularly likely to include obsolete activities.

Detailed discussion of the techniques of process improvement and re-engineering are beyond our scope here. But before you begin to assess present utilisation, start by checking that the processes which your people are operating are themselves well designed. Frank Price's book, *Right First Time*, published by Gower, provides a starting point.

Once you are satisfied that your processes are appropriate, you can look closely at the allocation of resources to each. There are a number of steps involved.

(i) Observe how long each operation takes, and how often it must be repeated.

(ii) Organise the operations into meaningful jobs, for an individual or a team. Each should be designed to strike an appropriate balance between specialisation and variety, routine and challenge – see Unit 13.

(iii) Make sure it is clear what the central purpose of each job is and what value it adds to the process it serves. Constantly review the tasks associated with it to make sure they are all necessary and cannot be done any other way.

(iv) Within each job, keep a careful eye on the allocation of time to particular activities. Table 2.1 illustrates a case where travelling and paperwork – non value-added activities for the customer – may be in danger of swamping the central purpose: that of understanding the customer's needs and wants.

Table 2.1 Analysis of a sales representative's day

Activity	Hours	Percentage of total hours
Customer contact	1.76	22
Travelling	2.88	36
Paper work	1.68	21
Waiting	0.48	6
Meals and social	1.20	15
Total	8.00	100

(v) Analyse key ratios, such as your productivity index, value added ratio, overtime and absence rates, to highlight inefficient use of time or effort. We will discuss the formulae that you can use to calculate these in Unit 22.

(vi) Calculate what proportion of your total expenditure is devoted to employee costs. Decide whether or not this is the best way of investing your money.

(vii) Examine the ratio of direct to indirect labour. All businesses employ some people who actually produce the goods or provide the services for which the organisation exists and some who provide clerical and administrative back-up. If the latter becomes too large a proportion of your workforce, this will prove an unproductive drain on your resources.

Regular analysis along these lines will enable you to identify areas where people are not being used to best effect.

'The importance of the sale is in the point of view – your job depends on it.'

Once you are sure that you are making the best possible use of your existing resources, and know what changes in demand business policy may cause, you are ready to move forward. But the identification of needs is not a once-for-all exercise. A whole range of other factors can influence your demand for particular numbers or types of employee. These factors include:

(*a*) market fluctuations, affecting demand for the firm's output, and hence the number of people required to produce it;

(*b*) changes in the availability of raw materials, affecting levels of production, and thence people;

(*c*) technological advances which obviate the need for some jobs and alter the skills required to perform others. Some changes – a decision to computerise certain systems, for instance – can usually be considered well in advance of the event, preventing panic reactions. Others will be a more immediate response to a technological breakthrough, and will need to be implemented straight away in order to keep abreast of the competition;

(*d*) government intervention (in health and safety, for example) may lead, directly or indirectly, to the creation of new jobs or the realignment of responsibilities in order to comply with legal obligations (see Unit 17);

(*e*) mergers and take-overs can affect every aspect of company life. Corporate objectives are likely to change, as may the climate of the whole organisation. Parts of the present organisation structure may therefore be rendered obsolete, and new additions may be required;

(*f*) internal problems, such as unexpected industrial relations difficulties, may also, through their effect on production, influence demand. Additional employees may be necessary to help make good the deficit in the short term. Alternatively, the disruption may lead to loss of orders and a subsequent decrease in demand;

(*g*) management thinking, highlighting 'a better way'. Even if they remain under the same ownership and management, few organisations have the same structure now as they did ten years ago. As management theory develops, cross-functional teams, delayering – to reduce the number of levels between boardroom and shop floor – or a demand for strategic business units to focus on the customer, take their place on top management agendas and subsequently alter the shape of the business;

(*h*) changes in the cost of labour relative to that of other resources.

Each of these factors forms a variable in the company planning process. It is never easy to predict what the future holds, but if we identify some of the areas of potential change, we can at least estimate the likely direction of future demand. In some instances we may wish to go further and try to be more precise through the use of more specialised management forecasting and decision-making techniques, such as time series analysis, linear programming, and probability theory. These are outside the scope of our present discussion but are dealt with in specialist texts on human resource planning.

In the light of the best information available you can proceed to draw up a basic planning chart for each part of the organisation. Software packages are available to help. Figure 2.1 illustrates how the plan might look for a two-year period, broken down into quarters. You may wish to enlarge it, to give you a month by month, or even week by week, picture. You might also wish to look further into the future, although the accuracy of your forecasts will tend to diminish with the addition of each extra year.

At the end of your deliberations concerning demand you should be in a position to fill in the appropriate figures in the demand column of Fig. 2.1. You will then need to consider what resources there will be within the organisation to meet this demand, so that you can complete the supply column and decide on recruitment and terminations.

KEY to Fig. 2.1:

D (Demand)	anticipated number required (assessed from demand information)
S (Supply)	estimated numbers available (assessed from internal supply information)
Recruit	estimated number to be recruited from outside the organisation (i.e. the excess of demand over internal supply, to be considered in the light of external supply information), see Unit 3
Terminate	estimated number to be dismissed (the excess of internal supply over demand), allowing for normal labour turnover (see Unit 20)
Note	Total demand should equal total supply, after recruitment and terminations.

2.3   Assessing Internal Supply

Our basic tasks now are to identify our existing position and to predict what proportion (and, if possible, who) of our existing workforce will remain with us through the planning period. Our estimates can be recorded in the supply columns of Fig. 2.1. They will, however, need to be based on as detailed an analysis of facts and trends as we can muster. The kind of data that we will require at this stage is listed below.

(*a*) **An age breakdown of** the existing workforce, to show where the concentrations occur, and to highlight any imbalances or likely problem areas. Figure 2.2 indicates one impending upheaval, in the shape of mass retirement among managers.

(*b*) **A skills matrix** or competence analysis to show how many people are proficient in the key skills required by the business. This can be dealt with in broad categories (managerial, clerical, manual), but the more precise you can be the better. On a departmental basis it is, in fact, possible to identify specific skills, such as word processing, filing and mailing, and calculate how many staff have the ability to cope adequately with each aspect. Figure 2.3 illustrates how this can be depicted on a chart or **job cover plan**, enabling you to highlight the areas of potential weakness.

	Year one								Year two								Remarks
	1st $\frac{1}{4}$		2nd $\frac{1}{4}$		3rd $\frac{1}{4}$		4th $\frac{1}{4}$		1st $\frac{1}{4}$		2nd $\frac{1}{4}$		3rd $\frac{1}{4}$		4th $\frac{1}{4}$		
	D	S	D	S	D	S	D	S	D	S	D	S	D	S	D	S	
Job category I (receptionist)																	
Job category II (general clerical)																	
Job category III (accounts clerks)																	
Job category IV (sales clerks)																	
Job category V (team leaders)																	
TOTAL Demand																	
Recruit category I																	
category II																	
category III																	
category IV																	
category V																	
Terminate category I																	
category II																	
category III																	
category IV																	
category V																	
TOTAL Supply																	

Fig. 2.1 A basic human resource planning chart

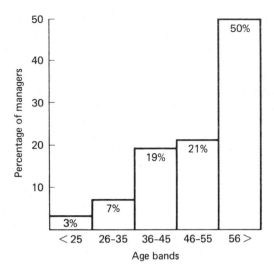

Fig. 2.2   An age breakdown chart

Task	Lisa Brown	Sarah Smith	Jackie Green	Barbara White	Simon Black	Remarks
Mail distribution	√				√	
Filing (invoices)	√	√			√	
Filing (statements)					√	
Word processing	√	√	√	√		
Desk-top publishing	√	√	√	√		

Fig. 2.3   A skills matrix or job cover plan

(*c*) **Training plans** to identify what can be done to improve and diversify the skills of the existing workforce. A system of performance appraisal designed, among other things, to monitor progress in this area, will be useful here (see Units 9 and 10).

(*d*) **A succession plan** to indicate who can succeed whom in the management structure. This will be discussed in more detail in Unit 11.

(*e*) **An analysis of labour turnover** for each category of employee, related if possible to the age analysis. This will again reveal potential problems, such as excessive wastage among trainees. This might mean that you will have a shortage of skilled workers in a few years.

The degree of sophistication required in this, as in other parts of the human resource planning process, will vary from business to business. Some large organisations – usually in areas of rapid technological change and employing upwards of 5,000 people – have established their own human resource planning departments to liaise with a corporate planning department and work with computerised planning models. These will project inflows and outflows of human resources and can demonstrate what the situation will be in three (or thirty) years' time if particular trends are maintained or assumptions prove to be true. Such systems can be made self-correcting, and can update the picture whenever fresh information about the current state of affairs is fed in.

Where the numbers employed are smaller, and the rate of change not as rapid, there is less need for a specialist department and advanced techniques. A basic knowledge of how to present and interpret simple statistical data can bring you to a much closer awareness of the present and likely future resources of your own business or department. The examples we have illustrated, though rudimentary, can form a starting point. Constant monitoring of the kind of statistical data discussed in Unit 22 and a few 'what if' calculations to see what will happen if, for instance, the current rate of labour turnover is maintained for a number of years, will help ensure that you can respond rapidly to changes in the underlying assumptions on which your planning is based.

Once you have identified what resources will be available within the organisation, you can compare it with the demand information we discussed in Unit 2.2 and illustrated in Fig. 2.1. Unless there is an exact match this will, in turn, lead you to one of two broad conclusions. Either you will have too many people or you will have too few. The picture may not be uniform throughout the organisation. In this case, it may be possible to consider moving people, with appropriate training, from one part of the business to another. This will help to avoid expensive redundancy payments and the loss of employees familiar with the organisation and its methods.

Whatever your general conclusions, however, your labour turnover is unlikely to occur in exactly the areas where you would wish it to. You are almost bound to find yourself having to look outside the company for at least some of your future resources. If this is the case, you will need to consider:

(*a*) availability outside the organisation (we will be discussing this in the next section);

(*b*) recruitment and selection procedures (these will form the subject of the next five units).

(If, on the other hand, you find you have a surplus of employees, you will need to consider the sorts of solutions which are put forward in Unit 20.)

2.4   Assessing External Supply

In order to assess the supply of people from outside the organisation, you will need to understand something about the **labour market**, that is, how the supply of and demand for people with particular types of skill is likely to match in a given geographical area. Your definition of the labour market will depend upon the type of work involved. Senior managers and professionals are likely to be mobile across regions and (often) internationally. If you are prepared to finance relocation you may be able to define the geographical boundaries quite broadly. If you are not, or if you are looking for less highly skilled employees, who may prefer to work locally, your supply will almost certainly be drawn from the area surrounding your premises.

If you are seeking employees on anything but a very small scale, there is a whole range of information that you will need about the labour market. Perhaps this can best be illustrated through the eyes of a company deciding whether or not to start up operations in a new area. The information required will include the following items:

(*a*) Population density at various distances from the workplace, to make sure that the area is sufficiently populated to provide some hope of finding employees locally.

(*b*) A general profile of that population, in terms of age and occupational category or socio-economic grouping, to prevent the kind of mismatch described in Unit 2.2.

(*c*) The pattern of immigration into and emigration from the area, to see if the population is growing, shrinking, or changing in composition. Plans for new residential developments will also be relevant here, to obtain a feel for how the place is developing.

(*d*) The nature of the output from the education system, to determine whether sufficient numbers of apprentices or trainees with the right educational background will be available.

(*e*) Local unemployment levels and, if possible, a profile of skills or occupational groupings. This will add to your knowledge of the availability of labour in the area.

(*f*) The competition for recruits, to help you gauge your ability to attract and retain employees of the right calibre. How many employers are there in the area with whom you will have to compete for major groups of staff? The existence of competitors need not deter you from moving in, but it may be necessary to identify more closely how they will compare as employers. Rates of pay, conditions of employment and local reputation are among the factors to be considered here. Once you are established in the area you will still need to keep a close eye on these aspects to ensure that you retain your desired place in the employers' market.

(*g*) Local transport facilities and patterns of travel to work, to prevent you opening up in an area which looks good on the map but where it will in fact be difficult to persuade people to work. Apart from deficiencies in local transport facilities (which might, if numbers warrant, be overcome by the provision of an employee bus), there is the possibility that some natural or man-made hazard will make travelling difficult. A motorway running north-south between your premises and your labour pool to the east will provide a very effective block if there is no east-west crossing point for some miles. In the Greater London area people are accustomed to travelling ten to twenty miles, and sometimes much further, to their places of work. This does not hold good in many other parts of the country, where much shorter distances are the norm. This will need to be considered when you are examining possible locations.

There are many factors other than employee availability which will have to be taken into account when deciding to relocate or open new premises. Proximity to or ease of access for raw material supplies, the availability of appropriate distribution channels or a situation close to your customers are among the other critical considerations. But you ignore the question of the supply of employees at your peril.

This kind of knowledge of the local labour market does not only apply to those contemplating major changes in location. However well established you may be in your area, and however familiar you may consider yourself to be with the local employment market, remember that we live in a fast-moving society. Although your business may feel fairly static, in the world outside its gates living patterns, educational standards, unemployment levels and career expectations are constantly changing. If you fail to take account of this, you may realise too late that your labour market has disappeared, leaving you with an acute shortage in an area where you can ill afford it.

2.5 Overcoming Problems

(a) Information
One of the major problems encountered by those who attempt to plan their need for, and the availability of, human resources lies in obtaining the right kind of information.

(i) People within the organisation may be reluctant to be specific about their objectives or their needs. Others may mistrust the whole idea of trying to plan in this way, assuming that this is just management's way of preparing for redundancies. A third group may feel that any attempt to plan ahead in a rapidly changing economic and technological environment is futile and resent the time spent on it.

Such problems are best overcome by involving those concerned in preliminary planning discussions, to try to win their backing for a process which, though less than perfect, is still immensely preferable to just letting events take their course.

(ii) Another difficulty may stem from the organisation's inexperience in planning ahead at the corporate level. We have seen how important it is that the planning of human resources and the formulation of corporate objectives go hand in hand. Rather than wait until the organisation as a whole has started its corporate planning, it may be possible to create an impetus in this direction by asking enough questions about the future aims of the company and their implications for employees.

(iii) Insufficiently developed personnel information systems may prove to be another problem. Without the right data, appropriately classified and stored in a system from which it can readily be retrieved, the assessment of supply from within the organisation will prove very difficult. This problem can best be overcome by making someone responsible for the regular collection and updating of the kind of information we have discussed. (In larger companies this tends to be a personnel department responsibility.) By anticipating, as far as possible, the kind of questions that you will need to answer, it should be possible to design an information system that will meet your needs. Its form will depend upon the number of employees and the sophistication of your requirements.

(iv) You may also suffer from a lack of knowledge of the labour market. This can be overcome, to a large extent, by familiarising yourself with the content of some published statistical sources, particularly census information and government employment statistics. You will also find it helpful to make and maintain contact with the managers of your local job centre/employment office, commercial recruitment agencies and the local authority planning office, all of whom can provide up-to-date local information about the labour market or other relevant factors. Formal and informal contacts with other employers, regular scanning of the local newspapers and an intelligent appraisal of current recruitment trends will help to complete the picture.

(b) Expertise

Sophisticated planning models require expertise to build. If your organisation is not big enough to warrant engaging the services of an expert, a general identification of future trends and possible problem areas can form a useful starting point until expertise is developed.

(c) Time

The kind of planning we have been discussing cannot be done overnight. It will take time to install the right kind of information systems and to interpret the data you can obtain. There are no shortcuts here except a systematic process of data collection and interpretation and a continuing concentration on what you are trying to achieve.

(d) Future Uncertainties

Few would claim to predict with certainty just what the future holds. Economic changes may affect the demand for your goods or services; technological changes may alter your methods of working; social and political changes may influence people's attitude to work and to the kind of work that they are prepared to undertake. We cannot pretend that this uncertainty does not exist. What we can do is to identify current trends, consider any likely changes in the factors which underlie those trends, and come up with a prediction which is as accurate as is possible in the circumstances. By constant monitoring of the actual situation as it unfolds to see how it compares with the plan, it should be possible to update both the plan and the premises upon which it is based, and to improve our planning expertise in the process. If there are times when we feel inclined to throw up our hands in despair at the complexities and uncertainties of the planning process, the more we persevere, the more likely it is that we shall reap the benefits described in Unit 2.1.

Once we have identified our future requirements, we can take steps to deal with any shortfall. This involves recruitment (attracting a field of candidates) and selection (picking one out).

Questions

1. If you were asked to inaugurate formal human resource planning in an organisation, how would you set about it?
2. What problems confront the planner in assessing future demand and supply? How can these be overcome or minimised?
3. In what ways can effective human resource planning contribute to the success of an organisation?

UNIT 3

Recruiting Employees

3.1 Introduction

We saw in Unit 1.3 how recruitment costs can mount up, so one of the guiding precepts when recruiting must be the search for cost-effectiveness. The ideal is to ensure maximum benefit, in terms of a recruit who can and will perform the job effectively, in return for minimum expenditure on advertising, consultants, candidate expenses and so on.

3.2 Confirming Vacancies

If you make it a practice to monitor employee utilisation in the manner suggested in Unit 2.2, it is unlikely that you will fall into the trap of filling positions that do not exist. In fact many organisations, acutely aware of the proportion of total costs that people represent, go to the opposite extreme. Documents for the requisitioning of recruits may be introduced, with a view to imposing top management scrutiny of requests even for routine replacements. While it may be important that there is some sort of check on *ad hoc* recruitment, the delays caused by the use of such methods may cause serious short-term difficulties where one job-holder leaves before a replacement can be found.

Whatever the circumstances, the departure of an employee does provide a unique opportunity to redesign, realign and rethink the job. There are three forces working against this.

(*a*) In some industries, trade unions may resist any attempt to reduce or alter jobs in this way.

(*b*) Some organisations appear to encourage an empire-building mentality through their reward systems. Thus a manager may find that any reduction in the number of subordinates will reduce points, and therefore salary, under the company's job-evaluation scheme. When this is added to the very human tendency to draw status and prestige from the size, in terms of people, of the section, the manager may view suggestions of managing without a replacement with scepticism, if not hostility.

(*c*) Management inertia may lead to taking the apparently easier route of like-for-like replacement.

Even so, and whether or not overall numbers are reduced as a result of such a review, the opportunity for internal reorganisation should be grasped wherever possible. It may be that you have someone in your section who could absorb part of the workload of the vacant position, thereby gaining more expertise and adding to the flexibility of your workforce. This may mean that part of that work is, in turn, redistributed, and a general restructuring will ensue.

If you have not already done so, now could be the time to start thinking even more laterally about the range of tasks you and your people perform, and to redefine them as team, rather than individual activities. Whether the resulting collection of tasks emerges as a separate job or a role within a team, it is helpful to record the key elements of it, as a basis for later stages in the selection process and for other purposes.

3.3 Describing the Job

There are a number of different ways of arriving at a job/role description.

(*a*) You can sit down and write a synopsis of the job as you see it, on the basis of your existing knowledge or specific observation.

(*b*) You can ask the present job-holder, if there is one, to produce a synopsis. Again, this can be done on the basis either of existing knowledge or aided by some self-observation and/or recording of activities, perhaps using a diary or checklist.

(*c*) You can interview the job-holder to produce an amalgamation of (*a*) and (*b*).

(*d*) You can talk to the job-holder's colleagues, particularly if the job is one which forms part of a team's remit. (If this is the case, make sure you include them at later stages of the process, too.)

(*e*) You can talk to the job-holder's customers. These are the people, inside or outside the business, who receive the outputs which the job produces – whether these take the form of information, ideas, products or services. They can help you understand the part the job plays in the total process, how it contributes to satisfying customers' wants, and what would happen if it didn't exist.

(*f*) You can employ a trained job analyst to compile the description based on one or a combination of the above.

Whichever method you adopt, the job description should provide an accurate reflection of the type of things the job-holder is called upon to do. Involvement of the incumbent himself is, therefore, vital, but care should be taken to make sure that a balanced picture is obtained, preferably by observing work in progress.

Once the data have been gathered, the next step is to organise the information into a usable document. This can be complicated by the fact that the job description can be used for a number of purposes apart from recruitment. Job-evaluation exercises, training needs analysis, performance appraisal and employee utilisation studies may all call for the existence of a working description.

Many attempts have been made to identify the most appropriate format for a job description. Two basic approaches emerge.

(a) An Open Approach

Information can be grouped under the following types of heading:

(i)	Job title:	
(ii)	Reports to:	
(iii)	Responsible for:	(who reports to the job-holder?)
(iv)	Job location:	
(v)	Number employed in this position:	
(vi)	Main purpose of job:	(why does it exist?)
(vii)	Key end results:	(what must it achieve?)
(viii)	Key tasks:	(what does the job-holder do?)
(ix)	Standards of performance:	(the task will be done satisfactorily when . . .)
(x)	Constraints:	(limitations of authority, time deadlines)
(xi)	Working conditions:	(heat, light, noise)
(xii)	Social conditions:	(who does the job-holder work with?)
(xiii)	Economic conditions:	(pay, fringe benefits)
(xiv)	Promotion prospects:	(where does the job lead?)
(xv)	Company context:	(structure, climate, aims)

This should provide a fairly comprehensive picture, but (viii) may tend to become rather unwieldy as there is no method for classifying the data.

(b) A Classified Approach

This can include all the items listed in (i) to (xv) above, but seeks to provide some way of categorising the information in (viii). The list of tasks is therefore subdivided to provide a more coherent grouping. Subheadings, such as those listed below, may prove helpful.

(i)	Methods:	(responsibility for establishing and revising/ maintaining corrcct working procedures)
(ii)	Money:	(responsibility for preparing or controlling budgets, controlling costs, administering pay)
(iii)	People:	(responsibility for determining requirements, recruiting, selecting, training, motivating or terminating employees)
(iv)	Materials:	(planning, controlling or optimising)
(v)	Machines:	(utilising or maintaining).

An alternative classification might include involvement with specific types of activity, such as sales, administration, security, customer relations, production or people management. Other variations structure the task list around the main competence areas of a relevant national vocational qualification – see Unit 10.5 or in-house framework of competences.

For more complex jobs, the classified approach will be the more useful. It will also be helpful where particular types of job evaluation are in use, as the categorisation can be used to reflect the factors chosen (see Unit 14).

Job descriptions, however, are only a means to an end. The art of compiling them lies in successfully walking the tightrope between a totally comprehensive, but extremely lengthy and inhibiting, coverage and a brief, broad, general approach which makes it difficult to differentiate between one role and another. The essential thing is that you provide yourself with a working document that tells you the 'what? why? when? where? and how?' of the job recognising the **range** of activities in which the job-holder may be involved.

The compilation of job descriptions is not a once-for-all exercise. Jobs are not static. Technological change, changes in product range, changes in company objectives or procedures will affect their content. Job-holders, too, may mould the job to suit their particular skills or inclinations, thereby introducing subtle changes which can render a job description obsolete within weeks of its being drawn up. Always make sure that it is still an accurate reflection of the job in question.

3.4 Producing a Personnel Specification

Once you have defined the nature of the role to be filled, the next step is a process of analysis to identify the attributes required in the person who is to fill it. These are the **criteria** on which your selection decision should be based. Traditionally, this analysis has been carried out clinically (using human judgment) rather than mechanically (using a computer). There is some evidence to suggest that the second method may have its value, as we shall see in Unit 3.4(*b*).

(a) Clinical Methods
Alec Rodger, J. Munro Fraser, Sydney and Brown, and Felix Lopez are among the better known of those who have devised checklists for use in compiling a personnel specification. Although still used, their approach is now somewhat out-dated.

(i) **The Seven Point Plan.** This was devised by Professor Rodger for the National Institute of Industrial Psychology. It draws attention to seven aspects of the individual:

Physique: health, strength, appearance, voice and other physical attributes.

Attainments: general education, job training and job experience.

General intelligence: capacity for complex mental work, general reasoning ability.

Special aptitudes: predisposition to acquire certain types of skill.

Interests: inclination towards intellectual, social, practical, constructive or physically active leisure pursuits.

Disposition: steadiness and reliability, degree of acceptability to and influence over others, self-reliance.

Circumstances: mobility, domicile.

(ii) The Five Point Plan. Munro Fraser designed the pentagonal peg system, upon which the minimum profile of the individual you seek can be plotted, as Fig. 3.1 illustrates. Each of the five points of a pentagon represents one aspect of the individual. The required level of each quality can be indicated on a scale extended from each of the points. When these levels are linked together the basic profile will emerge.

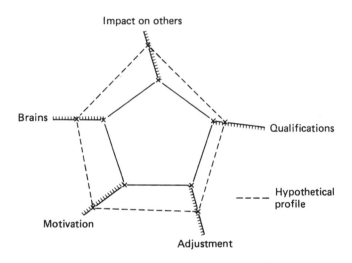

Fig. 3.1 The pentagonal peg

The points which Munro Fraser selected are:

Impact on others: relations with colleagues, customers and other contacts.

Qualifications: education, training and job experience.

Brains: innate abilities, quickness of apprehension.

Motivation: drive and initiative, personal standards and self-imposed goals.

Adjustment: ability to cope with stress and pressure, deviations from routine and general upsets.

The other two checklists we have mentioned conform to the same basic pattern but introduce some further aspects of the individual. Sydney and Brown include social roles and initiative in their nine-point list, while Lopez incorporates organisational identification (meaning loyalty, self-discipline, adherence to the established order) and potential for growth, as well as the more basic factors.

Some organisations use hybrid versions or their own variations. The headings of these plans help decide on the essential and the desirable attributes of the ideal job-holder.

(iii) Competences. The Five and Seven Point Plans tend to focus on attributes rather than behaviour. But it is often behaviour – that is, the way the person does the job – which matters more than innate personality or intellectual characteristics. A more direct and modern approach to establishing just what you need to look for is to consider what the job-holder must be able to **do** – that is, what competences are needed. If you can match these against the **demands** which the job will make, you are less likely to find that you have recruited someone who is incapable of performing to the required standard. If you also give some thought to the **rewards** which the job offers, in terms of pay and benefits, relationships and job satisfaction, you can then work out what individual **needs** these are likely to satisfy. If you recruit those whose needs are met by the rewards which the job offers, they are much more likely to stay and work hard.

The checklist in Table 3.1 provides a framework for this approach to compiling a personnel specification. To use it, first decide the extent to which the job does require each of the competences indicated by the headings in italics. Then consider exactly what is required. The suggestions under the headings will help you to focus on this. Be as precise as you can about how someone with the required ability would be expected to behave, and use Fig. 3.2 to draw up a list of the things that the person appointed must demonstrate the ability to do on day one in the job. (Remember, it may be possible to provide training on some aspects of the job – see Unit 10 – so allow for this when drawing up your list.)

For example, if you feel that 'working with words' forms part of the job, you need to focus on whether this will involve reading, writing, speaking, listening (or all of them). If writing is called for, what will the job-holder be required to write? If the answer is 'technical reports', and if the quality of these will be of some importance in determining whether or not the job is being done properly, you might put something like 'Write succinct reports which translate complex technical data into a form simple enough to be understood by those with no prior knowledge' on your list of selection criteria. When you design your selection procedure (see Unit 4.2) you will need to think how best you can establish whether or not the candidates are able to do this – and note it in one of the 'Assessment Method' columns on Fig. 3.2. Make sure you have some means of assessing every competence – and more than one for the most crucial. You will then be in a position to make objective comparisons between the behaviour of each candidate and that specified on your list.

Table 3.1   Checklist of competences and needs

Competences

Working with figures   Making calculations. Checking calculations. Interpreting numerical information. (Of what type? From what sources?)

Working with words   Reading (correspondence, reports, forms, technical information, instructions). Writing (correspondence, reports, forms, technical information, instructions). Speaking (lectures, presentations, interviews, giving instructions, meetings, telephone calls). Listening (lectures, presentations, interviews, receiving instructions, meetings, telephone calls).

Working with people   Leading/following. What style of leadership do they have/prefer? Motivating self or others. Persuading/ acquiescing. Organising. Directing/obeying. Coaching/being coached. Individual/team player. Customer orientation.

Working with ideas   Obtaining information. Understanding (concepts, arguments, technical issues). Developing (concepts, arguments, technical issues). Analysing situations and issues. Devising alternative creative interpretations and solutions. Problem solving.

Planning and prioritising   Identifying goals (short or long term). Planning own work/other people's. Getting on and doing. Meeting deadlines.

Making decisions   Short or long term. Scope and impact. Own work/other people's. Prescribed or discretionary. Monitoring and reviewing.

Ability to learn   Practical/technical/abstract – by doing/reading/observing.

Working with systems   Designing information systems. Using information systems. Designing job-related procedures (specify nature). Implementing job-related procedures (specify nature).

Specific knowledge/skill requirements   Legal, financial, political, geographical, procedural (specify nature), etc. Operation of particular machines/processes (specify).

Values   Seeing things through. Personal integrity. Rule bender/keeper. Learning and continuous-improvement orientated.

Availability and mobility   Working after hours. Travel and overnight stays. Driving licence.

Other requirements   Specify.

Table 3.1 (*cont*)

Needs

Existence Salary (amount and method of determining). Benefits (holidays, cars, pension, etc.). Welfare provisions (crèches, medical, counselling, etc.).

Relatedness Working with/for others. Nature of relationships. Quality of relationships.

Growth Self-fulfilment. Sense of personal achievement. Scope for learning and personal development.

Other Specify.

The development of National Vocational Qualifications (NVQs) based on the competences required to perform specific roles – from shop floor to senior management – has provided an effective short cut to competence-based personnel specifications. Instead of working from first principles, you can use the relevant job-specific list of competences and *could* choose to consider only those who have already attained the relevant NVQ. NVQs are discussed in Unit 10.

(b) Computerised Approaches

Recruitment and selection are basically about finding suitable ways of predicting, as accurately as possible, effective performance in a job. The clinical approaches we have been describing recognise this and attempt to deduce the qualities or competences demanded by the job. Although systematic in their approach, such methods rely heavily on human judgement and are therefore prone to being subjective, rather than objective, in their application.

A number of computer packages are now available to assist in identifying selection criteria and to help in short-listing planning interviews and other parts of the selection process. These typically require people familiar with the job to respond to questions about the frequency and importance of particular activities. From this the key criteria are derived. Such packages speed up and improve the objectivity of the specification.

To help identify those attributes which really make the difference to performance, greater sophistication can be introduced through an approach known as **selection profile analysis.** This involves taking a sample of people currently doing the job and identifying, through performance appraisal and other means, who can be classified as the real producers, who are the triers and who are the losers. A detailed questionnaire, covering such areas as educational background, attitudes to work, interests and job history, is then administered to each of the groups. By computer analysis of the results it is possible to identify the particular combinations of circumstances, attitudes

	Form	Test 1	Test 2	Simu-lation	Work sample	Inter-view 1	Inter-view 2	Refs	Medical
Job Title: _____ Date: _____ Department: _____									
			Assessment Method						
AREA OF COMPETENCE									
Working with figures:									
Working with words:									
Working with people:									
Working with ideas:									
Planning/prioritising:									
Making decisions:									
Ability to learn:									
Working with systems:									
Specific knowledge/skill:									
Values:									
Availability/mobility:									
Other:									
NEEDS									
Existence:									
Relatedness:									
Growth:									

Fig. 3.2   Assessment Plan

and achievements which distinguish the three groups. Assuming that the organisation will wish to recruit a majority of real producers, and possibly a few triers, in the future, the information relating to these categories can be used as a profile against which to measure potential candidates.

The management consultancy which developed this method claims that it does remove much of the subjectivity from the recruitment process. On the other hand, such an approach is only practicable where there are a number of people (probably between twenty and eighty) already doing the job, and where the appropriate software and expertise are available for analysis purposes.

If information regarding the identity of the losers gets into the wrong hands, or is used in the wrong way, that could have an adverse effect on morale and employee relations. This would detract from the undoubted value of the technique as an aid to effective recruitment.

3.5 Where to Look

In many cases where there is a job to be filled the best place to start looking will be inside the organisation. We will be considering the possible procedures for doing this in Unit 12 and have already seen, in Unit 1, the general advantages and disadvantages of pursuing such a course as a matter of policy.

Once we move outside the ranks of the existing workforce, we find a large array of recruitment services available. Some of them will be completely free or may only cost you the price of a drink or a meal. Others will cost as much as half a year's salary, plus expenses.

'You're exactly the type of man we need.'

Table 3.2   Recruitment services

Recruitment service	Approximate cost	Employee categories
Careers office*	Free	New/recent school-leavers
Job Centre/Employment office*	Free	Clerical/manual, skilled/unskilled
Careers conventions	Representative's time, publicity material	Future school/college leavers
University/college careers offices	Publicity material and hotel costs	New/recent graduates
Factory gate/shop window notices	Free/nominal cost	Clerical/manual
Local recruitment drives	Time, location and publicity costs	Clerical/manual, particularly part-time staff
Commercial employment agencies	10–20 per cent of starting salary	Clerical/specialist personnel plus some manual
Private recruitment consultants	15–25 per cent of starting salary and advertising costs	Managerial/specialist personnel
Executive search consultants	30–50 per cent of starting salary, plus expenses	Senior management/rare professional expertise
Press advertising ('give away', national, local, trade and professional)	From £10 to more than £100 per column centimetre	All types, depending on circulation (see Unit 3.6)
Commercial radio	Depends on audience and time of day	Clerical/manual, particularly for bulk recruitment
Word of mouth	Free/entertainment costs/introduction bonus	All categories but beware of indirect discrimination – see Unit 3.8

* State agencies.

Table 3.2 demonstrates the range of recruitment services currently available, together with an indication of cost levels and categories most likely to be found through their services.

Your choice of method will depend upon a number of factors.

(a) Candidate Expectations

The job-seeking habits of your target market are a prime consideration. Although it is difficult to generalise, certain patterns do emerge, as indicated in the right-hand column of Table 3.2. Thus you are more likely to recruit a competent systems analyst through a specialist agency or an advertisement in one of the computer journals than through a notice in the corner-shop window. Conversely, unskilled workers may well be found through a factory gate notice or some other local medium which suits their reading habits and expectations.

(b) Cost Considerations

Although important, cash alone is not an appropriate determinant of which recruitment method to use. Cost-effectiveness is what is important. Even if you only spend a few pounds on a classified advertisement in the local paper, those few pounds will be wasted if there is no response.

As a general rule, where you are seeking to recruit a number of people for the same kind of position, it will be more cost-effective to place the advertisement yourself, using an appropriate medium, rather than to engage the services of a consultant. This is because you will only pay for the advertisement once, however many candidates you subsequently select. If you work through a private agency or consultant, you will usually be required to pay a fee for each individual appointed.

(c) Company Policy

Some organisations, prompted either by social conscience and a public-spirited attempt to reduce the number of unemployed or by cost considerations, make it a policy to approach the government agencies first. Others use specific media for their product advertising and therefore try to keep their recruitment advertising in line. Yet others determine to keep their own involvement to a minimum by always using consultants to help fill senior appointments. You may be required to choose your recruitment media accordingly.

(d) Historical Factors

As we will see in the next section, whichever method you choose, it should be monitored to ascertain whether it does in fact produce the quality and quantity of replies for which you had hoped. Such monitoring should enable you to highlight the most effective methods for the employee categories you need. Usually this will be linked to the candidate expectations we have already discussed, but your monitoring procedure will enable you to pin this down specifically in relation to your own local situation.

(e) Legal Constraints

The Commission for Racial Equality's suggestions on this are discussed in Unit 3.8(b) together with the implications of the Sex Discrimination Acts 1975 and 1986, the Race Relations Act 1976 and the Trade Union and Labour Relations (Consolidation) Act 1992.

3.6 Using the Media

If a vacancy is pressing, there may be a temptation to go for saturation tactics, using every available medium. This is seldom wise. Not only do you incur excessive cash costs, but you also run the risk of attracting all manner of unsuitable responses from people who draw their conclusions as much from the placing of the advertisement or recruitment notice as from the actual content. Sifting these replies is time-consuming. It may also be expensive in terms of goodwill. Those who apply in good faith must be carefully treated.

The wisest course of action is usually to select one or possibly two media, according to the criteria outlined in the previous section. You should then ensure that all the appropriate information is incorporated and set up a system to monitor responses.

If you decide to use an agency or consultant, there is much to be said for acting on personal recommendation. Although there is a legal requirement for employment agencies to be licensed, and standards of conduct have improved in recent years, the agent is primarily a salesperson. It is worth building up a relationship with one or two agencies or consultants for each category of staff, and making sure that they learn enough about you and your organisation to be able to help. When they send you unsuitable applicants, tell them so. That way you will educate them to your requirements and make them realise that if they want to handle your recruitment business they must work for it.

It may be useful here to distinguish between the three major types of external recruitment service, and see what each has to offer.

(a) Employment Agencies

In return for basic information about the job to be filled (you should give them the job description and personnel specification), an agency will do some preliminary matching between your requirements and the individuals who are currently registered with them or who respond to an advertisement placed by them. The thoroughness of this matching process does on occasion leave something to be desired. Agencies of this type are operated both privately, under a number of familiar high-street facias, and by the government Employment Service. The latter operates under the Job Centre banner.

(b) Employment Consultants

When you engage the services of a consultant, he will normally come and visit your company and help you to compile the personnel specification. He will then examine his files to see if he is currently in contact with any suitable prospective applicants. If not, he will advertise on your behalf, preserving your company's anonymity if you so desire. (This may be useful if the forthcoming vacancy or its salary is politically sensitive in the organisation.) The consultant will then screen applicants, leaving you with a shortlist of candidates from whom you may make your final choice. Like the agencies, the consultancies operate on a sort of sale or return basis: if you don't select anyone, you don't pay a fee (although you may have to meet expenses).

(c) Executive Search Consultants

Some consultancies offer a special search facility for senior appointments. Operating almost entirely through personal contacts, they will seek out the one right person for the job in question and approach him or her with a view to discussing the possibilities. By building up detailed dossiers on people who may currently be employed by your competitors, they are able to match jobs and people down to a small shortlist. Although their methods have sometimes been derided as just an expensive form of poaching, for high-level vacancies where candidates are not actively seeking a job change and are therefore unlikely to respond to an advertisement, executive search may prove fruitful.

One other method of recruitment warrants particular attention:

(d) Word of Mouth

Although traditionally an inexpensive way of recruiting staff of all types, some organisations do make some sort of payment to members of their staff who introduce new recruits. It is advisable to add a proviso that the new entrant must remain with the organisation for, say, six months before the payment becomes due: otherwise it may be possible to find people making a living out of the introductory bonus scheme. The payments can be made in cash or in kind. Some firms, for instance, use holiday vouchers for this purpose. The main drawback from which word-of-mouth recruitment suffers is the danger that it will indirectly discriminate against groups not currently represented in the workforce (see Unit 3.8).

Whichever method you are using, the value of an effective **monitoring** system cannot be over-emphasised. With word-of-mouth recruitment, records are imperative if you are to keep track of who is entitled to payment. For all methods it is essential that you keep a simple record of the steps that you have taken, when, and how much they cost. You can subsequently enter the number of replies received, the number of candidates called for interview, the number shortlisted and the person selected. You may wish to follow through still further to consider the effectiveness of the new job-holder. This will link up with the validation of your selection procedure (see Unit 7.3).

In the next section we will consider how you can set about compiling a recruitment advertisement or notice. You may, of course, decide to employ a professional advertising agency to do this for you. In many circumstances this will be worthwhile, as the agency will obtain commission from the newspaper or journal where the advertisement appears, rather than payment from you. You may choose to use the same agency for both recruitment and product advertising, perhaps using your company symbol (logo) in both to facilitate instant recognition. The danger here is that both product and recruitment advertising are specialised fields and not all agencies are equally proficient in both.

3.7 Writing an Advertisement

Although we are primarily concerned in this section with the compilation of press advertisements, the basic principles apply to any recruitment notice or announcement.

(a) Basic Principles

The main aim of recruitment advertising is to produce, at minimum cost, a compact field of candidates, capable of doing the job and motivated to perform it to the required standard. The advertisement is a key link between the recruitment and selection phases. It attracts a field of candidates but, through the process of self-selection, it eliminates large sections of the population. By careful choice of both media and wording, the advertisement should strike home to the appropriate audience. Although, in one sense, the advertisement is a selling medium, giving information about the job and the organisation, it is vitally important at this, as well as at all other stages of the selection procedure, that the job is not oversold. The more the advertisement can convey the true atmosphere of the company, so that prospective candidates can identify whether or not it is the kind of environment which will suit them, the better. And bear in mind that each advertisement, whether for jobs or products, says something to the outside world about your organisation. So all advertisements can be used to build positive awareness and create a favourable future reaction among both prospective employees and prospective consumers of your products or services.

(b) How to Set About It

The advertisement comes after the personnel specification which, as we have seen, cannot be written until after the job description has been compiled. This sequence is important because the advertisement will need to include information from both these documents.

(c) What to Say

It is unproductive to try to lay down too many rules about recruitment advertising, as the original or the unique is always capable of attracting a good field of candidates in defiance of the rules. Some key points can be identified, although the order in which they are incorporated will vary.

(i) Identify the company.

(ii) Convey the flavour of the organisation (whether mechanistic or organic).

(iii) Give the job title and identify its main purpose and key components, by reference to the job description.

(iv) Specify the essential requirements of the job, from the personnel specification.

(v) Specify the benefits of the job, if possible including pay range. (Exclusion of pay may be mistrusted as indicative of an ill-thought-out pay policy, and could deter good candidates, who will use pay as a guide to the level of the job.)

(vi) Ensure that any hazards or unsocial aspects are included if they are likely to be significant in influencing candidates' decisions to accept or reject the job.

(vii) Identify job location.

(viii) Give directions as to whether you require applicants to write, telephone or call in. Telephone replies will speed things up and allow for a preliminary assessment to be made, but they require a competent person to deal with enquiries. Applicants should not be asked to submit a curriculum vitae if you have a standard application form for them to complete.

The key notes of effective recruitment advertising are relevance, factual information and the avoidance of ambiguity. These points can best be clarified by reference to a specific example, demonstrating some of the pitfalls (Fig. 3.3).

In the seven paragraphs of the advertisement, a valiant attempt has been made to incorporate most of the key features, but the result is a strangely conflicting series of impressions.

(i) The headline (1) is certainly eye-catching, and makes us want to read on.

(ii) The first paragraph (2) sets the tone of a friendly, informal kind of organisation, people-orientated and possibly rather chaotic.

(iii) This impression is confirmed in the second paragraph (3).

(iv) The next paragraph (4) tells us what the company does, and in (5) the job title is finally introduced.

(v) Not until paragraph (6) do we begin to find out in detail what the job actually is and what attributes are called for. (The advertiser has relied thus far on retaining our attention through an arresting headline and some interesting copy.) Whether the attributes indicated get us much further forward is a matter for debate. Flexibility and a strong personality are not traits that one can assess accurately in relation to oneself. Experience in personnel management is a more tangible commodity, but how much? Six weeks? Six years? The inclination to get involved with people opens the advertisement up to a range of welfare and social workers, as well as to personnel specialists, which may or may not be the advertiser's intention.

(vi) In paragraph (7) we find the benefits outlined. But what do we actually learn? Salaries are highly attractive – but perceptions of attractiveness will be coloured by our expectations and experience. To someone earning £13,000 pa, £14,000 pa may be attractive. To someone earning £14,500 pa, it is less likely to be so. Do comprehensive benefits include a non-contributory pension scheme and five weeks' holiday, or a contributory pension scheme and four weeks' holiday?

(vii) The final paragraph (8) leaves us wondering about two points. We have been directed to write or telephone, but we don't know to whom, and we have no telephone number. We have also been told to quote a reference number. This conveys a rather more bureaucratic and well-ordered approach than that suggested in the first paragraph (2).

Thus, while a cursory glance at the advertisement might suggest that it complies with the key points we have listed, advertising that may have cost £1000 has really left us with a conflicting picture of the organisation, no clear knowledge of the job content or the kind of person required, unanswered questions over salary and benefits, and uncertainty over whether to write, telephone, or forget the whole thing. If you really don't know what the job

Dealing with ①

You've heard the old line...
'You don't have to be mad to work here, but it helps'. It's like that at AOK, but in the nicest possible way. We

individuals

② believe that our Personnel Department should operate for the benefit of our staff, and not that staff should conform to statistical profiles. It doesn't make

demands

for an easy life, but dealing with people as individuals, rather than as numbers, certainly makes it a rewarding

a certain...

one.

...um...

We're committed to an enlightened personnel philosophy. We firmly believe that our staff are
③ our most important asset, and we go a long way both to attract the highest quality of people, and to retain them.

④ AOK is a company with a difference. We're a highly progressive, international organisation, one of the world's leading manufacturers in the medical electronics field.

...Character

⑤ As an expanding company, we now need another Personnel Generalist to join us at our UK Headquarters in Reigate, Surrey.

Essentially we're looking for an individual, a chameleon character who will assume an influential role in recruitment, employee relations, salary administration, compensation and benefits, or whatever the situation demands. The flexibility to interchange with various functions is vital.
⑥ Within your designated area, you'll experience a large degree of independence. You'll be a strong personality, probably already experienced in personnel management in a small company. Whatever your background you'll certainly be someone who likes to help people to help themselves and who is happy to get involved with people at all levels within the organisation.
Obviously, in a fast growing company with a positive emphasis on effective personnel work,
⑦ your prospects for promotion are excellent. Salaries are highly attractive and benefits are, of course, comprehensive.

So if you're the kind of individual who enjoys personal contact, problem solving, and will thrive on the high pace of a progressive, international
⑧ organisation, such as AOK, get in touch with us by writing or telephoning, quoting ref: 451/BPD, to AOK House, Reigate, Surrey.

Fig. 3.3 The pitfalls of compiling an advertisement

Table 3.3 Advantages and disadvantages in the placing of press advertisements

Medium	Advantages	Disadvantages
National press	Minimum delay before publication, wide and speedy circulation, good typesetting	High wastage factor (reaches an unnecessarily wide audience), has brief life, high volume of competing advertisements on page
Local press	Little delay before publication, can help local public relations	Quality of typesetting varies, not much read for senior appointments in most areas
Professional/trade journals	Compact and homogeneous readership, readers likely to scan advertisements automatically	May be long intervals between issues, slower circulation, tendency to mix recruitment and other types of advertisement in some journals

is or who you are looking for, you could probably say so much more suc-cinctly (and cheaply).

This is perhaps a little unfair to AOK; it probably does know what it wants but is possibly trying too hard to be different in its advertising. Despite its protestations to the contrary, the company sounds fairly traditional and well-ordered. So perhaps it would have been better to take a more traditional line and simply describe the company, the job, the person being sought, the salary and the address for applicants to write to.

(d) Where to Place the Advertisement
We considered, in the last section, the main determinants governing our choice of medium. Apart from general factors, relating to candidate expecta-tions and costs, there are a number of other points to consider when placing a press advertisement. These are outlined in Table 3.3.

Whichever type of medium you choose, your advertisement needs to be placed in a position on the page where the right people will read it. It should, preferably, be of a size and in a position where it will attract the attention of the casual reader, rather than just the ardent job-seeker. You may also like to give thought to the day of the week which will be most appropriate. Some of the major national newspapers devote one issue or more per week to special categories, such as managerial appointments. Midweek days are widely believed to be better than Mondays or Fridays.

3.8   Recruitment and the Law

Current legislation has a bearing both on whom you recruit (and subsequently select) and on how you set about it.

(a) Recruiting the Disabled and Young People

Although, as we shall see, the law specifies that you must not discriminate between applicants for the wrong reasons, there are only two categories of employee to whom there is a direct obligation: in the one case, to recruit, in the other, not to recruit.

(i) At present, all but the smallest employers are obliged to recruit 3 per cent of their workforce from among the ranks of the registered disabled. The Disabled Persons (Employment) Acts 1944 and 1958 require that employers with more than twenty employees take this quota from the register of disabled persons maintained by the government Employment Service. The forthcoming Disability Discrimination Act will make it illegal for those employing more than twenty people to discriminate against the disabled in recruitment, promotion, training or other aspects of employment. 'Reasonable' adjustments to working arrangements on physical layout will have to be made to avoid disadvantaging the disabled. Disabled people who believe they have suffered unlawful discrimination will be able to complain to an industrial tribunal – see pages 270–72. A statement of your policy regarding the employment of the disabled must appear in your Directors' Annual Report if more than 250 people are employed. There is a voluntary code of practice, available from the Employment Service, to help guide you in your dealings with disabled employees.

(ii) You may not employ any child under the age of thirteen years (Children and Young Persons Acts 1933 and 1969). Children (those under the compulsory school-leaving age of sixteen) may not be employed during school hours or for more than two hours on any day on which they are required to attend school. Nor must they be employed on heavy work which may cause injury to them. If you wish to employ a child aged between thirteen and sixteen, a permit must be obtained from the local education authority, and this will specify the conditions which will apply to the employment.

(b) How to Set About Recruitment

The Sex Discrimination Acts of 1975 and 1986 and the Race Relations Act of 1976 make it illegal to specify sex, marital status, colour, race or nationality when advertising or using any other method of recruitment. If you do, this is classified as **direct discrimination**. Neither may you specify qualifications or other requirements with which few people in a particular group will be able to comply, unless these are justified in relation to the job. If you do, this is **indirect discrimination**.

Thus if you were to state in a job advertisement that you required someone capable of lifting heavy weights with the intention of discouraging women from applying, and if this was not in fact essential for the position in question, any potential woman applicant who felt that she had been indirectly discriminated against could complain to an industrial tribunal. The tribunal could award her compensation for any loss, including injury to feelings, which she has suffered as a result of your action. (We will be looking at industrial tribunals in detail in Unit 18.)

In general only where sex or race constitute genuine occupational qualifications (such as a male actor or a Chinese waiter), or where the job is to be performed outside the UK, is discrimination permitted. It is, however, lawful to make special training arrangements to meet the needs of a sex or racial group which is currently under-represented in a particular occupation.

Both Acts apply regardless of how few employees you have.

The Commission for Racial Equality (CRE) has issued a Code of Practice for the Elimination of Racial Discrimination and the Promotion of Equality of Opportunity in Employment. This advises employers to extend the range of recruitment sources used, to avoid the discrimination that can creep in when there is too much reliance on word-of-mouth recruitment or jobs are only advertised in the 'white' press. Requiring candidates to have lived or worked in the UK for a specified period, or stipulation of UK rather than overseas educational qualifications, are also to be avoided. The Code further suggests that you should set out an equal opportunities policy (see Unit 19) and monitor the proportion of people from ethnic minorities who apply to you and are accepted – for comparison with the proportion in the local labour market.

While the Code does not have the force of law, its provisions can be taken into account by an industrial tribunal in deciding whether or not an employer has discriminated. **The Equal Opportunities Commission (EOC)** has produced an equivalent code relating to sex discrimination.

The practice of recruiting from the membership lists of recognised **trade unions** was once common in the UK, with the printing industry providing one of the most notorious examples. Wherever a **closed shop** or union membership agreement operated – see Unit 18 – this was a logical and cost-effective way of recruiting. Since the Trade Union and Labour Relations (Consolidation) Act 1992, it is no longer legal to refuse employment to someone who is, or is not, a member of a (particular) union and you may not restrict your recruitment efforts to those on the union list.

We will have cause to consider these aspects again in Unit 7, as they also affect the selection process.

(c) Government Employment Measures

Youth Training (YT) helps sixteen- and seventeen-year-olds to learn about the world of work. They do this through a programme of on- and off-job training which should lead to an appropriate National Vocational Qualification (NVQ) (see Unit 10).

As an employer, you can contribute to the development of the country's (and your own) future workforce by offering training places in your organisation. There is no obligation to offer trainees jobs at the end of the scheme and you do not pay them wages as they receive a grant. You can get details from your local Training and Enterprise Council (TEC) or Local Enterprise

Company (LEC) (see Unit 10). As well as helping to provide a worthwhile training and preparation for work for youngsters who might otherwise be unemployed, YT provides a useful source of additional help and potential recruits. If a permanent position becomes available, the trainee whom you have had a chance to observe and assess at work may be well worth considering in preference to an unknown outsider.

Modern apprenticeships offer craft-based training to NVQ level 3 or above for sixteen-year-olds. There are schemes in a number of employment sectors, including engineering, retailing and travel services, and more are to follow. Employers can set their own selection criteria but must agree a formal training plan with each recruit and have this approved by their local TEC. Although apprentices do receive a wage from their employer, at least part of the cost of training is met by the TEC. This is a potentially cost-effective way of making sure that those you recruit can make a long-term contribution to your industry.

Training for Work is designed mainly for those who have been unemployed for more than six months, although it is also open to the disabled, to ex-offenders and to others who might have particular difficulty in finding work. The scheme aims to train people in the skills they need to get and keep jobs – and the skills that employers need to avoid shortages.

The programme is administered by TECs and LECs. They have considerable discretion regarding the type of training provided. As with YT, there is no obligation for employers to offer jobs to those who undertake training placements with them as part of the scheme, but it provides another source of potential recruits.

Questions

1. How would you set about compiling and writing up a job description? To what uses might the finished document be put?
2. Compile a job description, personnel specification and recruitment advertisement for either your own job or that of someone you know. Where would you place the advertisement and how much would it cost you?
3. How would you set about ensuring that you attract a suitable field of candidates for an employment vacancy?

Selecting Employees: Preliminary Steps

4.1 Introduction

Once an appropriate field of candidates has been attracted, the next task is to pick out the individual who will be both willing and able to perform the job to your satisfaction. There are a number of tools that can assist you. We will consider the role of the interview in Unit 5 and of assessment centres, selection testing and work samples in Unit 6. Here we are concerned with the other basic elements of an effective selection process.

4.2 Setting up a Selection Procedure

Apart from the recruitment advertisement which, as we have seen, itself acts as a selection device, reaching some and not others, and attracting some and not others, there are five principal components in a conventional selection procedure. These are: application forms/letters of application, references, medical checks, interviews, and tests/simulations/work samples.

There are two sets of decisions to be made in setting up a selection procedure: which of the tools to use and in what order to use them.

(a) Selecting Tools for Selection: the Main Criteria

(i) Candidate expectations. All selection procedures are a two-way process: you are selecting the candidate and the candidate is selecting you. At the unskilled, manual end of the employment spectrum, applicants may not readily see the relevance of complicated application forms. Applicants who completed their education many years ago may look with suspicion on pencil and paper tests. But applicants at all levels would find it odd if they were not interviewed by someone, however briefly and however informally, before starting work.

(ii) Importance of specific attributes. If specific attributes such as a particular typing speed or A1 physical fitness really are essential then you should have candidates tested or examined yourself, rather than relying on ancient certificates and earnest assurances. You must be sure to avoid unfair discrimination through the use of inappropriate selection methods, though (see 'Content validity' on page 82).

(iii) The time available. Asking people to write or telephone for an application form, waiting for it to be completed and returned, arranging medical examinations, calling applicants for one, two or three interviews and administering a battery of tests is a lengthy process, stretching over weeks rather than days. You should always aim to spend the minimum of time compatible with both meeting candidates' expectations and thoroughly investigating their suitability for the job. But don't be stampeded into a hasty decision by the apparent urgency of filling the vacancy.

(iv) Cost. The longer you spend over selection, the more it will cost you, both directly and indirectly. In addition, the design and printing of application forms, test instructions, reference request forms and other documentation will involve further expenditure. But as we are concerned with cost-effectiveness, not just cost minimisation, if it is imperative that you assess accurately (and frequently) some key skill vital to the successful performance of an important job, time and money spent designing and validating (see Unit 6.4) a complex test to measure it will be worthwhile.

(b) Determining the Order: the Main Criteria
The selection process resembles a series of hurdles. Some of the contenders will fall at the first fence and others at the second, so that the field is progressively narrowed down to leave only one survivor. While the idea of making the first hurdle so difficult that few will surmount it has its attractions, candidate expectations or considerations of cost and time may weigh against this. As a general rule, you should try to strike a balance between the following:

(i) *Assess key criteria early in the procedure.* If, for instance, physical fitness is vital, don't leave the medical check to the end or you may find that none of those who have survived the other hurdles meets your health requirements.

(ii) *Try to whittle down numbers as fast as possible.* A well-designed application form can save hours of unnecessary interviewing or test administration; a test which can be administered to a group of applicants simultaneously will both save your time and, assuming the test is reliable and valid, sift out the unsuitable applicants.

(iii) *Avoid the procedure becoming too labour-intensive too soon.* Again, application forms and relevant tests can help if used early on.

(iv) *Bear in mind the candidates' expectations* and try to avoid rejecting people without due regard for their feelings. A candidate who is repeatedly turned down at the application form stage will become very dispirited, while someone who 'fails' at a selection test without the opportunity to vindicate himself in an interview may feel that he has not been given a fair chance. Attention to these points is not just sentimentality: disgruntled candidates are bad for public relations.

One mechanism which is useful at the beginning of the selection procedure is the application form.

4.3 Application Forms and Letters

Whatever method of recruitment you have used, and whatever the shape of the rest of your proposed selection procedure, it is helpful to obtain some basic information about the applicants so that you can assess who is worth interviewing or testing. Wherever possible, this information is best obtained by post in an application form or letter, so that you have time to study the details. However, it can be requested on the spot, a few minutes before you see the candidate if you have already decided to interview. For hourly-paid jobs (especially where applicants may currently be unemployed) the second method will be more acceptable to them, and quicker for you. If you have a large number of applicants to consider, it will be very time-wasting.

(a) The Letter of Application

Obtaining unstructured information from a candidate can play a useful, if limited, part in your selection procedure. It can identify the candidate's ability to express himself clearly and coherently in writing. It can tell you how good his spelling and grammar are. (If they are bad in a job application, the chances are that they are worse when he is not making a special effort.) It can give you a glimpse of his character, through his choice of words or possibly his handwriting. And if you need this kind of information in order to assess his suitability for the job, it will be helpful.

If, on the other hand, the applicant will not be required to write letters or express himself via the written word once employed, such data will largely be irrelevant to your selection decision.

Then too, being unstructured, the information contained in a letter of application is inevitably that which the candidate considers relevant to the job and favourable to himself. His assessment, particularly in relation to job relevance, may differ from yours, though a well-worded advertisement can help to guide his thoughts. You must, therefore, choose between rejecting a potentially worthwhile candidate because he has omitted to give you some information which you require and risking wasting your time through pursuing his application further.

(b) The Uses of an Application Form

(i) Well-designed forms will aid the selection of candidates to go forward to the next stage in the selection procedure. They enable you to compare like information with like, and to relate the facts, the **biodata**, that you have been given, to the requirements of the personnel specification.

(ii) A sophisticated application form (a **weighted biographical inventory**) can itself become an accurate predictor of ultimate job success. The design of this will be derived from the kind of analysis we discussed in Unit 3.4(*b*). The key areas of biodata which correlate with effective performance can be identified and weighted, so that the form itself goes a long way towards establishing the applicant's suitability for the job.

(iii) The application form provides a framework upon which a subsequent interview can be built. It obviates the need for the time-wasting collection of background facts, such as names and addresses of previous employers. By studying the form carefully prior to the interview, the interviewer will be able to identify any points which require investigation. Unanswered questions, or gaps in employment history, can be probed.

(iv) If the candidate is selected, the form can become the basis of his permanent personal record, encapsulating all the details of his life before joining the company.

(v) If the candidate is not selected, you may still wish to keep the form pending a suitable alternative vacancy in the future. There are two dangers here. The candidate was not quite good enough for this vacancy, so will he really be good enough for the next one? The job for which he applied has now been filled by someone else, so will the next job that becomes available be identical to it, with an identical personnel specification? Only if you are convinced that the candidate's attributes are right for the new job should you consider re-approaching him. Passage of time may have dulled your awareness of him. You may not even recognise him when you see him again. But he will feel fairly confident that he will be offered the job the second time. If you disappoint him, he will be (justifiably) disgruntled, or if you appoint him, you may find that you have made an embarrassing mistake.

(vi) Regardless of whether the applicant is selected, the application forms which have been completed will provide you with useful information for an analysis of the labour market: what kind of people are interested in joining you, where they live, what their pay expectations are. This will be of assistance in the assessment of the external availability of human resources which we discussed in Unit 2.4, and in monitoring your equal opportunity policy (see page 287).

(c) Designing an Application Form
Although a form can be used for any of the range of purposes we have mentioned, if it is poorly designed it may fail to meet all or any of them. Furthermore, it may antagonise candidates by making them feel frustrated or inadequate, or by giving the impression that your organisation sets too much store by form-filling. Consideration must be given to both content and layout. It will almost certainly be necessary to design more than one form, as different types of job require different information and emphasis. Data about hobbies and interests may be of great relevance to a position where the employee is required to socialise and entertain on behalf of the company, but they may be less so for jobs which do not require such activity. (There is a school of thought which claims that conclusions about a person's disposition can be drawn from a study of his leisure interests. While this is open to all sorts of counter-argument, where selection profile analysis has been used to identify correlations between interest in a particular pursuit and effective job performance, information about such interests could be relevant.)

(i) **Content.** A checklist for the kind of information you may require is given in Table 4.1, although circumstances will vary from job to job and

Table 4.1   Checklist of application form data

Identification
Name
Address
Telephone number
Date of birth
Name of post applied for
Recruitment source

Education
Schools attended: names and dates
Examinations passed
Higher education: names and dates of institutions attended
Examinations passed
Other qualifications and courses attended: names and dates

Occupation
Names and addresses of all previous employers
Dates of employment (month and year)
Job title
Synopsis of main responsibilities
Final salary
Reason for leaving

Recreation
Hobbies, sports and other pastimes

Miscellaneous
Health record: history of illness plus attendance record in last job
Driving licence/possession of own car
Positions of responsibility held (at school/college/socially)
Notes in support of application

from organisation to organisation. The acid test is whether the information
is something that you need to know in order to assess the candidate's suitability. Ask yourself **why** you think you need to know a person's religion or
nationality, or how many children he has. You may have plans to send him
abroad, in which case the first two *might* be relevant. You may have an
occupational pension scheme or other benefit arrangement which calls for
knowledge of whether or not he has dependants. But is the application form
really the right vehicle for such confidential details? Domestic information
and questions which can be construed as personal rather than job-related
should have no bearing on whether or not you decide to employ the candidate
and should be postponed until after selection. Including them at this stage
is likely to cause concern about potentially illegal discrimination.

The wording of questions must be clear and unambiguous, so that the candidate knows what is required. If some sections of the form are for office use only (and it is sometimes helpful to use parts of the form as an interview guide, or as a checklist for engagement documentation), these should be clearly labelled.

(ii) Layout. The questions asked will vary according to the type of job for which the form is designed. The space required in which to answer those questions will also vary. Candidates for positions where the educational requirements are high will need plenty of space to write their qualifications, and mature candidates will need space in which to list their past employment. School-leaver applicants for unskilled posts, on the other hand, will require little space for either educational qualifications or job history and are likely to feel inadequate if faced with a form which seems to suggest that they should have both.

As with any document for external use, your application form conveys an impression of your company. The quality of the paper and the reprographic process, as well as the actual design of the form, will induce some kind of reaction, whether favourable or unfavourable, conscious or unconscious, among prospective applicants. The more logical the sequence of questions and simple and uncluttered its appearance, the more inviting it will be to applicants to complete. And that, after all, is the essential first step.

4.4   References

A candidate can be asked to nominate referees who are prepared to supply information concerning the applicant's past life and character. Approaching past or present employers without the candidate's permission is bad employment practice. References can come in four main forms.

(a) Unsolicited Testimonials

These may be produced by a prospective employee. He will claim that a previous employer, headmaster or associate has written this (usually glowing) assertion that the bearer is honest, diligent and bursting with integrity. Such documents should be treated with caution. While many are, no doubt, genuine and sincere, they can all too readily be manufactured by anyone with access to his erstwhile employer's headed stationery.

(b) Letters

A response to a specific request for a reference may be obtained from the candidate's nominees. There have been cases of candidates providing names and addresses for reference purposes which belong to their friends and accomplices. But, by and large, this method is less prone to abuse than unsolicited testimonials. Names and addresses of companies can, in any case, be checked, perhaps by just using the telephone directory to make sure that they do exist. But this type of reference is normally unstructured and therefore suffers from the same kind of problem as the letter of application. You are only told what the writer wishes you to know, rather than what you need to know. You can, of course, go back to him for further information and elucidation, but this can be time-consuming and wasteful. It is probably preferable to adopt the next method from the start.

(c) Structured Reference Forms

These can be designed to ensure that you obtain information in a standard framework which will enable you to identify evasions and omissions. If you are employing a number of staff at different levels, you may, as with the application form, feel it appropriate to draw up more than one standard reference form, making each appropriate to a particular level of job.

The kind of general information to be obtained is outlined in Table 4.2.

Table 4.2 Checklist of reference form data

Proposed employment
Company name
Proposed job title
Summary of duties

Employment reference
Dates employed by referee
Capacity in which employed
Summary of main duties
Job performance assessment
Amount and frequency of absence and lateness
Final salary
Reason for leaving
Would you re-employ/do you know of any reason why we should not employ?

Personal assessment
Honesty
Relations with others
Comment on proposed employment

References of this type have a number of points to recommend them.

(i) They may reveal some previously unknown factor, regarding perhaps health, absence record or ability.

(ii) They make possible the verification of basic facts, such as dates of past employment. Any discrepancy between those provided by the candidate and those attested by the referee needs to be carefully investigated. It may add up to a dark and dubious period in the candidate's past – or a clerical error.

(iii) The questions that the referee omits or refuses to answer can be identified clearly and followed up.

(iv) The form can provide information about the actual performance of the candidate, albeit in a different company and job. If used carefully, this can be of more value than some of the predictions of interviewers and testers.

Regrettably, though, this type of reference also has a number of drawbacks.

(i) The referee may be reluctant to commit himself in writing. There is often uncertainty as to the extent to which reference information is actionable in law. In fact, a case for defamation of character by the subject of the reference would only be likely to succeed if the referee could be shown to have maliciously made unjustifiable statements. Negligent mis-statements which result in financial loss could provide grounds for a civil action for damages though.

(ii) The referee may be personally biased or have a particular reason for wanting to convey a favourable or unfavourable picture of the candidate. If, for instance, the present employer would dearly like to dismiss the employee, but has not yet exhausted his disciplinary procedure (see Unit 21), he may be only too happy to provide a glowing reference in order to speed the individual's voluntary departure.

(iii) As the recipient of a reference generally does not know the writer, it is not always easy to tell the real value of the reference. In large organisations, for instance, the completion of references for past or departing employees may be the task of a clerk in a personnel department whose information will only be as detailed and accurate as the facts contained in the individual's personal file.

(d) Telephone References

These may circumvent some of the difficulties if used as a substitute for, or in addition to, the other methods. Although some organisations are reluctant to provide such information over the telephone, others are willing to say things which they would hesitate to put down on paper. (The best way of obtaining references over the telephone is to call the referee and ask him if he would like to ring you back. That way, he has a chance to check that you are genuine.) A checklist of some kind (probably relating to the items in Table 4.2) will help you to ensure that you cover the key areas.

(e) Written Reasons for Dismissal

As we shall see in Unit 21, if an employee is dismissed by his employer he is entitled, under the Employment Protection (Consolidation) Act 1978, to be given a written statement of the reasons. While this is clearly not a substitute for the more detailed reference information that you may want, where an applicant claims that his last employer dismissed him, perusal of his written statement should throw light on the reasons for this.

References are a useful source of additional information about candidates for employment – but only if the major problems we have mentioned can be resolved. And however well the referee knows the candidate, and however honestly he tries to answer your questions, in the last analysis the decision about the applicant's suitability for this particular job, in this particular organisation, will be yours.

4.5 Medical Checks

There are five reasons why it may be advisable to arrange for a medical examination of prospective employees before they are appointed.

(*a*) To safeguard the health of those engaged on hazardous work. Medicals **must** be given to those involved in diving operations, working in compressed air or exposed to ionising radiation, significant levels of lead, asbestos above a certain level or any substance identified as requiring medical surveillance under the Control of Substances Hazardous to Health Regulations 1988.

(*b*) To safeguard the health of vulnerable groups. Epileptics, for instance, should not be employed where a seizure could place them in danger (for example, near moving machinery).

(*c*) To safeguard the health and safety of others. Employing individuals suffering from infectious diseases or violent mental disorders could directly jeopardise the safety of other employees. Employing someone with poor eyesight as a driver could create unnecessary danger for him and others.

(*d*) To ensure that some specific job requirement can be met. This can range from simple tests for colour blindness, administered to designers or electricians, to comprehensive physical examinations for North Sea divers, where peak physical condition is vital.

(*e*) Where there is an occupational pension scheme whose rules require that employees are examined.

In recruitment and selection, the twin considerations of cost and candidate reaction are always important. Both should tend to deter you from insisting on a comprehensive medical examination where a questionnaire to check for specific problems would suffice. Against this must be weighed the dangers of taking on someone who suffers from some disability or disorder for a job which is beyond his capabilities. The Health and Safety at Work Act 1974 and the Management of Health and Safety at Work Regulations 1992 (see Unit 17) have a bearing here.

The only real value of a medical check comes where a qualified medical practitioner, with a thorough knowledge of the physical and mental requirements of the job, assesses the physical and mental state of the applicants. In larger organisations a company doctor is sometimes retained for this purpose, and to treat existing employees at the work-place. He can provide valuable advice concerning the applicant's suitability for a particular job, and if the applicant is unsuitable, can suggest alternative types of work for which he might be considered.

If you need to obtain a medical report from the candidate's own doctor, the requirements of the Access to Medical Reports Act 1988 or the Access to Health Records Act 1990 may apply. This means that the doctor may be entitled to withhold certain information to safeguard the patient's health – as the latter is entitled to see the report.

Questions

1. What are the main tools for selection available today? How would you determine which ones to use in a particular situation?
2. Describe the procedure that you would adopt when selecting trainees for vacancies within an organisation with which you are familiar.
3. Assess the contribution which references and medical checks can make to effective selection procedures.

UNIT 5

Interviewing Candidates for Employment

5.1 Introduction

The interview remains our most commonly used selection tool, even though all too few interviewers are able to measure their success in a way which inspires much confidence in the method. Indeed, some research seems to show that scrapping the interview altogether and leaving the decision to pure chance would not have too startling an effect on the outcome of many selection procedures.

But candidate expectations, if nothing else, should deter us from being too hasty in abandoning the interview. Nor should we lose sight of the ways in which the interview can make a positive contribution to selection.

(*a*) It can provide an insight into the candidate's past behaviour – as an aid to predicting future performance.

(*b*) It can help candidates formulate a realistic picture of what it would be like to work for you, and *vice versa*. Other parts of the process can amend or confirm this, but there is no substitute for the chance to get to know each other face to face.

(*c*) It **involves** candidates in the assessment of their own suitability in a way that few other parts of the selection process do.

These last two points are particularly important if we accept that the outcome of the selection process will only really be satisfactory if both parties – the selector and the applicant – feel it to be right.

In this unit we will focus on how the selection interview can be used to best effect – always bearing in mind that it is only a part of the total process through which candidates and jobs should be matched.

5.2 Interview Preparation

(a) Documentation

An accurate job description and a carefully designed personnel specification expressed as far as possible in terms of what you want the candidate to be able to do, are essential prerequisites for effective interviewing. In addition, you need sufficient background information about the candidate to enable you to obtain a preliminary picture of his basic biographical details. In Unit

4.3 we discussed the relative merits of application forms and unstructured letters of application.

If you deal regularly with recruitment and selection, you may find it helpful to design standard letters to be sent to applicants. These might include:

(i) a letter requesting the completion and return of an application form, to be sent out with the form in response to initial enquiries;

(ii) a letter requesting attendance at an interview;

(iii) a letter politely rejecting candidates who prove unsuitable at any stage of the selection procedure (see Unit 7.3).

Prior thought given to this aspect of documentation will save time during the selection process.

(b) Administrative Arrangements
Before you start inviting candidates for interview, you must sort out where, when, how and by whom it is to be conducted.

(i) Decide when and where the interview is to be held (see 5.2(c)).

(ii) Decide who will be involved in conducting the interview (see 5.2(d)).

(iii) Notify other interviewers of the time and place, and arrange a meeting to plan the interview (see 5.2(e)).

(iv) Notify the candidates, in good time, of the time and place. Tell them how to get there, who to ask for, and roughly how long and what form the proceedings will take.

(v) Notify the receptionist/doorkeeper or other relevant person whom to expect and where to direct them.

(vi) Make arrangements to avoid being interrupted during the interview and give yourself enough time to be thorough.

(vii) If the interviewees have to travel some distance to the interview, make arrangements for their expenses to be reimbursed.

(viii) If candidate expectations and the timing of the interview warrant it, arrange to have tea or coffee served. If you are interviewing a candidate for a senior appointment, it may be appropriate to take him to lunch (if your budget will allow it).

(c) Environment
If the candidate who joins you is to work in archaic, badly designed and sparsely furnished surroundings, it may give quite the wrong impression if you conduct the interview in a plush modern office. It is more helpful to give something of the physical flavour of the environment he will meet if selected.

A second, and possibly conflicting, consideration is the need for the interview to be held somewhere private, where two (or more) people can sit and converse without interruptions or extraneous noises. (One way to solve this conflict is to take him to see the section where he would be working, after the interview. Even so, the memory he carries away could be of the interview room itself, as that will be where he spent most time.)

Candidate expectations and your own normal working environment will both need to be considered in determining what is desirable and feasible. There are a few general pointers which may be helpful. The things to avoid are:

(i) Extremes of light intensity, especially sunlight or direct lights shining in the candidate's eyes.

(ii) Extremes of heat and cold. The candidate may already be feeling inclined to perspire or shiver, without any help from the environment.

(iii) Chairs which are awkward to get in and out of, or inelegant to sit in.

(iv) Confusion over who sits where. Indicate the candidate's seat clearly to him.

(v) Eyeball to eyeball confrontation. This is particularly important where there is more than one interviewer present. A row of interviewers ranged against a lone interviewee is likely to make him feel tense and outnumbered. The solution is to arrange the chairs, perhaps in a circle, so that everyone can see everyone else without being drawn into sitting and staring at them.

(vi) Booby traps. Imagine the mortification of a candidate who sees the coat stand collapse under the weight of his coat or who makes a dignified exit into the storeroom.

While all of these should be avoided, if you intend to obtain the best from the interviewee and hence the interview, there are a couple of more positive points to bear in mind.

(i) Provide adequate space for the interviewee and his belongings, so that he doesn't feel that he is intruding.

(ii) Observe the basic social requirements. If smoking is permitted, provide the applicant with an ashtray: watching two inches of ash disintegrating over a man's best suit can be a distressing experience, particularly for the wearer. Similarly the provision of coffee and biscuits designed to relax the candidate will have precisely the opposite effect if he kicks his cup over for lack of a table to put it on or sheds biscuit crumbs all over his long-suffering suit for lack of a plate.

(d) Staffing

Trying to conduct an interview with more than one interviewer present is not an easy task, but it is often necessary. If the job requires that the employee reports to more than one person, the status and experience of his immediate boss may need to be backed up by the 'grandfather' figure of his own boss's boss; there may be a personnel section which has responsibility for vetting certain aspects of candidate suitability and needs to be represented at the interview, and the old adage 'two heads are better than one' brings home the fact that bias and unfair discrimination may be reduced by involving more than one person in the decision.

If someone else is to be involved, you have two alternatives: a two-person/panel interview, or two or more separate interviews. There are a number of factors to be taken into account in deciding which is more appropriate to your needs:

(i) The number of times the interview is to feature as a selection hurdle. If there is to be a preliminary screening interview to draw up a shortlist, followed by a more intensive interview for the 'survivors', these tasks can be shared out.

(ii) The relative status of the interviewers involved. It is sometimes difficult for more junior managers to ask appropriate questions and formulate an accurate assessment if they are inhibited by the presence of their own boss. They may be too inclined to defer to the boss's line of questioning or to be swayed by his apparent enthusiasm, or the lack of it. (If the applicant spots this, he can play one off against the other.)

(iii) Candidate expectations. At more senior levels, and in more mechanistic types of organisation, it is normal to have a panel of interviewers. Where, however, candidates are likely to be overawed by the presence of more than one interviewer (as with school-leavers), a sequential approach is preferable.

(iv) Candidate convenience. If candidates are travelling some distance to be interviewed, and if separate interviews would mean a return visit, a panel may again be preferable. A panel interview also prevents the candidate being asked the same questions again.

(v) The speed with which a decision is required. If all the people concerned see the candidates on the same occasion, they should be able to evaluate the information and make their decision immediately afterwards.

(vi) Simultaneous observation by the interviewers. If you feel that it is important that everyone should see the candidate in the same situation and in the same light, a panel will be the answer. This will be related to the degree of overlap which exists between the areas of interest of those involved. (If each interviewer needs to pursue a different aspect of the candidate's application, they may feel that it is not worth sitting through other people's questioning about things which are of no interest to themselves.)

(e) Planning

Before conducting any interview it is important to spend some time thinking about what you hope to achieve and planning how to set about it. If the interview is to be one in a sequence, it is vital to identify the purpose of each interview and the areas to be covered at each stage. If there is to be more than one interviewer present, it is important to meet beforehand to agree both your overall strategy and specific lines of questioning, so that everyone obtains the information he requires without confusing the candidate or causing undue repetition.

Your first task is to consider the structure of your interview and the overall strategy you will adopt.

5.3   Interviewing Strategy

There are four basic elements of good interviewing:

(a) Contact

Unless you make contact – establish rapport – with the interviewee, you are unlikely to persuade him to talk. If he does not talk, you will learn nothing.

(b) Content

Once he starts to talk, consideration must be given to what he is saying, to see how it relates to what you, as the interviewer, want to know. There is, therefore, a process of digestion and matching on the interviewer's part.

(c) Control

Rapport without a purpose can lead the interview to degenerate into a friendly chat which achieves little. It is vital that you retain control of the interview and can steer the discussion in an appropriate direction. This way you can find out what you need to know, within the time that you have available. Exercising control will mean bringing the interviewee gently back to the point and preventing him retreading ground that has already been satisfactorily covered.

(d) Structure

Maintaining control will be a lot easier if you work to a clear and relevant structure. It will also increase your chances of finding out what you really need to know, without confusing the candidate.

Should you opt for a blow by blow **biographical** account of the candidates' past lives, starting with early childhood? Or should you select what seem to you to be the turning points or **critical incidents** in their careers to date and explore those in detail? The answer is neither. The first will take too long and may fail to provide all the information you need to assess how your selection criteria are met. The second could miss the point altogether and may feel unduly like a hostile interrogation.

Far better to settle for a **criteria-based** approach, taking each of the competences you have identified and asking the **candidates** to give you examples of past occasions when each has been called into play. By letting them choose whether to draw these from education, work, social life or hobbies, you are more likely to discover both positive and negative examples of the relevant behaviour.

So if one of your criteria is to do with making bold decisions, you can ask 'can you think of a time when you really decided to take a risk on something? . . . Please tell me about it.' Don't just settle for one example, always ask for a second or third and look at each criterion from more than one angle. In this instance, you might try following up with 'what examples can you think of where you just knew you had to take the safest option?' There is more guidance on this in the example in the next section.

'Just a minute – who is interviewing whom?'

Within this broad framework you must decide on an overall strategy to achieve your ends. Should you introduce an element of stress, or will this give the candidate a bad impression of you and the organisation? If it puts him too much on the defensive you will not learn enough about him to reach a decision. Should you concentrate on trying to sell the job, or let him dominate the interview in his attempts to sell himself? Either of these courses of action may lead you into the sales trap: a sale at all costs, regardless of the suitability of the product for the purposes intended.

The best solution to the interviewer's dilemma is the adoption of what is known as a **joint problem-solving strategy**. This means:

(*a*) viewing the interview as a chance to help the candidate identify his own strengths and weaknesses, in relation to the job;

(*b*) working with the candidate to determine whether his weaknesses can be minimised and his strengths maximised to enable him to do the job to your mutual satisfaction.

The advantages of this approach are twofold.

(i) The interviewee will feel more committed to the decision made at the interview. If he can see clearly that the job would not be right for him, he is less likely to go away and spread disgruntled stories about you and your organisation. If, on the other hand, you both agree that he should be able to do an effective job, you both have a vested interest in proving yourselves right.

(ii) Increased information on which your joint decision can be based. If the interview becomes a shared exercise, rather than a game of hide and seek, there is more likelihood that the pertinent facts will emerge and an appropriate decision can be made.

Weighed against these two very important advantages must be the additional expertise and time that will be needed to carry through the strategy effectively.

In the next section we will consider the kind of questioning techniques which can help you here.

5.4 Questioning Techniques

Once you have broken the ice with a few pleasantries at the start of the interview, it will help to get both you and the interviewee on the right track if you explain the purpose of your meeting and the form that it will take.

The general rules of questioning are listed below.

(*a*) Ask open questions and listen to the replies.

(*b*) Link your questions to the candidate's replies or your own last question.

(*c*) Probe each reply to find out what the candidate is really saying, without putting him on the defensive. Summarise to check that you have understood.

(*d*) Keep to a logical sequence of questions so that you don't confuse him.

(*e*) Use pauses to give the interviewee time to think and to encourage him to say more.

(*f*) Make encouraging noises, nod, and look interested, to keep him talking.

(*g*) Use direct 'yes/no' questions sparingly just to help control the information flow from particularly talkative candidates.

(*h*) Avoid interrupting or putting words in the candidate's mouth.

(*i*) Avoid multiple, ambiguous or jargon-riddled questions which don't get you much further forward.

(*j*) Avoid using leading questions which predetermine the candidate's replies.

(*k*) Avoid criticising the candidate or his replies. This will put him on the defensive.

(*l*) Avoid using mannerisms that the candidate may find distracting.

In the case study that follows we can see some of the pitfalls that await the inexperienced interviewer. Both interviewers have identified the same selection criteria, but they have rather different strategies for assessing these.

Case Study

Jenny Jones, a school-leaver, is applying for the job of sales assistant in the perfumery department of a large store. Although quite bright, she is rather shy. She is being interviewed by the manager of the department.

Dialogue	Commentary
Manager: Hello. Come in. Sit down. So you've come about the job then, have you?	An abrupt introduction. A leading, rather obvious question.
Jenny: Er. . . . Yes.	
Manager: You've just left school then, have you? You've never worked in a store before, have you? Can you add up?	A multiple question, including implied criticism and three yes/no questions. Which should Jenny answer first? She isn't sure which to tackle and is already feeling defensive.
Jenny: (*blushing*) Er . . . Mum says I'll soon learn about customers.	
Manager: Eh? Oh yes, dare say you will. What's six bars of soap at 32p each?	Pounces with a test, with no lead in.
Jenny: Er. . . .	
Manager: Come on. You'd have to do it quicker than that if there was a customer waiting.	Criticism again, and unconcealed impatience.
Jenny: Er . . . £1.82.	Flustered by her aggressive manner.
Manager: No! We can't use people who can't add up. I don't know why they don't teach you better in school these days.	

Exit Jenny, in tears.

This particular manager has not done much to enhance the store's reputation as an employer. Nor has she found out enough about Jenny to know whether she would make a satisfactory sales assistant. Now let's have a look at how the situation might have been handled using a joint problem-solving approach and more open questions. It takes longer, but the outcome is more satisfactory for all concerned.

Dialogue	Commentary
Manager: Hello. (*Pause*)	Encourages response.
Jenny: Hello.	She's broken the ice and said something.
Manager: Thank you for coming to see me. My name is Alice Brown. I run the perfumery department here.	Jenny now knows who she is talking to. Alice Brown outlines her purpose in a positive and constructive way.
I know you have already had details of the job you've applied for, and I'll be happy to answer any questions you may have shortly. What I'd like to do for the first part of our interview is to take one or two key aspects of the work and see whether there are any things you've done, at school, in your hobbies, during holiday jobs and so on, which might help you in a job like this. I'd like you to think of **specific** examples wherever you can.	Sending out a copy of the job description in advance of the interview saves time and ensures all candidates are fully briefed. The contents and any other information given at interview will form part of any subsequent contract of employment.
We'll start by thinking of what it takes to provide our customers with the sort of service they expect. I know you haven't worked in a store before, but can you think of **any** occasion when you have gone out of your way to help someone recently, especially someone you didn't know well?	By allowing Jenny to choose her own examples Mrs Brown will get a much clearer picture of her capability. The question is phrased as a direct one, which might limit the response, but the encouraging tone of voice and the request for an example **should** get a more detailed reply.
Jenny: Well . . . there was the lady who was looking for the hospital last Saturday. Is that the sort of thing you mean?	Looks for guidance.

Manager: It sounds like it – tell me what happened.

Encourages and probes for more detail.

Jenny: Well, I'd never seen her before, but I was waiting at the bus stop and she stopped her car and asked for directions. She seemed a bit upset and couldn't seem to get what I was telling her so in the end I got in and took her there – it was only five minutes away.

Manager: Mm. And did she appreciate your help?

Probes for more insight into Jenny's reaction.

Jenny: Not really, she was too preoccupied. But it turned out her mother was very ill, so it was quite understandable.

Mrs Brown is beginning to build a picture of Jenny as a concerned and caring person, but is anxious to make sure she doesn't get a one-sided view.

Manager: Yes, indeed. Now I wonder if you can think of an instance when you thought it best to let someone sort out their own problems, rather than getting involved?

Jenny: Well ... I suppose ... *(Hesitates. Mrs Brown nods)* In some ways I shouldn't have gone with the lady on Saturday. You ought to be careful going off with strangers ... but she was **obviously** in trouble.

Encourages and gives her time to think.

Manager: What about any other examples?

Mrs Brown can continue to probe for both positive and negative instances until she is satisfied she understands how Jenny naturally reacts to others.

Fine. So although you've had no direct experience of working with customers you have had plenty of dealings with people, which should stand you in good stead.	Reassuring, and a link into the next area of questioning.
Now I wonder if we can think about another aspect of the job – working out how much change to give. Of course you would be trained in how to use our electronic tills, but there will always be the odd occasion when someone catches you with a quick question. What have you done that might help you there?	Instead of just pouncing, she has explained the reason for her interest and asked an open question which again puts the onus on Jenny to select her own examples.

Jenny:	Well, I was quite good at maths at schools.	Provides a lead.
Manager:	What did you do best?	Probes.
Jenny:	I suppose mainly addition and subtraction and that. I got a bit lost sometimes in algebra.	Identifies a possible weakness.
Manager:	Well, we don't need you to do algebra here. We're more concerned with adding and multiplying . . . Perhaps you could work out for me the kind of sum we do . . . What would you charge for six bars of soap at 32p each? *(Pause)*	Reassurance and encouragement. Linking Gives Jenny time to digest the question and think for a moment.

Jenny: £1.92

Manager: Well done! Let's try another couple. (*Jenny gets both the next two mental arithmetic questions right, establishing that she does know what she's doing.*

A mental arithmetic test like this will only be valid where the ability you need to test is mental, not written arithmetic.

The interview proceeds in this vein, exploring Mrs Brown's other selection criteria until she feels she has a full and fair picture of Jenny's abilities.) Now, Jenny, perhaps we can think back over the things we've been talking about, and see how we feel about the job . . . You're good at arithmetic, and you enjoy helping people. You have an interest in fashion in general and cosmetics in particular, and you like things to be neat and orderly. Have I missed anything?

Summarising, to see if they agree.

Mrs Brown has found out a lot more about Jenny than the previous interviewer did. Although each interview is different, and interviewees will react in different ways, the key skill lies in tailoring your interviewing pace and manner to each one.

Once you have obtained the information you need, the next task is to work out what it means.

5.5 Evaluating Information

In interviews such as the one we have just been considering, the information is being weighed up as soon as it is received. Mrs Brown is evaluating the information and deciding what to do with it. This is very necessary if she is to maintain control and direct the interview along appropriate paths. It is also important since she hopes, at the end of the interview, to have reached a decision as to the best course of action.

(In some instances, you may wish to do more of this evaluation after the event – see Unit 7. In that case, care must be taken when using a joint problem-solving approach that the decision you arrive at subsequently is not at variance with the general tenor of the interview.) We all evaluate information as we receive it. As we shall see in Unit 13.6, this is part of the nature of communication between one individual and another. During and after the interview every piece of information received must be weighed up and alternative interpretations examined.

The opposite of this careful weighing up and evaluation is the unconscious habit of jumping to conclusions – making up your mind about the applicant in the first few minutes of the interview or allowing prejudice to determine the outcome. This can take several forms.

(a) The Halo Effect

This occurs where one feature of the interviewee becomes an overriding factor which governs our perception of the person. A common pitfall is to assume that someone who is attractive and articulate is also intelligent.

(b) Prejudice/Bias

We tend to prejudge people, either favourably or unfavourably, because they belong to a particular group or remind us of a particular person. Common prejudices include the assumption that members of one race are more hard-working than those of another, or that women are less ambitious than men. These preconceptions will colour our interpretation of any comments they may make.

(c) Stereotypes

These take two forms.

(i) Good worker stereotypes. We may build up a picture in our minds of what a good worker is like, and then use the interview as a means of finding someone who matches that, rather than the personnel specification. We will be favourably disposed to those who appear to match, and more critical of those who do not. The most common stereotypes of the good worker are the 'boy scout' stereotype (a do-gooder and pillar of the community) and the 'human relations' stereotype (a jolly good sort whom everyone likes). Neither may be right for the job.

(ii) Physical trait stereotypes. We may identify one physical characteristic and assume that everyone who possesses that trait will be alike in character. Some examples are that people with red hair have quick tempers or that people whose eyes are close together are not to be trusted. Such unfounded assumptions will again colour our judgement and make it more difficult for us to evaluate information in a well-balanced way.

(d) Unfavourable Information

Most of us are more heavily influenced by people's bad points than by their good ones. Once we have formulated an adverse impression we are slow to change our minds. This, too, can be a barrier to effective evaluation of all the information that has emerged during the interview.

The evidence for the existence of this range of human failings comes mainly from a series of American studies, carried out some years ago at McGill University and in Minnesota. It is unlikely that we can really free ourselves from them. All we can do is to recognise that they exist and try and come to terms with our own particular weaknesses. One useful exercise is to ask a colleague to sit in with you during an interview and challenge all your conclusions at the end, to see if you can justify them rationally.

But before you make a final decision about whom to select, you might like to consider the contribution that a more rounded assessment process can make.

Questions

1. Describe the steps that you would take if you were inviting a group of candidates in to your company for interview.
2. Compile a list of the open and probe questions that you might use when interviewing a woman returning to work after raising a family, who is applying for a position as a hotel receptionist.
3. The interview, although the most widely used selection tool, has certain inherent disadvantages. What are these and how might they be overcome?

UNIT 6

Assessment Centres, Tests and Work Samples

6.1 Introduction

For some jobs the interview remains the key component of the selection process. In recent years, partly as a response to research evidence highlighting the poor predictive power of conventional interviews, there has been a marked increase in the use of additional methods to complement or compensate.

School- and college-leavers and many more experienced candidates now regularly face assessment centres as a follow-up to a brief first interview. Team selection for shop floor employees is also increasingly sophisticated, with the use of simulations and work samples becoming quite routine.

6.2 Assessment Centres

Some organisations do indeed have a 'centre' where assessment takes place – a physical location, a company training centre perhaps, which is permanently set up for assessment purposes. Many others use the term to describe the collection of exercises, simulations, interviews and tests through which they obtain samples of candidates' behaviour to match against competence-/behaviour-based selection criteria.

The concept is by no means new. During World War II the War Office was confronted with an acute shortage of officers. The War Office Selection Board was therefore set up by expert psychologists in order to provide a mechanism for identifying officer potential as accurately as possible, within the tight time constraints imposed by the military situation. The group selection programmes that the boards devised were designed to measure a whole range of attributes, using traditional test and interview methods. But they also tried, wherever possible, to create the kind of situations where the candidates' physical stamina, leadership ability, problem-solving and deductive powers, communication skills and so on could be clearly demonstrated and observed.

Modern Army Officer Selection Board procedure has adhered to this idea. An assault course assists in the assessment of physical prowess. A physical task, in which the candidate is required to use the resources of the rest of the group of candidates in order to solve some problem (be it transporting equipment across a stream or barrels over a pit) provides a forum for leadership skills and problem-solving ability. A leaderless group discussion, again problem-centred, is used to see who emerges as an authoritative leader to whom the others will listen, and to see who makes the most practical suggestions for the resolution of the problem. Candidates are asked to deliver a five-minute talk to the rest of the candidate group and the assessors, so that their powers of oral communication can be examined. Thus each activity is carefully designed to simulate parts of the job and to enable a team of trained assessors to see how each candidate actually does perform, not just what skills he seems to possess.

The civil service and many business organisations have adapted the approach to include business simulations, case studies, in-tray exercises to assess priority setting and time management, and a raft of other elements. Specialist assessment consultants such as DDI (Development Dimensions International) offer a complete service, from training assessors to designing tailor-made exercises and assessing results.

Professionally run assessment centres have three main advantages.

(i) Research generally indicates that they provide a more accurate basis for predicting job performance than conventional interviews and tests.

(ii) Because they are and are seen to be both thorough and relevant, even those candidates who are initially wary of them generally feel they are fair.

(iii) Because they highlight where individual candidate's strengths and weaknesses lie, they can also be used internally, for development purposes. We will discuss this aspect in Unit 11.

An assessment centre is not something that can be undertaken lightly. Detailed analysis of the job, expert activity design, fully trained assessors and up to forty-eight hours with a group of candidates are required. This all adds up to a more expensive and sophisticated selection procedure than most small companies are prepared to justify, rightly or wrongly. There are several less elaborate ways of testing particular selection criteria. We will consider each in turn.

6.3   Types of Tests

If we want to know whether a candidate possesses a particular skill or can perform a particular task we have two alternatives. Either we ask him, relying on the accuracy of his own assessment and his honesty, or we test him, thereby providing ourselves with the opportunity to assess his abilities and measure them against the standards for which we know (from our personnel specification) that we are looking.

Tests can be administered either before or after the interview. They have the advantages that most types can be administered to a group of people simultaneously, saving time, and supervision of the simpler tests can be delegated to quite junior staff, provided they have been properly trained in test administration.

The tests fall into five main categories. The simplest can be designed by an amateur who pays attention to the basic principles which we will discuss in Unit 6.4. More sophisticated tests require professional expertise in both design and interpretation. 'Dabbling' by amateurs can be dangerous and only those certified competent by the British Psychological Society are authorised to use the more complex aptitude, intelligence and personality tests.

(a) Performance Tests

These are tests to measure specific skills required in a job. A shorthand and typing or word-processing test, for instance, can indicate both the speed and accuracy of candidates for secretarial positions. Similarly, a driving test can indicate the proficiency of, say, a heavy goods vehicle driver.

The attraction of performance tests is that they can be related closely to the job for which the applicant is being considered. He is, in fact, being tested on his ability to do a part of the job to a specified standard. Where skills are clearly differentiated and standards are known, this is very helpful. In more complex, managerial jobs, for instance, it may not be so easy to isolate the important component skills, and still less easy to design tests to measure actual performance.

The logical extension of the performance test is the **work sample**. These examine performance across a whole task rather than individual skills and are explored in Unit 6.6.

(b) Knowledge Tests

These are designed to assess what an applicant knows about a subject relevant to the job. Many applicants will possess certificates from various examining bodies, indicating that they have anything from a GCSE to an honours degree in, say, geography. If this was obtained some time ago, or if you need to be sure that a candidate does have sufficient knowledge of the geography of Europe to be able to perform satisfactorily as, for instance, a travel sales adviser, you could devise your own mental or written test.

(c) Aptitude Tests

These differ from the two previous types of test in that they are not designed to measure something that candidates have already learnt. Aptitude tests are designed instead to assess whether candidates have the basic abilities to develop particular skills or knowledge in the future. They take two main forms:
(i) General aptitude tests. There is a whole range of aptitudes which some of us possess to a greater degree than others. Hand–eye co-ordination, manipulative dexterity, mechanical reasoning, spatial ability, numeracy, word-fluency, visual perception and critical thinking are just some of them. Many commercially available tests are designed to measure such aptitudes. Thus, by testing someone's ability to place rods in holes in a board, you may assess whether his hand and his eye are sufficiently well co-ordinated for him to learn a particular job on the assembly line. Similarly, by giving an applicant a written series of pairs of words, some (but not all) of which are identical, and asking him to identify the mismatches, you can assess whether he has enough clerical aptitude to be able to check accurately through written data.

The design of such aptitude tests requires a two-stage approach, which makes it more complex, and generally less satisfactory, than the basic performance test. In both cases you need to examine the job and identify the key skills, but in devising an aptitude test of this type you then need to determine the basic aptitudes that a person would need in order to be able to develop those skills. Only then can you design the test.

(ii) Trainability tests. These are an attempt to return to measuring actual performance, rather than the aptitudes which are thought to underlie it. They are a means of resolving the dilemma of how to measure the performance of someone who has not yet learnt how to do a task. It would, for example, be futile to attempt to administer a sewing machine performance test to someone who had never learnt to sew on a machine. But if you were prepared to teach recruits to use the machine once they had joined you, what you really need to know is whether they will be able to learn to use it within a given time. So you take a small part of the job and, under standardised conditions, instruct the applicants in how to carry it out. You then test to see if they can do the task.

This method has been used successfully for jobs as diverse as building society manager and sewing machinist. It has the added advantage that it enables the applicant to experience some of the actual job content. This can be a very powerful self-selection device. Either he likes what he sees, in which case his motivation to do well is increased, or he does not like it, in which case he may decide to withdraw his application. Both parties will then be saved the expense and frustration that would be caused if the candidate's aversion to the job was not discovered until after he had joined the company. Trainability tests require more time to administer than ordinary aptitude tests, as the candidate must be taught the task first. They also need a trainer to give instruction and a careful analysis of the task and relevant standards of performance. Even so, the benefits can certainly outweigh the extra effort.

(d) Intelligence Tests
In some senses these too are a form of aptitude test. They have, nevertheless, tended to emerge as a separate category because of the complex but fundamental nature of the aptitude concerned.

The concept of intelligence is not an easy one to define. There are some who would put it no more specifically than 'that combination of abilities important within a given culture'. For our purposes we will define it as an aptitude for general reasoning and the ability to relate one concept to another. The design of intelligence tests is more specialised than for most of the other types we have so far considered. The most widely known example is the old 11+ examination, where sequences of words, pictures and numbers were used to measure the individual's ability to relate the items in the series. Although tests of this kind can be used in the workplace, it is much easier to identify how much manual dexterity is required to do a job than to work out how much of this more nebulous quality called intelligence is needed.

(e) Personality Tests

Like intelligence testing our final category is definitely not an area for the amateur. Personality is a complex web of factors which reflect the whole of a person's character: it includes the extent to which he is introvert or extrovert, happy-go-lucky, proud, expedient and practical. Pencil and paper tests that have been designed to assess personality usually take the form of a self-recognition exercise, such as those popularised by some of the newspapers and women's magazines which purport to help you identify how good a wife, husband or parent you are.

One of the more widely used tests is **Cattell's 16 PF (Personality Factor) Test.** Here you are presented with a series of written statements and, for each set of statements, you are asked to indicate, as spontaneously as possible, the one with which you most readily identify. (The questions are of the 'If I had a choice I would rather spend my time at a football match/walking in the country/don't know' type.) Some questions are designed to cross-check your response to earlier sets of questions, to act as a lie detector and to ensure that a balanced picture is obtained. When all the questions have been answered, a score is derived for each of the sixteen personality factors that the test is designed to measure. This score is then compared with the standard score for people of the same age, sex and cultural background. The result is plotted on a chart or **personality profile** to show the shape of your personality. This can then be compared with the ideal shape for the job in question. Unfortunately the derivation of this ideal shape is not an easy task, as two people with completely different combinations of personality factors may do the job equally well. Such tests are also particularly prone to faking by candidates (see Unit 6.5).

Although most of the personality tests used for selection claim to be non-evaluative (they do not say whether it is good or bad to be extrovert, simply that you do or do not match the level required for the job), we all tend to be rather sensitive about our personalities. Great harm can be done to an individual by ill-advised feeding back of results.

There are several other approaches to the study of personality, apart from the tests we have mentioned. We can find out what sort of person a candidate is by asking him to supply an **interest inventory** giving details of his leisure activities. We can also apply what are known as **projective techniques**, which involve procedures such as word association and pictorial interpretation, more commonly associated with the psychiatrist's couch and too specialised for general application.

6.4 Using Tests

From the comments we have made so far, it will be clear that the design, administration and interpretation of tests requires considerable care. Like any other part of your selection procedure, tests are only worthwhile if they act as a fair and accurate predictor of effective job performance.

(a) Considerations in Test Design

There are a number of steps which can help you in setting up your own test procedure:

(i) Refer to the job description to identify the key component tasks in the job.

(ii) Analyse each to see what competences are required, as listed in your personnel specification.

(iii) Separate what you need someone to be able to do when he starts work (base skills and knowledge) from those things for which you will train him (aptitudes), and from the more general attitudes and personality factors.

(iv) Consider the base skills and knowledge. What exactly must the newcomer be able to do? Shorthand at 120 words per minute with no errors? Add up five-figure columns using a calculator with a maximum 2 per cent error rate? What can the present job-holder do? How fast? How accurately? In what conditions of heat, light, noise and with what equipment? Your answers to questions like these will help to formulate both the shape of the test and the standards that you set for success. What you are seeking is as much realism as possible. If the job is done standing up, the test should be done standing up. If there is a particular type of machine that the recruit will be expected to use, the test to assess performance should be on that machine.

(v) Now consider the aptitudes. Let's suppose that the job involves rapid finger movements, perhaps operating a keyboard. So you are looking for someone with finger dexterity. How nimble can you expect his fingers to be before he has received training and practice? How nimble were the present effective job-holders when they started? (It's no use considering how nimble they are now, after years of practice.) How best can you simulate the kind of movement that is needed in the job? Again, the closer you can get to reality without putting the inexperienced candidate at a disadvantage, the better. If the job requires that both hands should be moved, the test should require that both hands are moved. If the job requires the use of all the fingers and the thumbs, the test should require the use of all the fingers and the thumbs.

The example we have used is a physical one, a **psychomotor skill**. A similar process could be used for assessing mental skills such as numeracy or clerical aptitude.

If you consider that you need a more complete assessment of intelligence, do not attempt to design your own test. Approach a body such as the National Foundation for Educational Research (NFER) who will be able to give you specific guidance.

(vi) Finally, consider the general area of mental attitudes to work. This brings us to attitude measurement and personality testing, so again reference to experts will be necessary.

For many jobs, it will not be sufficient to mount just one test: a complete battery may be needed to form an assessment over the whole series of tasks that the job-holder will be called upon to perform.

(b) Setting the Cut-off Points

However well-designed the test is, if the standard set for passing (the acceptable level of performance) is too high or too low, the test will not be much help. But establishing the cut-off points is not easy, particularly, as we have seen, where you are dealing with aptitudes. Your present workers will have turned their aptitudes into skills and inexperienced candidates cannot be expected to match these performance levels. There are two main possibilities:

(i) Design or buy the test, administer it to applicants, and place their scores in a sealed envelope. You can then select your new recruit(s) on the basis of interview and other selection data, without looking at the test scores. Once those selected have been doing the job for long enough for you to identify the good performers of the task, as distinct from the not so good, take out the test scores. What did the worst of the good performers score? If your test has satisfactory predictive validity (see below), that will be your cut-off point for this particular test in relation to this particular job.

(ii) Use the norms provided by the designer of commercially produced tests. For each such test there is usually a norm or standard score for particular types of job. Care must be taken here to ensure that the conditions under which the test is administered and the task for which it is used are exactly as prescribed.

(c) Validating the Test

There are a number of different kinds of validity, some of which are more relevant than others when using tests for selection.

(i) Face validity. Although apparently the most superficial aspect of validity, this basic question of 'Does it look right?' is very important. If it doesn't look right to the tester, he will lack confidence in it and may be inclined to dilute the results. If it doesn't look right to the candidate, he may either refuse to do it, or do it half-heartedly, neither of which will help you to ensure that you appoint the right candidate. You can assess face validity by asking candidates whether they can see the relevance of the test and would be prepared to undergo it.

(ii) Predictive validity. It doesn't matter how right the test looks, though, if it is not predicting success in the job. This will be judged according to the criteria that you determine for measuring effectiveness: your **criterion data**. Length of stay, salary progression, promotion rate and performance appraisal ratings provide possible yardsticks.

You can use the sealed envelope technique that we have already described to establish, first and foremost, whether there is any relationship at all between the test scores and effective performance. Do all the good performers score high on this test? Do all the bad performers score low? Or, given a reasonable sample size – say thirty – do at least a significant proportion of the two types of performer fall into the appropriate scoring category? If so, you will probably be justified in using the test to try to predict into which performance category an applicant with fall. (You may find that some tests seem to differentiate well between the good and mediocre performers, but not so well between the mediocre and the bad. Other tests may be good at predicting female success, but not so good at predicting male success. You may therefore need to take into account such moderator variables as sex and age, and to think in terms of practical, rather than purely statistical, validity. You may also find that in some instances the good performers score low, while the bad performers score high. What matters is that the test can distinguish between the two groups.)

(iii) Content validity. Although there may be a high correlation between test results and performance of a specific task, it is important to ensure that the test is measuring something which is relevant to the overall job. The use of inappropriate or badly designed selection methods can lead you to discriminate unfairly against some applicants – who could do the job but who cannot cope with your selection procedures. A test of shorthand ability will have low content validity if the job in fact involves only audio typing. You can assess content validity by checking to ensure that the competence that you are measuring is still relevant to the current personnel specification for the job in question.

(iv) Concurrent validity. This is the extent to which a test can differentiate between your present employees. It may be less relevant in selection, for reasons which we have discussed. You can, however, assess it by asking your present employees to do the test, and then examining the relationship between their results in the test and their actual job performance (assessed by other means).

(v) Construct validity. This is the extent to which a test measures what it sets out to measure. You can assess this by using more than one method of measuring the same construct or aspect, and cross-checking the results. One test which is designed to measure the testee's powers of deduction, for instance, requires that he disregards his own previous experience and deduces his answers from the information given in the test. It may be questioned whether the construct measured by this test is indeed deductive powers or rather the testee's ability to divorce himself from reality.

(d) Ensuring Reliability

Although it is very important that tests are properly validated, the reliability of the test is also significant. A reliable test is one which will produce consistent results when repeated on a number of occasions. If your test is not reliable, you might select people on one occasion whom you would have rejected on another. Reliability can be affected both by the actual design of the test and by the conditions under which it is administered. You can assess reliability by administering the test to a number of groups of people who might be expected to achieve a similar pattern of scores. This is preferable to asking individuals to repeat the test, as familiarity will affect their results.

(e) Administering the Test

In the interests of reliability and of courtesy to candidates, the conditions under which the test is administered should be carefully standardised.

(i) The reason for the test should be explained, so that candidates can see its relevance to the job and in order to allay their doubts and suspicions. Test instructions must be clear, so that the candidates know what is expected of them and how long they have available. Any materials needed should be provided at the outset. There should be no distractions while the test is in progress.

(ii) When the test is completed, the same standards should be applied to the assessment of each candidate's work. If one assessor gives people the benefit of the doubt for an answer which is half right, then all assessors should do so, or the results will be worthless. If you are using a commercially produced test, you should make sure that you understand the scoring system and are using it properly.

(f) Interpreting the Results

The interpretation which you put on the results of performance, knowledge, aptitude and intelligence tests will be dictated by the cut-off points that you have established. The interpretation of a personality profile is a job for a trained psychologist.

(g) Communicating the Results

In many ways modern society is divisive. People are separated by income, education and the nebulous concept of class. Wherever possible we should avoid categorising them and, more particularly, branding them as failures. It is therefore important to put a constructive interpretation on even the most disappointing test result. If the individual's skills clearly do not lie in the area of manual dexterity, for instance, a positive attempt should be made to help him identify which other areas might be better suited to his talents. As this applies to the outcome of the whole selection process, we will discuss it further in the next unit.

'It seems, Mr Willis, that Jack of all trades and master of none is exactly what you're suited to be.'

6.5   Test Limitations

Apart from the general considerations of time, expertise and patience, there are a number of specific limitations which should be borne in mind.

(i) At best, test scores simply tell you that a greater proportion of people who achieve a certain score will be successful in the performance of the task than of those who do not achieve this score. They cannot predict whether one specific individual will succeed or fail.

(ii) Tests do not tell you **why** someone does well or badly.

(iii) Test validity and reliability may be reduced by the existence of stress, faking or familiarity, each of which will tend to distort the results. If candidates are particularly nervous, they may well underperform on the test. If they have seen the test before they may have an unfair advantage. The problems of faking were clearly revealed in one American knowledge test devised to assess whether potential cigarette salesmen were familiar with the night club world. Testees were asked to explain a number of slang expressions associated with the business. Candidates clearly assumed that they should not confess to knowing anything about such socially questionable things and professed ignorance of the meaning of all the terms. The test completely backfired.

(iv) Knowledge of results may have an adverse effect. If the applicant learns of his results on a particular test, this may either undermine his confidence or give him an inflated sense of his own ability. If, on the other hand, his boss or colleagues are aware of his results, this can influence their judgements of him and provide him with undue help or hindrance in the job. This is likely to influence his overall job performance in the direction indicated by the test, turning it into a self-fulfilling prophecy.

(v) Tests may be discriminatory. We will see in Unit 7 how important it is that every aspect of your selection procedure should be examined to make sure that it does not unjustifiably include methods or criteria with which one group may find it particularly hard to cope. Some types of test are more difficult for people from some cultures to succeed in than for others. Intelligence tests are a good example. Many people educated outside the western world will be unfamiliar with some of the concepts applied in intelligence tests. Pictorial representation is introduced into some such tests, to overcome language problems and try to make the tests fair to people from different cultures. But in fact, this may have the opposite effect. We do know how to translate words from one language to another; our knowledge of how to translate concepts and pictures is much more doubtful. In fact, any kind of symbolism may have vastly different meaning for people from different cultural backgrounds.

Even a language test can be regarded as discriminatory, as the British Steel Corporation found to its cost at Scunthorpe. The Corporation had refused to re-hire seven Bangladeshi ex-employees who failed a newly introduced English language test which had not been properly constructed or validated. The workers brought the case before an industrial tribunal, but an agreed settlement was eventually reached between BSC and the Commission for Racial Equality, involving payments totalling £10,000 to be made by the

Corporation to its ex-employees. The men concerned were also offered labouring jobs with the Corporation until such time as their attendance at English language classes (during working hours) should render them sufficiently proficient in the language to pass a properly supervised test and enable them to gain promotion into production area jobs.

(vi) There is a certain amount of hostility towards tests on the grounds that they constitute an invasion of privacy. The testee may unwittingly give away information about himself which he would rather not disclose. He has far less control over this in a test, where he cannot understand the mechanism to which he is being exposed, than in an interview.

(vii) Most tests only provide an accurate prediction of job performance about 16 per cent of the time. This is, at least partly, because of the two-stage process necessary to design tests of aptitude, intelligence and personality.

All this is not necessarily an argument for abandoning the use of tests altogether. It is additional evidence that tests must be properly constructed, administered and validated. And the closer we can move towards sampling actual job performance the better.

6.6 Work Samples

Obtaining an adequate sample of job performance is easy enough after your new recruit has started work. But by then you will both have invested time, effort and emotion in what could turn out to be a mistake. Far better, if you can, to assess the candidate's competence as it relates directly to key elements of the job **before** you commit yourselves.

One way to do this is via the relevant National Vocational Qualification (see Unit 10.5). Another is to ask candidates to produce a **work sample** related to one or more of the key tasks in the job description.

You can use work samples to test anything from the culinary competence of aspiring cooks to the telephone manner of potential receptionists. One college allegedly staffed a course for several weeks by inviting shortlisted candidates for a teaching post to conduct one session each while being observed by a member of the selection panel. The observer was trained to record instances of particular types of behaviour against a checklist and then to rate the candidate's competence in each element.

This is potentially a valid means of assessing teaching competence – though the students' reactions are not recorded! In a business setting, shortlisted candidates for senior management posts have been invited to spend two or more days in a company, to conduct their own assessment of key priorities as a prelude to presenting their business plans to the selectors.

Even if you lack the time or resources to sample directly, it may be possible to ask candidates to bring samples with them from previous employment or college. In some fields this is standard practice. Designers, for instance, will expect to show a portfolio of their work.

This can be a good substitute for on-the-spot samples. The risks are:

(*a*) you have no way of knowing whether the contents are genuinely theirs;

(*b*) not all candidates will have an equal opportunity to obtain samples from previous employers – and in some cases the work may remain the employer's property;

(*c*) as each sample will have been produced under different conditions it will also be harder to set a consistent standard.

Work samples generally have high **face validity**. Make sure they are **content valid** by testing only tasks which form part of the current job description. They will have **predictive value** only if observers/assessors have a clear understanding of what competent performance actually looks like and are trained to recognise it when they see it. To be fair to all the candidates, you must take care to give each the same time, resources, conditions and opportunity. The clarity and consistency of candidate briefing are vital.

Provided they are not too demanding or time-consuming work samples are arguably one of the best means of assessing experienced candidates. You can use them as part of an assessment centre, in conjunction with other tests, or on their own. You can incorporate them into an interview – like the building foreman who placed a bag of cement on the candidates' interview seat. They had to move the bag before they sat down. He got a sample of their work. (This particular practice is not recommended. If the candidate has not been trained in handling and lifting techniques – see Unit 17 – it could backfire!)

Where you **cannot** use them effectively is:

(*a*) for work involving equipment or procedures specific to your organisation;

(*b*) for those with no prior experience of the type of work.

Your best alternative in these circumstances will be either a trainability test or a simulation of some sort.

Questions

1. Describe the various types of test which can be used in selection, giving an example of where and why you would use each.
2. Describe how you would set about designing a test to assess the aptitudes or skills of applicants for a job of your choice.
3. What types of test validity are important in selection? How would you assess whether a test that you were using possessed these various forms of validity?

UNIT 7

Selecting Employees: Completing the Process

7.1 Introduction

The use of all the selection tools that we have been discussing is a means to an end: the making of a decision to appoint someone who will turn out to be a success in the job and in the organisation. The decision itself is only a starting point for further action. And in making the decision we must bear in mind not only the information that we have gathered, but also the legal constraints affecting the selection process.

7.2 Making a Decision

Deciding on the outcome of the selection process is seldom an easy task. You are dealing with people, all of whom are likely to find failure or rejection unpalatable. You are also trying to determine, on the basis of a few samples of behaviour, something which has an important bearing on the future success of your business. There are a number of things that you should do to try and make sure that your decision is the right one.

(a) Make sure that you have gathered all the information you need from the applicants: there should be no unanswered questions or gaps in your data. An assessment record, constructed along the same lines as your personnel specification, can be helpful here (see Fig. 7.1). It should include space for you to relate your interview findings, test and assessment centre results, and reference data to the criteria that you laid down in your specification at the start of the procedure.

(b) Evaluate **all** the information, bearing in mind the points we have made about bias, prejudice and the role of unfavourable information, and about the limitations of test and reference information.

(c) Use the rating system in Fig. 7.1 to record how each of the applicants matches your criteria. The best candidate will be the one who is the closest overall match, probably rated 3 or 4 on everything – not necessarily the one with the highest total.

(d) Review your own reactions and those of other people who have been involved. If you are going to have to work with the new recruit, are you going to be able to make it a successful relationship? Do you have any niggling

	Test 1	Test 2	Simu-lation	Work sample	Inter-view 1	Inter-view 2	Refs	Overall	Notes
Name: _____ **Date:** _____									
Assessor: _____ Rating									
AREA OF COMPETENCE									
Working with figures:									
Working with words:									
Working with people:									
Working with ideas:									
Planning/prioritising:									
Making decisions:									
Ability to learn:									
Working with systems:									
Specific knowledge/skill:									
Values:									
Availability /mobility:									
Other:									
NEEDS									
Existence:									
Relatedness:									
Growth:									

Ratings:

5 = far exceeds required standard
4 = exceeds required standard
3 = meets required standard
2 = marginally below required standard
1 = falls well short of required standard

Notes:

Fig. 7.1   Assessment record

doubts? If you do, perhaps you ought to review the information again; try to identify what is wrong and, if necessary, invite the candidate back for a further interview or tests.

(*e*) When you are sure that you have found the right person for the job, the organisation and you, stop to ask yourself whether they are all right for him. If you have adopted a joint problem-solving approach in an interview with him, you should be in a position to do this. (This is, in fact, one argument for leaving the interview until the end of the selection process. That way, the rest of the information will already be available to you and can be evaluated, together with the interview data, immediately after the interview, when recollections are fresh.)

7.3 Follow Up

(a) Unsuccessful Applicants
You should adopt a policy of informing unsuccessful candidates at the earliest opportunity. If the decision is formulated during a joint problem-solving interview, there is much to be said for bringing the applicant round to a realisation of his unsuitability during the interview. But if the decision is delayed you should write to him as soon as possible. We have already made the point that no applicant should be made to feel a failure, but it is worth repeating. Wherever possible, something constructive should emerge. This may be no more than the candidate's recognition that, if he isn't offered this job, he will pursue a different type of work in future. That gives him a positive new direction, rather than just a sense of failure.

This is why any standard letters that you compile, at any stage in the procedure, to advise candidates that you will not be offering them the job, should be as personalised as possible. That way, the candidate will not be misled into thinking that his application has not received your careful attention. Particularly if the applicant reached interview, you might introduce a paragraph highlighting some aspect of his application or past experience which you found especially interesting, and make some encouraging comment about it.

(b) The Successful Candidate
The person selected should be notified speedily. If he has applied for other, similar jobs, there is a chance that he will be offered one of the others first and you will lose him. (He may, of course, change his mind even after he has accepted your offer, so you may feel inclined to leave open some channel of communication to one of the other applicants, just in case. This will only be feasible if he, too, matches your requirements and came a close second in the decision-making process.)

In order to make certain that the appointment proceeds smoothly from this stage, you should give careful thought to a number of different pieces of documentation:

(i) **The offer letter.** This is an important legal document. Once accepted, it forms the basis of the contract of employment (see Unit 8.5). It tells the applicant that you are offering him the job, subject perhaps to the receipt of satisfactory references or the results of a medical examination, if these have not already been obtained. The letter may suggest a joining date, and should include details of the salary and main terms and conditions of employment. It should also advise the recruit of any action that you require him to take, attending departmental or project briefing meetings or submitting his birth certificate for pension purposes, for instance. You may wish to offer him the job subject to a satisfactory trial period (see Unit 8.4).

Where the selection procedure has been carried out on a word-of-mouth basis, with no previous correspondence and a starting date which is almost immediate, an offer letter may be superfluous. It is better to tell the candidate personally or over the telephone. But it will still be necessary to provide him subsequently with written particulars of his terms and conditions of employment (see Unit 8.5).

(ii) Joining instructions. When the starting date has been finalised, you will need to give your new employee precise information about when, where and to whom he should report for work. He will also need to be told about any equipment he is to bring with him and where he can park his car on arrival.

(iii) Company information. If you offer an occupational pension scheme or a sports and social club, you can either send the details out in advance or wait for induction. The same applies to the contract of employment or statement of employment particulars which you are required to issue within two months of the start of employment to anyone whose employment will last more than one month.

In addition to the preparation of this formal documentation, you also need to make arrangements for the welcome and induction of the new employee. These will be discussed in Unit 8.

(c) General Follow Up

Once you have appointed the successful applicant, you may feel tempted to sit back and relax, until the next time you need to recruit. In fact, now is the moment to look back over the whole of your recruitment and selection procedure, to see which parts of it have gone well and to set up a system for the validation of your selection.

You will only know if the right candidate has been appointed when he has been doing the job for several months. Then you can look at specific criterion data by which to judge your selection decision. Is the new recruit still in the job? Is he doing the work to the required standard? Is he ready for an increase in pay or a promotion? If you wish to learn from your decisions, you will find it helpful to use the assessment record (Fig. 7.1) to predict which aspects of the job he will be particularly good at, and which he will find more difficult. You can now check back to see if you were right.

If he is not doing as well in the job as you had hoped, or if he has left it altogether, you will need to consider the reasons for his departure. Did he find the job too hard or not sufficiently challenging? This would indicate that the job was either undersold or oversold to him at interview. (One way to find out why he has left is to discuss it with him in an 'exit' interview.) If

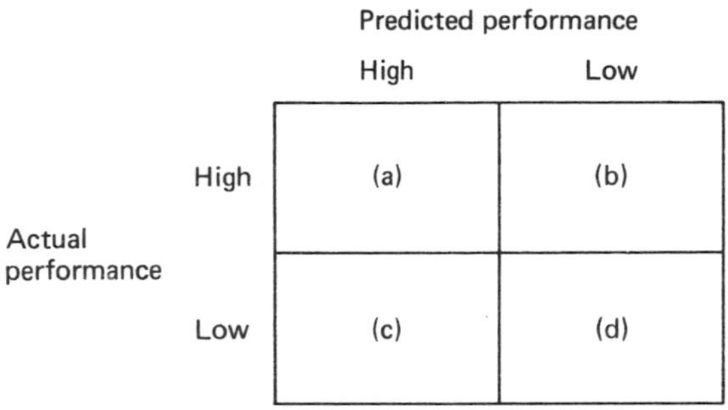

Predicted performance

	High	Low
High	(a)	(b)
Low	(c)	(d)

Actual performance

Fig. 7.2 Gellerman's grid

he is not proving effective, is this because you made your selection decision without a sufficiently thorough evaluation of all the available information, or were you perhaps looking for the wrong things in the first place? Perhaps you ought to rethink your evaluation process or go back and have another look at what should go into the personnel specification.

You can keep a diagrammatic record of your successes and failures, in the form of a chart such as that illustrated in Fig. 7.2. This is known as **Gellerman's grid**. To do this, you need to divide your job applicants into two categories when they join the company: those who are predicted to be good performers in the job and those who are predicted to be poor performers. You can then divide actual job performance into the same two categories of high and low performance. For someone who was predicted during selection to be a high performer, and who now actually is a high performer, you should place a cross in box (*a*). For someone who was predicted to be a high performer and who has turned out a low performer, place a cross in box (*c*), and so on. A good selection procedure should result in a roughly equal number of crosses in boxes (*a*) and (*d*), and very few crosses in either of the other two boxes.

From this we can see that validation does not have to be a negative process. You can follow up your successes as well as your failures. The group you don't usually have a chance to examine is the one you rejected.

You can also go back one stage further and consider the recruiting methods that you used, and analyse the quality and quantity of the response from which your new recruit was drawn. We discussed this aspect in Unit 3.6, while in Unit 3.8 the desirability of monitoring the proportion of each gender and each ethnic group who survive each selection hurdle was mentioned.

But you cannot judge your success only by internal criteria. Your decision must be legal, as well as right.

'There's no prejudice against women here. In fact my typist has a PhD and outstanding ability.'

7.4   Selection and the Law

The law intervenes in the selection process to prevent discrimination.

(a) Sex Discrimination

As we saw in Unit 3, the Sex Discrimination Acts 1975 and 1986 make it unlawful to discriminate against individuals, either directly or indirectly, on the grounds of sex or marital status. In selecting new employees (and in training and promoting existing ones) you must therefore avoid both these types of discrimination throughout selection.

(i) Selection criteria.   As we saw in recruitment, your specification must relate to the actual demands of the job and must not include unfounded requirements with which either men or women, married or unmarried, will have difficulty in complying. In one case involving entry into the Civil Service, an industrial tribunal held that the rule which stated that all applicants for direct entry at Executive Officer level must be less than twenty-eight years old involved unlawful discrimination. Fewer women than men are able to apply in their twenties because of the demands of having and raising children. The tribunal decided that there was no justifiable foundation for the rule, so it should cease to operate.

Beware, too, of making assumptions about one sex or the other in relation to your selection criteria. Travelling, late hours, overnight stays and so on should be discussed with **all** candidates. Never assume that a woman or someone with young children is unlikely to be suitable for such a job. And never assume that a woman will be less reliable or that she 'needs the work less' than a man.

(ii) Selection procedures.   The questions you ask during an interview, the content of and briefing for tests, simulations and work samples, even the comments the receptionist or the administrator makes, can all have a bearing on candidate reactions. Those who have been asked, for instance, whether they plan to start a family can be so disconcerted that they fail to do themselves justice during the rest of an interview. Claims of sex discrimination have been brought, and won, on such grounds.

Even though you believe you are simply taking a natural interest in the welfare of the children, you should also avoid questions about child-care arrangements. It is for the applicants to sort out their domestic affairs. You only need to know that they will be both punctual and reliable. You can check this, for both men and women, by:

(*a*) making clear the genuine demands that the job will make and asking whether the applicant foresees any difficulty in meeting them;

(*b*) establishing how often they have been absent or late in the past year or so.

(b) Racial Discrimination

As in the earlier stages of recruitment, race is not a characteristic you can take into account, either directly or indirectly, in deciding who to employ. Equally important, you must make sure that none of the assessment methods used will discriminate unfairly.

Asking candidates to complete complicated application forms which require an understanding of English beyond that needed in the job could discriminate against those for whom English is not their first language. If you do need the information, make sure candidates are provided with help in completing the form.

As we saw in Unit 6.5, poorly designed selection tests can lead to difficulties, as can procedures which fail to take account of differences in language or conduct. In some cultures it is seen as appropriate to take educational and other certificates along to interview. The interviewer who is dismissive of or derides these could leave the candidate confused or angry and detract from interview performance.

Provided:

(*a*) all your assessors and interviewers have been properly trained;

(*b*) your procedure has been carefully designed to be an accurate and reliable predictor of subsequent job performance,

you are unlikely to run into difficulties. But where you cannot show that there is a relationship between assessment results and job performance, you could find yourself accused of race discrimination.

(c) Discrimination against the Disabled

When the Disability Discrimination Act becomes law, those who believe they have been discriminated against on the grounds of their disability will be able to bring claims against those employing more than twenty people. You should not allow physical or mental disability to prevent you selecting someone to a job which they would be competent to perform.

(d) Discrimination against Ex-offenders

Under the Rehabilitation of Offenders Act 1974, people who have had a previous police conviction but have kept out of trouble for a specified length of time must not have their past crime held against them: their conviction is 'spent'. The length of time before a conviction becomes spent varies according to its original severity: a period of between six and thirty months in jail will not become spent until ten years have elapsed. More serious offences can never be spent, and in some professions, including the law, medicine and accountancy, the Act does not apply.

Where a conviction has become spent, you cannot refuse to employ a person because of his past offence; nor is he obliged to inform you of it.

Although sometimes misunderstood as some kind of villains' charter, this law is in fact just an attempt to enable individuals to live down their past, comparatively minor, transgressions, and live a normal life.

(e) Discrimination on Grounds of Trade Union Membership or Non-Membership

The Trade Union and Labour Relations (Consolidation) Act 1992 made it unlawful to refuse employment because someone is, or is not, a member of a (particular) trade union. As we saw in Unit 3.8, the once widespread practice of using the union's 'list' as a short cut to recruitment is no longer acceptable. Nor should the union be asked to approve appointments.

(f) Selecting Foreign Nationals

If the person you have chosen is not a UK citizen or a national from the European Economic Area, you will need to apply to the Department of Trade and Industry for permission to go ahead. (The European Economic Area includes Iceland, Norway and Switzerland as well as the members of the European Union.)

Although the applicant may claim to have a work permit, this is not transferable from one employer to another, so you must reapply. A permit is valid for a period from twelve months to two years, with the right to apply for an extension for up to four years. The Department of Trade and Industry will not grant one unless some specific conditions are met.

Before applying on Form WP1, you should have taken steps to ensure there is no suitably qualified European Union national available. Such steps would normally include notifying the Employment service, advertising the vacancy widely and undertaking to pay the fares of any potentially suitable resident to travel to interview.

Even if you have done this, a permit will usually only be granted if the work requires special qualifications, skills or experience which the overseas worker has. You will be required to supply original references for the employee to verify this, plus a set of your own company's audited accounts.

In the case of internal transfers within multi-national companies, or for positions at board level, rather less information is usually required. It is also somewhat easier in cases where there is a recognised shortage of workers or where the employment is essential to an inward investment project, bringing capital investment and more jobs to the UK.

If you are considering employing someone who will need a permit, you would be well advised to consult your local Employment Office or Job Centre manager at an early stage, to establish whether your candidate is likely to fall within the eligible categories.

Having selected your candidates, the next task is to introduce them into the organisation.

Questions

1. Describe how you would set about determining which of the candidates called for interview and tests for a particular position was to be offered the job.
2. How should the outcome of a selection procedure be notified to candidates, successful and unsuccessful? Give reasons for your answer.
3. Describe the steps that you would take to monitor the effectiveness of a recruitment and selection procedure.
4. Discuss the implications of employment legislation for the designers of recruitment and selection procedures.

UNIT 8

New Employees

8.1 Introduction

We saw in Unit 1 that the first three or four months of employment can be the most critical in determining whether a new recruit will stay with you. The reception he is given on his first day and the help and guidance he receives while he is settling in may be very important.

Once you have agreed a starting date for the newcomer, it is a good idea to compile a checklist of things to do so that you are ready for him when he arrives.

(*a*) Inform the people who need to know about his appointment. This could include other people with whom he will need to liaise or consult or those for whom he will be working.

(*b*) Arrange for overalls, safety wear or other necessary equipment and materials to be available and in good order.

(*c*) Allocate working space, and make sure that it is as clean, tidy and welcoming as circumstances will allow.

(*d*) Allocate a locker or key for the locker room, if appropriate.

(*e*) Brief someone to act as guide and mentor during the first few weeks: to accompany the new recruit to lunch breaks, perhaps, and answer informal queries. This is known as a 'sponsor' or 'buddy' system.

(*f*) Provide details to the pay section (and personnel and training sections, if appropriate).

(*g*) Decide who is to induct the new recruit into the organisation and make the necessary arrangements (see Unit 8.2).

(*h*) If you will not be inducting him personally, set aside some time yourself to welcome the newcomer.

8.2 Induction Training

The main purpose of induction training is to orientate the new recruit to the company and its way of life. Think carefully about the kind of things he will need to know in order to settle in as quickly as possible. A standard induction checklist might contain the following items:

(*a*) Essential safety information – the location and use of first aid equipment and fire extinguishers, what to do in the event of fire, areas where protective clothing is required, procedures for handling hazardous substances or equipment.

(*b*) A tour of the building, to locate fire exits, rest and recreational facilities/ canteen, lavatories, cloakroom, staff entrance, car park, pay office and other sections relevant to the newcomer personally.

(*c*) Information about the organisation, to give him a more detailed idea of the company's operation, what business it is in, its history and future plans, its values and vision of the future (see Unit 19.3). This will serve to reinforce any written information or details given at interview, but care must be taken to put the information over in a way that will be both interesting and directly relevant. (The recruit may be less impressed with a detailed history of the life of the founder than he will be by a succinct account, perhaps illustrated by charts and diagrams, of how the work done in his section relates to the activities of the company as a whole.)

(*d*) Information about terms and conditions of employment, to reinforce and answer any queries on the contract of employment or statement of employment particulars (see Unit 8.5). If these were not sent out in advance, they should be handed over during induction. The main points to which attention should be drawn are hours of work, the timing and length of lunch breaks, holiday entitlement and who he should see to book his leave or ask for other time off. Specific rules should also be explained, such as first aid procedures, when and where he may smoke, or what he should do if he is ever unwell and unable to come to work.

(*e*) Information about the job, including a job description if he has not already been given one, can be dealt with during induction. The job should be discussed in some depth, so that any misconceptions can be ironed out now or during preliminary job training.

(*f*) Introductions, to the people with and for whom he will be working, especially his guide and mentor, and to the providers of essential services, like the pay clerk.

(*g*) Issue of clothing and equipment so the new recruit will not feel an odd one out for too long.

You may find it useful to put yourself in the recruit's shoes. Given that he knows nothing and no one in the organisation at present, how much of this information does he need to have on his first day? Could some items be taken care of later, to strike a better balance between overloading him with information, which he will have difficulty in remembering, and telling him enough to survive? Bear in mind that he will be registering many new experiences, not all of which may be in line with his expectations.

You will also need to weigh up the relative advantages of different ways of putting over the information. The written word, the spoken word, films and pictures can all contribute, but much will depend on the nature of the material. Who will be the best person to put it across? Should you do it all yourself, or should part of it be delegated? The more general guidance on learning methods in Unit 10.3 will help you decide.

Once you have welcomed the new recruit and begun to acclimatise him to the organisation, your next task, in his interests and your own, is to ensure that he is in a position to do his job effectively as soon as possible.

8.3   Preliminary Job Training

The difference between the competences that you listed on your personnel specification and those actually possessed by the new recruit is the **training gap**. An analysis of his current skills and knowledge in relation to the requirements of the job will enable you to highlight what he needs to learn before he can be expected to perform to the required standard. The width of the training gap will vary according to whether the individual has done the same or similar types of work before.

The basic principles involved in identifying the skills and knowledge for which training may be required are given in Unit 10. There, too, we will discuss the range of training methods which are available to help you impart them. Here it is sufficient for us to recognise the possible existence of a gap that can be filled by training.

8.4   Trial Periods

If the training gap is wide, or if there were factors which emerged during selection which made you less than 100 per cent certain about your choice of candidate, you may feel it is desirable to build in some kind of safeguard in case things do not go according to plan. It is easy to say that if you are in doubt as to the wisdom of your selection decision you should wait until you find a candidate about whom you are certain. But if the vacancy is pressing or your doubts comparatively minor, it will be less easy to do. A trial period alerts your new employee to the fact that you feel that further assessment is necessary. It also gives you the chance to assess actual performance rather than relying on the selection process.

If you do feel that a trial period is necessary, you can specify when you write your offer letter to the new recruit that the appointment is subject to, say, a three-month trial period. You can then build in a procedure for monitoring his performance during that time. Don't wait until the three months are up before giving any indication that you are not satisfied with performance. And don't assume that you can dismiss the employee at will during the trial period. He will still be entitled to written particulars of employment (see Unit 8.5) and must be treated in accordance with these even though some of their terms may be less generous than for those in confirmed employment.

Whether or not there is a formal trial period, you should discuss progress with all new recruits at regular intervals. The basic principles to apply are those given in Unit 9 in relation to performance appraisal. If someone does not progress as rapidly as you had anticipated, try to find out why. Have you underestimated the width of the training gap? If so, it may be a lot quicker and cheaper to reassess and meet his training needs than to dismiss him and start the recruitment and selection process all over again. Only when you are certain that there is no likelihood of your recruit reaching the required standard of performance within a reasonable time limit should you actually terminate his employment, giving due notice of your intention to do so and making sure you have acted fully in accordance with your disciplinary procedure (see Unit 19).

8.5 New Employees and the Law

You and your new recruit have entered into a **wage–work bargain**. The fact that you have agreed to pay him for the work that he will do, that you are both competent in the eyes of the law to enter into such an agreement and that the agreement is not for unlawful purposes means that there is a contract between you. If this contract is a contract of employment (rather than a contract for services such as is made with an independent contractor) your employee automatically becomes entitled to protection under employment law. It is implied in the contract that you will treat your employee in accordance with the law on, for instance, health and safety, discrimination, equal pay, dismissal and collective rights. Other terms agreed orally at interview may also form part of the contract. The main particulars of your agreement must, however, be written down in the form of a formal statement, in accordance with the Employment Protection (Consolidation) Act 1978 and the Trade Union Reform and Employment Rights Act 1993.

(a) Written Particulars

All employees expected to work for one month or more must be issued with a written statement of the terms of their employment. This statement must be issued by the employer within two months of the start of employment. It should contain the following points:

(i) The names and addresses of the parties (employer and employee).

(ii) The date on which the employment began. This will normally be his starting date, but if the employee has previously been employed by another company in the same group, which will count as part of his continuous employment, this should be indicated.

(iii) The scale or rate of pay or the method of calculating pay (including overtime arrangements, piece rates and so on).

(iv) The intervals at which payment is made (weekly, monthly).

(v) Hours and place of work – or if the employee is required to work at various locations, an indication of this together with the address of the employer.

(vi) Holiday entitlement, including bank and public holidays and holiday pay. (This section should give the employee sufficient detail to enable him to work out exactly what his holiday entitlement is, and what his accrued entitlement will be if he leaves your employ at any time in the year.)

(vii) The title of the job which the employee is to perform or a brief description of it.

(viii) Sickness or injury absence arrangements and details of any sick pay scheme which applies to him.

(ix) Details of any occupational pension scheme which is contracted out of the state scheme and a statement about whether there is a contracting out certificate under the Social Security Pensions Act 1975 (see Unit 15).

(x) The disciplinary rules governing the behaviour of the employee.

(xi) The details of any disciplinary procedure relating to the employment.

(xii) The details of any grievance procedure relating to the employment.

(xiii) The length of notice which the employee is obliged to give and entitled to receive before terminating employment.

(xiv) Details of any relevant collective agreements (see Unit 18) which directly affect the employee's terms and conditions of work.

You do not need to spell out all the details of these various items within the statement itself. Provided the first seven are included in your first or **principal statement** the rest can be issued in later statements. For full details of items (viii) to (xiv) the employee may be referred to some other document(s) which he has reasonable opportunity of seeing in the course of his employment. So a file of separate advice notes, accessible to all (and known by all to be so) or a notice board which everyone has the opportunity to consult from time to time could be the answer.

You must notify each employee of any change in any of these items. This can be done by issuing a further written statement to draw attention to it within one month of the date on which the change becomes effective, or by updating the reference documents. In order to avoid debate about whether or not a written statement has been issued, it is advisable for both parties to sign and retain copies of the document.

We will be dealing, in subsequent units, with the ways in which you can ensure that your procedures and arrangements for pay, discipline, grievances and so on are in line with further legal requirements and good employment practice. But first we must look at item (xiii), periods of notice, as these are also covered by the Employment Protection (Consolidation) Act.

(b) Notice Entitlement

As soon as an employee has been with you for one month, even if no written statement of particulars has as yet been given, he is entitled to receive a minimum of one week's notice if you wish to terminate his employment. The employee's entitlement to notice increases with length of service, as set out in Table 8.1, although he is not obliged to give you a corresponding increase in notice if he wishes to leave.

If you think there are circumstances in which you may wish to pay the employee in lieu of notice, it is advisable to specify these in the contract. The notice periods laid down in the Act are minimum periods only, and you are perfectly at liberty to specify longer periods, for either side, in the contract

Table 8.1   Notice entitlement

Period of employment	Notice to employee	Notice to employer
4 weeks–2 years	1 week	1 week
2–3 years	2 weeks	1 week
3–4 years	3 weeks	1 week
4–5 years	4 weeks	1 week
5–6 years	5 weeks	1 week
6–7 years	6 weeks	1 week
7–8 years	7 weeks	1 week
8–9 years	8 weeks	1 week
9–10 years	9 weeks	1 week
10–11 years	10 weeks	1 week
11–12 years	11 weeks	1 week
More than 12 years	12 weeks	1 week

or statement of particulars itself. Managers, for instance, are quite often put on three months' notice on either side, although it is rare for the employer to take action against an employee who fails to observe the required notice period. The most commonly applied sanction is for the employer to mention the fact in references he may subsequently provide for the employee.

Tempting as it may be to withhold holiday pay or sick pay from an employee who has tendered his resignation, the law forbids this. All aspects of pay and other conditions must comply with the agreed terms until the employee actually leaves.

Once the new employee is safely in his post and the legal requirements have been complied with, you can start to think about how you can train and develop him to help him maximise his contribution. In order to do this you will need to monitor his work and behaviour to assess whether or not these are developing as you would both wish. You can do this informally but it sometimes helps both parties to avoid misunderstandings if a more formal arrangement is adopted. Performance appraisal can help here.

Questions
1. Why is the induction period important? What can be done to make it successful?
2. In the context of your own organisation, draw up a checklist of the kind of general information that a new recruit would need during his first month with the company. State when, where, how and by whom this information could be imparted.
3. Draft a contract of employment between your organisation and a new recruit for a job of your choice. Prepare a script for use by someone seeking to explain the contract during induction.

Appraising Performance

9.1 Introduction

Performance appraisal is the name given to the regular (usually six-monthly or annual) formalised and recorded review of the way in which an individual is performing in his job. It is normally carried out by the job-holder's immediate boss. From this point on, concepts of what appraisal is **for** and how it should be used diverge. In the past it tended to be seen purely as a management tool, designed to make sure every employee was meeting company standards. The history of its development paralleled changes in management thinking along the continuum from 'autocratic' to 'democratic' (see Unit 1.4). Below we will review the approaches to appraisal which resulted.

But, as we also saw in Unit 1.4, there is another, different philosophy which is beginning to gain ground – the concept of 'empowerment'. This challenges many of the assumptions on which earlier approaches were based. Coaching and empowerment, to unlock the talents of **all** employees and cast aside self- or organisationally-imposed limits on personal attainment, bring a whole new perspective to the review of performance. We will begin to explore this in Unit 9.4, and develop the philosophy more fully in Units 10 and 11.

9.2 Traditional Approaches

(a) Traits-orientated
This involves the appraisal of personal qualities, such as appearance, punctuality, leadership skills, co-operativeness.

(b) Results-orientated
This requires that the outcomes or results achieved by the job-holder form the basis of the appraisal. Sales figures, wastage rate, complaints received and costs incurred provide examples.

(c) Competence-based
This recognises the importance of the way a person goes about his work, rather than just the results he achieves. What does the effective performer do, and how does he do it? What specific competences does he exhibit?

A further dimension is given to any discussion of performance appraisal by the split between open and closed systems.

(i) In an **open system** – as the name implies – the appraisee has the opportunity to discuss his performance with his boss and to contribute, to a greater or lesser extent, to the record of the appraisal.

(ii) **Closed systems**, on the other hand, are those where the boss assesses and records without discussion.

As pressure has increased for more employee participation and a more open approach to management, there has been a trend towards more openness in appraisal. Schemes also differ in the extent to which they are designed to be judgemental or developmental.

(iii) **Judgemental systems** are essentially about **assessing** past performance with a view to remedying deficiencies. They typically include some form of rating or scoring system to record how well (or badly) each person is performing (see Unit 9.3).

(iv) **Developmental systems** are more concerned to **review** past performance with a view to learning how to do things differently in future. Often renamed 'performance reviews', many find it hard to entirely escape a judgemental element – particularly where the onus is on the boss to produce the report. One solution is suggested in Unit 9.4.

(d) Use of Appraisal

Performance appraisal **can** be very useful. A regular review of each individual's performance provides information about the competence and aspirations of the workforce – essential for planning. The system can also encourage commitment to corporate goals and conformity with work group norms (expected patterns of behaviour – see Unit 19.2). Thus most organisations have unwritten rules which reflect their value system. Senior management may wish all managers to adopt a particular style of management. If style as well as results are discussed at an appraisal interview, all managers will recognise the importance placed upon this issue.

In addition, performance appraisal can serve a wide range of specific uses for the individual and the manager. The first five are relatively uncontentious. The last three should be viewed with caution.

(i) **Identifying training needs.** Unless some mechanism is devised for reviewing an employee's level of competence in his job, any areas of shortfall in that competence may be difficult to identify. You may know that someone is not 100 per cent effective. You may think that you know why. But it is only when you come to look at the requirements of his job in detail, and compare it with what he is actually doing, that the scope and nature of the problem may fully emerge. If you go further and actually discuss this, all sorts of things may be revealed. He may never have realised that some specific task was his responsibility, or he may never have learnt how to do it properly. He may have been taught and then lapsed into bad habits. He may have learnt to operate a process slightly different from the one now in use and simply be translating his old work habits into a new system, for lack of clear guidance to the contrary.

(ii) Identifying key skills. Even after you have selected an employee, carefully matching competences to the requirements of the job and of the organisation, many changes can occur, as neither the job itself nor the employee will remain static. The job may change and no longer utilise some of the employee's talents, or he may acquire new competences. The performance appraisal interview should provide an opportunity for the mismatch to be identified. Perhaps the individual could now contribute more effectively in another job or the limits of his present one could be redesigned to afford him the opportunity of using wider talents, to the benefit of the organisation.

(iii) Improving present performance. There are many reasons why employees may fail to meet required standards of performance or to maximise their contribution to the business. The existence of bad inter-personal relationships within the department, financial worries, domestic problems, misunderstanding over what is required, ignorance of the effect low work standards have on others, as well as the more specific training needs we have discussed, can all tend to drag standards of performance downwards. The performance appraisal interview should provide an opportunity for discovering such barriers to effective performance and for considering how they can be removed.

(iv) Improving communications. 'I don't need to appraise my people. We see each other every day.' Yes, but does seeing mean **communicating**? Does it mean finding out how the other person sees a problem or what solutions he may have to offer? Does it mean explaining clearly what is required and helping him to see how he can build on his strengths in order to achieve it? Does it mean listening to what he has to say and understanding his point of view? Or does it just mean a cursory 'Hello. How's things?' with no real time to talk around the wider issues or think where you are both going? The importance of communicating with employees is something that we will discuss further in Unit 13. Here we will simply point out that a quick word exchanged amid the pressures of the working environment is not really communication in the true sense of the word.

The performance appraisal interview forces a constructive dialogue between you and your people: a chance to see things in perspective, and to plan together. So although the basis for your discussion will be your day-to-day activities, the opportunity to discuss them in detail does not present itself every day.

(v) Enhancing commitment. Performance reviews provide a chance to talk to employees as individuals and to let them know that their contribution is valued. Although it *can* lead to over-dependence and approval seeking (see Unit 13.6), appropriate recognition of effort and achievement is important.

(vi) Identifying potential. If you feel it appropriate to try and plan the succession to key jobs (a point which we will consider in Unit 11) you will need some objective data on which to base your decisions. Competence-based performance appraisal in particular should give a more objective picture than simply relying on informal personal assessment of the individual. It can indicate how he is likely to cope, at least with those aspects of the new job which closely resemble the present one. The employee may also welcome the chance to discuss future prospects to help in personal career planning. This needs careful handling, though, to avoid creating expectations which the organisation may not be able to fulfil. The differences between the present and future role may be such that you would do better to rely on other methods of identifying potential (see Unit 11).

(vii) Disciplinary documentation. As we shall see in Unit 21, if and when you have to dismiss one of your employees for misconduct or poor performance, it will be important that you have documentary evidence to support your assertion, perhaps before an industrial tribunal. You will not only need to show that the employee was unsatisfactory, you will also have to demonstrate that he knew that this was the case and had been given an opportunity to improve.

Performance appraisal records can help in both these respects, though the review itself is not a disciplinary device. The manager who saves up a year's misdemeanours for correction at appraisal time will bring both himself and the appraisal system into disrepute or worse, as Unit 21.3(*l*) highlights, without improving discipline. As Unit 19 will show, discipline must be immediate and clearly related to the offence if it is to have the desired result (an improvement in behaviour). What is important is that the appraisal should reflect consistently the individual's actual standard of performance and behaviour. This way, you will avoid the embarrassment (and cost) of a tribunal finding that an apparently isolated episode did not warrant dismissal.

(viii) Determining pay. The link between performance appraisal and pay has long been a bone of contention. If pay is not performance-related, rewarding each individual according to his contribution, however measured, the argument does not arise. But where it is the quality of overall performance which determines that 'Mary' receives more than 'Debbie' for doing the same job (see Unit 14), there needs to be some means of assessing them as fairly as possible. The performance appraisal scheme might seem the obvious answer.

The only trouble is that if people think performance appraisal is to determine pay rises, any other benefit may be lost in an argument over money. The pragmatic answer is to space out the two events, dealing with them in separate interviews, several months apart. That way, the appraisal interview can also be used for any of the other purposes above.

(e) Limitations

Appraisal can create more problems than it resolves. Many organisations, particularly small ones, or those with an organic climate (see Unit 1.4), do not have any formal system and do not appear any the worse for it. Even the most long-established and apparently well-designed schemes have their critics, and there are, indeed, many pitfalls. These are of three main types.

(i) Administrative problems. It takes time and money to develop and administer a system. Those who are required to appraise others must be trained and will spend much time planning the appraisals. Appraisal interviews will mean time away from the job for both appraiser and appraisee, and in a large department the manager can be tied up with appraisals for days or even weeks.

(ii) Implementation problems.   There is always the danger that the system will not be used for the purposes intended – perhaps because people have lost sight of its original objectives. Many schemes fall into the trap of creating expectations which become (or maybe always were) unrealistic. Systems which create expectations of promotion, for instance, will lead to frustration and disillusion if the organisation stops growing or starts 'de-layering' by reducing the number of managers. Systems which are designed to identify training needs may encourage individual managers to abdicate their responsibilities by simply asking employees what they would like and then passing the burden on to a central training department, if there is one. This can lead to the provision of the courses people want, not the training they need. As we have seen, the links with pay and discipline can also have undesirable effects.

(iii) Assessment problems.   Arbitrary assessment, as the case in Unit 21.3(*b*) shows, is contrary to good employment practice. Bias can creep in, even to well-organised systems. Halo effects, stereotyping and an over-emphasis on negative information, which we discussed in connection with selection (Unit 5.5), can also play a part. Leniency too may be a problem, with appraisers reluctant to 'play God' or judge their appraisees too harshly. Although these difficulties are particularly likely to occur with traits-orientated judgemental systems, no scheme is immune. In results-orientated systems, there is also the problem of accurately measuring results, and attributing them to the right people. Some people who appear to have done a good job may in fact be taking the credit for the work of others. Often poor results are not so much a reflection on the job-holder as on other factors: the economic situation, the design of the job, natural variation in the work process, lack of support from others, including perhaps the appraiser. In addition, even where the assessment is accurate in relation to the present job, there may be difficulties in using this as a basis for the prediction of performance in other, more senior, posts which may make different demands and call for different approaches.

Although not all these problems are inevitable, many are hard to avoid. Having weighed up the costs, the pitfalls and the benefits, you may or may not decide that you want such a system. As a rough guide, if you are in a mechanistic organisation where there are systems for everything, people will probably accept the idea of a system of appraisal (though oddly enough its introduction into UK public service organisations was relatively slow). If you are dealing with jobs where the job-holder has scope to influence the way the work is done – rather than simply responding to a machine or carrying out a predetermined sequence of actions – you are likely to be able to realise more of the benefits. But if the system is set up or allowed to continue without clear objectives and regular evaluation of its effectiveness in meeting them (see Unit 9.7), it will be a waste of time and money.

'Are the salary increases here automatic, or do you have to work to earn them?'

9.3 Introducing a Traditional Appraisal Scheme

(a) Deciding on Objectives

Appraisal should never be introduced into an organisation without careful thought about the objectives it is designed to serve. The best starting point for this lies in a discussion with other managers concerned, to consider the kind of problems that they have encountered in dealing with their people.

'We always seem to live from one crisis to another. I never really get a chance to talk to them.'

'Most of my people are doing quite well, but I dare say they could all do more if we had some way of getting to grips with it.'

'I seem to spend a fortune sending people away on the best outside training courses, but I'm not sure they're really any better at their jobs afterwards.'

'I'm all for paying each person what he deserves, but I often find it difficult to be sure that I'm really being fair to people.'

Each of these statements is symptomatic of a different problem. The first may mean that there is a lack of communication between the manager and his staff. The second could signify failure to identify key skills or lack of opportunity to improve present performance. The third may indicate that training needs are not being correctly assessed, while the fourth points to the lack of an effective measure of performance.

Performance appraisal can help with each of these problems, but only if it is designed to do so. You will not improve communications by introducing a closed appraisal scheme. You will not provide an objective measure of performance for pay purposes by designing a traits-orientated system. You will not assist the identification of training needs by focusing too much on pay.

This preliminary identification of problems should not only help in designing a scheme which will serve some useful purpose, it can also help to ensure that all managers who use it are committed to the idea.

It should, incidentally, act as an antidote to the temptation to design a performance appraisal system by plagiarising other people's. The paperwork of performance appraisal is a means to an end: once you have clarified the end that you wish your scheme to serve, you can identify your own route for getting there.

(b) Obtaining Commitment

Commitment to the operation of the scheme is all important. This means commitment to the methods, as well as the principle, if the benefits are to be spread through the organisation. It can only be achieved if three conditions are met.

(i) All who use the scheme must be trained in its use, in terms of knowledge of how to operate the system and, in the case of an open, judgemental system, skills in interviewing and assessing.

(ii) The system must be seen to be used for the purposes intended. If managers have identified problems which the scheme is designed to help resolve, constant monitoring will be necessary to see if the appraisal system is working.

(iii) Each appraiser should himself be appraised by his own boss, preferably before he starts appraising his own team.

Clear objectives and full commitment are fundamental if appraisal is to get off the ground. Both the substance of the appraisal and the paperwork that accompanies the scheme warrant consideration.

(c) Deciding What to Appraise

We have already identified the three traditional possibilities: traits, results or competence.

If you opt for a **traits-orientated approach**, you tend to limit the acceptability (and therefore the workability) of the scheme in three ways.

(*a*) The assessment is subjective, based on one person's perception of what another is like, rather than on what he does and what he achieves.

(*b*) It becomes more difficult to work constructively for the future. A five-point plan on restructuring your personality is a lot more difficult to agree and adhere to than a five-point plan on how to improve sales figures or minimise costs next year.

(*c*) This method overlooks the fact that the main things that matter to you as an employer or manager are probably the way people do their jobs and the results, of all kinds, that they achieve. You cannot afford to employ people just because they are 'nice'; you need to help them to become nice, **productive** people.

If you opt, on the other hand, for a **results-orientated approach**, you will need to think carefully about the kinds of measurable results that you expect from your people and the kind of constraints and difficulties that they face in trying to achieve them.

The third line of approach, **competence-based**, will involve you in trying to determine how a good performer behaves. This method can help you to focus on why it is that someone is or is not effective. It does, however, presuppose that you have some overall criteria for separating out the good and bad performers. It can also be time-consuming and costly to develop, and it may be difficult to reach agreement on the relevant behaviours or competences.

Having decided which of these approaches to adopt, we still have to determine just what particular traits, results or behaviour are relevant to the jobs in question. There are six main possibilities.

(i) Using the job description. You can start by working through the job description, perhaps jointly with the job-holder, to sort out which are the **key tasks**: those which have a major bearing on the achievement of the job's overall purpose. This will ensure that you do not lose sight of what the appraisee is supposed to be doing. You will also need to think about the standards of performance that are required in each of the key tasks. You can then assess how well the appraisee is coping with the tasks he is required to perform, and consider whether or not he is meeting the required standard. A secretary's job description, for instance, might include the task of word processing standard letters to clients, which will be done satisfactorily when, say, forty letters a day are produced, without typographical errors and in accordance with the house style of the company. That is the standard of performance against which you can appraise the secretary.

Apart from the time needed to sort out which are the key tasks, which may, of course, be numerous, the major drawback to this line of approach is that it is easier to see whether the employee is doing the job to the required standard than it is to determine why his performance is falling short and what needs to be done to improve it. It is therefore of most use for judgemental results-orientated systems.

(ii) Using a committee. A group of managers who are familiar with the organisation and its requirements can sit down and work out a list of the attributes (traits-orientated) or outcomes (results-orientated) against which employees can be appraised. They can also consider the 'how' aspect to help in clarifying what will distinguish the effective performer's way of working (competence). This method, too, has its problems. Apart from the fundamental difficulties of working through a committee, there is the strong likelihood that the team will be short on knowledge of some of the jobs whose holders are to be appraised. This may lead them to overlook or place too little emphasis on some factors, while over-emphasising others.

(iii) Conducting in-depth interviews. As a basis for a competence-based system, job-holders can be asked to specify those parts of their job which take up most of their time, occur most frequently or are most crucial to success in the job. The common elements of such tasks can then be examined, providing an indication of the range of activities and elements involved. The interviews can be followed up by further interviews or with questionnaires administered to the job-holders' bosses to establish, for each activity, what effective behaviour looks like. The findings can be translated into a checklist against which actual performance can be appraised. Though time-consuming, this technique (which is known as the **repertory grid**) is more likely to give you an accurate picture of the things which really are important to the job and the organisation than do the job-description or committee methods. But it does call for some degree of expertise in interviewing and cross-questioning, to identify the key elements.

(iv) Applying the critical incident technique. You can ask a sample of employees, chosen at random, what was the most difficult problem they have had to deal with in, say, the last three months (the time span will vary according to the level of the jobs under consideration). You should ask them for full details of what happened, and with what consequences. After a number of interviews of this kind, a picture of the things that really determine success in the organisation will begin to emerge. These criteria for success can then be translated into an appraisal checklist. This method is known as the **critical incident technique**, and although not as thorough as the in-depth interview, it should serve to highlight the key areas that you need to consider in appraisal of results or competence.

(v) Analysing documents. By examining reports and other documents in current use inside the company, you will begin to see what really goes on in particular jobs. An example of this might be to analyse a sales representative's customer reports, looking for the kinds of problem that he is actually having to deal with and the sort of skills that he needs in order to be able to cope. For jobs where specific paper or oral transactions can be analysed, this **content analysis technique** will provide at least a starting point in determining what is important in the job and what measures of performance will be relevant to it.

(vi) Consulting relevant competence lists. For jobs which are covered by National Vocational Qualifications the competence statement on which assessment is based can provide a useful framework for appraisal. For example, for the competences associated with managerial and supervisory positions, the Management Charter Initiative (MCI) has produced an assessment package with just this end in view – short-circuiting the need to create a fresh list for each job or organisation.

These methods are not mutually exclusive. The one you choose will depend on the time and expertise that you have available and your degree of determination to find a list of performance criteria which fully reflects the values of the organisation and the contents of the jobs under consideration. If you can find the time and expertise to adopt one of the interview- or analysis-based techniques, it will pay dividends, for there is no point in appraising people on the performance of tasks which are not important or the achievement of results which the organisation does not regard as significant.

(d) Appraisal Reporting Techniques

Most performance appraisal systems require that some sort of record be kept. In an open system, such a record might be completed jointly by the appraiser and the appraisee, both agreeing to the final version. In closed systems, the appraising manager will complete the report alone. In either case, though, a 'grandfather' figure, such as the appraiser's own boss, may examine and countersign the completed forms to ensure that they are being used properly and to learn about his direct subordinates through their appraisal of others.

The final destination of such forms must be dictated by their purpose. If they are to be used for the identification of training needs, the training officer (if there is one) will want to see them. If pay is linked to performance, the person responsible for pay decisions will need to have a look at them.

There are four main methods of approaching the recording of performance information. All of these can be applied to either an open or a closed system and to traits-, results- or competence-based approaches. The first two sit relatively comfortably with either a judgemental or a developmental approach. The second two are more inherently judgemental in style. Each has its own problems and limitations, but each also has its own value.

(i) **Descriptive approach.** This involves asking the appraiser to give an unstructured narrative report on the appraisee and/or his job performance. Its basic advantage is that it allows the appraiser free rein to include those attributes/behaviours and parts of the job which he considers relevant; but herein also lies its biggest disadvantage. As we saw in the case of unstructured letters of application or references, much that is important may be left unsaid. And appraisers who find it difficult to tackle those aspects of a subordinate's performance or personality which are most in need of development can take the easy way out by avoiding reference to it. A descriptive section may, nevertheless, be a useful addition to an appraisal form, if one of the other methods is used to record the basic information.

(ii) **Checklists.** These provide some structure for a descriptive report, serving as a reminder of the areas which should be appraised. They can take the form of a list of key results areas, or of competences or traits on which to comment. Provided that such lists are carefully worked out, using the kind of techniques we discussed in the last section, they can help to overcome the basic criticisms of the descriptive approach. Unfortunately they still leave plenty of scope for appraiser vagueness. Because he is free to make whatever comment he likes in relation to the items on the list, the appraiser may tend to use judgemental words without a definite value, like 'excellent', 'good' or 'poor'. As one person's standard will differ from another's on what constitutes 'excellence', this can make comparisons between the subordinates of different managers misleading. If you are using the scheme to help predict potential or for a link with pay, this can have unfortunate effects for the subordinates of the manager who is more sparing with his praise.

One variation where judgement is required is to specify that the comments made should be divided into strengths and weaknesses. The appraiser is obliged to weigh up each of his remarks and identify those aspects where the appraisee does not perform effectively, as well as those where he does. Further rigour can be added to the proceedings in both this and our next method by encouraging the appraiser to specify examples and the deciding factor which led him to his conclusions.

(iii) Ratings.   These provide yet more structure for judgement, by requiring that the appraisee be scored against the checklist. Ratings can be numerical, alphabetical or **behaviourally anchored** – that is, a description of different types of behaviour which the job-holder could be expected to exhibit. Simple descriptive scales are also used: for example 'far exceeds required standard', 'exceeds required standard', 'meets required standard', 'below required standard' or 'well below required standard'.

This example demonstrates one of the pitfalls of rating systems: that of **central tendency.** Because there are an odd number of comments from which to choose, there will be a tendency for appraisers to pick the middle one. It may, therefore, be more useful to limit the choice to four categories, as to extend the scale further makes it increasingly difficult to distinguish between shades of grey. Where numbers are used, these tend to give a falsely scientific and precise air to what is, particularly in traits-orientated schemes, an entirely subjective process. You may or may not want to encourage this pseudo-scientificality. But if you wish to be in a position to give your appraisees a score, perhaps to apply a formula for a link with pay (see Unit 14.3), or for an analysis of overall performance standards, numerical rating will be helpful.

(iv) Comparisons between people.   These can take the form of ranking individuals (Joe is the best performer, Grace is the second best, Bill the third, and so on), or they can follow a normal curve of distribution (10 per cent of your people will be significantly below average, 80 per cent will be around average and 10 per cent will be significantly above average). This allows the appraiser in a judgemental system to compare people against each other, rather than against some absolute standard. This is something that tends to come more naturally to people. Its major drawback lies in what is known as the **zero sum effect.** That is, it assumes that someone will always be best and someone will always be worst. This can mean that however hard an employee at the bottom of the ladder may try to improve, if those people above him are also improving, he cannot move upwards. So, rather like riding a nailed-down bicycle, however hard you pedal, you remain in the same place. This is a frustrating and demotivating experience.

It will be clear from all this that there is no perfect format for performance appraisal. What is important, even with traditional approaches, is the training that users receive to enable them to apply the system consistently and effectively – and their commitment to using it to achieve the intended objectives.

It should also by now be clear that conventional appraisal can have at least as many limitations as benefits. In fact few such schemes, however well designed and administered, survive for more than a few years without overhaul or redesign. As a management tool, appraisal needs regular oiling.

One possible explanation is that, in organisations facing rapid change, the relatively static, backward-looking perspective implicit in all three of the traditional approaches is inappropriate. Another is that most schemes, whether overtly judgemental or developmental, are based on the assumption that it is the **manager** who controls performance. He may consent to involve his people in the review. But he is the boss. He is responsible. He must judge.

9.4 Coaching and Appraisal

In a climate where the ingenuity of individual employees provides the real competitive advantage, a much more dynamic, future-orientated, employee-centred approach is called for. This is only possible where managers are prepared to **share** control with their people, rather than exercise it unilaterally. They must be prepared to stop appraising and start coaching.

This has several important implications. It means:

(*a*) embracing the belief that each one of us is capable of more than we at present think possible;

(*b*) accepting that true **responsibility** depends on having a choice. You can tell someone to do something, and he may or may not comply. Even if he does, that does not mean he will feel responsible for it. If he encounters difficulties, he will more than likely come back to ask you to sort them out. After all, it's you that wants the job done. But the decision to **own** the task, and see it through to completion, can only be taken by the individual concerned. Responsibility is not given, it is taken;

(*c*) recognising that **awareness** and **understanding** of the relevant facts provides the key to improved performance. That awareness must be developed through focus and attention by the individual – not 'telling' by others. **Questions** are the best way of enabling someone to focus on and become aware of relevant issues;

(*d*) understanding the process through which learning, and hence improved performance, takes place. This in turn depends on –

(i) clear, attainable yet challenging personal **goals**

(ii) a thorough exploration of the situation as it is now – to raise awareness of present **reality**

(iii) careful identification and subsequent evaluation of all the things the individual **might** do to improve the situation – the **options**

(iv) a decision about what he or she **will** do, within what time scale, to meet the original goal – including plans to overcome any obstacles likely to be encountered and to obtain any help that may be needed.

This simple model is explained fully by John Whitmore in his book *Coaching to improve performance*. He calls it the **GROW** model – GOAL, REALITY, OPTIONS, WILL. We will refer to it again in later units.

It renders obsolete the debate about whether to appraise traits, results or behaviour, using checklists or ratings or comparisons between people. It also makes the word 'appraisal' itself sound unacceptably judgemental, although we will continue to use it in the context of this unit.

Working to the GROW model:

(*a*) the skilled appraiser/coach invites the employee to identify what he sees as key goals for the planning period of, say, six months. These should be selected within the broad context of organisation and department goals and should be framed to reflect what the employee feels it will be possible to deliver. Goals may initially be expressed as end **results** – e.g. sales of £x thousand. Often it will be more helpful to focus on specific parts of the **process** – e.g. 'introducing an additional item to every customer';

(*b*) the coach asks questions to raise awareness, not to criticise or challenge. If the goals first selected are woolly, hard to measure or completely unrelated to the job to be done, the coach will seek clarification: 'How will you know when you are making progress?' 'How will that help the business as a whole?' If necessary, he will revisit the goal several times in the course of the discussion to confirm that it is still the one the employee wants to aim at;

(*c*) for each goal – and for a six-month planning period two or three challenging ones are better than a dozen minor ones – the coach will ask 'How would you rate yourself now in relation to that – on a scale from one to ten? . . . Where would you like to be? . . . By when? . . . Is that realistic for you?'

(*d*) once the goals are defined, the coach questions, in detail, the 'what', 'when', 'who', 'how often', 'how many' of the current situation. This is to raise the employee's awareness of all the factors underlying and surrounding present performance against the goal. Sometimes the appraisee will suddenly realise something that has been preventing progress and need no further coaching;

(*e*) with the goal and reality understood by the employee, the coach will ask 'What **could** you do?' not 'What **will** you do?' or 'What **should** you do?' The aim is for the employee to generate as many ideas as possible, without evaluating them in any way – yet. When he runs out of spontaneous ideas, the coach will prompt with questions like:

'What if you had unlimited time?'
'What if you had unlimited money?'
'What if you were the boss?'
'What if you were a real expert?'
'What if you knew the answer – what could you do then?'

The coach will not put in any suggestions, unless invited to do so. The closest he should get is 'Would you like another suggestion?' – and not be hurt or surprised if the answer is 'no';

(*f*) once the employee is satisfied with the number of options, the coach can ask how he wants to evaluate them – what criteria he will use and how each option matches up. If it becomes apparent that the employee is lacking some relevant information which the coach has, the latter will resist the temptation to say 'What if I told you . . .?' Instead he should ask 'Is there any other information you think you need?' It is for the employee to narrow down the choice, not the coach;

(*g*) usually the process of evaluation will lead to one or two options emerging as natural to adopt. The coach won't settle for that. Instead he will ask:

'So what **will** you do?'
'What obstacles might you meet?'
'What help might you need?'
'How likely is it that, if you do that, you will achieve your goal?'
'What else could you do to increase the chances?'
'How do you rate the likelihood that you will do everything in your power to make it happen?'

Unless the employee has an action plan which he rates the chances of implementing as at least nine out of ten, the coach will question further to find out what else is needed to increase the chances of success;
(*h*) the coach and the employee will agree who will write up the key points, especially the goal and the action plan, as an *aide mémoire* for both parties.

By adopting this sort of approach, it is possible to achieve any or all of the objectives listed in Unit 9.2 – though any link with pay must be avoided, for reasons which are discussed in Unit 15. Most of the assessment and implementation problems we identified should disappear. You are also likely to find that the goals which employees set for themselves are more challenging than you would have dared to set – and that they are met more often.

Substituting coaching for conventional appraisal is relatively new and not widely tested. Those who have tried it instinctively feel it is a more open, more productive and more forward-looking process. But it cannot be introduced effectively into an autocratic or bureaucratic organisation culture without a lot of other simultaneous changes – some of which we will explore in later units.

9.5 Upward Appraisal

Applying coaching principles to the appraisal process changes its character from implicitly **judgemental** to truly **developmental**. It is no longer something the boss does to his people – instead it is something he does **with** them.

Even so, it remains a one-way process. Some companies, including, for example, WH Smith, challenge the value of this. If 'appraisal' is about helping people learn to do better, why shouldn't it be something colleagues do with each other? Why stop there? Why shouldn't employees do it with their bosses as well as the other way round?

The practice of 180-degree appraisal (employees to boss) is spreading. In theory, it could work in just the way outlined in Unit 9.4, but with the roles reversed.

In practice, most users have adopted a less direct approach. Each employee is asked to complete a questionnaire reviewing the boss's behaviour against a checklist of appropriate behaviour. The boss has a chance to reflect on what his people have said, perhaps with professional counselling support, at least to begin with. This is then followed by a discussion session during which the team give further feedback and examples and help identify alternative ways for the boss to behave.

Introducing 180-degree appraisal requires real commitment to open communications. Initially the feedback is likely to be painful. The scheme **must** focus on suggesting alternative behaviours rather than condemning existing ones.

The next step, 360-degree appraisal, is beginning to be used in some team-based organisations. It allows all team members, of whatever level, to give and receive feedback from each of their colleagues as a basis for team development.

In both cases, the more the appraisal sessions resemble upward or lateral coaching, the more productive they are likely to be.

Whichever type of appraisal scheme you adopt, the next section highlights some basic points to think about before and during the discussion.

9.6 Interview Preparation

Before each meeting, make sure you are familiar with:

(i) the job that the employee is required to do;

(ii) the goals agreed at the last meeting;

(iii) the employee's progress – gleaned from day-to-day observation, written reports and other tangible indicators (sales figures, numbers of complaints) and information from others with and/or for whom he has worked;

(iv) the general circumstances surrounding the employee and his job inside and outside the department, such as problems beyond his control either at work or at home;

(v) the mechanics of the appraisal system, such as reporting requirements and the arrangements for employee participation and appeal;

(vi) the general policy of the company as regards training, transfer, promotion, pay and other matters likely to crop up in relation to particular individuals, together with up-to-date information on what might or might not be available to help the employee and resolve problems.

Plan as carefully as for any other type of interview. In particular:

(a) choose a location where you will not be interrupted;

(b) be relaxed but professional in your manner;

(c) encourage the employee to take a lead in identifying what is happening and what's to be done;

(d) ask open questions – never lead;

(e) probe fully – to make sure all the issues and options emerge;

(f) summarise regularly;

(g) don't patronise. Indiscriminate 'thank-yous' or 'well dones' make it sound as though you think your people work hard for **you**. Far better if they do it because they want to.

9.7 Acting on Appraisal

Without effective follow up, the benefits of a well-conducted appraisal or coaching interview will be dissipated.

(a) Completing the Report

This will be the first step, during or immediately after the interview, and may be done by either party. You should ensure that only items which have been discussed are included and try to make it an accurate record of agreement reached and plans laid. The precise format will be dictated by the style of paperwork that you have chosen (see Unit 9.3).

(b) Keeping Promises

If you have promised someone that you will investigate the possibility of off-job training, you must do just that. (You should have known before the interview whether this was likely, in general terms, to be feasible, otherwise you will have raised expectations which cannot be fulfilled.) If you have said that you will meet again to discuss a particular problem or to review progress, you must do so, within any time limit that you may have specified. If you have said you will talk to your own boss, you must do so, and so on.

(c) Analysing Information

The completed appraisal forms of a number of managers may be useful in providing a picture of the current state of the business and of the needs of the people within it. Training needs can be examined collectively; potential can be looked at in relation to your succession plans; present performance can be considered in terms of your company objectives. Minor problems, whether individual or collective, can be revealed and dealt with before they become major ones.

(d) Ongoing Activity

Important as performance appraisal may be as a formal process, you should not forget that it is, in fact, only the tip of a very large iceberg. If you are managing people effectively, you will be finding out about them and their performance on a continuous basis. And you will be giving them regular coaching and guidance as and when they need it, not just when the calendar says that appraisal is due again.

(e) Evaluating Effectiveness

Setting up a performance appraisal system is time-consuming and costly. It is important that a review of the system and its operation takes place at regular intervals, to ensure that it is meeting the needs which led to its introduction, and that those needs are themselves still valid. You can do this through renewed discussions with those using the system and by analysis of the uses to which the information generated by appraisal is being put. The questions to ask are: 'What is our performance appraisal system doing for us?', 'Do we need that done?' and 'Could we do it more cheaply or more effectively by some other means?'

Whatever form appraisal takes, and however effective or ineffective it is in meeting its objectives, it is more than likely that the process itself will create expectations of further training for those who want or need it. This is the subject of Unit 10.

Questions

1. What do you understand by the term 'performance appraisal'? In what ways can a system of performance appraisal assist managers?
2. Describe the performance appraisal system in operation in an organisation with which you are familiar. What are its objectives and how far do you consider that it achieves them?
3. If you were called in, as a management consultant, to introduce performance appraisal into an organisation, how would you set about it?

UNIT 10

Training Employees

10.1 Introduction

Well-trained employees will have the confidence and the competence to produce better-quality goods and services, quicker and with less waste. They are also more likely to be able to suggest and implement improvements in the way work is done and the results achieved. Before we consider this area in more detail, it is important to distinguish between four words which sometimes cause confusion.

Education is the process of acquiring background knowledge or skills. It is person rather than job or company orientated.

Development is a course of action designed to enable the individual to realise his potential for growth in the organisation. It often relates to future skill demands rather than present tasks. We will consider this in Unit 11.

Training is concerned with the acquisition of a body of knowledge and skills which can be applied directly to work of a particular type. Changing technology and patterns of work mean that training must be a continuous process throughout a working life. Skills acquired for one job may have to be transferred, modified and supplemented for other jobs. If core skills common to a group of jobs can be identified, flexibility can be enhanced.

Learning is the process through which particular patterns of behaviour are 'taken on board' (internalised) and become the norm, for an individual, a group or the organisation as a whole. Although generally seen as something that happens as a **result** of education, development or training, it often occurs in spite of them – or by other means altogether.

Learning takes place when we reflect on something we have experienced, formulate a view about alternative ways of doing it, test out the alternatives and then decide which to adopt in future. This is the **learning cycle** which is explained more fully by David Kolb in *Organisational Psychology: A Book of Readings*.

This is not always a conscious process, nor do events always follow exactly the same sequence. Some people typically act first and then reflect, while others formulate a theory and then test it. But for complete learning all four steps are necessary. As we saw in Unit 9, the more acute the learner's awareness of what is happening and the stronger his sense of responsibility for his own learning, the more effective the process is likely to be.

If your organisation is or aspires to be one in which learning is a way of life, you will take a broad view of learning and value it for its own sake. Ford provides one example of a company which encourages employees to learn anything and everything – on the basis that those who are in the habit of learning are best equipped to bring about change. Resources are made available to help people acquire skills and knowledge which have no direct relevance to their jobs – as well as those that do.

In this unit we will start by looking more narrowly at the processes through which job and company-specific training needs can be identified and met. In Unit 11 we will return to some of these broader learning issues.

10.2 Analysing Training Needs

In analysing training needs, our focus should be first on the job or job-group and what it requires and secondly on the job-holder and how he is able to meet those requirements. There are three basic levels of approach, which are best followed in sequence.

(a) The Company

The overall goals of the company and its future business plans are vital:

(i) in terms of numbers of people to be trained: expansion may mean more junior managers or more skilled employees;

(ii) in terms of the types of jobs for which they will have to be trained: more automation may mean different skills; diversification could demand whole new skill categories;

(iii) in terms of the attendant policies for promoting or transferring employees which will be developed to help meet corporate objectives and which will have an impact on who is to be trained or retrained.

Much of this information will not be new to you if you are engaged in planning your long-term human resource needs and availability. But it will be helpful to bring it all together to identify training needs and to guide the formulation of training policies and priorities on a broad basis. Discussions with managers and sensible use of forward planning information are your best tools at both this and the next level.

(b) The Department

In Unit 2 we discussed the relevance of identifying key skills and who possesses them. When we look at training from the departmental or team point of view we can consider:

(i) the advantages of flexibility that might be gained from giving job-holders broader-based job training: this way they can help each other at busy periods and be more able to adapt to other work if required;

(ii) who needs to be able to do what, to cope with the present workload;

(iii) who needs to be able to do what, to cope with expected changes in workload, work systems or workforce;

(iv) who needs to be able to do what to ensure that continuous improvement is the norm.

(c) The Individual

Although it is the individual who is to be trained, there is little point in spending time and effort identifying and meeting training needs for him if changes at the department or company level are about to render them obsolete. The company and departmental facts established, the analysis of individual training needs should follow a logical sequence.

(i) Examine the job description to ensure that it is up to date and sufficiently detailed to give an accurate picture of the job or job-group.

(ii) Identify the key task areas, together with the techniques and procedures they involve. This will tell you what 'competences' are needed to do the job.

(iii) Identify what is required to perform those tasks, as in the derivation of a personnel specification. This time, though, you will find it helpful to write out a preliminary task analysis along the lines illustrated in Table 10.1. In this example it is part of the job of a canteen supervisor which is being examined. We can see how just four of the tasks which are listed in the supervisor's job description can be broken down to reveal what the job-holder must know or be able to do.

(iv) Assess the trainee's current competence. This can be done by performance appraisal, but observation, reference to specific performance data and the other information-gathering preliminaries will need to be done carefully. Exposure to situations designed to test knowledge and skills or an assessment centre (see Unit 6.2) may be more helpful on occasion.

Table 10.1 A preliminary task analysis

Task	Knowledge	Skills
1. Devise menu	Nutritional values, food preparation times and methods, budget constraints	Creating a varied menu
2. Cost menu	Food costs, company costing methods	Numerical ability
3. Order catering supplies	Company ordering procedure/forms	
4. Oversee food preparation to ensure that hygiene and catering standards are met	Food preparation methods, company standards and statutory hygiene regulations	Motivating, advising and correcting cooks

Discussions with the trainee should form an integral part of this analysis. In some instances you might discover that he has a basic lack of confidence in his own ability to do the job. Training may therefore be required not so much to teach him how to do the job as to assure him that he does know how.

Conversely, a job-holder may not recognise that he is not coping effectively with his present job and therefore be resentful of the idea of training. Some managers are tempted to overcome this by selling training as a reward. The danger here is that the trainee may then choose to regard the training as a holiday, deriving little benefit himself and interfering with the learning of other participants. An effective coaching approach to performance appraisal is likely to be a better antidote to this attitude.

Once you have identified who needs training and for what, the next step is to consider how these training needs can best be met.

10.3   Designing a Training Programme

A training programme is a summary of all the training required to enable an individual to perform a particular job to the required standard. It involves a number of different sets of decisions.

(a) Identifying Learning Objectives

A learning objective is a statement of what the trainee will be able to do, that is, what competences he will be able to demonstrate, to what standard and in what circumstances, at the end of the programme. The overall objective can then be subdivided for particular sections of the programme: for example, 'At the end of this part of the training programme, the trainee will be able, given product details and customer information, to complete all sections of an inland despatch docket without error and within the space of one minute, assessed by a timed test on a sample docket.' Such an objective clearly relates back to a key task in the trainee's job and to a specific procedure with which he is required to comply at a given speed. This speed can be calculated using work measurement techniques applied to experienced workers. It is known as the **experienced worker standard**.

The content of the training programme will be determined by the number and type of learning objectives that it is designed to meet.

(b) Specifying the Sequence

For learning to take place effectively, the learner will need to build from the known to the unknown. But there will also be some parts of the job which are so much part of his everyday activities that you will want him to master these first, so a balance must be struck to ensure that you do not deprive the trainee of the underlying logic and structure that he needs. It would, for instance, be futile to try to teach someone to add up before he had learnt to count. In an industrial context a little knowledge can be a dangerous thing, and it is particularly important that a trainee learns about any safety devices and how to use them before he learns to operate the machine itself.

(c) Choosing the Learning Methods

This aspect must be dictated by the learning objectives. An indication of the range of possible learning methods is given in Table 10.2. The list is divided into two main sections: those which can be applied on the job and those which call for off-job training. The right-hand side of the chart indicates the areas of learning for which each method is most useful.

Table 10.2 Learning methods

Method	Explanation	Area of learning
1. *On-job training*		
Demonstrations	Trainer shows trainee how to (e.g. operate machine)	Knowledge – how to
Training manuals	Written collection of instructions (e.g. how to operate machine)	Knowledge – how to, standards required
Computer-based training embedded in the system	Computer 'trains' operator step by step as he/she carries out a computerised task	Practical – how to
Work samples	Trainer watches trainee (e.g. operate machine)	Practical – how to
Specific projects	Trainer asks trainee to research and report on specific topic (e.g. availability of raw materials)	Knowledge – facts, investigating and problem-solving skills
Coaching	Trainee takes responsibility for own learning and uses on-job instructor as coach to raise awareness	All
2. *Off-job training*		
Films/tape-slide presentations/ video recordings	Sound and vision projections	Knowledge – how to, preparation for skills training
Demonstrations	Trainer shows trainees how to	Knowledge – how to, preparation for skills training

Table 10.2 (*cont*)

Programmed learning/ computer-based training	Book/machine which paces reader and checks knowledge through periodic questioning	Knowledge – facts, occasionally skills
Interactive video	Computer-linked video recording which allows trainee to respond to questions	Knowledge – facts and some skills
Multi-media	Integrated sound, graphics, video and computer packages accessed using CD-Rom	Knowledge – facts and some skills
Lectures and presentations	Trainer delivers prepared exposition	Knowledge – facts and opinions
Tutorials/seminars	Discussion of work produced by trainees	Critical examination of knowledge and opinions
Discussion groups	Discussion, chaired sometimes by trainer, of specific topic	Inter-personal skills, changing attitudes
Briefing groups	Short exposition by trainer, followed by questions and discussion	Knowledge – facts and opinions and how to
Practicals	Trainees operate under trainer's supervision and receive feedback	Practical – how to
Role plays	Trainee puts himself in 'someone clse's shoes' for purposes of practical exercise	Changing attitudes, developing interpersonal skills, e.g. interview skills training
Business games/ computer simulations	Board games or computer-assisted evolving case studies which allow participants to see the consequences of their decisions in given situations	Practical – analysing and deciding

Table 10.2 (*cont*)

Team tasks	Practical indoor or outdoor exercises or simulations	Planning, organising, team and interpersonal skills
Case studies	Write-up of an incident, with questions for analysis	Practical – analysing and deciding
Incident method	Trainees are given last item in sequence of events and asked to re-construct circumstances through questioning trainer	Practical – analysing and questioning
In-tray exercises	Trainees are given a series of memos and other papers, to be put in order of priority	Practical – assessing priorities, deciding
Group/individual projects	Investigation and report, usually with recommendations, on issues of concern to the organisation	Knowledge – facts, investigative, analytical and problem-solving skills and, for groups, team/interpersonal skills
Coaching	Trainee takes responsibility for own learning and uses off-job trainer as coach	All

The important thing in choosing a method is to recognise the nature of the learning that you wish to take place, and to select one which will facilitate that. The biggest pitfall lies in failing to realise the distinction between memorising and learning. The fact that you have told someone repeatedly how to operate a machine means little. Even if he is able, on questioning, to repeat to you exactly how the machine should be operated, that does not mean he can actually operate it. The only way to make sure that he can is to let him try.

This is one reason why the use of coaching, either on or off the job, is so powerful. It makes sure that the learner really is internalising and understanding the process, not just memorising it.

(d) Choosing the Locations

The learning objectives and the learning method will, between them, dictate where the training should take place. The possibility of distance learning should not be overlooked, but the basic choice is between on-job training and off-job training.

You may find off-job training helpful if:

    (i) there is a group of trainees with the same training needs that can more economically be taught as one unit;

    (ii) the work process is such that on-job training would cause an unacceptable level of disruption. This can apply equally to operatives on a fast-moving line and to managers whose errors would be difficult to undo and costly in terms of employee or other relations.

    (iii) there is no one at the workplace qualified to coach on-job;

    (iv) there is no one at the workplace with time to coach;

    (v) the distractions of the workplace might impede learning.

On-job training, on the other hand, has three positive advantages.

    (i) It may seem of more immediate relevance to the trainee.

    (ii) It can facilitate the **transfer of learning**. This is the name sometimes given to the process by which a trainee applies what he has learnt during training to his own job. This can become a particular problem where complex skills are learnt in isolation from one another and from the work environment. Our despatch clerk may be able to fill in his despatch dockets perfectly in one minute flat in the peace and quiet of the training room, but doing it in a hectic despatch department, with a telephone in one hand and a parcel in the other, will be quite a different matter.

    (iii) It is likely to be less expensive at least in terms of capital outlay. If all your training could be done on-job, there would be no need to set aside an area as a training room or to buy expensive equipment to simulate the machines on your shop floor. Where training is needed you must weigh up the costs of doing the training effectively against the costs of not doing it at all.

(e) Choosing the Trainers

The only real consideration here should be the competence of the person in question in using the chosen learning method to reach the required learning objectives. The following points are vital in this respect.

    (i) Trainers should be skilled in coaching and committed to helping trainees learn. This will usually, but not always, be linked to expertise in the subject to be studied. They may be line managers, specialists or consultants.

    (ii) Trainers must have credibility with the trainees.

    (iii) Trainers must be able to use the chosen learning methods to meet the learning objectives.

    (iv) The chosen trainers must be available at the appropriate time.

Table 10.3 Drawing up a training programme

Training programme (pro forma)

Learning objectives
1. At the end of the programme trainees will: . . . .
2. ”   ”   ”   ”   ”   ”   . . . .
3. ”   ”   ”   ”   ”   ”   . . . .
4. ”   ”   ”   ”   ”   ”   . . . .
5. ”   ”   ”   ”   ”   ”   . . . .

	Day/Time	Method	Trainer	Location
1.				
2.				
3.				
4.				
5.				

Unless all of these conditions are met, your trainees will not learn as much as you need them to. (We will consider how the individual trainers should best prepare themselves in the next section.)

(f) Drawing up the Programme
The final stage is to bring together the 'what, when, how, where and who' that we have been discussing, and produce a training programme. Table 10.3 indicates the kind of format that you might use for this, to bring together the component parts, not just for a training course, but for a whole programme incorporating both on- and off-job elements.

But drawing up the programme is only the beginning. Unless you can actually put it into operation to satisfy the training needs, it will be worthless.

10.4 Implementing a Training Programme

Each of the elements of the programme must be considered to ensure that the training happens according to plan, and with the desired results.

(a) Learning Objectives
These must be broken down to provide specific objectives for each component part of the total training programme.

(b) Learning Sequence

This, together with the overall objectives, should be explained to the trainees and trainers before the start of the programme, so that they can see where they are going and how the various parts of the programme, on- and off-job, fit together.

(c) Learning Methods

These must be examined, together with the objectives, so that each trainer can prepare appropriately and the necessary administrative arrangements can be made. This will be particularly important if you are organising some off-job in-house training. You may need to liaise with trainers over the preparation of some of the following items.

(i) Handout material.   This can be used to reinforce points made during sessions and will constitute a permanent reminder for the trainees.

(ii) Visual aids.   Trainees need to use as many of their senses as possible if they are to learn effectively. If they can look at a video, demonstration, overhead projector transparency or wall board as well as hear, they will learn more.

(iii) Teaching guides.   Each trainer should be given a clear (preferably written) brief, so that he knows precisely what is expected of him. This briefing should take place well in advance of the programme, as the trainers will need time to prepare their own material and consider how they are going to present it.

(iv) Special technical facilities.   A video player or tape-slide equipment can be a useful aid to learning, as can tape recorders, computers, interactive video and other devices. If they are to be used, they will need to be acquired and tested before the session. They must also be operated by someone competent to do so, otherwise they will tend to hinder, rather than assist, the learning of the trainees.

This sort of detailed preparation will not be necessary if you are simply arranging for your trainees to attend an external training course. You will need instead to investigate the course and its methods, and secure places on it for the required number of trainees.

(d) The Location

Where in-house training is involved, the room where it is to take place must be made available and kept free from extraneous activity during the period of the training. If you are able to set aside an area as a training room for off-job training, you will need to think how best it can be equipped to meet your needs. A black or white board, wall boards, flip charts, an overhead projector, screen and possibly video equipment are among the items you might consider. Variable seating, rather than fixed rows, will increase flexibility. In selecting and equipping such a training room or in using on-job locations, some specific factors should be borne in mind.

(i) Basic environmental considerations, such as the temperature, lighting, ventilation and noise factors, must be examined. Extremes of temperature, bad ventilation and noise are not conducive to concentration.

(ii) All the facilities required during relevant phases of the programme must be capable of being used in your chosen location. If you are using overhead projector transparencies, for instance, you will need a power point, as well as a projector, screen and possibly window blinds.

(iii) Chairs and tables may be needed, and you may want to experiment with a layout more conducive to discussion or other forms of participation than the serried rows of the traditional classroom.

(iv) Information about the location – where it is, how to get to it – will need to be given to the trainees to help ensure that they turn up in the right place.

(e) The Trainers

We have mentioned the importance of briefing trainers well in advance. Any questions that they have or doubts they may express should be dealt with early on. If you find yourself required to make a formal presentation or give a talk, here are a few basic rules that you may find helpful.

(i) Prepare thoroughly, making sure that you are fully conversant with your subject and have thought about it from a number of angles. If possible, rehearse your presentation, but not to the point where you become bored.

(ii) Look at the subject through the eyes of the trainees. What do they already know that may help them in achieving these new learning objectives? What sort of presentation will they gain most from? Might a lighter, more humorous approach bring a weighty subject to life or would this be totally out of keeping with the character and expectations of your audience?

(iii) Let them know what you're going to tell them, tell them it, then tell them what you've told them. This is a time-hallowed but unbeatable dictum, which applies to all types of presentation. The actual telling can happen through any of the media listed in Table 10.2, but the introduction and the summary are still vital.

(iv) Work with methods and equipment that you know and are happy with, provided of course that they are appropriate for the achievement of the desired learning objective. Experiment to develop your expertise only where doing so will not jeopardise the trainees' learning.

(v) Remember that the quality of your input can only be measured by one standard: the extent to which the learning objectives are achieved. An Oscar-winning performance may be very enjoyable for all concerned, but if the trainees actually learn nothing, it is misplaced. By all means entertain your audience, but remember that they are there to learn.

(vi) Look for, and use, feedback. If the trainees have gone to sleep, they are not learning. The same applies if they are fidgeting or looking bored. Encourage them to ask questions and involve them in discussions to make sure that everyone is on the same wavelength. And ask them questions, formally and informally, to check their understanding.

(vii) Wherever you can, abandon the set-piece presentation altogether in favour of a coaching approach. Involve the audience in agreeing the goal and use questions as a means of raising awareness.

(f) The Programme

Use your programme to provide yourself with a point of comparison through-out the implementation of the training. You should check regularly to ensure that the timing and sequence are being adhered to. But most important, you should also use it as a checklist against which to measure progress towards the achievement of learning objectives.

While most of our discussion in this section has been more relevant for those contemplating involvement with in-house training, in the next section we will be placing more emphasis on the nature and contribution of external courses as part of a training programme.

10.5   Training Courses

Our discussion so far should indicate that 'training' is not synonymous with 'course' and that courses are not necessarily external. We considered, in Unit 10.3, the relative uses of on- and off-job training. Here we will look at some of the respective merits of in-house and external training courses and at the types of external course that are available.

(a) In-house Training Courses

If the training can be organised and conducted on an in-company basis, there will be a number of benefits.

(i) Course content will be tailor-made to suit the learning objectives of your trainees, in the context of your company.

(ii) Real company examples can be used, which will have a high degree of relevance for the trainees.

(iii) The trainees are more likely to find themselves among people that they know and will therefore have to spend less time becoming acclimatised socially, and possibly geographically. They should therefore be able to start learning sooner.

(iv) The training can more readily be integrated with on-job coaching and practice, as the company will have control over the timetables for both and can arrange for half a day's off-job training to be followed by half a day's on-job practice to reinforce it.

(v) If you have the necessary resources and expertise within your company, it will be more economical to use these to supply the needs of a group of trainees, rather than paying course fees for them all to attend some other institution. You can always supplement it by selective use of external guest speakers or invite a consultant to design and run the whole course for you.

(b) External Courses

These too have a range of advantages which can make them a more attractive proposition in certain circumstances.

(i) They can bring together the expertise of a number of specialists, over a range of subjects, which might not be available in-house.

(ii) They can bring together a range of facilities which would not be economically viable on a small training budget.

(iii) They can allow for a valuable cross-fertilisation of ideas between companies, which can prevent the sort of stagnation which occurs when an organisation becomes too introspective. Provided that this does not lead to leakage of confidential company information or loss of personnel through 'poaching', this can be a very useful spin-off from external training.

(iv) They create an opportunity for learning to take place away from the distractions and interruptions of company life. If there is a sudden crisis, it is all too easy to knock on the door of the in-house training room and ask for 'Pam' to come out and help downstairs for a little while. If Pam is out of the building at an external training establishment, there is a lot less chance of this happening.

While these advantages and disadvantages will need to be weighed up carefully, the deciding factor in many cases will be the availability of a suitable external course. These fall into two basic categories.

(c) Qualification Courses

In the UK these are provided by colleges of further education, technical colleges, universities and specialist colleges, who operate under the general aegis of the government's Department for Education and Employment. They may also be offered by private institutions. Some courses are designed and approved (**validated**) by the institution concerned, as is the case with most university degree courses. Others such as City & Guilds and BTEC courses are centrally designed or validated and are offered by a number of different institutions.

Many courses are geared to providing the individual with background knowledge and skills, usually in a range of interrelated subjects. They can therefore be used for all age groups and all types of employee. The British education system provides for everything from learning another language or brushing up your maths, to obtaining a master's degree in management or business administration. Courses can be undertaken on a distance learning, evening class, day-release, block-release, sandwich course or full-time basis.

A more practical, competence-based approach is taken by those offering a National Vocational Qualification (NVQ) or Scottish Vocational Qualification (SVQ). These relate to a specific industry, vocation or profession and are intended to operate at six levels. A shop assistant or a skilled factory worker may aim at level one or two initially, a supervisor at level three and standards for directors may eventually be set at level six. Specialists in the relevant sector contribute to the development of NVQs through what are known as **lead bodies** – often an existing industry or professional association.

NVQs do not necessarily entail attending formal courses, as the qualifications are intended to reflect competences acquired at work. Those who enrol may have to produce a portfolio of examples of things they have done at work and be observed by a qualified internal or external assessor.

*'I understand you've been taking unfair advantage of
our Day Release scheme.'*

If they satisfy the assessor that they meet the relevant **performance criteria** for each of a number of designated **elements of competence**, they will be credited with the relevant **unit of competence**. Once they have the required number of units, the NVQ, which is validated by an external **awarding body** such as City & Guilds, BTEC or the Industry Training Organisation (see Unit 10.7) will be awarded. General NVQs are available through schools and colleges as a more practical alternative to academic qualifications.

With many different courses available, it can be hard to tell how one relates to another in terms of qualification level, so the National Council for Vocational Qualifications (NCVQ) liaises with employers and examining and validating bodies to bring new and existing vocational qualifications into a national framework with agreed standards of competence. Hence most courses now have an NVQ equivalent level.

Time spent making the acquaintance of the heads of the relevant departments of your local colleges will help you to formulate a clear idea of how they can help you. This will be more effective than simply looking at a heap of prospectuses.

You can also approach your local Training and Enterprise Council (TEC) or Local Enterprise Council (LEC) (see Unit 10.7). They may be able to help with information from the NCVQ national database.

(d) Short Courses

Colleges, universities and many other bodies, from the manufacturers of computers to professional associations and from specialist training companies to individual consultants, offer courses of job-related training, usually for specific skills.

On short courses, varying in length from a day or two to several months, you can learn to program a computer or to conduct a selection interview, acquiring skills which are job-, not company-, related. In fact, many such courses are open to people who are not currently employed in the particular field concerned, but who are taking part in the Training for Work scheme (see Unit 3.8) or are paying their own fees.

As with educational courses, tracking down the one that is right for you can be a problem. Your local TEC or LEC should be able to provide some guidance from their database of local providers. Their roles are discussed more fully in Unit 10.7. Outside the local area, the National Training Index or a commercial database like OMTRAC can help you explore what is available and will provide some objective assessment of quality.

Most providers will be happy to send you details of the courses they offer on either an open or in-house basis so you can form your own judgement. But bear in mind that short-course brochures tend to be designed as marketing tools rather than objective appraisals. Wherever possible, make contact with past users before committing yourself.

It is in the area of external skills training courses that complaints of irrelevance to the in-company situation tend to crop up. And where such training is provided to all comers, on a non-selective basis, across different types of industry and every level of ability, it will inevitably be difficult to please all the people all the time. There are two ways of combating this when you are considering external training.

(i) Study the learning objectives of the course very carefully to make sure that they really do match the needs of your delegates.

(ii) Examine the possibility of the training providers concerned running the course on a private basis, for your participants only. This need not be much more expensive than sending delegates to an open course, and it will probably also be considerably more effective. This way, you receive the benefits of external expertise and, if desired, location, without the disadvantages which arise from an attempt to meet all needs. The feasibility of such a venture will also depend on how many of your employees really do share the same training needs. Once you start adding people just to make up the numbers, you might as well abandon the whole scheme.

The important thing about implementing your training through external courses is that you must not lose sight of the vital link between the job and the training. Debriefing sessions, where trainees can examine what they have learnt on the course in relation to their jobs, will be of immense value. And remember that the most effective training programmes are often an amalgam of activities, on-job and off-job, in-company and out-of-company. The art lies in knowing how to mix them to derive maximum benefit from each to satisfy learning objectives and meet training needs at minimum cost.

10.6 Evaluating Training

You can waste a great deal of money on training if you do not bother to check to see if it has been worthwhile. This evaluation of a training programme, or a component of it, can be carried out at four different levels.

(a) Reactions Level

The way in which the trainees react to the training in terms of enjoyment and perceived learning is one basic, but sometimes unreliable, yardstick. The fact that trainees have enjoyed themselves may indicate that they found themselves in a congenial social group, rather than that they have actually learnt anything. And the fact that they **think** they have learnt something may be a reflection of their unwillingness to admit that such a happy social event was, from the learning point of view, a waste of time.

Evaluation at this level can be either informal or formal.

(i) Informal. Trainees give oral feedback in answer to general questions such as 'How did you enjoy it?' or 'Which parts were of most use to you?' If the trainer himself asks these questions, particularly on an individual basis, it can become embarrassing for both parties. If it is done on a group basis, at the end of a training course, for instance, it needs careful handling to ensure that it remains both constructive and representative of the majority view.

(ii) Formal. A questionnaire can be designed to elicit trainees' reactions to the course as a whole and to specific aspects of it. The interest and relevance of the content, the appropriateness of the learning methods, the quality of instruction, and so, on can all be brought under the microscope in this way. Depending on how and when the questionnaire is administered to trainees, you will get a more or less considered and responsible set of replies.

It is also possible to introduce formalised self-assessment, where you ask participants to mark on a scale the level of their knowledge or skill at the start of the training and repeat the process at the end. As trainees have no yardstick against which to measure themselves at the beginning, and may tend to underrate their own abilities anyway, such methods can produce distorted results. You may even find that trainees profess to know less at the end of the training than they did at the beginning. This could mean that you have succeeded in confusing them to the point where they really do know less. Alternatively, it may simply indicate an over-optimistic preliminary assessment being modified in the light of greater awareness.

(b) Immediate Outcome/Learning Level

Your learning objectives, if properly stated, will have included some method of assessing whether or not the desired learning has taken place. In the example we used in Unit 10.3 the assessment takes the form of giving the trainee one minute in which to complete an error-free inland despatch docket. If he can complete the docket in the time allowed, we can assume that learning has taken place. If, however, we want to make quite sure that the learning happened as a result of the training, we should administer the same test both before and after the training session, to make sure that we are not teaching the trainee something that he already knows.

For many courses, evaluation at this level takes the form of an examination or test of some kind. This is designed to sample the kind of learning that the training was designed to provide. There are a number of difficulties to consider.

(i) You may inadvertently introduce an additional variable into the situation. If, for instance, instead of asking the trainee actually to complete the docket we had asked him to write a paragraph explaining how he would do so, we would be adding quite a new dimension. He may have difficulty in expressing himself fluently in written English. Or he may not be able to analyse his own actions. So he will not do himself justice, and we will not know whether he can, in fact, write out a despatch docket in the correct manner. All such post-training tests must have **construct validity**. That means, as we saw in Unit 6.4, that they really do measure what they set out to measure.

(ii) All tests and examinations tend to produce unnatural behaviour of one kind or another. The stress of the situation may lead the trainee to forget things which he knows perfectly well. If the test is practical, the feeling of being under scrutiny, added to the worry of what happens in the event of failure, may lead the individual to behave in a way which is quite out of character. These and other problems associated with testing were discussed more fully in Unit 6. The difficulties can be reduced if the tests are explained as a means of giving feedback to the trainer, so that he knows whether the trainee can now fill in the despatch docket or whether he needs more training. For qualification courses – especially those examined centrally – this argument wears rather thin. The examinee may be only too well aware that his job prospects depend on his results.

(iii) The time and trouble necessary to construct valid tests may seem to make their use something of a chore. Depending on the nature of the test, marking it can be even more arduous. It is therefore all too easy to lose sight of the significance of the result for the individual. Some types of test, particularly those calling for essay-type answers or tester observation, may also tend to produce rather a subjective and not totally valid assessment.

In spite of these drawbacks, some immediate feedback is necessary, and if you have thought through your learning objectives properly, an appropriate means of testing whether they have been achieved will almost certainly suggest itself. But evaluation at this immediate outcome stage has one further limitation. It cannot tell you whether the trainee will actually **apply** his new knowledge or skill to his job. The transfer of learning cannot be measured through a post-course test or examination and the next level of evaluation will be of more help here.

(c) Intermediate Outcome/Job Behaviour Level

If the training has been carried out in response to a clearly identified training need, arising out of the way in which the trainee was doing his job prior to the start of the programme, it should be possible to evaluate the training by seeing whether his job performance has changed for the better. The ease with which this can be done will vary with the size and complexity of the job and the factors affecting it.

In the case of our despatch clerk, a decrease in the number of dockets returned as illegible might be one control mechanism through which to monitor the effectiveness of the training. The volume of work he handles in a day might be another, provided nothing else has changed in the meantime. But take the case of a sales assistant in the swimwear department of a large store. Her return from a three-day selling-skills course in June coincided with the start of an anticyclone which was to last all summer. Swimwear sales rocketed. Much as the trainer would have liked to take the credit for this, the intervening variables, in the shape of temperatures of 30°C, cannot be ignored.

Care, therefore, needs to be taken to ensure that the effects of training can be isolated. In our last example, comparison with other weather-influenced departments, garden furniture or sunglasses, for instance, might give an indication of the sort of percentage increase in sales which might be attributable to the good weather. Comparative figures for other stores in the group might also be of value, provided that they have not sent anyone for training recently and have enjoyed the anticyclone too.

But what if a further variable had been introduced, in the shape of a change of buyer for the department? This could mean that the stock which our sales assistant is selling so rapidly has been chosen according to new criteria this year. It may be that this stock is more saleable than last year's, thereby apparently reducing still further the trainee's contribution to this meteoric rise in sales.

The possibilities are endless. And the more likely the trainee's job is to be influenced by external circumstances, such as the action or inaction of others, or the availability of raw materials, the more difficult the task of evaluation becomes.

It is difficult, but not impossible. If we observe the trainee at work after the training, as well as before, we can obtain a comparison. Or we can set up test situations at work, to see how the trainee copes with them, before and after the training. It may be more difficult to distinguish between specific parts of the training if the whole has been brought together and blended into the way the trainee does his job. But the remedying of shortfall in key results areas should not be too hard to spot. (If no improvement has occurred, we must ask ourselves whether this is because the training was ineffective or because the training needs were wrongly identified in the first place.)

(d) Ultimate Outcome/Organisation Change Level

In Unit 10.2 we established the importance of relating overall training policy and plans to the goals of the organisation. The ultimate evaluation of training comes when the organisation either does or does not manage to sustain those goals. Some people would argue that this is the only truly significant level of evaluation. It doesn't matter how well trained your staff are if the company is not achieving what it should. This is also the most difficult level of evaluation to carry out and, for that reason, the most rarely applied. The problems identified in relation to job behaviour level evaluation are multiplied by the number of other compatible or conflicting moves being made by the organisation while training is being planned and implemented. Examples include changes in recruitment or pay policies affecting the calibre of person employed; new technology or changed marketing strategy affecting production or sales for better or worse; and the external constraints of changing markets, changing competition, and the rest. If you succeed, is it because of training or some other factor? If you fail, the same question applies.

10.7 National Initiatives

In spite of the difficulties of **proving** the effectiveness of training, most progressive organisations now firmly believe that it is the key to future success. The government has actively encouraged this view and has reflected it in several important initiatives.

(a) The National Standard for Investors in People (IIP)
Organisations which can demonstrate that they:

   (i) are publicly committed to developing all their employees in order to achieve their business objectives;
   (ii) regularly review the training and development needs of all employees;
   (iii) plan and conduct effective training for new and existing employees;
   (iv) evaluate its effectiveness and contribution to the achievement of business objectives

may be awarded the special IIP 'kite-mark' which they are authorised to use for three years.

   The standard is a rigorous one. Organisations are assessed by trained assessors who report back to the appropriate Training and Enterprise Council. Those aspiring to recognition as an Investor in People must prepare detailed documentary evidence that they meet all the elements of the standard. The assessor will also spend time interviewing and observing employees at all levels against the twenty-four detailed assessment indicators to make sure that commitment to learning is truly organisation-wide.

(b) National Targets for Education and Training
(i) **Foundation learning.** The government's aim is that by 1997 80 per cent of young people will have qualifications at NVQ level II or equivalent and that training and education to level III will be available to all young people who can benefit from it. By the year 2000 the goal is that 50 per cent of young people will have reached level III or equivalent. The type of training given should be such as to encourage self-reliance, flexibility and breadth at the beginning of people's careers.

(ii) Lifetime learning. As we have seen, 'once and for all' training is no longer an option for any of us. The government's aim is that by 1996 **all** employees should be taking part in training or development activities, that 50 per cent of the workforce should be aiming for NVQs or units towards them and that 50 per cent of medium to large organisations should have attained the IIP standard. Their goal for the year 2000 is for 50 per cent of the workforce to be qualified to at least NVQ level III or equivalent.

(c) National Training Awards

Each year organisations and individuals who believe that a particular training initiative has made a positive contribution to their business performance are invited to compete for a national award. Full details of the training and verification of its impact are submitted to a panel of judges. The winners receive national publicity as well as the kudos of the award and a trophy. There are a number of special categories, including training of women, ethnic minorities and those with specialist needs, and one for those who have been active in developing the Modern Apprenticeship programme (see Unit 3.8).

(d) Training Infrastructure

Training and Enterprise Councils (TECs) provide a focal point for local information and funding for training. They are independent companies, operating under licence to the **Training, Enterprise and Education Directorate (TEED)** which in turn is part of the Department for Education and Employment. In Scotland the same functions are fulfilled by Scottish Enterprise/Highlands and Islands Enterprise.

Each TEC has between nine and sixteen directors, at least two-thirds of whom are private sector chairpersons, chief executives or top operational managers. The balance may be drawn from the public sector, trade unions, voluntary organisations and so on. They generally operate through a series of special committees or working groups with wider membership and have a small staff of permanent employees.

Their budgets are allocated on the basis of population, economic conditions and bids for specific funding. Each develops a network of local training providers drawn from existing colleges and private providers. Their training responsibilities include:

(i) working towards the achievement of the National Targets for Education and Training in their area – including IIP standard;

(ii) the delivery of youth and adult national training programmes (Youth Training, Training for Work);

(iii) support for new enterprises and expanding businesses;

(iv) promoting closer links between business and education;

(v) encouraging employers to provide training for their own employees.

Industry Training Organisations (ITOs) set training standards and aim to ensure the training needs of their particular industry are met. They assess future skill requirements and in some cases provide a direct training service, particularly in industry-specific skills.

In the main, ITOs have replaced the old **Industry Training Boards (ITBs)**, though two ITBs are still functioning – one in construction, the other in engineering construction. While ITBs are funded by a statutory levy on employers of a set percentage of payroll expenditure, ITOs raise money by subscription from members and charges for their products and services. They are normally run by management committees and some also act as Industry Lead Bodies for the development of relevant NVQs. They are linked through the National Council for Industry Training Organisations.

Questions

1. What is the distinction between 'education', 'development' and 'training'? Is it important? Give reasons for your answer.
2. Taking a job with which you are familiar, compile first a job description and then a task analysis to identify the knowledge and skills required of the job-holder.
3. Prepare a training programme for a new recruit into the job analysed in question 2. Explain the reasons behind your choice of sequence and learning methods.
4. Discuss the relative merits of: (*a*) off-job versus on-job training; (*b*) in-house versus external training.
5. How would you set about evaluating an off-job training course which you have attended?

UNIT 11

Developing Employees

11.1 Introduction

At a global conference on lifelong learning in 1994, the managing director of the Rover Learning Business, part of the Rover car group, said: 'It is a fundamental responsibility of every organisation to create an environment of continuous learning and development'. Yet for many organisations, and for much of this century, 'employee development' has in fact meant **'management development'**.

Once each employee's initial training gap had been identified and filled, further training would only be given in response to specific changes in working methods or individual responsibilities. Opportunities for development were largely limited to those identified as having potential for more senior roles.

In this unit we will start by exploring some of the factors which have led many organisations to redefine the scope of their development activities and discuss what this means in practice. We will return to the specific issue of management development in Unit 11.4.

11.2 Development Needs

For many people specific, task-related skills are now only the start. Of course the machine operator must be able to operate the machine safely and to produce the required quality and quantity of output. Of course the clerical assistant must be able to transfer the correct information from computer screen to customer or supplier – or *vice versa* – speedily and without errors. Of course the sales assistant must be able to communicate the features, advantages and benefits of the products and collect the correct payment efficiently and pleasantly. But all three – and most other employees – need to be able to do much more besides.

More and more organisations are seeking to become **world class**. In brief, that means:

(*a*) putting the **customer** first;

(*b*) refusing to trade-off **quality, value** and **service**. All three must exceed customer expectations;

(*c*) working continuously to **improve processes** and reduce the number of defects or errors;

(*d*) working to eliminate **waste**. This includes inspection (which shouldn't be necessary if things are done right to begin with), transportation time, re-work time, storage time – none of which adds any value for the customer though all may add considerably to costs;

(*e*) rethinking the way progress is **measured** and success is judged – to make sure that only those activities which add value for the customer are encouraged;

(*f*) **empowering** the workforce to identify and implement new ideas and ways of improving processes – drawing on the creativity and problem-solving skills of every member of the team, not just the boss.

Among the many tactics adopted to support the drive to become world class are **business process re-engineering** and **total quality management** programmes (see Unit 1), **BS5750**, **IS09000** and **IIP** (see Unit 10.7). For employees this means:

(i) they are expected to **think** much more about what they are doing and how it could be done better;

(ii) they may work in multi-skilled **teams** rather than as individuals. This means learning not only to operate another machine or two, or to work with other data or products, but also to relate to other members of the team, to ensure that the combined output is greater than the sum of the parts. It may also mean getting used to a new layout and methods of passing work on – a 'u-shaped' module rather than an assembly line in a factory, for instance;

(iii) they may be responsible for monitoring and measuring their own work, perhaps drawing up their own charts to record anything from absences to customer complaints, machine breakdown time to running temperatures, response times to machine tolerances. In some cases, they will need to master the techniques of **statistical process control** so that they can make sense of their data over time and distinguish between normal fluctuations and those which indicate that special problems are arising;

(iv) they need to know about their **customers** – the people who make use of the output from their part of the process. Sometimes this will be those who actually buy the finished product or service. Often they will be 'internal' customers – the people who carry out the next steps in the process of getting the output to the final customer.

Bringing this about calls for:

(*a*) **effective communication** of the reasons for change and the development of a shared concept of what change will mean – for the organisation as a whole, its component parts and individual members;

(*b*) **redefinition of management roles** – from boss to team leader, from giver of orders to coach and facilitator of creative problem-solving – with a whole new philosophy and set of skills for managers to master;

(*c*) **commitment to continuous learning**. For many, learning to learn is the first step in this process. To begin with, **what** is learned matters less than the fact that movement around the learning cycle restarts;

(*d*) **specific training** in new equipment, processes and techniques;
(*e*) **team work** skill development;
(*f*) **coaching**, on an ongoing basis, and including self-coaching and cross-coaching between colleagues for all involved.

Depending on the size, complexity, structure and climate of the organisation, such change can take years to implement – and will never be finished. Because each is different, it is dangerous to attempt any 'how to do it' prescription. Table 11.1 highlights some of the key elements involved – but for every business which has worked methodically right through the process, there are several others who have begun in the middle and worked outwards or jumped about within the sequence.

Table 11.1   Key elements of the change process

Element	Comment

1. Identify need for change
  – diagnosis of current situation
  – comparison with competitors
  – identification of strengths, weaknesses, opportunities and threats facing the business
	Commercial pressure or impending disaster are the most common triggers. Executive foresight is a better foundation

2. Educate management team
  – raise awareness of need for change
  – introduce key concepts
	Programme should familiarise them with current management thinking and its application

3. Provide open access to learning for all employees	For example, by arrangements with local colleges, libraries, in-house facilities
4. Develop vision of what the world will be like when the change is complete	See Unit 19.3
5. Formulate specific mission	This is what the management team is paid to achieve
6. Identify critical success factors	These are the things which, if not achieved, will thwart fulfilment of the mission and mean the vision remains a dream
7. Determine when and by whom progress will be measured	Establish measures, baselines, goals and milestones

Table 11.1 (*cont*)

8. Identify and review core business processes – the linked activities which underpin the critical success factors	Focus on those which add value for the customer
9. Decide which processes are most in need of 'transformation'	Those where improvements will make a real difference
10. Devise a detailed programme for change	See text
11. Design skill development programme	See Table 11.2
12. Communicate vision, critical success factors and outline programme	Generate enthusiasm and start to build commitment. Evangelical realism is key
13. Involve as many people as possible and keep them involved	See Unit 18.9

Some opt for total employee involvement from the start, on the basis that you cannot introduce openness and empowerment from behind closed doors. Others have devoted proportionately more time to winning the hearts and minds of senior and middle managers first, on the basis that they are the ones who will have to manage the change through the organisation and must have time to adapt to new ways of thinking and/or acquire new skills themselves before they start involving others.

Which is 'right' depends on the starting point and how each is carried through in practice. Asking people to pack their bags for a journey before anyone has the slightest idea where they are going or how they will get there can cause unnecessary alarm. Waiting until 'management has got it all worked out' is clearly not right either.

One contribution you may be able to make if you find yourself caught up in such a programme of change is to help build a sensible development programme for your own team. Table 11.2 shows the sort of things you could include. There are several factors to balance when working out precisely what sequence to adopt.

(*a*) Learning that cannot be put into practice is soon lost. Development activities scheduled on a 'just-in-time' basis, i.e. when they are needed, are likely to be the most effective.

(*b*) Much of this learning will require un-learning of old patterns of behaviour. That takes time and demands constant reinforcement. A three-day coaching or team-building event, on its own, will be nowhere near enough to change the habits of a lifetime. Opportunities for practice and additional

Table 11.2   Skill Development Programme

Element	Participants
1. Team building for management team and for other groups expected to work to common goals and standards	Relevant teams
2. Customer care – what it means for the business	All
3. Customer care – what it means for us	Each team – to identify who its customers are and what actions it can take to improve its service
4. Coaching skills	All who manage people, then team members too
5. Process improvement – what it means for the business	All
6. Process improvement – what it means for us	Each team – to identify and work to eliminate waste in its work process
7. Uses and application of process improvement techniques, including statistical process control	Those identified as process improvement leaders
8. Use of specific process improvement techniques	All employees, as needed
9. Systematic problem solving	All
10. Project management	Those charged with delivering more complex projects
11. Facilitation skills	Individuals designated to assist project and process improvement team leaders
12. Job skills	Those who will operate more or different processes in future

coaching must be made available. This is one argument in favour of helping others with managerial responsibilities first. Unless they have themselves had time and encouragement to 'groove in' the new ways, they may be unable or unwilling to help their people do so.

(c) The amount of new learning which people can take must be considered. There is plenty of synergy between, for instance, team building and coaching, and many people find it helpful to work on both more or less simultaneously. Expecting them to master statistical process control as part of the same learning event could be asking too much. Far better to space things out and have a chance to practise each element before the next is added.

(*d*) Until the programme is under way, it is almost impossible to anticipate what extra help may be needed. Teams working to identify how better to serve their customers may uncover all sorts of barriers to improved performance which will take time to remove. It is therefore essential to retain some flexibility to allow time and funds for unforeseen elements.

(*e*) Unless all other activities cease while changes are made (an unlikely luxury except in a brand new operation), learning must be phased to allow for business as usual. That may mean that groups who ideally should learn together find this difficult. One solution is to use non-work time – evenings or weekends – for some essential elements. Team building in fact lends itself quite well to an off-duty timetable, provided the vital commitment building is already underway.

11.3 Development Methods

Some of the methods outlined in Table 10.2 can be applied to development as well as training. There is, however, one method which is fundamental to employee development.

(a) Coaching

If your employee development programme is to be sustainable, as much of it as possible should be self-directed by the learner. Only by building a climate where people take responsibility for their own learning can you hope to create the momentum you will need. Arguably, if enough of your people are effective coaches, you will not need any other development methods. They will coach each other to develop the required skills.

The GROW model outlined in Unit 9.4 provides a framework. Whatever an employee wants to learn, being clear about specific goals and the present position in relation to them must be the starting point. Encouraging experimentation and reflection, rather than simply 'telling', will enhance ownership and a sense of responsibility for learning.

Enquiring 'What do you notice? . . . What do you feel? What is happening?' while the learner is trying something new may be all that is needed to help him focus, raise his awareness – and learn.

In the next section we will outline the type of events which can assist the development of team skills. But we could equally well use coaching as a means of developing them. The process might be roughly as follows.

(i) The coach could ask the team members to identify the sorts of behaviour they feel are the hallmarks of an effective team. This could be done at a team meeting or as part of a training session.

(ii) He would then ask each team member, privately, to rate both the team and himself in relation to each behaviour.

(iii) The team scores would be shared and aggregated, with no opportunity for challenge or recrimination.

(iv) The team members would select the behaviour on which they wished to work first. A little time might be spent probing for examples to ensure general understanding of the nature of the issue, before asking them what sort of rating they would aim to be able to give themselves – and when.

(v) During the working day the awareness raised by steps (i) to (iv) would go a long way towards sensitising the group and some change in the relevant behaviour would be likely.

(vi) To boost awareness further, the coach would make a point of asking questions at intervals throughout the day – not just when there was a particularly good or bad example of the behaviour. 'What is happening now? . . . Who is affected? . . . What else do you notice?' This might be followed with 'What **could** you do? . . . What else?'

(vii) At the agreed time the team members would rate themselves again on the relevant behaviour – and then agree whether to set themselves a new goal in relation to it or start work on a fresh behaviour.

(viii) Over a period of days or weeks, the team members could tackle each of the behaviours they initially identified. Periodically the coach could ask whether they wished to extend their list, and whether they wanted to revisit any of the behaviours tackled earlier.

(ix) Once established as a way of working, the team may quite naturally wish to continue being coached. Eventually though, the new behaviours would become second nature and the coach's questions redundant.

Where the team work closely together and the coach is on the spot to ask questions, this sort of gradual on-the-job build-up of team effectiveness can work very well. There are, of course, circumstances in which it may be more appropriate to take the group away to start the process. This will be particularly important where interactions between team members are less frequent or less visible – or where the need for a 'fresh start' is felt.

(b) Team building

The hallmarks of an effective team include trust, adaptability, unselfishness and co-operation. These can be developed in any context which forces group members to work together – not necessarily a work context.

For that reason, much team building activity takes place out of doors. Here it is possible to create visible interactions on which the group can reflect. There are many programmes on offer – the more extreme of which have received rather a mixed press. The key elements are usually:

(i) a series of progressively more complex tasks, requiring group effort to resolve. Defusing mythical 'bombs' or transporting people or objects along planks or over obstacles are favourites. Participants learn the value of being clear about their objectives and resources, planning, sharing information and ideas, listening to and supporting each other and co-operating to achieve team goals;

(ii) an element of (controlled) risk. Unwanted dousing in cold water, a night without food or shelter or even personal injury might feature. Physical challenges ranging from caving to subaqua sports or rock climbing may have to be mastered – under tuition. Participants learn to value each other's abilities, understand their own and others' physical and emotional limitations and to trust each other;

(iii) a major exercise, sometimes extending over two days or more, calling on all the skills developed in the previous stages. The more daunting the task seems and the more challenging the team finds it, the greater the sense of 'oneness' they generally develop when they have achieved their goal.

If you are involved in choosing someone to provide this sort of experience, there are two vital things to check:

(i) **Safety standards.** Established providers, like the Leadership Trust in Ross on Wye, take great pains to remove any real risk from such events. Medical checks for participants before the course, rigorous training and competence testing for the instructors involved in the physical elements and psychiatric help on hand if it all gets too much are the sort of things you should look for. Even if you are 100 per cent satisfied, don't forget to check the insurance position with both the provider and your own insurers. In case the worst **should** happen, you must make sure you are covered.

(ii) **Learning support.** Just doing the tasks or accomplishing 'mission impossible' may be good fun – but it does not take people round the learning cycle. You must have someone – and probably a team of people – available to help the team members clarify their development goals and to raise awareness of what is actually happening. The tutor may not be as closely involved in the event as the coach in our workplace example in the previous section, but he must be in a position to question and draw out the learning.

To get the best from the programme, it is important to get the **whole** team together. Leaving out one or two who can't make the date may not seem vital. But if the programme works for the others, they will always be at a disadvantage.

And if it is **team building** you need, make sure your team will stay together for most of the course. There **is** value in individuals attending open programmes and mixing with delegates from other companies. The learning gained will be about the leadership and/or team membership skills of the individual. This should help him to be a more effective member of his own team, but will have done little to enhance the performance of the team overall.

Most of the other development methods we will discuss do in fact focus on the individual rather than the team. They can be used to help particular employees develop their understanding of the broader business – and equip them to contribute more flexibly to its development. Business process reviews are again team-based.

(c) Business process reviews

Helping a team to conduct a review of its business processes is a particular form of development activity which falls somewhere between a meeting and a training event. In so far as their objectives are to raise awareness of alternative ways of exceeding customer expectations, they are undoubtedly developmental for the participants.

Such reviews are best led by the manager or team leader responsible for the process in question. As the 'process owner' he is the person charged with maximising its efficiency and effectiveness. The other key participant is a facilitator or coach. He typically takes little part in the discussion but coaches the leader before and after meetings, manages the time and the flip chart during meetings, asks questions to clarify or raise awareness on particular issues and keeps the records.

The others involved should be all those who work within the process. They will provide information and ideas and undertake to research particular issues or test out ideas between meetings. The precise content of the review will depend on the process under discussion. The common elements are likely to be:

(i) an agreed goal – a (quantified) statement of what participants would like to be the result of the review – be it a reduction in customer complaints, an increase in repeat orders, a reduction in delivery times or a less time-consuming way of planning and organising work schedules. Without a shared belief that the process is capable of improvement, the exercise is a waste of time;

(ii) some agreed outcomes – things which will be different as a result of the team's effort. These could include revised documents, retrained staff, redesigned systems;

(iii) a shared understanding of the scope of the team and of other changes which will be needed elsewhere in the business to avoid limiting their effectiveness;

(iv) a method of working closely modelled on the coaching framework – using the GROW model rigorously to explore, chart and measure current reality and future options;

(v) creative use of problem-solving techniques – silent brainstorming, cause-and-effect diagrams, affinity diagrams, interrelationship diagraphs and other visual methods of triggering and ordering ideas. You can obtain more information about these from Process Management International (PMI) in Coventry (their telephone number is 01203 419089);

(vi) regular testing of ideas and measurement to assess the effect;

(vii) incorporation of effective ideas into standard operating procedures.

(d) Other Methods

There are a number of ways of helping **individual** employees to develop their potential to contribute. Some of the most common are outlined here.

(i) Job rotation.   Moving a person from one job to another, or a chance to learn from an experienced mentor, will broaden his horizons. If it is to be fully effective, coaching should be an integral part of the process.

(ii) Understudying. Making someone assistant to a more experienced person will provide insight into what goes on in the other's job and may help in grooming the understudy for that job. Again, coaching and/or mentoring can play a vital role.

(iii) Specific projects. Tasks of any size, from planning a new layout for the office to making recommendations for strategic business development, can be tackled by someone seconded to the project for a period of days, weeks or even years. In the process, the individual should learn all sorts of things about the organisation and the people in it, as well as about the particular subject in hand.

(iv) Task forces and working parties. Some organisations find it helpful, from time to time, to call together groups of people from different parts of the organisation, either to carry through a particular exercise (task force) or to consider possible future courses of action and make recommendations (working parties). Thus, if you were launching a new product you might call together people from marketing and sales, production, distribution, and finance to work out and implement specifications, warehousing and packaging requirements, distribution arrangements, marketing and sales strategies, and so on. These people would forget their normal, formal reporting relationships and work as a team to get the job done and launch the product successfully. (It is possible to run an organisation permanently on this sort of task force basis, without a formal hierarchical structure. This is sometimes referred to as **matrix management.**)

A working party, on the other hand, is more likely to be concerned with the earlier stages in the product launch, discussing its feasibility and the implications for the organisation, making recommendations rather than actually doing anything.

To include someone on either of these types of group as part of his development programme is to provide him with a first-class opportunity:

(*a*) to obtain an overview of the implications of particular courses of action for the organisation as a whole;

(*b*) to see things from the point of view of those in other parts of the company;

(*c*) to get used to working as a member of a team;

(*d*) to let him try out his ideas on people with the experience to help him develop them;

(*e*) to learn about whatever it is that the working party or task force was set up to deal with.

As with all the other methods we have so far discussed, the value of the experience will be lost unless the individual is briefed and debriefed properly. Only thus can he be brought to recognise the learning that he has gained from the experience.

(v) In-company learning events. These take several forms, including the following.

(*a*) Courses to develop specific abilities, such as problem-solving, project management, process improvement techniques, finance or interpersonal skills. They can be offered to all comers or targeted first at those who have an immediate need.

(*b*) Group problem-centred training or tutorials, where participants bring their problems along to a tutorial session and have the opportunity to discuss them with others who may have similar or different problems.

(*c*) Attitude training of various types, where participants are encouraged to review their own preconceived ideas about their work and the company, and to develop new ones. It is, of course, particularly important that any such change is in line with the company's overall development programme, if there is one.

(*d*) Team or departmental meetings at which a trainer is invited to provide feedback to the participants about their behaviour in the group. It may be helpful, for instance, to ask a skilled training specialist or consultant to attend your regular departmental discussions or briefing groups. By observing the process of your discussions, rather than the actual content, he may be able to help you to see undercurrents in your relationship with your people or between the team members themselves that you didn't know were there. Once you do know, perhaps you can use them or work round them: you can in any case develop your management style in the light of increased awareness.

The techniques used for in-house developmental activities will run from the highly participative, such as group discussions and role play (which will be most useful in the field of attitude change and skills development), through to straight lecture sessions to impart knowledge (perhaps as background input to solving financial problems).

In general, though, such courses need to be highly participative and conducted in a coaching rather than a teaching style.

Learning objectives are just as vital to development as they are to training. It is also important that participants are properly briefed so that they have appropriate expectations and do not feel threatened.

(vi) External courses and consultants.   The advantages and disadvantages of external training discussed in Unit 10.5 apply in a development context just as much as to training. When it comes to the broader change process, consultants can provide vital guidance.

Transforming a business is not a job for a novice. Few organisations manage it without a few false starts or wrong turns. Too many of these, and the whole process loses credibility with employees, shareholders and customers. The experience and expertise of someone who has helped others through the change process can be invaluable.

Such help does not come cheap, though. You will need to budget between £1,000 and £2,000 per consultant per day – and much more for the real leaders in the field.

In choosing a consultant do bear in mind that no two organisations are identical. A style of approach that suits one won't necessarily fit the culture of another. Use them selectively, and on the basis of personal recommendation. A chief executive with a clear vision (see Unit 19.3) and a management team committed to helping achieve it are likely to be the real factors determining success or failure.

11.4 Management Development

In a climate of change such as we have described, planning the future shape of the organisation and the skills that will be needed in particular roles is a real challenge. The roles which exist today may not be there next year – let alone in five years' time. If they are, they may call for quite different skills and knowledge.

For the individual career path, too, it has profound implications. Instead of a nice straight ladder to climb, with plenty of rungs on the way up, the down-sized, de-layered, decentralised organisation of today offers a far from clear-cut career structure.

What is clear is that the future will belong to those organisations which both make the most of the resourcefulness and creativity of **all** their employees **and** are led by people with the competences needed to constantly push back the boundaries of what is possible. Visionary leaders, strategic thinkers, shrewd entrepreneurs and effective coaches will all be needed to manage the businesses of the twenty-first century.

So how can you set about identifying those with the potential to take your organisation forward?

Apart from subjective personal opinion, there are three possible approaches to the identification of management potential.

(a) Development Centres

These are, in effect, assessment centres (see Unit 6.2) used for development purposes. Their big advantage in the present context lies in the fact that they sample actual behaviour rather than make deductions about how the individual is likely to behave. Let us take the case of a team leader whom we are considering for 'other things'. There are four steps that we should follow.

(i) Specify the nature of these 'other things'. If possible, we should refine it down either to a particular type of job or a collection of competences required in a range of jobs. We can then attempt, using the kind of techniques discussed in Unit 9.3, in particular the interview and critical incident techniques, to identify the criteria for assessing effective behaviour.

(ii) Design exercises which will give the team leader an opportunity to show whether his behaviour matches the pattern for effective performance. One key area for a managerial job might be the ability to determine priorities. An in-tray exercise could be designed to confront the assessee with the mixture of urgent and non-urgent memos, letters, reports and other communications that might typically be found in the in-tray of a manager at the level for which he is being assessed. The team leader can be asked to reply to, redirect or otherwise deal with each of the in-tray items, as if he were the manager alone in the building for, say, an hour before catching a plane to some far-off destination which will make him unavailable for follow-up or consultation for the next week or so. His approach to this task will help you to identify his sense of priorities and his knowledge of appropriate courses of action. So an in-tray exercise could form one of your series of development centre activities.

(iii) Train observers who will be able to assess the behaviour of our team leader, identifying his strengths and weaknesses in relation to the desired behaviour pattern.

(iv) Give feedback to the assessee and agree a personal development plan to help him in the future.

By providing the opportunity for an analysis of behaviour over a series of exercises – some individual, some group-based – a development centre can, if carefully designed, provide a picture of the likely potential for development of the team leader, together with an indication of the directions that such development might take.

(b) Track Record

The individual's achievements to date, whether formally recorded through performance appraisal or not, will help to demonstrate where his particular strengths lie. If he has always been able to cope with tight deadlines, production pressures and internal conflicts, and has managed to achieve satisfactory results in spite of them, we may feel safe in deciding that he will be able to cope at more senior levels, where the pressures are even greater. Unfortunately, every managerial job – even those at the same level in the same organisation – tends to have its own peculiarities. Although equally acute, the pressures may be of a different nature higher up the ladder. They may, for instance, involve decisions about people, rather than decisions about materials. So achievements in one sphere will not necessarily provide a valid predictor of achievements in other spheres. You will need to look for the differences, as well as the similarities, between the assessee's present job and his proposed future one.

(c) Performance Appraisal

We have already noted, in Unit 9.2, the pitfalls and limitations of performance appraisal as a means of identifying potential. In so far as your system really does provide an insight into behaviour and aspirations, it **can** provide a useful reference point. The dangers of assuming that performance in one job will automatically predict performance in another cannot be over-emphasised.

In spite of their limitations, these three strategies can help you to spot those with management potential in your organisation. Your next task is to refine further your ideas about where they are going, before you try to work out the best ways of getting them there.

11.5 Designing a Succession Plan

Succession planning is normally taken to mean identifying the key jobs in the organisation and ensuring that if anything, planned or unplanned, were to remove the present job-holder from his post, there would be someone ready to take his place. This benefits the company by ensuring that there are no expensive gaps or panic measures to fill them. It benefits the individual by providing opportunities for advancement. The approach is broadly as follows:

(*a*) Decide which are the **key jobs** in the organisation as a whole. In this context, 'key' means those jobs whose incumbents need a particular blend of qualities, experience and company knowledge, which is not readily available and cannot speedily be acquired. These will normally correspond with the top two or three layers of your organisation chart. It is possible to move further down the organisation, but in practice this becomes very unwieldy. You could try to plan the internal succession within your own department or section, working out who will succeed whom in which jobs in the departmental hierarchy. The danger of planning in isolation like this lies in thinking that your present staff will best be served by remaining in the department and in overlooking people in other departments who might serve you better. Organisation succession planning really needs to be a 'top down' activity.

(*b*) Identify, through the mechanisms we have discussed, who has the potential and inclination to fill these positions.

(*c*) Take a copy of the company's organisation chart and fill in the names of the present incumbent and of the person destined to succeed to each post.

The difficulty with such detailed succession planning is that the unplanned events may never actually happen and the planned ones may be a long way off. People who have been developed to the point where they are ready to take over a more senior job are unlikely to wait indefinitely for that job to become available. You may therefore prefer to legislate only for those events which are planned in the foreseeable future, perhaps using a chart like Table 11.3 to help you identify the schedule to which you must work.

In our example, the retirement of the personnel director in May 1997 and of the chief executive in July 1999 give rise to a series of moves. **Cashman** must be equipped to take over as chief executive and will benefit from a spell in personnel. But **Hastle** is eventually to assume the personnel director's role and needs a period in line management first. His return to personnel, over the head of **Doer**, who will by then have had similar experience of both functions, could cause problems though. The chart also highlights the absence of any clear successor in the finance field when **Moneypenny** takes over to release **Cashman** for other duties.

On this chart we have allowed only for the briefest takeover periods, sending **Cashman** to personnel, for instance, during the month preceding **Mann's** departure. The timing of the handover warrants careful thought, though: there may be a case for present and future incumbent to work together in double harness for a rather longer time than this.

Table 11.3   A succession planning chart

Jobs	1996	1997	1998	1999	2000
Chief Executive	*Bossman* ——————————→			retires in July/	
				Cashman ——————→	
Functional Manager					
Personnel	*Mann* ——→ retires in				
		May/*Cashman* ——→	to chief executive in		
			June/*Hastle* ——→		
Finance	*Cashman* —→ to personnel				
		in April/			
		Moneypenny ———————————————→			
Sales	*Lineman* _____→				
Marketing	*Adman* _____→				
Number Two					
Personnel	*Hastle* ———→ to sales in				
		March/*Doer* ————————————————→			
Finance	*Moneypenny* ——→ to finance				
		director in			
		April/?	?	?	?
Sales	*Doer* ———→ to personnel				
		in March/			
		Hastle ———————→ to personnel			
			director in		
			May/*Trier* ——→		
Marketing	*Sellers* ————————————————————————→				

There are three other questions which require consideration.

(*a*) What will happen if **Cashman's** spell in personnel causes us to doubt his capacity as a future chief executive? The chances of this happening can be minimised by careful selection for promotion and thorough development, but if we have made a mistake, we will have to face up to it and look elsewhere for our new chief executive.

(*b*) Should we tell people where they figure in the company's succession plan? If we do, it may adversely affect their behaviour and also make it more difficult for you to change your decision and not promote them. If we don't, then **Hastle** may doubt our motives for pushing him into sales and leave the company in 1998. The answer may lie in counselling the individual in general terms about his future, but avoiding promises of specific jobs at specific dates.

(c) What if the organisation structure changes during the next five years? The personnel function might be decentralised, or sales and marketing combined and the organisation structured around particular product or customer groups.

To allow for such changes, a competence-based approach would afford more flexibility. Instead of simply relating to job titles, the plan might distinguish between strategic decision-makers, tacticians and operational management across relevant areas of functional expertise or specific business processes. Instead of naming just one possible successor, the goal would be to ensure that there is always a pool of people with the relevant competences.

As we saw in Unit 2, wherever possible existing competences should help shape corporate development. So **before** any restructuring takes place, the succession chart should always be examined: not to act as a deterrent to change, but rather to make sure that it **will** be possible to staff the new structure in the medium term. If there are doubts about this, immediate action should be set in train to broaden or deepen the competences of those concerned.

In the final analysis, the succession plan serves only one real purpose. That is to alert senior management to possible future problems – so that steps can be taken to avert them.

11.6 Designing a Career Plan

While the needs of the organisation determine the succession plan, the needs of the individual will be reflected more clearly in his own career plan. The two are, of course, overlapping, in that the individual's career should be planned to enable him to take the opportunities provided by the succession plan and to perform effectively at all the points en route.

In Table 11.4 we can examine the sort of career plan that might be drawn up for Mr Hastle. This allows us to plot his personal progress in more detail, highlighting specific training requirements along the way. We could create similar charts for all the other individuals who feature in our succession plan and for others who are not yet ready for promotion, but who would benefit from a broadening of their experience.

There are a number of questions to be considered in designing a career plan.

(i) Where is the individual going eventually? Are there openings revealed by your succession plan for which he could be equipped?

(ii) Where do his interests and aspirations lie? These will inevitably act as a moderator on the company's plans and can best be determined in discussion with the individual concerned.

(iii) What additional experience and learning does he need to help him fulfil his own aspirations and those of the company? How might these be provided? Practical experience and formal training both feature in the plan that we have illustrated.

Table 11.4   A career plan

Name: Hastle, D. J.

Year	Position	Training required
1996	Personnel (number two)	
1997	Move to sales management in March (as number two), to broaden experience of company operations	Coaching by sales manager
1998	Sales management	Senior management development programme
1999	Promote to personnel director (designate) in May	
2000	Consolidation in personnel management	
2001	? further progression	

The career plan will plot out the main stages in the individual's personal development. But simply doing each of the jobs we have identified for him will not necessarily equip him for his ultimate role. Yet again, the key to his learning will be effective coaching – either self-coaching or with help from his new boss. This can be supported, where appropriate, by any of the other methods discussed in Unit 11.3. Attendance at an external management development programme at a leading business school or perhaps an MBA programme on a block-release or distance learning basis might help. The Open University offers a modular approach to study which can be used selectively to help fill gaps in specific functional areas.

Some organisations extend their career planning process well beyond the few top jobs to develop a **'fast track'** through the company for those who are seen to have particular potential. These are often linked to graduate entry schemes and provide a mixture of work experience, specific responsibilities, training and development. They can be an effective way of ensuring that there is always a pool of potential candidates for the most senior roles but care must be taken to provide an appropriate level of continuity in the jobs through which the participants pass.

Another disadvantage is that those who are **not** part of the scheme may feel they are treated as second-class citizens and denied promotion or career development opportunities of which they consider themselves capable. The best safeguards are to:

(i) make sure the criteria for entry to such schemes are clear, fair and objective and, ideally, that existing employees have a chance to apply;

(ii) adopt appropriate standards for allowing individuals to remain on the scheme. Those who are seen to fail in jobs en route should, of course, have a chance to redeem themselves – but no more so than any other employee;

(iii) prevent the scheme being seen as a 'meal ticket' or passport to senior jobs by requiring participants to apply for some or all of their career moves and be assessed against other candidates;

(iv) ensure that key development roles which form part of the fast track are not blocked by long-term incumbents. The criteria for selection for such jobs can include potential for further movement. It must be clear from the start that any fast track member who is inclined to settle into one of these roles will be barred from doing so.

As we have seen, no career or succession plan can ever be taken as definitive. Their greatest value lies in their ability to signal blockages or dead ends for the individual – and competence shortfalls for the organisation. Where **employee** development is taken seriously, free and open application for career moves and promotion opportunities will be an essential adjunct to such plans.

Questions

1. What do you understand by the concept of 'employee development'? What might be the benefits for an organisation of ensuring all employees have the opportunity to participate?
2. Describe how you would set about identifying those people within your organisation who have potential for development to managerial positions.
3. What do you understand by the terms: (*a*) succession planning; (*b*) career planning? What are the problems associated with each and how might these be overcome?
4. What part can coaching play in employee development?

UNIT 12

Career Moves

12.1 Introduction

We discussed in Unit 1 the advantages and disadvantages of pursuing a policy of promotion from within the organisation. Much of our discussion in Unit 11 was based on the assumption that you do wish to develop and promote your own employees. Here we will look at how this can be done fairly and effectively.

We are not suggesting that promotion from within is invariably the best course of action, but when it is done it must be done well.

Nor are we suggesting that all moves within the organisation should be upwards. Lateral movement to broaden understanding of the business and extend an individual's skills is an essential part of employee development and can be approached in the ways outlined in this unit.

12.2 Identifying the Candidates

The way in which you approach this will depend partly on your management style, partly on the sophistication of your information and assessment procedures and partly on whether or not the succession has already been planned. When an opportunity for movement arises, there are two broad options.

(a) Candidates Nominate Themselves

With external recruitment, you have no way of knowing precisely who is out there waiting to respond to your advertisement. You can operate exactly the same tactics in an internal situation. Simply circularise the details, conforming to the same sort of pattern as you would in an external advertisement, but possibly omitting some of the company detail, and await the replies. If you have:

    (i) a concern to ensure equality of opportunity for all your employees;
    (ii) a participative style of management and do not wish to be thought of as controlling the destinies of your employees;
    (iii) a trade union which insists upon open advertisement;
    (iv) no other information base upon which to proceed

'If you'd had more ambition you could be living in quiet seclusion now instead of complete obscurity.'

you will find that candidate initiative is the best way of highlighting the aspirations of your employees and can reveal people of whom you might never have thought, but who could be very effective in the job in question. If the system is to work effectively, though, you will need to ensure that everyone learns of the vacancy, perhaps through a notice board, house magazine or special circulars. You will also need time to sort carefully through the replies and counsel the unsuccessful applicants.

If you have already planned the succession, candidate self-nomination will be superfluous. It will, in fact, be counterproductive to encourage people to apply for a job which is not really available. Only if you are in doubt about the nominated successor and wish to see who else is interested will it be worthwhile.

(b) Company Nomination

The mechanisms which the company can use in deciding who to nominate are those which we discussed in Unit 11, namely, development centres, performance appraisal and track record. The combined information from these three sources can be retained on personal files, stored either manually or by computer and referred to when a vacancy arises. Where the succession to the job is already planned, this is the method to use. The difficulties lie:

(i) in devising an information system which will enable you to identify the appropriate people without hours of searching;

(ii) in the fact that such information will quickly date and may therefore give an inaccurate picture;

(iii) in the problems inherent in applying each of the three methods of collecting the information, which we have already discussed.

Particularly if you have a small number of employees, you may feel that you can dispense with the more formal methods of assessment and act on the basis of your own personal knowledge in moving individuals. But how sure can you be that you are not letting yourself be ruled by an ill-founded general impression? And can you be certain that your personal feelings, rather than the facts, are not dictating your decision? If it is dangerous to assume that effective performance in one job equates with effective performance in more senior jobs, it is doubly dangerous to give promotion to someone who 'deserves' it by dint of long and faithful service rather than someone who merits it on the basis of his capacity to develop in the future.

Whenever nominations come from the company rather than from the employees, there is a danger that people will draw unfavourable conclusions. They may feel that favouritism is being exercised and that only those who catch the boss's eye have a chance. They may feel that the whole system is autocratic or discriminates against particular groups. And there is also the chance that you might overlook a good candidate because you don't think that he would be interested, or nominate someone who does not want the job.

If candidates nominate themselves you will overcome these difficulties. At the same time, you will find it easier to draw up a shortlist if you can call on the sort of objective information on which the company nomination method is based. This can be considered alongside specially requested reports and the candidates' letters of application.

12.3 Selection Procedure

In Table 12.1 we can see the similarities between procedures for selection in external and internal appointments. This is the procedure which should be followed when candidates nominate themselves. Where the company nominates the candidates, the first two items may be dispensed with. If the company has nominated only one candidate, in line with the succession plan, then selection has already taken place and our discussion in most of the remainder of this unit will not apply.

Although minor modifications will be appropriate, there is much to be said for making your internal transfer and promotion procedure as rigorous and carefully thought out and validated as your external procedure. Unless candidates have already been assessed at a development centre, setting one up as a prelude to a new appointment can pay dividends. It will not only provide a fair and objective basis for selection; it will also enable you to agree appropriate development plans for both the successful and unsuccessful candidates. The formality of an interview may seem misplaced, but however well you think you know the candidates, the chances are that you have never talked to them about promotion to this particular position before. Only if the

Table 12.1 Procedures for selection in external and internal appointments

External recruitment	Internal appointments
1. Advertisement/recruitment method	Advertisement/company information system
2. Application form	Letter of application (forms are less usual)
3. Interview(s)	Interview(s)
4. Tests	Tests
5. Assessment centre	Development centre
6. References	Discussions with other managers, examination of past records, appraisal reports and special reports
7. Medical checks	Medical checks, if nature of new job requires them

appointment is simply a change in job grade rather than true promotion might you be justified in omitting the interview.

12.4 Interviewing for Career Moves

Because the candidates are already employed by the company and familiar with its ways, there may be a temptation to take short cuts. All the preparation and attention to strategy and questioning technique which we advocated in Unit 5 are equally relevant here. Only the sources of your information about the candidates prior to interview will differ. You must take particular care not to assume that the candidate knows more about the job and what it involves than he actually does.

Your purposes remain those of finding out more about the candidate and assessing his suitability, while enabling him to learn more about the job. Your best overall approach remains a joint problem-solving one.

After the interview, you should apply the same rigour to your evaluation and decision-making process. It is particularly important to try and see the candidate in relation to the personnel specification for this position, rather than as 'old Joe' whom you know so well. For the long-term benefit of the company, promotion and transfer decisions must be based purely on suitability for the new job. You should therefore weigh up interview data and all the other available information before making your decision.

12.5 The Successful Candidate

Once you have made your decision, you should of course notify all the candidates as soon as possible. As far as the successful candidate is concerned, there are a number of vital things to consider. Let's take the case of Rachel

Green, the assistant manager of the Shrewsbury branch of a chain of retail shops, who has just been selected to become manager of the company's branch in York. Our list of items divides into two.

(a) Domestic Arrangements

(i) **Moving house.** Rachel owns her house in Shrewsbury, and buying and selling property can be an expensive, time-consuming and worrying business. What can the company do to help? Since the move is at the company's request, the least it can do is to ensure that Rachel does not end up out of pocket. Estate agents' fees, legal fees, furniture removal costs and a relocation allowance to cover the costs of replacing carpets and curtains which won't fit in the new house should all be provided by the company. If they are not, Rachel's enthusiasm for the job in York is likely to disappear rapidly. In addition, Rachel could be granted a disturbance allowance to compensate her for the inconvenience and problems of moving.

Then, too, the cost of rail fares or car usage will have to be met when Rachel and her partner go to York to look for a new house. And they may need to go more than once. If Rachel has to start work in York before her family can move, her living expenses will need to be met. If her house in Shrewsbury proves difficult to sell, the company may need to help out with bridging finance so that Rachel and her family can move into their new home before the old one has been sold. If houses are more expensive in York than in Shrewsbury the company may need to consider providing more long-term finance.

Apart from meeting the cash costs, the company should consider how else it can make the move easier. It will remove a lot of the anxiety if Rachel knows exactly whom to approach for what and when. Who, for example, will authorise the payment of legal fees? Does she have to pay them herself and then wait for the company to reimburse her or does the company pay them direct? This is just one of the many questions that the company will need to anticipate. If the promotion and relocation of employees is a regular occurrence, it will be worth spelling out the procedure in a leaflet or management advice note.

(ii) **Family commitments.** Rachel has school-age children and will be reluctant for them to change schools in the middle of a term. Can the company postpone the date for Rachel to start her new job in York or will it enable her partner to stay in Shrewsbury until the end of the term? He has a job which he will have to give up. Can the company help him to find another in the York area? What arrangements and introductions can be made to help Rachel and her family settle down, socially and educationally, as soon as possible after arrival?

(b) Job Implications

(i) Rachel is leaving Shrewsbury. Who will replace her as assistant manager? Will there be another promotion or should the company look outside? Either way, urgent steps will have to be taken if the Shrewsbury branch is not to be left without an assistant manager for a prolonged period.

(ii) What sort of timescale are we working to? When must Rachel be operational in the York branch? Will she need to spend some time with the present manager before she actually takes over? If so, what is the deadline for the present manager's departure?

(iii) Apart from a period with the outgoing manager, what other induction will Rachel need into her new job? Is there a regional manager who can help her through the first few weeks, introducing her to people, places and systems? Is there some job training that she lacks? It is a regrettable but frequent phenomenon for people to be promoted into jobs for which they have not been trained and to be sent on a training course to be taught how to do it some six months after they have learned it for themselves, the hard way. If she has not already attended one, Rachel should be included on a branch managers' training course right away.

(iv) Is the job ready for Rachel? Has everyone involved been told that she is coming, and when? Is the outgoing manager leaving things in reasonable shape, returns up to date, paperwork in order, stock in good condition? It will not always be possible to ensure that everything is running smoothly as it depends upon the circumstances of the promotion. But it is unwise to stack the odds too heavily against the new person's chance of success in the job.

(v) Rachel's job title and some of her terms and conditions of employment will change when she becomes manager of the York shop and her contract of employment must be amended accordingly. She should be given a new job description and starting details for the new job.

All of the job-related points that we have made in connection with Rachel's move will apply even if the promotion takes place within the same geographical location. If Rachel were moving overseas, of course, the question of her domestic arrangements would be considerably more complex.

12.6 The Unsuccessful Candidates

We will leave Rachel poised to start her new job in York and turn to consider the other candidates for the position. Most of them are reliable and effective employees, whose loyalty and contribution to the organisation we wish to maintain. Each of them thought himself capable of running the York shop. Some of them probably are almost ready to do so, others are less well-equipped for a managerial position. What can we do to ensure that none of these rejected applicants becomes bitter and disillusioned?

(*a*) We must ensure that our selection decision is, and is seen to be, soundly based. The person appointed should be someone who matches those parts of the personnel specification to which we drew attention in our initial circular or advertisement. All applicants should have been fairly treated and given an opportunity to state their case, either in a letter of application or at interview, or both. Remember, too, that the provisions of the Race Relations Act 1976 and the Sex Discrimination Acts 1975 and 1986 also apply to promotion and transfer decisions. Indeed, many of the cases lost by employers at industrial tribunals have occurred where internal applicants were turned down for promotion as a result of either direct or, more commonly, indirect discrimination.

(*b*) Promotion interviews should be conducted in a joint problem-solving vein. This will help to ensure that all the applicants have a reasonably realistic measure of their own strengths and weaknesses in relation to the job.

(*c*) We need to help the unsuccessful candidates to strive in directions which are appropriate to their own particular strengths. Rather than wait for the next performance appraisal interview, it would be a good idea to talk with each of the candidates about his aspirations. A counselling approach, to help him identify suitable channels for his talents, can be adopted, either by his immediate boss or by whoever was making the promotion.

If there are frequent opportunities for movement, the good candidates will find a suitable one sooner or later. But the weaker candidates will need regular help, through training and development, appraisal and counselling, to equip them for a move or to come to terms with the lack of it. The emphasis must be on building constructively for the future, rather than indulging in recriminations about the past.

But disillusion is not something which is restricted to rejected promotion candidates. All your employees need to have a reason to work – and to work hard – for you. It is to this that we will now turn.

Questions

1. What other aspects of employment policy and practice might be affected by a decision to promote solely from within the organisation?
2. Consider the possible methods of identifying candidates for promotion. Discuss the advantages and limitations of each.
3. How would you try to ensure that all candidates for internal transfer or promotion, unsuccessful as well as successful, benefited from the experience?

Motivating and Communicating with Employees

13.1 Introduction

Man is a rational animal: when he behaves in a certain way, he does it for a reason. A motive is something which impels a person to act, a reason for behaviour. If, therefore, we want people to behave in a certain way so that the organisation can achieve its goals, we need to understand the kind of motives that will prompt them to do so. Motivation is not about manipulation. It is about understanding the needs or urges which prompt people to do things and providing ways of helping them to satisfy those needs through the organisation, while at the same time harnessing their contribution to satisfy its needs.

We will devote this unit to a discussion of motivation, starting with a brief look at some theories of motivation and moving on to see how you, as a manager, can build a motivated team.

13.2 Why People Work

Early management thinkers explored two main sources of motivation to work. One was the job as an end in itself, the other was the end towards which the job provides the means.

(a) Intrinsic Satisfaction

This means deriving the satisfaction of your needs, and therefore your motivation, from the work itself. A considerable weight of behavioural science research has been devoted to the pursuit of this concept.

(i) **Abraham Maslow.** The hierarchy of needs, first formulated in 1943, is an attempt to explain motivation as a series of ascending urges. Figure 13.1 illustrates this. While an urge or need remains unsatisfied, it acts as a motivator, but once it has been satisfied, according to Maslow, it ceases to motivate and the next higher need in the pyramid comes into play.

When you have managed to acquire the basic necessities of life, you cease to be prompted by a need to get more. Your safety needs then become paramount, and so on through to the need for self-actualisation or self-fulfilment.

The major problem with Maslow's hypothesis is the value system that is inevitably built into this kind of hierarchy. Thus a higher order need, such

Self-
actualisation
needs

Esteem needs,
self-respect

Social needs, belonging to
a group, acceptance by others

Safety needs, an environment free
from threat

Physiological needs, food, water, the essentials
of life

Fig 13.1

as self-actualisation, becomes more respectable than a lower order need
such as cash to supply the basic necessities. This approach also assumes
that once a need has been satisfied, it will remain so for ever. This is not
necessarily so.

(ii) Frederick Herzberg.   The two-factor theory, devised in 1959, is perhaps
the best known of many theories of motivation. From his research among
American accountants and engineers, Herzberg concluded that there are two
sets of forces at work on the individual. One set he termed **hygiene factors**,
the other **motivators**. The hygiene factors include such things as pay, fringe
benefits, working conditions and quality of supervision. If there is something
wrong with any of these, it will be a source of dissatisfaction to the individual
and should be rectified. But however much attention is paid to getting them
right, they can never provide a source of motivation. Only the motivator factors, such as recognition, advancement, a sense of achievement or of personal
growth and fulfilment in the job, can do that. Herzberg's theory has earned
much adverse criticism since its initial acclaim in the 1960s. His research
methodology has been attacked by some; others maintain that his hypothesis
may hold good for American white-collar workers, but certainly does not do
so for British blue-collar workers. His work has, nevertheless, given substance
to the idea of job enrichment, which we will be considering further in Unit
13.4.

(iii) Clayton Alderfer.   ERG theory, devised in 1972, overcomes some of the
difficulties associated with Maslow's theories by putting forward just three
types of need: **existence, relatedness and growth** – hence ERG. These three
needs are placed together in a straight line relationship, a continuum. An
individual may move from one part of the line to another and back again,

Fig 13.2

and there is no value system built in. (The relationship between Alderfer's needs and those identified by Maslow is illustrated in Fig. 13.2.)

(iv) David McClelland. One particular personality variable, the need for achievement, **N ach.** (as distinct from need for affiliation, **N aff.**), was distinguished by McClelland, in 1961, as being an important source of motivation for **some** individuals, but his extensive research indicates that this is of more significance in some cultures than in others. In the UK a more recent study does seem to indicate that a high **N ach.** (as evidenced by success in the driving test at an early age) does correlate with subsequent career advancement among recent graduates. People with a great need for achievement will be more prepared to tackle challenging situations than those who are prompted by a fear of being blamed for failure.

Each of these theories regards motivation as being at least partly connected with the content of the job itself. But there is also another approach.

(b) Extrinsic Satisfaction

This means deriving satisfaction of needs using work as a means to an end; it is also sometimes termed an **instrumental** approach. Work provides us with money, money enables us to obtain satisfaction. So money, not the intrinsic satisfaction of the job, is the main motivator according to this school of thought.

(i) F. W. Taylor. Taylor is sometimes referred to as the father of scientific management. He was perhaps the first person to give serious thought to the question of why people work or, more specifically, how they could be made to work harder. His answer was to relate pay to output: the more people produced, the more they were paid. Although Taylor was working at the very beginning of the twentieth century, many of his ideas about how work should be divided into simple tasks are still current in some industries. His search for a true science of work gave birth to the technique of work study.

(ii) The Luton Studies. These were a series of investigations carried out among car workers in Luton in the late 1960s. The researchers found that many car workers were not interested in their jobs at all, except as a means to earn money. They were using their highly paid assembly work purely as a means to that end. Even the social relationships of the workplace meant nothing to them. Their aim was to maximise their earnings and enjoy their leisure.

None of these theories provides a fully satisfactory explanation of what motivates people. One reason for this is that most of them attempt to find one specific law of behaviour which will hold good in all circumstances. It may well be that we are not all motivated by the same needs or that at different stages in our careers different needs may be paramount.

(c) Process Theories

More recent research has taken a broader look at the **process** of motivation and stressed the importance of the individual's own assessment of and influence over his situation.

(i) Expectancy theory. This derives from work carried out in America, initially by Vroom in 1964 and later by Lawler. Its main tenet is that people will be motivated to increase their effort if they believe that this will lead to their obtaining some reward or goal which they see as worth having. These rewards may or may not be financial. Each employee will have different value goals – the employee's beliefs about the relationship between effort, performance and reward are crucial. The required performance must be clearly defined, so that he can see what is expected, and the rewards available must be understood. It is also essential that employees are properly selected and trained, so that they have the capacity, as well as the will, to achieve the desired level of performance.

(ii) Equity theory. Jaques and Adams both put forward ideas in the 1960s which suggest that it is not the absolute value of a reward which motivates, but the individual's view of how fair (equitable) that reward is. Jaques saw equitability in terms of the level of work performed – his ideas are explained more fully in Unit 14.2. Adams suggested that employees consider the fairness of rewards both in relation to effort and in relation to what other people are getting. Where individuals believe that there is a 'disequilibrium' between 'inputs' (what they are putting in) and 'outputs' (what they are getting out) they will attempt to restore the balance. If they feel they are overpaid, they will either work harder or produce better quality. Equity theory reinforces the need for reward structures which are clearly related to the demands of the job and the efforts of the individual. In Units 14 and 15 we will consider some ways of providing this.

(iii) Reactance and attribution theory. Brehm, who developed reactance theory in 1966, like Adams, sees employees as motivated by a desire to control or reduce uncertainty or imbalances in the factors which influence their rewards. Where they cannot see what these factors are – such as in a promotion system where the criteria for promotion are unclear – they may eventually give up and stop trying. Also important is the extent to which individuals see themselves as having control in the first place. Some people will be inclined to put a sudden pay rise down to luck – that is, beyond their control; others will attribute it to hard work. The employee who attributes his pay rise to luck will not be motivated to work harder, because he does not believe that will influence his pay. The employee who attributes it to hard work will believe that by working harder still he can earn even more – that is, he believes he has control, and will be motivated to keep trying.

Much research has been devoted to the study of motivation over the years. One study which serves to highlight the complexity of the reasons for employee behaviour was carried out at Ashridge Management College in the early 1970s, among a sample of 2,500 senior executives. Six different motivational groups emerged: material reward, leadership, variety and challenge, status and prestige, job interest and security and social orientations. So, depending upon the needs of the individual at a given period, anything from a pay rise to a rubber plant in his office, or from a pat on the back to a Christmas party, may act as a motivator.

It may be that it is still worth seeking a universal motivator. We might do better, though, by turning our attention to the expectancy theory idea of identifying the things which matter to our own employees, either as groups or as individuals. One useful mechanism for this is the kind of attitude or **opinion survey** practised, for instance, by IBM as a means of testing employee response to management action or the lack of it. Designing an attitude survey is a complex task, beyond the scope of our present discussion. There are standardised questionnaires available, such as the American 'Work Motivation Inventory', which is based on the work of Maslow and seeks to highlight the needs of subordinates. But care needs to be taken interpreting the results of a questionnaire designed originally for use in another country.

Whether you do it formally or informally, it is a good idea to find out from your employees about the things that they see as important and about their needs in relation to the job.

13.3 Pay and Motivation

The case for pay as a motivator is, at best, 'not proven'. In Unit 14 we will examine the range of available pay systems. As we shall see, some of these systems allow differentiation between individuals, doing the same job, on grounds of performance. These are based on the assumption that pay is indeed a motivator. Whether or not that is so, there are two other general points which have a bearing.

(a) Fairness

If pay is to motivate, or indeed have any positive influence at all, it should be felt to be fair, in relation both to the work done and to other people doing the same or similar work. Equitable pay is, however, an elusive concept, because what looks fair to the person earning £300 per week will not necessarily look fair to the person earning £150 per week. Even if agreement can be reached between employees as to what is fair, the company must decide whether it can afford to be fair, in terms of finding the cash to foot the bill. If pay is not felt to be fair, one of three things may happen:

(i) Employees collectively, through their trade union, will exercise the kind of sanctions that we will be discussing in Unit 18.

(ii) Individual employees will withdraw their labour, either completely, by seeking other jobs, thereby raising labour turnover, or in part, by absenting themselves or restricting their output.

(iii) It will become increasingly difficult to recruit new employees of an appropriate calibre.

Fair pay does not necessarily mean high pay. Individuals will find other compensating factors – fringe benefits, working conditions or intrinsic rewards. It is pay relative to effort and relative to others that is significant. Even those who believe that positive motivation can only come from intrinsic satisfaction would not dispute that unhappiness over relative pay can lead to very real dissatisfaction.

(b) Pay Secrecy
Some research, by Lawler, suggests that secrecy may reduce the ability of pay to motivate. If employees do not know what their colleagues are earning, it makes it difficult for them to be sure that pay is indeed fair.

13.4   Job Satisfaction

The Herzberg school of thought, as we have seen, places great value on the work itself as a means of motivating people. If we accept the importance of intrinsic motivation, careful attention will have to be paid to designing the jobs and the managerial policies of the organisation in such a way that employees derive maximum satisfaction of their needs through them. Even if we don't accept the link with motivation, such methods can still improve the quality of working life. There are a number of issues that we should examine in this context. Some – job enrichment, for instance – arise directly from Herzberg's thesis. Others simply represent a carefully thought out approach to job design and management.

(a) Ergonomics
This is a branch of psychology designed with a view to increasing efficiency rather than job satisfaction. By designing jobs to fit people, rather than the other way around, it may nevertheless contribute to job satisfaction or to the avoidance of frustration. The science of ergonomics first emerged during World War II, when technology was advancing very rapidly and creating completely new types of job. It was realised that you cannot design a job without thinking about the limitations of the human body. The classic, if somewhat exaggerated, example is the machine that requires someone five feet tall with arms four feet in length (and preferably three of them) to operate it effectively. Modern applications include everything from the height, shape and swivel capacity of a keyboard operator's chair to the internal design of a space capsule.

(b) Job Rotation

This has been cynically defined as 'swapping one boring monotonous job for another boring monotonous job'. The idea is that employees will derive greater satisfaction if they experience variety in their work and can understand more of the range of operations in which the organisation is involved. It has the added advantage of creating greater flexibility and improved utilisation of human resources. Its limitations lie in the facts that:

(i) The basic level of work in which the employee is engaged remains the same. He simply moves further down the assembly line, to a different sales counter or on to a different set of clerical entries. The amount of additional satisfaction to be derived is therefore marginal.

(ii) It fails to recognise the lines of demarcation still drawn by a few trade unions with a view to preserving the jobs of their members.

(c) Job Enlargement

This idea is closely related to job rotation, but instead of changing jobs from time to time the job itself is made bigger by the introduction of new tasks. This gives greater variety in job content, but again its value is limited as the nature of the new tasks is broadly similar to that of the old ones. Thus one assembly worker will now carry out three different operations during his work cycle, rather than repeating the same one over and over again. This means that the length of time before each task is repeated will be increased, thereby alleviating monotony.

Job enlargement may have some immediate benefits in terms of increased intrinsic satisfaction, but the danger is that either management or employees may see it as a ploy for getting more work out of people for the same money. Job enlargement can only work if you recognise that the addition of new tasks means reducing the number of times that the old ones are repeated during the working cycle.

(d) Job Enrichment

Unlike job enlargement and job rotation, job enrichment involves adding to the work cycle work of a more responsible, rather than just a different, nature. One of the first European examples was the Volvo car production operation at Kalmar in Sweden. Here the traditional assembly line principle, which used to figure so largely in British car production, was set aside in favour of the creation of autonomous work groups. This meant that a group of workers, without supervision, became responsible for the production of a complete vehicle. It was entirely up to the group to organise itself in the most effective way to maintain production standards, so there was a considerable element of job enlargement and job rotation. But over and above this, the fact that the group had the authority to make its own decisions and maintain its own quality control standards added a whole new dimension of responsibility, designed to meet the workers' need for challenging and responsible work and for knowledge of their own results. This helped Kalmar to become the most labour-efficient of the company's Swedish plants.

13.5   Empowerment

Japanese production systems go beyond job enrichment. Multi-skilled teams, equipped with the tools of statistical process control and an array of problem-solving skills, not only maintain their own quality standards, they also continuously and inexorably drive out defects in production.

Working without the stockpiles of work in progress typical of many UK operations, they use the **Kanban** system for just-in-time replenishment of raw materials and components. Machine change-over and set-up times are drastically reduced by creative engineering. Designers work in close harmony with manufacturing to make sure that products are not only appealing to customers but also easy to make with zero defects. Those who work in such teams, whether in Japanese car plants in the UK or, increasingly, in many British factories, are dedicated to the elimination of waste and the improvement of processes. (Although the work is very different, the same sort of approach is also taken in some service organisations and administrative functions – where the 'product' is less tangible.)

Beyond that, they are empowered to take decisions which historically would have been a management prerogative. Their training and development have equipped them to be a highly flexible, committed team. It is not their factory layout or the manufacturing system that makes the difference. It is a fundamental difference in philosophy.

Empowerment is based on the belief that everyone wants to 'be the best they can be'. Employees do not come to work intending to do a bad job, defraud their employer or be idle. Many management systems and controls assume they do. People are not machines to be programmed, nor do they want to leave their brains behind when they come to work. Many work processes assume they are and so they do. Empowerment assumes the opposite. True empowerment demands a fundamental rethink of job design, systems and management style.

(a)   Job design
Every job must:

- have clear and relevant goals;
- provide plenty of variety and challenge;
- make full use of the skills and potential of the incumbent;
- give as much chance as possible to work on meaningful tasks which produce an identifiable output the employee can 'own';
- enable the employee to take responsibility for as many decisions as possible;
- allow the employee to assess how the process is working and to act to improve it.

(b)   Systems
Each of the organisation's systems for dealing with people must truly reflect the value it places on them. This includes:

  - communication systems designed to treat employees as intelligent adults not wayward children (see Unit 13.6);
  - payment systems which recognise that people are not donkeys to be enticed with carrots or beaten with sticks, nor are they 'units of labour' (see Unit 14);
  - benefits systems which recognise that differential privileges based on hierarchy signal an 'us and them' approach and should be abolished (see Unit 14.6);
  - systems for ensuring that employees' ideas on improvements are actively sought and promptly acted upon every day;
  - the demolition of systems designed to check up on employees on the assumption that they are incompetent or untrustworthy.

(c) Management style

This should be based on coaching not commanding. Hire-and-fire approaches, favouritism, lack of trust and looking over people's shoulders are all symptoms of a management which has not yet learnt to empower. More subtly, management reaction to everyday events can be very revealing. Table 13. 1 highlights some of the differences between the empowering manager and his colleagues.

As we saw in Unit 11, empowerment is not something that happens overnight. For many managers it means a major philosophical shift and a complete rethink of their role. Instead of adding value by telling other people what to do, they now add value by helping other people do it better. Instead of making decisions **for** their people, they now supply their people with data or other support to help **them** decide. This is disorientating.

In other ways, too, empowerment may need careful handling.

(i) If people at the bottom of the hierarchy take more responsibility, people in the middle will tend to have less. The effects on managers and supervisors need careful consideration.

(ii) Not everybody instinctively **wants** to be empowered. Some may say they prefer just to do a routine job which leaves them free to think about other things. Thinking about the job would be an unwelcome intrusion or just too taxing.

Arguably, it is the system under which they have worked for so long that makes them feel this way. If the evidence of your daily experience is that your skills are not valued or you are not fit to think, eventually you will begin to believe it and act accordingly. Empowering those who feel like this will take time and patience to demonstrate that things really are different now.

(iii) Some trade unions are still somewhat wary of the implications for traditional skill boundaries and for pay. These will need to be thoroughly examined – by management and unions together.

(iv) Empowerment presupposes that you are prepared to invest in training and developing your people to cope with the new way of working. Motivation may or may not come through the pursuit of challenging new goals. It certainly will not come if people are unsure what is expected of them, or if they lack the skills and knowledge to perform to their own satisfaction.

Table 13.1   Management Reactions

Non-empowering	Empowering
'I'll decide' or 'The committee will decide.'	'If it makes sense, get on and do it.'
'That's *management* information.'	'If it will help you to understand our goal, I'd like to share it with you.'
'That was a mistake. You've got one more chance.'	'That didn't achieve the results we'd hoped. What can we learn?'
'That will be good enough.'	'How could we make that even better?'
'That looks like too much hassle.'	'Could that be a way forward?'
'We've got to play it by the book.'	'The only rule is "do whatever it takes to exceed your customer's expectations".'
'We can't do everything. If the price comes down, the quality will too.'	'We *can* do everything. We can look for ways of eliminating waste.'
'We've found a way that works. What's the point of changing?'	'We've found a way that works. How can we improve it?'
'Don't waste time thinking – just get on with it.'	'If you think you can find a better way, how much time would you need to explore it?'
'That's a good idea but . . .'	'How do you see that working?'
'What you've got to do is . . .'	'Our goal is . . . what are the options?'
'This is how you do it.'	'What have you tried so far . . . what effect did that have?'
I'm very pleased with what you've done.'	'How do you feel about what you've achieved?'

Whether or not you are ready to empower **your** workforce, there are clearly a large number of ways in which you can influence the degree of satisfaction which your employees derive from their jobs. Day-to-day issues, such as the way you greet them in the morning, the way you handle their mistakes and their suggestions, the way you respond to their requests for help, the freedom to experiment which you allow them and the way you deal with their requests for time off or special treatment, all have a vital bearing on how your management style is perceived and on the satisfaction that your employees gain from working for you.

One aspect which does warrant more detailed consideration is the extent to which your communications with employees can influence their motivation.

13.6 Communicating with Employees

We will define communications as the passing and receiving of signals from one human being to another. This may happen either directly, through written, spoken or non-verbal language, or indirectly, through technology: telephone, television, radio, fax, computer networks. It is with the first of these types of communication that we will primarily concern ourselves. We will begin by looking at the basic purposes of communication, and at their connection with our discussion of motivation.

(a) Purposes of Communication

There are three main, but inter-connected, reasons why people communicate with each other.

(i) To increase knowledge or understanding. Examples of this include the communication which takes place between teachers and pupils, instructors and trainees, and the makers of television documentaries and their audiences. Every time you tell your employees about a new work process, new terms and conditions of employment or new company products, you are trying to increase their knowledge and understanding of their jobs, the company and their relationship with it. You may or may not want them to change their behaviour directly as a result of the communication.

(ii) To influence or change attitudes. As we have seen, the area of attitude change is a difficult one. Although a straight 'telling' may be designed with a view to changing attitudes, it is unlikely to do so. Group communication (through discussions), role-play training (where one person has to adopt a new attitude in order to play his role effectively) or coaching are more likely to succeed. These methods all tend to confront people with the consequences of their present attitudes, and thereby induce change.

(iii) To instigate or influence action or behaviour. Ultimately all communication, particularly in the workplace, is arguably geared to this end. Although we seek to increase knowledge or change attitudes, we will only know that we have done so if behaviour changes as a result. If a pupil can solve a complex mathematical problem which was previously beyond him, we may say that there has been a change in behaviour, made possible through increased knowledge. Some communications are intended to have an immediate impact on action. If you tell someone to switch off a machine, you expect him to do so. If you sound a bell which has traditionally been the signal to break for lunch, you expect people to stop work and head for the canteen. So their behaviour after receiving the communication will be a direct response to that communication. As we shall see, such responses are not always the ones that the communicator intended.

(b) Communication and Motivation

Communication impinges on motivation in three main areas: training, setting objectives and knowledge of results.

(i) Training.   The questions which the coach asks to raise awareness and the directions which the instructor gives for specific action are, at one level, simply different forms of communication. All types of training involve communication and all training can have a powerful influence on whether the jobholder can do his job to his own, and your, satisfaction. An employee who is told to operate a machine but not told how will do one of two things. Either he will decide it can't be done, and will leave well alone, or he will attempt to operate the machine and do so in a way which may damage himself, the material, the machine, or possibly all three. Either way, he is likely to end up feeling frustrated and demotivated.

(ii) Setting objectives.   If employees do not know what they are expected to achieve, the pursuit of intrinsic job satisfaction is more elusive than ever. Although a few people thrive on the challenge of seemingly insuperable odds, such as the ascent of Everest or a single-handed circumnavigation of the globe, most of us prefer, in our day-to-day existence, to minimise the odds against us. If we do not know where we are going or how we are going to get there, we quickly become frustrated. The importance of clarity of communication and understanding of what is required can be demonstrated by a conversation between a manager and one of his sales representatives, Jane Johnson, during an appraisal interview. Jane's overall performance seems, to her manager, to be rather patchy.

> *Manager:* You must be very pleased with your sales figures for last month, Jane. I wonder how we might work on your customer information reports to provide a more general input to the department.
>
> *Jane:* What customer information reports? I always fill in my sales reports. I didn't know there was anything else we were supposed to do.
>
> *Manager:* Yes, don't you remember? We decided at the last sales conference that we needed to know about the sales that don't come off. You remember, I came back and told everyone at the first departmental meeting after the conference. I gave you all samples of the new form, and told you what we wanted.
>
> *Jane:* Well, you didn't tell me. When was this conference? I don't remember any meeting.
>
> (*It transpires that the meeting in fact took place while Jane was away from work, having her appendix removed.*)

After the interview, Jane feels rather hard done by, notwithstanding her manager's apology and a promise of instruction in the use of the new report. She feels that she has been appraised on the basis of an objective she didn't know she had, and is probably wondering what will crop up next year to detract from her good sales results. So this failure to communicate what is required may have an adverse effect on her motivation.

(iii) Knowledge of results. Ideally, work processes should be designed in such a way that people can see for themselves whether or not they are achieving their objectives. Where this is not the case and feedback is communicated verbally, then the focus should be on facts not feelings. A snatch of conversation between a clerk, Joseph, and his supervisor, Gloria Case, will illustrate this.

Gloria Case: Well done, Joseph, you've got all the invoices up to date. I really am very pleased.

Joseph: Oh. Er . . . good.
(*Thinks . . . that's good, with any luck I'll be able to ease up for a bit.*)

Gloria Case's praise may be well intentioned and genuine. By choosing to communicate this, rather than the simple fact that the invoices are up to date, she runs the risk of reducing Joseph's personal ownership of his job. Joseph works to achieve his objectives – not to give pleasure to Gloria Case.

This may sound harsh, but it **could** lead to him becoming much more dependent on his boss than he needs to be. If he is to continue to develop in his job, he must take **personal** responsibility, not wait for Gloria Case's approval.

In these three important ways – what to do, how to do it and with what results – communication influences the individual and his motivation. More generally, there is a relationship between the communication structure, the amount of information available to a group, and the satisfaction and performance of members of that group. In an experiment where various channels of communication were blocked and members had limited access to information, Leavitt, writing in the *Journal of Abnormal and Social Psychology*, showed that where information is shared within the group members tend to be more satisfied than where there is one central figure to whom they must all apply for information. The central figure himself, on the other hand, may derive much satisfaction from the importance of his position, and that sort of formation can sometimes be quicker to produce solutions to a problem.

Motivation can be influenced by the method, as well as the content of the communication.

(c) Methods of Spoken Communication

Although all spoken communication involves the use of the human voice, it can be applied in a number of different ways in the workplace. Some of these are listed below.

(i) **One-to-one directives and questions:** 'do it this way' or 'how do you plan to do it?'.

(ii) **One-to-one discussions:** the appraisal or coaching interview.

(iii) **One person to a group:** a lecture or non-participative briefing group.

(iv) **Group discussions** (with or without a chairperson): task forces, working parties, participative meetings or briefing groups.

Each of these may be appropriate in different circumstances. If there is only one person whom you need to involve, the individual approach will be better than wasting the time of others in the group by holding a meeting. On the other hand, if you are trying to bring about a change in one person's attitude, you may need the power of the team to help you. If there are a number of people who are to receive identical information of a non-personal nature, it will save time and ensure more uniformity of both transmission and reception of information if you tell them all at once. It may, however, be more difficult to tell whether each one has received and understood the message than it would be in a one-to-one situation. You will also need to think about the extent to which you require the communication to be a two-way affair. If there are things which your hearers will need to tell you, then there must be an opportunity for them to do so. What they will tell you may be something which will, in turn, influence what you have to tell them. Or maybe their contribution will simply take the form of repeating your message to you, to show that they have understood it. Whichever method you choose, take a few minutes beforehand to clarify your objectives and start every encounter by checking that your objectives line up with those of the other people involved.

In addition to thinking about objectives and the form that the encounter is to take, you will also need to pay careful attention to your choice of words and the way in which you say things. Your choice of words will be equally important where written communication is concerned, and we will be considering that later in this section. But the tone of your voice, your facial expressions, your hand and body movements, your physical stance and the clarity of your speech will all influence the way in which the content of your communication is received. There are two general points that you should bear in mind.

(i) All your non-verbal signals should add to, rather than conflict with, your basic message. If you are pleased or imparting good news, smile; if the news is bad, look serious. If you are addressing a group as friends and colleagues, adopt a relaxed, non-authoritarian position. This will mean that if they are sitting, you should sit. If you have called them together at lunchtime and asked them to bring their coffee and sandwiches with them, you should have your coffee and sandwiches there, too. If they are questioning you, show by the tone of your voice and the deliberation of your answer that you think their questions are worthwhile, not a waste of your valuable time.

(ii) The physical surroundings in which the meeting takes place should also facilitate the right kind of communication. If there is noise, people may not be able to hear, let alone concentrate on what is being said. The general principles concerning environment that we discussed in relation to selection interviews will act as a guide to what may be appropriate.

'You buzzed, yelled and thumped, sir. . .?'

As a footnote to these points on spoken communication, if your communication is indirect – perhaps on the telephone – you will need to pay special attention to the way in which your tone of voice adds to your message. Smiling and nodding your head will not get you very far.

Even if the meeting is relatively informal, don't hesitate to capture points of agreement and proposed actions in writing as you go – preferably on a flip chart where everyone can see it.

(d) Methods of Written Communication

Notes or minutes of meetings are an important way of recording the outcomes of spoken communication.

More generally you can use the written word to communicate with your employees via any of the following media.

(i) **Letters:** of engagement, termination, congratulation, condolence (mainly personal in their content).

(ii) **Legal documents:** contract of employment, addressed to an individual.

(iii) **Memoranda:** for internal communication, in relation either to the job or personal matters.

(iv) **Notice boards:** for notices and announcements of general interest, but not of major importance or urgency as you cannot be sure that everyone will see, let alone read, them.

(v) **House magazines:** for items of general interest and to build corporate spirit. More detailed coverage can be given than would be possible on a notice board, but the time interval between issues, production costs and patchy readership will limit its value for important messages.

(vi)   **Circulation lists:** memoranda or notices can be passed from hand to hand, each person signing against a list of those to whom the item is to be circulated to show that he has seen it. Seeing does not of course equate with reading and understanding, but it does mean that the item is brought to people's attention, and you can identify anyone who has been missed by checking through the list after circulation to see if anyone's signature is absent.

(vii)   **Manuals of instruction/management advice:** these can relate to both general policies and specific procedures. They can be kept in a department for reference purposes, to be consulted either by all employees or on a restricted access basis. If the manual is designed in a loose-leaf format, it can be updated by the reissue of a page, with instructions to remove the old one.

(viii)   **Pay packet communication slips:** where information of a personal nature is to be distributed to a large number. Where changes in national insurance contributions are concerned, this may be an appropriate medium. But where the content is of major personal significance, such as notification of redundancy, the method should not be used.

(ix)   **Job descriptions:** we discussed these in detail in Unit 3. They can provide a reference point for the employee, telling him what he is supposed to be doing.

(x)   **Organisation charts:** to show people who's who in the organisation and what the official reporting channels are. These are the channels that should normally be used for communication. So your subordinates communicate with you, you tell your boss, and he tells his. What often happens in organisations is that an informal set of communication channels is opened up. This may bear little or no relation to the formal channels indicated on the organisation chart. Thus you will tend to approach someone other than your boss, if you feel that by doing so you will elicit the right action more quickly.

(xi)   **External media:** the trade, national or local press can provide information for your employees at the same time as they provide it for the rest of their readers. This is not a method to be recommended for the communication of information that affects your employees personally, such as plant closures. They will feel a justifiable resentment at not having been told before the news became public knowledge. Where the press may be useful is to enable employees to keep up to date with non-central issues, without the necessity for setting up an expensive internal mechanism. One large retail company, for instance, found it uneconomic to keep its geographically scattered branch managers informed about which product advertisements were to appear in the national press each Sunday. It was cheaper to allow each branch manager to buy the appropriate Sunday newspaper and charge it to the company, thereby providing a useful fringe benefit as well.

Your choice between these methods will be influenced not only by the nature and content of your message, but also by the general climate of the company. Some more bureaucratic organisations, for instance, cannot exist without piles of paper. The memorandum is therefore the preferred form of communication, and telephone conversations will always be confirmed in writing, as will face-to-face encounters. In others, e-mail networks, the electronic equivalent of a postal service, are being used to replace the printed word. As a general principle, if a decision has been made or an instruction given, it is useful to have some sort of record of it, in case there is uncertainty in the future.

Various other general factors will influence the way your communication is viewed in the organisation. If you have chosen to put a notice on the notice board, for example, this will indicate that the message is not private to any one individual. The words 'private and confidential' on the corner of an envelope should indicate the opposite. If you habitually address your employees by their first names, to start a letter 'Dear Sir' will have an ominous ring. Quality of paper and size of envelope may, in some organisations, take on their own special significance.

(e) Choosing your Words

The basic rule for both written and spoken communication is to choose words which your audience will understand and are likely to interpret correctly (perhaps with graphics as a back-up). Do not insult their intelligence by speaking or writing only in words of one syllable; but bear in mind the existence of a device known as the **fog index**. This is a method of measuring roughly the number of years' education which the reader of a piece of written communication would need to have in order to understand it. It is calculated by taking the percentage of words in the passage which have three or more syllables, adding the average number of words per sentence, and multiplying by 0.4. A passage with an index of twelve should be intelligible to someone with about twelve years' schooling. But even if they comprehend your words, the way in which people will interpret them will depend upon a number of factors.

(i) Private conventions. From childhood we tend, as individuals or as families, to develop our own particular code words as a form of shorthand. An example might be using the words 'next door' to mean the local pub, deriving from a time when the family did live next door to a public house. If words which have a special private meaning are used in another context, they will tend, even if only momentarily, to obscure the real meaning of what is being said. This is very difficult to avoid completely, but perhaps provides an argument for communicating important parts of messages twice, using different words, in order to avoid confusion.

(ii) Group conventions. Group pressures can distort the meaning of a communication or condition the reactions of the recipients. It may be that the people with whom you are trying to communicate in the working group have developed their own private shorthand conventions, which will tend to compound the problem mentioned above. In addition, the existence of group norms – accepted standards of behaviour enforced by group members – may complicate communication. Katz and Lazarsfield, in their book *Personal Influence: the Part Played by People in the Flow of Mass Communication*, suggested that communication is in fact a two-stage process. The seeing or hearing of a message is stage one; the interpretation and action which results is stage two. But this second step is determined not by the communicator, but by the response of an influential member of the group to which the recipients belong. Because the group can be a closely knit entity, seeking approval from and conformity with its members, this 'influential', as he is called, will determine whether the group responds in the way intended by the communicator. There may be different influentials for different parts of the work activity. So one person might be influential on matters of pay, another on social aspects, a third on company politics. Sometimes (but not always) the influential person will draw his influence from his own position. Thus a shop steward may be the reference point or influential for the group on all matters relating to the job and conditions of employment. Even where the original message was addressed to one person, he may still refer it to his group influential before acting upon it. (We will be discussing group norms and their more general implications in Unit 19.)

(iii) Conventions deriving from hierarchy. The fact that there are different levels in most organisations tends to mean that different sets of norms will apply at those different levels and that different influentials will emerge. So a statement made to managers may be interpreted in quite a different way from that in which a group of foremen would interpret the same statement. More than this, a statement made by someone at a given level in the hierarchy will derive its particular significance from that fact. This may or may not be connected with the traditional authority structure: it doesn't always follow that the more senior the communicator, the more weight will be given to his words. But as a general rule, your response to the words 'I think it would be a good idea if you took tomorrow off' will differ according to whether it is your boss or a colleague who utters them.

(iv) Conventions deriving from past experience. Human beings, and animals too, can be conditioned to respond in a certain way given certain stimuli. The phone or the fire alarm provide the trigger for a series of semi-automatic actions. Even where conditioning is not so obvious, expectations deriving from past experience can have an effect on, for example, attempts to change a traditional relationship and create a feeling of trust. Take the words: 'I can assure you, lads, management have your best interests at heart.' In some companies, those words uttered to you by a trusted shop steward would ring very differently than if they were said to you by a member of management. This would not be because of the difference in status between the two, but because of your past dealings with both. Management may only ever have said this kind of thing as a prelude to doing something which, it seems to you, is quite clearly not in your best interests.

(v) Expectations deriving from education, social class and culture. In some instances our expectations may be so strongly influenced by these factors that we cannot interpret a communication correctly. Examples of this can be found whenever you hear the words: 'But I didn't believe you could really mean that.' At the end of World War II, when British officers were ordered to assist in the repatriation of Russian prisoners and refugees, a number of them felt that they had misunderstood their instructions because it was so much against British tradition to send people back to what was almost bound to be death or a labour camp.

These are some of the difficulties which may arise when people try to interpret and act upon our communications. In some cases the expectations may be so strong that people think they know what we are going to say before we have even said it. The people who chime in to finish your sentence with you believe that they are one step ahead of you. If you say something that they did not anticipate, they may not even hear you.

This range of conventions and expectations in itself poses quite a problem to the would-be communicator. To them can be added the difficulty of choosing an appropriate method and the basic human barriers to communication: failure to listen, failure to speak clearly, bad handwriting, poor telephone lines. But these must not be allowed to interfere with the exchange of information within an organisation more than is absolutely unavoidable.

(f) Using Symbols

The saying 'actions speak louder than words' is an important one to remember when you are trying to communicate. What you **do** symbolises what you really mean and can either support or detract from your message. So the managing director who proclaims that from now on all pay rises will be awarded strictly on merit will lose all credibility if in the following week he gives a substantial increase to someone whom everyone else believes to be totally incompetent.

Effective communication is vital if the right things are to be achieved, at the right time and in the right way. It is also, as we have seen, an important part of motivation. So too is the next area to which we must turn.

Questions

1. What do you understand by the word 'motivation'? How can an understanding of motivation assist a manager?
2. Describe three theories of employee motivation and assess their implications for the day-to-day relationships between managers and their staff.
3. What is empowerment? What would you have to change in **your** organisation to make it a reality?
4. How would you set about ensuring that communications – upwards, downwards and laterally – in an organisation were effective? What are the factors which may tend to reduce their effectiveness?
5. What might be the consequences for an organisation of an ineffective system of internal communication?

UNIT 14

Pay

14.1 Introduction

As Table 14.1 illustrates, there is a complex range of factors which confronts a manager whenever he starts to think about pay. The sort of issues that he faces include determining and maintaining appropriate differentials between jobs, determining and maintaining a way of rewarding individuals for their personal contribution, fixing rates of pay that will suit the company, employees and the external situation, thinking through the implications of having a workforce divided by methods of payment into salaried staff and weekly paid, working out the relationship between pay and fringe benefits in a way that suits both company and employees, and keeping the whole edifice on the right side of the law. In the next two units we will be looking at all these issues, examining the factors which underlie them and the ways in which you can cope with them.

Table 14.1 The pay package

Basic pay	(hourly, weekly, monthly rate)
plus	
Bonus/incentive payments/premium payments	(overtime, shift allowance, etc.)
plus	
Cash benefits	(holiday pay, sickness benefit, etc.)
equals	
Gross pay	
minus	
Deductions	(National Insurance, pensions and other contributions, Income Tax, etc.)
equals	
Take home pay	

14.2 Devising a Pay Structure

A pay structure is a pattern of internal differentials between the pay levels for various jobs, often expressed as a series of ascending grades or points. Such a structure provides a reference point for employer and employee alike. The employer benefits because decisions about pay take place within a closely defined framework and can therefore be made lower down in the organisation, thereby saving senior management time. He can also forecast pay costs more effectively and justify his decisions against a specific framework. From the employees' point of view, a published structure helps them as individuals to see where they stand in the organisation, and to what levels they can aspire. It also helps employees collectively to feel that there is some sort of rational system, rather than just managerial whim, which determines their rewards and provides a degree of uniformity among employees doing similar work and appropriate differentials for those engaged in more skilled tasks. Equal pay legislation (see Unit 14.7) makes this particularly important.

In real life it is seldom possible to start with a clean sheet of paper in devising a pay structure which is both rational and fair. The normal process is a series of updates and rethinks, all of which are inevitably coloured by the history of what has gone before. There are four general approaches which can contribute to the devising of a pay structure. We will consider each in turn.

(a) *Ad hoc* Pay Structures

Small, organic types of business often exist without a formally agreed pay structure of any kind, but have a loose arrangement that develops on an *ad hoc* basis. When the founder takes on a new recruit, probably to do a rather ill-defined job, he pays him whatever rate is necessary to persuade the individual to join him. Someone else then comes along and the cycle is repeated. Soon the first recruit comes back and asks for a pay rise. Either he gets it, or he doesn't, according to the boss's assessment of the consequences of each action. ('Can the company afford it?' 'Will the employee leave if he doesn't get it?')

This is rather a simplistic view, perhaps, but a workable one where people's value to the organisation is person-related (relates to them as individuals), rather than job-related (comes from the sort of job they are employed to perform). In fact, in such situations, a sort of subconscious structure may be dictating that the assistant doesn't actually end up earning more than the boss and that some conception of natural justice is served by the arrangement.

The problems with *ad hoc* pay structures arise as the organisation grows and a number of people are employed to do the same kind of job, but find themselves on totally different rates of pay. Once the job starts to prescribe the nature of the contribution that the individual can make, so that job worth becomes as important to the organisation as person worth, it is time to start thinking about devising a more soundly based structure. Otherwise unhealthy suspicion and jealousy between employees and a policy of 'he who shouts loudest gets most' will tend to take over. If you are dependent on having a certain number of employees, with certain types of skill, you cannot afford to let this happen.

(b) Externally Imposed Structures

National agreements, arrived at between employers' associations and trade unions, provide, for those groups of employees covered by them, a basic pattern of differentials between jobs. The actual rates of pay are less important to our present discussion than the pattern which emerges between skilled, semi-skilled and unskilled jobs and between different crafts or types of employee category. In fact, many employers exceed the basic cash minima required by national agreements, but the shape of their pay structure still follows the same broad outline. We will be talking further about the collective bargaining process, at local and at national level, in Unit 18.

(c) Local Collective Bargaining Arrangements

We have seen the influence that national agreements may have, but at the local level the pay rates and differentials agreed by employer and union have a vital bearing on the shape of the structure. Particularly significant here may be the comparative power of the different unions with which, in a multi-union workforce, an employer may have to negotiate. Unions with a stronger bargaining position, acquired perhaps through weight of numbers or through the centrality of their members' jobs to the success of the enterprise, may be able to win for themselves higher rates of pay than their less well-organised or less important colleagues, thereby influencing the pattern of differentials for the organisation.

What each of these first three approaches has in common is the fact that each involves starting with the money – the rate agreed either individually or collectively – and working backwards to see what sort of structure emerges from the pattern of differentials. This can cause problems under equal pay legislation (Unit 14.7) if the jobs done by women tend to emerge low down in the pecking order. The fourth method of determining a pay structure should reduce this risk. For most methods of job evaluation, the rate is immaterial until the structure has been determined by reference to the actual content of the jobs themselves.

(d) Job-evaluated Pay Structures

Job evaluation can be defined as a method of establishing the relative worth of jobs, using criteria drawn from the content of the jobs themselves. Most people have a feeling that some jobs warrant more payment than others. The criteria that we instinctively use are probably the level of responsibility, pleasantness or unpleasantness of the work, and the level of skills and training required. Where we tend to disagree is in applying these to specific jobs.

Job evaluation is a means of harnessing this instinct in order to try to provide some rational and defensible basis for the differential rates of pay that

Table 14.2 A grade description for job evaluation

Grade	Definition
1	Simple tasks involving light manual effort, closely supervised at all times
2	Simple tasks involving light manual effort, according to prescribed procedures
3	Tasks involving manual effort plus some areas of discretion in applying prescribed procedures
4	Tasks involving manual work plus some responsibility for the work of others

inevitably arise between jobs. Some form of job evaluation is used by most of Britain's largest companies (those employing more than 10,000 people), though it is less widely used by smaller firms. It falls into three main types, each of which has its own contribution to make. We will consider each of them, before moving on to a more general summary of the strengths and weaknesses of job evaluation. Most non-computerised systems, if they are to be applied effectively, require a panel of evaluators (a job-evaluation committee, preferably including employee representatives); an appeals procedure; accurate role descriptions; and a focus on the job, not the job-holder.

(i) Non-analytical/whole-job systems. You can evaluate a job as a whole unit, either by comparing it with other jobs (ranking) or by comparing it with a series of grade descriptions to find the best fit (**grading** or **classification**). A simplified example of such a grade description is given in Table 14.2.

While such methods are easy to understand and quick to operate, they tend to be subjective. Even where a detailed job description is used to supplement the evaluators' knowledge of the job content, it is sometimes difficult to separate the job from its present incumbent. This, in turn, may make it difficult to justify the results of the job evaluation. Although these whole-job methods will provide a reasonably acceptable 'pecking order' where the number of jobs is small, the greater the number of grades the harder it can be to differentiate. They also pose problems if a measure of the size of the difference between jobs is sought or where equal pay for work of equal value is at issue.

These problems are at least partly circumvented by the **direct consensus method**. This involves taking a panel of judges, drawn from all the interested parties, and examining a sample of jobs, on a paired comparison basis. Ranking forms are drawn up to enable each job to be compared with all the other jobs under consideration, one by one; the judges indicate which job in each pair has the greater value. The results are then fed into a computer to produce the overall order.

Competence-based job family systems are an up-to-date variant of grade classification. By focusing on competence levels – perhaps linked to NVQ standards (see Unit 10.5) – broad job families can be created. In delayed organisations where most jobs can be fitted into relatively few grades, such a **broadbanding** can provide a workable structure. If progression within each grade is limited to the acquisition of additional skills (see page 197) objectivity is increased and much of the divisiveness associated with more traditional methods is removed.

(ii) Analytical/job factor systems. These take a number of different forms, some copyright to particular management consultancies, others more generally available. Most lend themselves to shared management employee involvement in designing and/or implementing the scheme. Some are largely computer-based. What they have in common is the breaking down of the job into a number of factors and the assigning of points to each factor. One method which is widely used in the UK is the points rating method. The steps involved are:

Decide on the factors which are of significance to your organisation in distinguishing between jobs (competences required, responsibilites, working conditions).

Decide on any necessary subdivision of factors. Should competences be divided to distinguish between personal competences, technical competences and managerial competences?

Assign weights to each of the factors you have chosen in order to reflect their overall value to the organisation. Thus the maximum score for problem solving might be 25, whereas a factor which was thought to be more important, specific professional expertise perhaps, could be assigned a maximum 75 points.

Divide the factors into degrees or levels, using degree definitions on the same principle as the grade level descriptions shown in Table 14.2. You should then be in a position to draw up a rating plan, using your chosen factors and levels, and incorporating the weights, as illustrated in Table 14.3.

Draw up comprehensive job descriptions for all the jobs which are to be evaluated.

Select a number of jobs which will serve as a representative of each of the currently identifiable groups of jobs. These are known as benchmark jobs, and are best selected from fairly static jobs whose grades are not under dispute.

Evaluate the benchmark jobs, using the factors and weights that you have devised, to allocate a score or points rating on each factor. The purpose of this is to check that the evaluation does produce a reasonable outcome by placing the jobs in an appropriate order.

If the evaluation of the benchmarks is satisfactory, you can then proceed to evaluate the remainder of the jobs. If it is not, you may need to rethink either the factors used or the weights allocated to them.

Table 14.3 A points rating table

Factors	1st degree	2nd degree	3rd degree	4th degree	5th degree
1. *Competences required*					
planning and prioritising	5	10	15	20	25
problem solving	5	10	15	20	25
inter-personal	5	10	15	20	25
decision making	15	30	45	60	75
specific professional					
expertise	15	30	45	60	75
2. *Responsibilities*					
management of operations	10	20	30	40	50
financial management	5	10	15	20	25
management of people	15	30	45	60	75
management of					
information	15	30	45	60	75
3. *Effort required*					
physical demands	5	10	15	20	25
abnormal position	5	10	15	20	25
4. *Job conditions*					
disagreeableness	5	10	15	–	–
unavoidable hazards	5	10	15	–	–

This brings you to the stage where you have a score for each job in the organisation. You should then group jobs with like scores into an appropriate number of grades. We will be discussing shortly how this can be done. (An illustration of the way your system will take shape is given in Table 14.3.)

A points system lends itself to evaluation based on whatever factors the organisation finds appropriate. Other analytical approaches concentrate on specific groups of factors, which are held to be of general applicability. The **Hay guide chart profile** is the most widely used in this group. It uses the dimensions of know-how, problem solving and accountability. Know-how means the knowledge, skills and experience necessary for effective job performance, plus the managerial scope of the job in terms of planning, organising, evaluating, developing and co-ordinating. Accountability means the degree to which the individual has freedom to act in pursuit of results, and the degree of impact the job has on the organisation's objectives. Problem solving relates to the amount of original thought required in the job in analysing problems, evaluating information, making deductions and arriving at conclusions. These factors are dealt with on what is basically a points rating system, although there is a clear geometric progression in the number of points which can be

Table 14.4   Paterson's decision band method

Band E	Policy-making
Band D	Programming, planning how to carry out the policies
Band C	Interpreting, deciding how to implement the plans
Band B	Routine, deciding which tasks need to be done to achieve the interpretation
Band A	Automatic, allocating the techniques and the tasks to others
Band O	Defined, following a defined procedure to carry out a task, making decision on how to follow the procedure

assigned to particular levels or degrees of a given factor. In practice, each degree is worth approximately 15 points more than the step below it.

While giving a semblance of scientific objectivity, this so-called analytical group of job evaluation methods still has its shortcomings. One indeed lies in the degree of subjectivity which still remains. The drawing up of job descriptions, the selection of factors, the assigning of weights to those factors, the choice and evaluation of the benchmark jobs, the evaluation of the remaining jobs and the grouping of jobs into grades are all steps which involve an element of human judgement. In addition, the complexity of some systems, together with the time and expertise necessary for their introduction, tend to make them a less attractive proposition than the non-analytical methods. In their favour, however, we should point out that they do provide a consistent framework and generally logical approach, which are useful as a point of reference when jobs change or new ones are created and have to be fitted into the existing pay structure. There is also something specific at which to point if employees query the grades assigned to them.

(iii) Single-factor evaluation methods.   The single factor which is used as a means of distinguishing between jobs is that of differences in decision-making. **Paterson's decision band method** provides an example. Paterson distinguishes six levels or bands of decision-making. These are listed in Table 14.4. Each band is divided into two grades, and allocation to a grade depends on whether the job-holder is making the decisions himself or co-ordinating the work of other people making that type of decision. A job is assigned to the lowest band in which any of its tasks fall. But if even one of its tasks involves co-ordinating the activities of others, it will be assigned to the higher of the two grades within that band.

The main difficulties with the Paterson method arise from the choice of differences in decision-making as the sole criterion. This deliberately over-looks the other factors, such as skill, experience and general responsibility, which have traditionally been regarded, by employer and employee alike, as having a bearing on pay. The method is therefore less likely to be acceptable to non-managerial employees. Nor is subjectivity really any further removed from this method than from the other analytical methods we have discussed. In addition, the fact that a job will be placed in the higher grade even if only one of its tasks involves co-ordinating other people's activities may be an open invitation to job-holders to try to formalise any informal authority they may have over their colleagues. In an organic or empowered organisation, this will run directly counter to the general climate; even in a bureaucratic one it will tend to add to the rigidity of the hierarchy.

One other method of job evaluation based on differences in decision-making warrants our consideration: the **time span of discretion** developed by Elliott Jaques, a consultant famous for his work with the Glacier Metal Company. The criterion for distinguishing between jobs should be, according to Jaques, the length of time that it takes for marginally sub-standard decisions, rather than unmistakable blunders, made by the job-holder to be identified. This length of time is his time span of discretion. The longer it is, the more the job-holder should be paid. Jaques goes further, in devising what he called an equitable payment chart. This shows the payments which are appropriate for each length of time span and can be updated by reference to the wages index. These payments, according to Jaques, correspond to **felt fair pay** – the money the job-holder feels to be a fair reward for the level of responsibility carried. Again, the method has its critics. The relationship between the equitable payment chart and felt fair pay has been cast in doubt by subsequent research and the use of the time span of discretion as a sole criterion creates the same sort of difficulties as those encountered with the Paterson method when you attempt to apply it to jobs where the decision-making element is not obvious. In addition, an employee could earn more under a negligent manager who allows his decisions to go unchecked for a long period than he would under someone more conscientious. But because the length of a time span can be quantified, the method does seem to be less subjective than some of the others we have discussed.

It will be clear from our discussion so far that job evaluation is a large topic, to which a variety of different approaches can be applied. All that we can do here is to give a brief indication of those different approaches for you to follow up by further reading.

We have mentioned some of the specific problems relating to particular systems. Here we will look at some of the more general difficulties of job evaluation as a method of determining a pay structure.

(i) Although some methods of job evaluation appear scientific, they are almost all highly subjective in their design and application.

(ii) As jobs change, constant updating is necessary if the structure is to keep pace. Especially with systems where points are allocated in relation to specific factors, even a small change in job content may give rise to claims that more points are due. The factors themselves can become outdated as new issues gain importance.

(iii) It is difficult to find a set of factors which are universally applicable. Some points rating systems concentrate on factors which are more appropriate to manual jobs. Decision-based systems tend to be more suited to managerial jobs.

(iv) Jobs which are evaluated as being of equal size may not be equally attractive to employees. This will affect the ease with which people can be recruited or retained in certain jobs. Taken in conjunction with the general forces of the labour market, where certain skills may be in short supply, this can tend to upset the job-evaluated structure. This can be avoided by allocating special weightings or allowances to compensate, but care must be taken lest these become permanently built into the system.

(v) A carefully negotiated job-evaluated structure can become a strait-jacket for managers who feel unable to respond to changing circumstances by going outside the established grading structure. It can also make it difficult to reward flexibility – which is increasingly important to many employers. In an empowered organisation committed to continuous improvement, this can be a particular problem. Many systems seem calculated to act as a disincentive to the use of discretion and initiative by those in the lower grades.

(vi) Where team working exists, tight evaluation of the jobs of individual members may be unhelpful. The overlap and inter-dependence between roles may be such that defining fixed jobs for job evaluation purposes is impossible. Competence-based job family systems are probably the best solution here. All the jobs in a given team may belong to the same family, but individuals can still be rewarded according to their personal contribution or skill.

(vii) Not all trade unions have traditionally welcomed job evaluation. Equal pay legislation has tended to modify this view, and many are now favourably disposed towards it as a means of ensuring fair rewards for their members. There is a strong argument for encouraging as much employee involvement in both the design and implementation of a scheme as possible.

(viii) Job evaluation tends to be expensive as pay rates for present job-holders will not be reduced even if the revised structure shows them to have been overgraded. This leads to the practice of **red circling** (maintaining employees at their present rate or grade on a personal basis, but recruiting newcomers to the job at the job-evaluated grade). Some problems arose over this after the Equal Pay Act became operative in December 1975. Where the new recruits were women, recruited to comply with the Sex Discrimination Act, they found themselves being paid less than the men, even though they were doing the same work. This difference was in fact based on sex, because no women had previously been accepted into the jobs. It was therefore ruled by the Employment Appeal Tribunal, in the case of *Snoxell and Davies* v. *Vauxhall Motors* 1977, to be in contravention of the Equal Pay Act.

(ix) Job evaluation merely establishes a pecking order; it does not, generally, tell you what you should pay.

Although job evaluation is clearly not a perfect method for determining a pay structure, it is arguably the most rational that is available. And it does have some specific benefits.

(i) It can provide a valuable framework for dealing with grievances over pay, for establishing equal pay for work of equal value and for coping with changes in job content.

(ii) The consistency and acceptability of decisions over pay is likely to be greater, for the majority of employees, than more *ad hoc* methods. This will be especially true if employees are themselves represented during the evaluation procedure. Nor is there any reason to regard job evaluation and collective bargaining as mutually exclusive: one can provide a framework for the other.

(iii) A carefully devised method will enable the organisation to reward those factors which it considers to be of importance, rather than succumbing blindly to outside pressures.

(iv) The procedures involved in designing and implementing job evaluation can have other spin-offs for the company. An improvement in employer-employee understanding, a better knowledge of job content and/or key competences, leading to more rational job design and organisation structure, and better recruitment and selection are among the possible side-effects.

But the process of job evaluation does not, by itself, lead to the establishment of a rational and equitable pay structure. Unless some form of grade classification has been used, it is necessary to take the rank order or points derived from the application of your chosen system and use them to arrive at a grading scheme. Some methods of job evaluation specify their own ways of doing this. The Hay guide chart profile, for instance, provides not only for a predetermined grade structure to reflect points values, but also includes a salary survey to give information to companies using this system about current rates of pay for jobs evaluated on each level.

The most generally applicable procedure is as follows:

Examine the results of the job-evaluation exercise.

Group the jobs with similar scores together, perhaps plotting them on a graph, showing job values against existing rates of pay. Usually a number of natural breaks will appear, identifying the groups of job scores which can be treated together.

Decide how many grades you need. You should consider both the number of points at which significant changes in job scores, and so job content, occur and the need to create an adequate differential between grades to encourage promotion and development among the employees. If you are devising one grade structure for all the jobs at once, you will need a longer structure than if you are dealing separately with different functions and levels.

You may like to *review your grade structure* once you have established the top and bottom cash limits for your pay scale. If you determine that 15 per cent differential between the midpoints of the grades is essential, in order to provide an incentive for promotion, the number of grades in your structure will be calculated by seeing how many points, each 15 per cent greater than the one below it, the range will divide into. (You may decide that you wish the size of the differential to change near the top of the structure; this will create a convex curve if plotted on a graph, where the differentials get smaller towards the top; where the differentials get larger towards the top the line will be concave. The latter has its advantages where people at the top end are otherwise going to be hit unduly hard by higher tax rates.)

Decide whether the grades will actually be single rates or include a range of payment. We will be pursuing some of the possibilities in the next section.

Consider present market rates before actually fixing the rates to be applied to each grade. This will form the subject of Unit 14.4.

Once you have made your decisions, *cost out the new structure* and decide how you are going to deal with people who are at present over- or under-paid.

The final step is *implementation*. This should not take place without full explanation to employees about what is happening and why. You should set up appropriate procedures for monitoring the system, for coping with the creation of new jobs and for dealing with appeals. Ideally, these will all be included in a manual, together with a detailed breakdown of the system and how it is applied, to serve for future reference.

14.3   Choosing a Pay System

A pay system is a method for differentiating between the pay received by individuals doing the same or similar jobs. A number of jobs may be grouped at the same grade, and a number of people may be employed to do identical work. But because of differences in output, skill, age, length of service or some other variable, you may feel it appropriate to reward the job-holders at different rates.

In theory, you should reward individuals by the criteria which best reflect their value to the organisation. In practice, the history of the situation and in particular employee and managerial attitudes will have an important influence. Whichever method you choose, you must make sure the basis of your decisions is objective and legally defensible – to avoid equal pay claims (see Unit 14.7).

The subject of pay systems divides into two halves: wages and salaries. The case for amalgamating the two will be discussed in Unit 14.6.

(a)   Wage Payment Systems
Employees who are paid on an hourly, daily or weekly rate are described as **wage earners.** Traditionally, a number of different systems have been applied, but we will deal here only with those which are designed to separate one individual from another in terms of regular weekly pay. Bonuses of various kinds will be dealt with in Unit 15, and productivity bargains will be discussed in Unit 18.

(i) Payment by results systems (PBR).   These are designed to reward the employee for the number of units he produces (money piecework) or the time he takes to do a given amount of work (time piecework). Appropriate output or time rates are calculated, using the work study technique of effort rating. A base for all employees is normally applied, but the worker who produces more or takes less time can earn more than the base rate. This additional payment may take the form of proportional piecework (the additional pay increases in direct proportion to the extra output) or differential piecework (beyond a given point, the additional pay increases either faster or more slowly than the increase in output). The first is known as a **progressive system** of differential piecework; the second is a **regressive system**.

Piecework is used in Britain mainly for production, maintenance and toolroom work. The underlying theory follows F. W. Taylor's thesis that money provides the motivation for additional performance. Its supporters claim that PBR satisfies the needs of both management and employees, by providing high wages in return for high output. It also permits an accurate assessment of how much it will cost to produce each additional unit and generally requires less supervision to keep production high.

PBR has many drawbacks. There is some evidence that employees, perhaps driven by the need to belong to and be accepted as one of the work group, set norms of output for themselves and then restrict their production to meet those norms. They may also tend to avoid drawing attention to the attainability of measured time or piece rates, for fear of finding the work study team hastening back to reassess the rates.

Another serious problem with PBR systems is the pressure that they may produce for employees to cut corners, with adverse effects on product quality, customer care and employee safety. In addition, changes in job design will be resisted, in case they result in a downward revision of rates, while conflict may be increased through jealousy, suspicion and the uncertainty of a variable income, particularly where output is basically paced by the machine or dictated by circumstances beyond the employee's control. PBR can also seduce managers into neglecting their responsibility for motivating their employees. Rather than managing output, they may leave the scheme to do it for them. Underlying these problems is a much more fundamental flaw. Piecework is based on a 'carrot and stick' view of human behaviour. Managers who make this sort of assumption are likely to be repaid in kind. If you treat people like donkeys you should not be surprised if there is a certain mulish-ness in their behaviour. The signal conveyed by PBR is that management does not trust the workforce to take responsibility for their own output. Piecework is not compatible with empowerment.

(ii) Measured day work. This system is designed to level out earnings from week to week. So when an employee reaches a certain output over a period of, say, two weeks, he is paid at the rate for that level of performance. Several levels may be set, using work-measurement techniques, and the employee progresses through them as he becomes more proficient. In theory, measured day work can overcome the problems produced by the variations of piecework, but is still essentially a 'carrot and stick' approach. It relies

heavily on supervision and social pressures to encourage employees to maintain their level of output but is less overtly mistrustful in its assumptions.
(iii) Flat-rate systems (also known as day rate, day work, time rate or hourly rate). These provide that the employee receives an agreed rate of payment in return for a given period of work: for example, £6.00 per hour or £240.00 per week. This rate is fixed periodically, through collective bargaining or by reference to local rates. Pay varies only with the hours worked, not with the rate of output, and it therefore eliminates much of the day-to-day conflict and unpredictability of PBR. Where output is controlled by the machine, supplies of raw materials or other circumstances beyond the control of the individual employee, this is more likely to be felt fair. What it does not do is to allow for the kind of differentiation between employees which will reward those who contribute more, more highly. Any individual relationship between effort, performance and reward is therefore lost.

A flat-rate system is best treated as a contract with your employees. This means agreeing not only the rate per hour, day or week, but also establishing the standards of performance that are required. If the standard is not attained, through the fault of the employee rather than through that of management, you then have the normal sanctions of discipline and, ultimately, dismissal. The individual has the sanctions available to him through his trade union or your grievance procedure, if he feels that he has been unfairly treated.

If it is installed with full employee co-operation and participation, and if there is a system to monitor whether people are performing to the agreed standard, it can overcome many of the difficulties associated with other systems, while still allowing management to keep some control over the pay:output equation.
(iv) Performance-related pay. This allows for differentiation between individuals on the basis of performance. Increases may be either **fixed** or **variable. Fixed systems** establish a specific relationship between performance ratings and size of increment. In a performance rating system with a possible top score of 100, those scoring more than 80 might receive a 6 per cent pay rise, those scoring 65 to 79 might get 4 per cent, while 50 to 64 would warrant 2 per cent. The rest would receive no merit payment. The amount of money available for distribution in this manner can be calculated in advance and the formula worked out accordingly.

Variable systems leave a manager – or the team itself – free to award increases as he sees fit. The only constraint will be the size of the overall pay budget. There is no set formula. If the budget allows for payroll costs to rise by 4 per cent overall, it is then possible for one individual to get all the available cash, perhaps doubling his pay. In practice it is much more likely that everyone will get a little – although the basis for this may not always be as clear as with a fixed system.

To be felt fair, performance-related pay must be based on specific aspects of the employee's contribution – quality of work, participation in the team, ideas for improvement and so on. Unless the criteria are both clear and relevant, the system will quickly fall into disrepute. An element of team assessment can be introduced into both this and the next approach.

(v) Competence-based payments/pay for skills. Where multi-skilling is a goal, rewarding employees on the basis of the number of skills they have mastered makes sense. Those who can operate more than one part of the process warrant higher rewards than those who can only cope with one – they are more flexible and therefore in a position to make a greater contribution. This will usually be seen as fair – and may act as an incentive for more employees to become multi-skilled. It does require that all employees have equal opportunity to acquire the relevant skills, and that there is some means of assessing competence, either through the NVQ system or less formally. It is also important to be clear whether **possession** of a competence is enough to qualify or whether it must actually be used in the job. The former gives employees a guarantee that extra learning is worthwhile – but overlooks the fact that competence dissipates without practice. The latter can provide useful back-pressure on management, or the team, to rotate tasks to ensure that everyone's skills are kept topped up. In cash terms it is of course potentially much more expensive.

(vi) Service increments. If you are trying to build a core of stable, competent employees, one way of recognising their increasing value to the business without setting up potentially divisive performance criteria is to reward length of service. A **fixed increment** each year for a number of years appropriate to the complexity of the jobs and the length of time it takes to really master them can be granted automatically. This makes the system very easy to administer but means poor performers benefit too.

A **variable increment** allows for an element of discretion in determining the speed at which an individual's pay progresses. Increments can be withheld from those who fail to perform. This can be important. Incremental systems have a habit of degenerating into a reward for time-servers. If that happens, newer more capable people may become demotivated or hard to recruit.

(vii) Team-based systems. We have already indicated that team members can be involved in the assessment of each other's pay. Instead of looking for ways of differentiating between members of the team, the whole team can be rewarded – on the basis of its performance or overall competence level. It could then be for the team to decide whether everyone deserves an equal share or whether some alternative basis for distribution should be used. Alternatively, the team's effort may be rewarded through some form of bonus. We will discuss these in Unit 15.

Important as the team focus may be, it is also necessary to remember that the contract of employment is an individual contract. As most team members will agree, individual effort should count for something, provided it is directed towards the achievement of the team goal.

There are no absolute rights and wrongs in the field of selecting a payment system. What will work effectively in one set of circumstances will not do so in all. It is important to take into account the range of variables which affect the operation of the payment system. These variables include the type of technology, the product market, physical conditions, interpersonal relationships and the social and cultural backgrounds of employees, the state of trade unionism, the labour market and management style – in addition to actual job content.

This approach, known as **contingency theory**, represents a major advance over the prescriptive approaches which preceded it. It may be, though, that the crucial factor on which the success of a system depends is the **way** in which it is introduced and operated. Whichever scheme is chosen, it is more likely to be effective if it is set up as a result of extensive consultation with those affected, rather than by managerial decree. It is thus possible that the design of the payment system is less important than the message the scheme conveys to the workforce about the wider relationship between management and themselves. How this message is interpreted will depend, to some degree, on the existing relationship. In a hostile industrial relations climate, a new payment system is a good excuse for a fight. In a positive and constructive one, the pay system is, for all concerned, less likely to be contentious.

(b) Salaries
Employees who are paid on a monthly basis or at longer intervals are described as salaried. PBR and measured day work are not usually applied to salaried employees, although commission payments which allow sales staff a percentage of the value of items sold provide a parallel to PBR. All the other systems outlined in relation to wage payments **can** be applied. Flat-rate systems, with no scope for differentiation between individuals except through promotion to another job (**deferred gratification**), are less common among salaried staff. One possible explanation for this is the slower development of trade unionism among white-collar workers. The unions tend to emphasise the importance of equal treatment.

Historically, the public sector was known for its fixed incremental systems. As employees in this sector are public servants, it no doubt seemed appropriate to reward and encourage loyalty – that most valued of servants' attributes. Today, in common with many other sectors, the move is towards some form of performance-related pay – perhaps linked in with a wider system of **performance management**. This should comprise:

(*a*) clear definition of goals and objectives, for the team and/or the individual;

(*b*) performance coaching;

(*c*) some form of performance review or tracking to chart progress and record achievement at key stages leading to comprehensive learning and development plans;

(*d*) a well-worked out system for linking performance ratings to pay. The way this is done varies from organisation to organisation. Some financial services businesses claim to have had a positive response to some firmly 'fixed' formulae. Others have found that too tight a link between performance and pay has overtones of 'carrot and stick' and is counter-productive.

Your choice between salary systems will again be determined by a range of factors. By their nature, fixed-incremental systems seem more suited to a bureaucratic kind of organisation, where everything is clearly defined and laid down. At the other end of the spectrum, a variable performance-related system might appear to be better suited to the flexibility of an organic organisation climate, where the contribution that each employee makes is seen to be determined by person worth rather than job worth. These are generalisations. What seems to suit the needs of the organisation may not suit the needs of the people within it, and the two must somehow be brought into harmony.

Perhaps the most innovative approach to the question of pay determination is the one taken by the Semco company in Brazil. Instead of management developing systems to decide what each person would be paid, employees were invited to 'name their price'. Each was asked to review his or her career to date and present role and given copies of internal and national salary surveys. Then they had to tell their boss what they thought they should be paid.

The result was not the sort of pay explosion many might have feared. Instead, virtually everyone set salaries in line with what management thought reasonable. Of the half-dozen who didn't, five set lower figures. The fact that everyone knew what everyone else was paid probably helped to keep the claims reasonable. Those who overpaid themselves would have to live with their colleagues knowing they had overvalued their worth.

At Semco, these changes came only after a number of other steps to empowerment. They were introduced slowly to include first of all the top 5 per cent of employees, then the next 25 per cent. So far shop-floor employees have not been included, but the hope is that one day they will be.

14.4 Determining Market Rates

We have spent the last two sections discussing how we are to differentiate one job from another and one person from another in terms of pay. We have not yet talked about establishing the cash value of the job or the person. In order to do this, we must obtain some idea of what the jobs are worth, not just in relation to others but in absolute terms. The mechanism for doing this is the pay survey.

There is a certain amount of published information available which will give you a guide as to wage rates and how they are moving. Government publications, such as the *Employment Gazette* and the *New Earnings Survey*, indicate national pay trends. The wages index, looked at in conjunction with the retail price index, will provide an indication of the sort of inflationary pressures that can influence pay. Publications under the Incomes Data Services banner can help you keep abreast of what is happening to pay generally by providing information about pay settlements, current trends, the incidence of particular fringe benefits and payment systems. But if you need to know how much people in your locality are paying their maintenance fitters, their sales ledger supervisors, their financial director or any other specific position, you will almost certainly need to consult a pay survey.

These take two main forms: published and private surveys.

(a) Published Surveys

A number of bodies produce surveys, particularly in the salaries area. Professional associations, private consultancies and agencies, and trade unions are all active in this field. In addition, there are publications for particular specialist areas, such as computing or accountancy.

Some of these surveys attempt to cover all types of staff, others select a particular group or section of the industry. Sample sizes (the number of people whose pay is taken into account) vary from the very large – 65,000 in the case of one trade union survey – to the very small (180 for one professional institute). Some surveys consider only UK pay rates; others, such as those provided by Employment Conditions Abroad apply to other parts of the world.

(b) Private Surveys

If the information that you need is purely local, and you need it immediately, these may be two strong arguments for trying to collect your own information about pay rates. You can do this informally, perhaps by looking at the job advertisements in your local paper to see what your competitors are paying. This is likely to give you a somewhat distorted picture, as not all of them will have current vacancies, not all of them will have chosen that medium for recruitment and not all of them will state pay, anyway. An alternative is to approach the manager of your local job centre or a commercial agency. Much the same problems will apply, although they may have been able to analyse the information over a period of time.

For a more precise and reliable indication, the construction of your own pay survey can be the answer. You should follow, as far as possible, the steps listed below.

(i) Identify the jobs which you wish to compare.

(ii) Make sure that you have an accurate and up-to-date job description for each of them.

(iii) Decide on the degree of precision that you require. This will influence your sample size and whether you feel it necessary to examine anything other than basic pay.

(iv) Select an appropriate number of companies whom you have reason to believe employ the same categories of staff as you do, in the same geographical location or labour market. You may find that there is already a ready-made group of employers, represented through an employers' association or some other grouping, who will be willing to participate. They may even be prepared to join together for an annual survey among themselves, each company taking it in turns to do the research. The size of your sample will depend partly upon the number of possible respondents in the area and partly upon the degree of precision required. Allowing for some lack of response, if you start off with twelve to fifteen neighbouring employers, this should give you a fairly accurate feel for the situation. One other point to watch is whether to include only those in the same sort of business as yourself. Some industries, such as the oil industry, are traditionally high payers, and even though you may employ similar categories of staff, particularly on the clerical side, you need only take their rates of pay into account if you are in direct competition with them for staff.

(v) Decide what information you need from the companies in your sample. Basic rates of pay for each job are the obvious starting point, but won't mean much on their own if there are piecework rates or other forms of bonus being paid in addition. Total gross earnings can provide a more reliable yardstick, though if these are likely to be fluctuating you may need to take an average over a period of, say, six weeks. Even total gross earnings are only part of the picture. For salaried staff, as we have seen, there may be a range of pay within a grade. So, ideally, you need to know the top and bottom limits, the basis of progression through the grades and any points at which people tend to cluster. Fringe benefits of various kinds should also be considered, as should basic company information, to enable you to see the jobs in context: the company size, department sizes, organisation structure, frequency of pay reviews and the date of the last review may all have a bearing on your final analysis of the situation.

(vi) Decide whether you wish to send out a questionnaire by post, deliver it personally or use it as a checklist for yourself during an interview. Each has its advantages, but personal contact is usually very helpful in these circumstances, provided that it can be combined with a structured exchange of information.

(vii) Approach your chosen companies to find out if they are willing to co-operate and to confirm that they have sufficient staff in the right categories to be of assistance to you. It will be helpful to give them an abbreviated job description for each of the jobs in the survey so that they can pick out the comparable positions in their own organisation.

(viii) Collect your data, making sure this doesn't take more than about one month at the most. You must avoid the possibility that rates may have changed while the survey was in progress.

(ix) Analyse your information, comparing each company's response, job by job. You can draw out the mean (the average gross earnings for the group) to compare your own company data with it. Other statistics which may be helpful are the median (that rate which has as many people paying above it as below) and the mode (the most common rate of pay). Or you can simply look at the highest rate and the lowest rate and see whereabouts you come in the spectrum. You will need to qualify your conclusions by reference to the compensating fringe benefits which may either improve or worsen your position relative to other companies.

(x) Your final task is to decide how to use the information. We will be considering this in the next section, but you should not omit to notify your respondents of your findings and thank them for helping.

Conducting a pay survey is time-consuming and there are many pitfalls. Most of them also apply to the published surveys.

(i) The sample may be biased and therefore not representative. Only the clients of a particular consultancy or the readers of a particular publication may be involved.

(ii) Comparing like with like may be very difficult. The organisations in the sample may not have exactly identical jobs so a certain amount of distortion will occur.

(iii) Forming a true picture of differences in rewards for various jobs will be complicated by the existence of fringe benefits and working conditions whose compensating value to the employee will be difficult to quantify.

(iv) Statistical terms, particularly when used in the published surveys, can be misleading. The average may be skewed upwards if there are a few employers paying very high rates, so it is important to analyse the figures in a number of different ways, if you can.

(v) Outdating can be a problem if the information was collected even a few months ago. You cannot be sure how a new round of pay negotiation will have affected the figures.

(vi) If the survey extends beyond the UK, you will need to consider the implications of different taxation systems and different costs and standards of living.

Even with all these shortcomings, pay surveys can give you valuable information about current rates of pay. You can supplement this by information from other sources, be they government statistics, an employers' association, trade unions, your own employees or other contacts. What you need is an adequate knowledge of prevailing rates before you move on to fix the rate for the jobs under your control.

14.5 Fixing the Rate for the Job

Although current market rates must be taken into consideration if you wish to recruit and retain staff, this is not the sole criterion.

(a) Company Pay Policy

Some organisations deliberately set out to be market leaders on matters of pay, others prefer to be market followers or to strike a middle-of-the-road position. If you choose to be market leader, then people will look upon you as a high-paying employer and you may tend to attract people who are motivated mainly by material rewards. This may or may not suit the aims of your organisation. You may choose to be a market follower because you have a paternalistic attitude towards your employees and want to attract people who are looking for a happy working environment and a secure job, with perhaps reasonable fringe benefits. But the choice may not be something which is presented to you. Cost considerations, our second factor, may be the real determinant of both your pay policy and the rate for individual jobs.

'Boy, did we extract some fantastic pay rises before the firm went broke.'

(b) Cost Considerations

Although you might wish to be a market leader, you may not have the money available to pay at that level. The financial state of your business is bound to have an effect. An extra £10.00 per week for one job could mean an extra £10.00 per week for fifty people for fifty-two weeks per year. There does, though, come a point at which the company just has to afford its employees if it is to continue to produce. This is where the difficult decisions over investing in people or investing in machines may come into play.

(c) Collective Bargaining

The third factor which determines the rate for any one job in the company is the bargaining power of the group of employees concerned. We have already seen how collective bargaining may shape the pay structure. But bargaining over actual pay rates, wages and salaries is a very significant influence in many industries. It may, in fact, force the employer to override the affordability considerations, at least in the short term. Even if he cannot really afford the extra £10.00 per week, still less can he afford to lose all production through a lengthy strike.

(d) Relative Position in the Pay Structure

For any one job in the hierarchy, the precise rate of pay which can be allocated to it is bound to be circumscribed by the rates of pay for the jobs immediately above and below it in the structure. So if job A is graded 5 and is paid £180.00 per week, and job C is graded 7 and paid £220.00 per week, job B on grade 6 is bound to fall somewhere between the two, perhaps on £200.00 per week.

(e) Wages Councils

Until 1993 wages councils were an influence in some industries. Where the bargaining process was less fully developed, they prescribed minimum rates. Since their abolition, employers have been free to determine pay rates by reference only to the items above – and of course the individual's contract of employment (see Unit 14.7).

14.6　Monthly versus Weekly Pay

The distinction between manual wage-earners and clerical, managerial and professional salaried staff owes its origin, at least in part, to historical economic circumstances. In the past, demand for manual workers tended to fluctuate from week to week or even day to day, in response to fluctuations in workload or the availability of raw materials. Demand for other categories of staff remained constant. Because of this, our second group of employees obtained security of tenure in their jobs, reflected in monthly pay, now paid by cheque or bank transfer, pension schemes, paid holidays, sick pay and other white-collar benefits designed to secure and reflect their commitment to the firm. Blue-collar workers were kept on a weekly or hourly wage, paid in cash, which made it far easier to dispense with their services as circumstances dictated.

There is now a strong argument in favour of staff status for all employees. The principle of job security and the right to work has been extended by the Redundancy Payments Act (see Unit 20), the Trade Union and Labour Relations Act, the Employment Protection (Consolidation) Act, the Employment Acts and the Trade Union Reform and Employment Rights Act (see Unit 21). Manual workers can no longer be regarded as a dispensable commodity, best kept on an hourly rate so that they need not be retained a moment longer than necessary. Any organisation which aspires to an empowered workforce will quickly engender cynicism if it is not prepared to address this issue. There are three possible approaches to the question of single status for all employees.

(a) Abolition of Weekly Payroll

This provides uniformity of payment arrangements and removes the superficial distinction between monthly- and weekly-paid employees. It may also save the company administration costs and insurance premiums, as pay is 'cashless', and it should no longer be necessary to keep large sums of money on the premises. The spread of cashless pay was relatively slow in the UK because until January 1987 manual workers had the right to insist on being paid in cash. This general right was removed by the Wages Act 1986 though it remains in some individual contracts. Many more companies have now moved to cashless monthly pay for all.

(b) Equalisation of Terms and Conditions

This involves common pension scheme arrangements, where an occupational pension is contracted out of the state scheme; equal hours and the abolition of clocking in; equal sick pay and holiday entitlements; and shared eating and washing facilities, as well as the monthly pay cheque. The outcome of one important legal case – *Hayward* v. *Cammell Laird Shipbuilders Ltd* 1988 – created additional pressure for the harmonisation of terms and conditions between different sections of the workforce. The case was brought under the Equal Pay (Amendment) Regulations 1983 (see Unit 14.7). The House of Lords eventually took the view that each term of the contract of employment, rather than just basic pay, should be taken into account when comparing the remuneration of male painters and fitters and a female cook. Clearly such comparisons are easier to make if there are common terms and conditions for all groups.

Many employers are reluctant to move too rapidly to harmonise pay and conditions, because of the increased labour costs they will incur. In some industries, however, the costs of a move to single status are being offset by the benefits to be obtained from a single-union, no-strike agreement (see Unit 18.7).

(c) Change in Management–Worker Relationships

Some companies, especially capital-intensive, high-technology firms and those starting up on a 'greenfield' (new) site, have recognised that staff status for all, in its fullest sense, requires a fundamental rethink of traditional relationships and attitudes. Among the changes that need to accompany equalisation of terms and conditions will be reduction in the degree of supervision to match that accorded to non-manual employees; shared participation in briefing groups and representation in discussions at departmental and higher levels; and the abolition of paid overtime. Where small amounts of overtime are worked, the employee will be expected to stay late for no extra pay, in the same way as salaried staff have traditionally done. Where larger amounts of time are involved, he will be compensated by time off in lieu. This paves the way for what is known as the 'clean salary', where there are no add-ons to the basic rate. Although the cause of empowerment dictates that this must be a sensible direction in which to proceed, it is not without its drawbacks.

(i) Clean salaries may be less attractive, even to traditionally salaried staff, as there is much less prospect of wage drift, through loose piece-rates or overtime payments, and the employee has little room to manipulate the system.

(ii) Despite the demise of the hire-and-fire concept on which the distinction between wages and salaries was originally based, it is still more difficult to anticipate staffing levels in relation to workload for manual jobs than it is for clerical and managerial levels where minor fluctuations in workload can be carried more easily. It may therefore be necessary for manual workers to work large amounts of overtime, without receiving compensating time off until a much later date. (The concept of **annual hours**, see page 228, could help here.)

From our discussion it will be clear that single status can be far more than just the abolition of weekly pay. It is a question of fundamental beliefs about whether employees should be treated as a whole or separately. As we have seen, some recent changes in the law are likely to affect this issue. The law also affects a number of other aspects of remuneration.

14.7   Pay and the Law

For legal purposes the amount of wages or salary to be paid to an employee is determined by the contract of employment. The contract terms will either reflect rates agreed between the employer and the individual or between the employer and a trade union negotiating on behalf of the employee and his colleagues collectively.

Elsewhere in Europe minimum rates of pay are set by government. The 1989 European Social Charter states that a 'decent wage' must be established in each EC country, 'either by law or by collective agreement . . . or in accordance with national practices'. In the UK the state currently has only a limited influence on pay rates.

(a) The Fixing of Pay Rates

(i) **The Equal Pay Act 1970.**   This became operative in December 1975. It established the right of men and women to receive equal treatment as regards terms and conditions of employment, when they are employed on the same or broadly similar work or work which, though different, has been assigned equal value under a properly conducted job evaluation scheme. ('Properly conducted' means that jobs have been studied thoroughly and the results impartially applied. If management has to make a **conscious** decision as to where on the payscale an employee falls, the scheme will not be acceptable to an industrial tribunal as the basis for refuting an equal pay claim. The points value of the **job**, not the characteristics of the individual, should determine where it fits.) Taken in conjunction with the Sex Discrimination Acts, which we discussed in Unit 7.4, the Equal Pay Act means that you must generally employ women on the same work as men, and on the same terms and conditions.

The Equal Pay (Amendment) Regulations, which came into operation in 1984, have wider implications than the original Act. If a woman feels that her work is of equal value – that is, it calls for the same sort of effort, skill and decision-making – as that of a man, she can claim equal pay even though the two jobs have **not** been evaluated as equal by the employer. Although a soundly based job evaluation scheme, properly implemented, should help you to refute such claims, all job evaluation schemes should be examined closely to make sure that neither the factors on which they are based nor the way the points have been allocated are tending to overvalue male characteristics – such as physical strength – or to undervalue female ones – such as manipulative dexterity. Particular problems may occur where the female employee is covered by one job evaluation scheme, perhaps for clerical grades, while the man with whom she compares herself is covered by a manual or professional employee scheme. You need to review the overlap and compatibility of all schemes and, if the industrial relations climate permits, perhaps consider a move towards a consolidated scheme. The implications for other benefits must also be considered, as the *Cammell Laird* case (page 205) shows.

Failure to comply with the Equal Pay Act or Regulations entitles the woman who feels that she should be paid at the same rate as a male colleague (or vice versa) to complain to an industrial tribunal. If the tribunal finds in her favour, it can award arrears of pay and damages for a period of up to two years before the complaint was made.

(ii) Government pay policy. During the 1970s the Wilson and Callaghan Labour administrations imposed pay restraints ranging from £6.00 per week, through 5 per cent (with a minimum of £2.50 and a maximum of £4.00), to 10 per cent and back to 5 per cent, in various years. The basis of this restraint was voluntary. The concept of a **social contract** was accepted by the trade unions, who agreed to work with the government to reduce the rate of inflation, then running at an annual rate of about 25 per cent. The basic principle of a twelve-month gap between pay awards was enshrined in the contract and, with few exceptions, proved workable. The social contract was never intended to be a permanent feature of British industrial relations, and a change of government in 1979 saw the return of free collective bargaining.

Since then there has been no formalised general pay policy – although pay increases for many public sector employees have been limited by restrictions on the budgets of local and central government departments. During the early 1980s, high levels of unemployment and fears of redundancy, combined with much lower levels of inflation, tended to reduce the size of annual pay rises in the private sector. Some organisations had to ask employees to forgo an increase, sometimes two or three years running, or to take a pay cut. Others moved to a two-year interval between negotiations. By the end of the decade, with inflation rising and unemployment falling, employers were once again under pressure to concede double-figure percentage increases. In the 1990s, after another recession and with inflation at its lowest levels for thirty years, settlements are again in low single figures.

(b) Specific Entitlements
(i) Itemised pay statements (Employment Protection (Consolidation) Act 1978). All employees must be given an itemised statement to explain the

contents of each wage packet or salary cheque. This should specify the gross amount of pay, the net amount after deductions and what deductions have been made. These deductions are either fixed, such as union dues or other subscriptions, or variable, like income tax or national insurance which are calculated as a percentage of earnings.

(ii) Deductions from pay (Attachment of Earnings Act 1971 and Wages Act 1986). Apart from payments required by law such as income tax and national insurance contributions, you cannot make any deductions from an employee's pay unless they have been specifically agreed in writing or are part of the contract of employment. Deductions for trade union subscriptions under the 'check-off' system and subscriptions to sports clubs, savings clubs, charities and other bodies must all have the employee's express agreement.

The only exceptions are in retail – where in certain circumstances and provided the contract allows for it deductions of up to 10 per cent of salary may be made to cover cash or stock shortages – and payments under a court order. If you are ordered to make an **attachment of earnings**, you should deduct the amount specified and pay it over to the court. An employee who falls behind in maintenance payments to his divorced wife, for example, may have his earnings attached in this way so that his wife can be paid.

(iii) Guarantee pay (Employment Protection (Consolidation) Act 1978). Guarantee payments, not exceeding a specified figure, must be paid to employees of over one month's standing who are not provided with work on a day when they would normally work. If an employee refuses a reasonable offer of alternative employment, or is idle as a result of a trade dispute involving any of his employer's other employees, or those of an associated employer, the provisions do not apply. The year is divided into quarters and you are only obliged to make guarantee payments for five days in each quarter. If you don't make the payments, your employees can appeal to an industrial tribunal and you will be ordered to pay.

(iv) Statutory maternity pay (SMP). A woman who has worked for you for twenty-six weeks or more up until the fifteenth week before the expected birth of her baby is entitled to statutory maternity pay when she is absent for the birth of the child provided she earns more than the lower earnings limit for national insurance. Payment should be at the rate of nine-tenths of her average weekly earnings for the first six weeks and at a lower, prescribed, rate for a further twelve weeks. 92 per cent of SMP can be reclaimed from the state by the employer deducting the amount paid out from his national insurance payments. (Details of entitlement to maternity leave are given in Unit 15.8.)

(v) Time off with pay (Employment Protection (Consolidation) Act 1978, Employment Act 1980 and 1989). There are a number of circumstances in which you must give your employees time off with pay. If an employee is carrying out certain official duties or being trained to carry out such duties concerned with industrial relations between employer and employee or with health and safety at work, he must be given reasonable time off. (The Code of Practice on Time Off for Trade Union Duties and Activities and the Code of Practice on Time Off for the Training of Safety Representatives provide further guidance on this.) If he is being dismissed as redundant under the terms of the Redundancy Payments Act (see Unit 20), he is entitled to time off to look for a new job. If he is suspended on medical grounds, not because he is incapable of work but because it would be dangerous for him to continue working on that particular job, he is entitled to payment for up to six months, provided he does not unreasonably refuse an offer of alternative work. Pregnant employees are entitled to reasonable time off for ante-natal care. In addition to these periods of paid absence, the Act specifies that individuals who hold public office, such as justices of the peace, or are members of public bodies, such as the local council, be given reasonable time off, without pay, to attend to their duties.

(vi) Holiday pay. In the UK most of the workforce, apart from young people working in factories, has traditionally received its holidays as a result of voluntary agreement between employers and trade unions, or under terms and conditions specified by the employer in the contract of employment. If the European Working Time Directive comes into force, employers may have to observe specified minimum requirements for holiday pay and rest periods.

(vii) Statutory Sick Pay (SSP) (Social Security and Housing Benefits Act 1982). This changed the basis of payments to employees who are temporarily unable to work because of sickness. SSP was introduced as part of a general programme of reducing the number of civil servants needed to administer state benefits and as a means of making state sick pay taxable. Whenever an employee, however short his service, has a period of incapacity for work (PIW), and that PIW is part of a period of entitlement (PE), then he will be paid statutory sick pay for each qualifying day (Q day) after a three-day waiting period. A PIW is one where the employee is absent for at least four consecutive days. A period of entitlement starts with the first day of absence and ends with the return to work, the exhaustion of twenty-eight weeks SSP or the ending of the contract of employment, whichever occurs first. Qualifying days are the days on which the employee would normally have worked and should be agreed between employer and employee.

The rate at which SSP is paid is currently £52.50 per week for those earning more than £58 per week. It is payable for up to twenty-eight weeks in any one PIW. After that the employee may be eligible to receive benefit from the state. Although you pay your employees their SSP, if your SSP costs exceed 13 per cent of your company national insurance contributions you can reclaim the excess – by deducting from the amounts due to be paid by way of employer's national insurance contributions. All entitlements to and payments of SSP must be properly recorded and monitored, as inspectors from the Department of Social Security may require proof that the scheme is being properly operated. (From 1997 employers will be able to opt out of SSP if their own occupational sick pay schemes are more generous.)

So far, we have talked about basic pay strategies. But the role of other elements in a total remuneration package is becoming increasingly important. It is to these that we will now turn.

Questions

1. What do you understand by the terms (*a*) pay structure; (*b*) payment system? What are the factors determining each in your organisation?
2. What are the strengths and weaknesses of job evaluation?
3. Your managing director has asked you to conduct a pay survey for a range of manual and clerical jobs in your organisation. Describe how you would set about complying with his request.
4. What is meant by the term 'staff status for all'? What are the implications of a move in this direction?
5. In what ways does the law prescribe employers' behaviour in the field of pay?

UNIT 15

Employee Benefits

15.1 Introduction

Additions to pay and payments in kind, which may or may not form part of your terms and conditions of employment, are sometimes referred to as fringe benefits. This is somewhat misleading, as many of the items are of far more central importance than the word fringe implies. Such benefits are also referred to as 'perks', but this has overtones of slightly underhand dealings, not really appropriate in the majority of cases. 'Compensation package' also has its drawbacks as a description. Compensation is normally associated with making recompense for our transgressions, perhaps by paying a sum of money to an employee who has suffered injury as a result of our negligence. We will therefore think of employee benefits as part of the total remuneration or pay package, avoiding the doubtful connotations of the other titles.

There are four main reasons why total remuneration, rather than just basic pay, is important today.

(a) Employee Expectations

Certain benefits, such as sick pay and pensions, were once regarded as welfare provisions. Employee expectations, bolstered in the case of pensions by the law, have moved them into the area where they are regarded, certainly by salaried staff, almost as a right. These expectations are, in some instances, translated into positive demands, such as where a trade union negotiates for an extra three days' paid holiday. In others, they are just something against which it is difficult to argue, if you wish to attract and retain the right kind of employees. Although phrases in job advertisements in the vein 'plus the benefits you would expect from a leading company' are, as we saw in Unit 3, fairly meaningless, the fact that employers feel that they can use them implies some sort of recognisable pattern of expectations.

(b) Employee Retention

Although clearly linked with employee expectations, the use of fringe benefits for employee retention purposes is something which warrants separate consideration. The Americans, as we saw in Unit 1, have coined the term 'golden handcuffs' to describe those benefits which, though attractive, tend to shackle the unwary employee to the company even after he has lost all intrinsic satisfaction in his job. Mortgages at rates well below those charged to the private borrower are an example. Although the employee may find a bank or building society to take over the unexpired part of the loan should he leave the company, in theory he will be deterred from doing so by the need to start paying interest at market rates. In practice there are now so many companies in the commercial sector offering this facility that employees may move from one to another with comparative ease.

In using fringe benefits as a means of improving employee retention we are, in fact, seeing the other side of the argument we put forward in Unit 14.6. We are trying to induce the loyalty of salaried staff by such benefits, rather than rewarding them for their past commitment.

(c) Employee Motivation

Apart from the basic motivation to join or leave the organisation, for certain groups of employees benefits may provide a more positive source of motivation. We referred, in Unit 13.2, to research carried out at Ashridge into executive motivation. For the groups who have a drive for material rewards and for those who seek status and prestige, benefits will be very important. The first group may see them in terms of their cash equivalent, but the second will view the provision of an expensive company car or benefits in the 'key to the executive washroom' vein as definite signs, to themselves and others, that they have 'arrived' and are recognised.

Unfortunately many of those who do **not** receive the benefits may also see them in this light. Differences in benefits can be divisive and demotivating and, as we saw in Unit 14, may not be conducive to the development of an empowered workforce.

Other benefits which we will be considering in this unit may have a more positive motivational impact and can be shared more widely. Bonus schemes, especially those linked to company profitability in some way, are often designed to motivate all employees to contribute maximum effort to achieve company goals.

(d) Tax Implications

To give an employee who pays tax at the standard rate an extra £100 spending power, it will actually cost you nearer £200. This will allow him to pay his national insurance contributions and income tax, and you to pay your employers' national insurance contribution, and still leave him with £100 in his pocket at the end of the day. If the employee is on top rates of tax, and you want him to end up with an additional £1000, you will need to budget for between two and three times that amount.

Although some benefits do attract income tax, they can still ease the tax burden considerably. Membership of a private medical insurance scheme provides an example. Group rates for entry to such schemes, especially where the company has a number of members who have been participating for some time, may cost, for each additional member, only about half what it would cost the employee if he were to enter the scheme as a private individual. We will take the figures as £100 for the employer to purchase membership for the employee and his family, and £200 if the employee buys it himself. In the first case, the employer will need to find about £150 in order to pay the membership fee and to enable the employee to pay tax at standard rate on the benefit without ending up out of pocket. It will cost him nearly £400 if he tries to get a net £200 into his employee's pocket to enable him to buy the benefit himself, allowing for all the deductions that we have seen a cash payment will entail.

This therefore is a powerful argument, from the employer's point of view, for paying in kind rather than in cash. From the employee's point of view, if it enables him to have something which he wants, such as medical insurance, at less cost to himself (because the chances are his employer would not be forthcoming with the full amount for tax and insurance), he too will benefit.

The obvious flaw in the argument is that the employee may not want free medical insurance, or he may not want it as much as he wants something else. The role of employee benefits in the fight against the tax inspector has been likened to that of the tail bestowed by God on the philosophical donkey in George Orwell's *Animal Farm* in order to keep off the flies. Although the tail was useful in this respect, the donkey would rather have had no tail and no flies.

For all these reasons, employee benefits are something which, if you are thinking about remuneration generally, you cannot afford to ignore.

15.2 Constructing a Benefits Package

There are five basic considerations to take into account.

(a) Objectives
As with so much else in the field of management, the first task is to clarify your objectives. Are you designing a package just to meet current employee expectations, or will it be helpful to anticipate future demands? A look at the sort of benefits being offered by some of the more enlightened large companies may give you a clue here. (The Reward Group, tel. 01758 813566, publishes a periodic survey which you might find useful.) Is employee retention a factor that you need to consider? What about tax implications if you are trying to minimise costs for yourself, your employees, or both? Will your package need to have high motivational value, or is that already catered for through the pay system?

(b) Policy Considerations
We saw in Unit 14 the part that decisions about policy can play. In devising a benefits package you will need to consider how it relates to your basic pay policy. You may be tempted to compensate for low basic pay through a policy of generous benefits. This is not usually very effective, unless the benefits are geared towards the security and social needs of employees.

(c) Cost Considerations

However attractive a benefits package may look, if the company cannot afford it there is little future in pursuing it – unless the consequences of not doing so will be even worse than the costs of going ahead. All benefits need careful costing, particularly if, like occupational pension schemes, they will involve the company in a long-term commitment.

(d) Compatibility with Company Objectives and Employee Needs

You must make sure that any benefits you introduce are in line with the direction in which the company is travelling. A share option scheme, for instance, presupposes that you are happy with the idea of your employees having a vote as company shareholders. Bonus schemes involving a high degree of disclosure of information and participation in target-setting may not be compatible with a closed and authoritarian management style. But neither of these will be of any use if employees don't want them.

Nor should we always assume that employees will want the kind of benefits which are the most expensive for the employer to provide. In one American company it turned out that employees had a marked preference for a comparatively inexpensive dental insurance scheme, rather than a much more costly life assurance scheme. Their rationale was apparently that death was probably a long way off, but their next dentist's bill was just around the corner.

'You used to complain we didn't plough profits back – now we do, you complain there's nothing left in the kitty for bargaining.'

(e) Impact on Internal Relationships

If you are thinking of giving one group of employees five weeks' holiday, how will that affect other groups of employees, in terms of workload, morale and demands for equal treatment or a compensating increase to maintain their relative position? Our discussion on the equalisation of terms and conditions (Unit 14.6) is relevant here.

These are the preliminaries. In subsequent sections we will be looking at some of the elements that you might include.

15.3 Bonuses and Share Option Schemes

Bonuses more closely resemble a straight addition to pay than most of the other benefits we will be considering. With the exception of what we will call Traditional Bonuses, they are normally payable in relation to some specified criterion, such as profit or productivity, rather than as gifts from employer to employee. They do, however, tend to become a right, rather than a benefit, in the eyes of employees. A general difficulty associated with all forms of bonus or incentive payments is that of calculating the proportion of total earnings that they should reasonably constitute. Presumably you will not want it to be so high that in a bad year your employees will be practically destitute. But if you make it too small, your employees are unlikely to value it at all.

If introduced as part of a genuine move to enable **all** employees to share in the success of the business, an appropriately designed scheme **can** enhance employee involvement. Bonuses paid only to executives or other senior groups can have the opposite effect. They take several forms.

(a) Traditional Bonuses

Some organisations have a practice of making additional payments to employees at particular points in the year. Extra cash or goods at Christmas may be given to all employees, perhaps graded by seniority. More generally a feature of paternalistic organisations, their motivational value must be doubted. What tends to happen is that, if the bonus is worth having, few staff will leave in the period immediately before it becomes payable, but there may be a mass exodus afterwards. Unless you can gear your bonus payment to come at the end of your peak period, this can cause real problems.

While Christmas is the traditional time for such largesse, an extra week or two's pay by way of holiday bonus is provided by some companies. This may be paid immediately before or immediately after the holiday. In the UK we have not yet developed the fourteenth month bonus or additional month's holiday payment system which is part of basic terms and conditions of employment in some European countries. These, too, are geared towards providing extra money for each employee, so that effectively he is paid double while on holiday.

(b) Continued Good Service Bonuses

These are paid to individual employees, often those who have reached the top of their pay grade and cannot be promoted. They are designed to encourage loyalty and maintain motivation. In practice, though, when you have rewarded an employee in this way once, you may find it difficult to withdraw the privilege without demotivating him, and the criteria on which it was originally granted may become blurred.

(c) Merit Bonuses

These, again, are individual bonuses paid to employees, sometimes only those at senior level, in recognition of their attainment of specific targets. Achievement of sales increases, cost control or other objectives can be rewarded on either an *ad hoc* basis or according to a pre-set formula. They can also be adapted to reward groups. Some of these bonuses are profit-related. We will consider these under the next heading.

(d) Profit-related Pay (PRP) and Profit-related Bonuses

(i) **Profit-related pay.**   A growing number of companies now seek to increase employee involvement and commitment by linking bonus payments to profit. A bonus trigger point is usually determined, below which no payment is due. The trigger may be a fixed level of profit, return on assets or capital employed, or some other measure – or it may be varied from year to year. The bonus is usually a percentage of normal pay. Its size depends on the amount by which the trigger point is passed.

If they comply with Inland Revenue rules, which specify that a percentage of normal pay must become profit dependent, PRP schemes can have significant tax advantages for the employee and employer. Such schemes can be introduced for the whole company or for any division or unit, provided its accounts are audited separately. To qualify, at least 80 per cent of those employed in the unit must participate in the scheme, and the link between PRP and profit must be clearly specified – either by allocating a specific proportion of profits or according to a formula. PRP was first introduced in 1987 and was extended under the 1989 and 1991 Finance Acts. In 1988 there were 616 such schemes approved by the Inland Revenue with just under 90,000 participants. By 1994 there were several thousand schemes and more than two million participants.

(ii) **Executive bonuses.**   At senior level it is quite common for salaries to be enhanced by very sizeable profit-related bonuses, for individuals whose contribution is perceived as being worthwhile. Sometimes there is a specific formula related to the division's return on investment ratio or to its improvement in profitability. With some bonuses for chief executives running well into six figures, they can attract adverse publicity. They also become difficult to operate fairly where the achievement of objectives is very much a group effort.

(iii) **Group bonuses.**   These can be calculated according to profit formulae like those already mentioned. Each member of a unit or division can then participate through a points system which may, in turn, be related to status, length of service or merit. Alternatively the bonus may be expressed as a percentage of salary.

(e) Team-based productivity schemes

Some companies have moved away from the kind of PBR individual incentives we discussed in Unit 14 and instead have adopted a team-based productivity arrangement. Such schemes can focus people's attention not just on output but on cost of output and should mean that employees are encouraged to come forward with suggestions for increasing output or reducing costs – or both.

On the other hand, because such bonuses are usually paid out at fairly lengthy intervals – quarterly or even annually – their incentive value may be less than that which can be incorporated in the pay system direct.

Such schemes can be applied to individual teams or plant-wide. There are two traditional forms of plant-wide scheme. Both can be adapted to work with smaller units and the basis of the calculation can be modified to suit particular circumstances.

The Scanlon Plan. This was originally an American invention, but was introduced in the UK by the Rootes Company which at one time operated the Linwood car plant in Scotland. It includes both direct and indirect labour. The basic steps involved are:

Determine your current ratio of labour costs to sales revenue.

Using this ratio, *draw up an allowed payroll* (what you think it should cost in labour this year to make the number of items you intend to sell in order to make this year's sales revenue).

At the end of the year, *calculate the actual payroll* (what you actually did spend in labour costs).

Work out your participating payroll, to reflect the amount of time worked by individuals.

Subtract your actual payroll from your allowed payroll.

Some of the difference may go into a reserve; of the remainder, some goes to the company and the rest is divided among the participating payroll.

What you are effectively doing is rewarding your employees for reducing labour costs in relation to sales revenue. You are, however, highly dependent upon sales remaining buoyant. Once they start to decline, unless labour costs also decline, the bonus is squeezed out of existence, as actual payroll exceeds allowed payroll. This is, in fact, what happened at the Linwood plant.

Nevertheless, the degree of employee participation which you can obtain in launching such a scheme will prove beneficial in improving communication and trust generally, providing it does not founder too quickly.

The Rucker Plan. This has as its underlying basis the *value added* by the workforce to the raw materials or the products which the company buys, works on and sells. The steps are:

Calculate production value by deducting the cost of incoming materials and services from sales revenue.

Calculate your total employment costs.

Work out the relationship between employment costs and production value, if possible comparing the ratio over several years.

Determine the appropriate ratio for your company, by comparing it, if possible, with other companies in the same industry.

If the ratio falls so that employee costs constitute a smaller part of production value, a bonus will be payable in that period. If the ratio increases beyond the acceptable level, no bonus will be due.

Decide on an appropriate scale of bonus, in relation to the ratio, and devise a table so that employees can see what percentage of their salary they will get in bonus, at any given ratio level. You may wish to set a minimum cash level, too, so that even low-paid employees will derive a significant bonus.

(f) Share Schemes

Whichever formula is used for calculating a bonus, and whether it is paid on an individual, group or plant-wide basis, the practice of paying a bonus in the form of company shares, rather than in cash, is growing.

While most cash bonuses attract income tax and national insurance deductions, shares allocated under an Inland Revenue approved profit-sharing scheme do not – provided certain conditions are met. Under such schemes, the company allocates money to a trust fund which acquires shares in the company on behalf of the employees. Employees cannot normally sell their shares during the first two years, and if they sell them within five years income tax is payable. After five years the employee is free to dispose of the shares (though capital gains tax may be payable if he makes a lot of profit on disposal).

Although they have long been popular in America, where deferred profit-sharing schemes are widespread, until 1978 the British tax system limited its introduction here. Employees were generally subject to taxation both on receipt and subsequent sale of the shares. Since 1978 there has been an upsurge of interest in such schemes as well as in other types of share option and ownership trust arrangements. Share ownership has generally become a more popular form of investment, a trend encouraged by the well-publicised issue of shares in companies like British Telecom, British Gas, the Trustee Savings Bank and the water and electricity companies.

There are other variations on the share ownership theme, through offering shares at preferential or on a 'buy one, get one free' matching basis. The usefulness of this rather depends on whether share ownership is the form of investment favoured by your employees.

This general concept of allowing employees to participate in the equity of the company has its attractions. It is argued that it encourages employees to think more about the long-term viability of the company. They automatically reap a dividend if the company is profitable, and therefore have a vested interest in making it so. We will be discussing the wider aspects of employee participation in Unit 18. But for companies who wish to see additional employee involvement in company affairs, share ownership may be a step in an appropriate direction.

The counter-argument claims that such schemes force employees to 'put all their eggs in one basket'. This is fine if the company is profitable, but if its position is not sound, employees may lose both their jobs and their investments simultaneously. Its opponents also suggest that giving shares, and therefore a share dividend, to non-investors, acts as a disincentive to genuine investment. (We might respond that investment of labour is just as important as investment of capital.) And the more widely accepted equity participation becomes, the more unfair it will be for those employed in the public sector or those in struggling areas of the private sector who, despite their individual efforts, can never benefit.

There is, however, a growing body of research evidence, from both the UK and America, which suggests that companies with employee share-ownership schemes tend to fare rather better, by a number of important business criteria, than those without.

In some senses, employees may regard profit-sharing and share-option schemes as deferred pay. A company's occupational pension scheme, too, can provide a future benefit for present employees.

15.4 Occupational Pension Schemes

The Social Security Pensions Act 1975, which came into operation in 1978, made the state pension scheme more attractive to employer and employee alike. Apart from a basic weekly pension, for which all employed persons who contribute through national insurance are eligible, there is a state earnings-related pension (SERPS). Each week a retired employee receives one-eightieth of his average weekly earnings, between certain limits, for every year of service since 1978, up to a maximum of twenty years. (For those retiring after the end of the century the proportion declines to one-hundredth per year of service, in accordance with the Social Security Act 1986.) Earnings are revalued in terms of the earnings level current in the last complete tax year before state retirement age. There is also state provision for benefits for widows, which take the form of either a pension or allowance, depending on age.

Both earlier pieces of legislation are now incorporated within the Social Security Contributions and Benefits Act 1992 and the Pension Schemes Act

1993. The latter also specifies that men and women must have equal access to occupational pension schemes.

The earnings-related tier is proving very costly. It has already been revised and may eventually be abolished. In any case, there is still much to be said for offering your employees their own occupational pension scheme. You cannot opt out of the basic state pension and its contributions but you can contract out of SERPS. If you do so, your national insurance contributions and those of your employees will be correspondingly reduced. You will be able to put that money, plus, if you wish, additional contributions, which are allowable against tax for both employer and employee, into a scheme which provides better benefits than the state scheme.

Some of the additional benefits that you might consider are:

(*a*) calculating a pension on the basis of sixtieths of weekly earnings, rather than eightieths or hundredths;

(*b*) calculating a pension on the basis of **all** the years served by the employee, up to a maximum of forty years. This would mean that instead of a pension of twenty-eightieths (one-quarter) of his previous weekly earnings each week, he could receive as much as forty-sixtieths (two-thirds);

(*c*) allowing the employee to commute part of his pension entitlement into a lump sum;

(*d*) providing a lump-sum benefit to the spouse in the event of the employee dying while in your service and a more generous pension for the spouse and dependants than the state scheme allows.

Any or all of these additional benefits may be of value to you in building your image as an employer who is concerned for the well-being of his employees. They may also prove an aid to employee retention, particularly among older employees, although since July 1988 it has been possible for employees to take out personal pensions instead of belonging to their employer's occupational scheme. The fact that the contributions to, and some of the benefits from, an occupational pension are tax free makes deferred pay, in the form of enhanced pensions rights, a way of rewarding senior staff whose tax burden is already high. (You should bear in mind, though, that there is now an 'earnings cap' which limits the benefits payable to top earners.)

Then too, as in a number of areas where the law has intervened to regulate arrangements between employer and employee, trade unions tend to view the state scheme as a starting point. More generous provision is something for which they are prepared to bargain. This means that once you and your employees have contracted out of the second tier of the state scheme, you will need to be prepared for them to discuss pensions as a form of deferred pay and to nominate some of the trustees of the scheme.

The field of pensions is a specialist one. The regulations governing the funding and administration of schemes are being tightened up in the wake of the notorious Maxwell affair in order to protect members from unscrupulous company proprietors. You should take expert advice if you are thinking of developing your own scheme. It is not always necessary for you to run it yourself, though, as many insurance companies will manage the funds for you and administer the whole scheme.

A benefit such as an occupational pension scheme may be of limited value to employees whose current financial concerns are more pressing.

15.5 Loans

You can lend your employees money at preferential rates of interest, or even interest free, for any purpose from house purchase to the cost of an annual season ticket for travelling to work. The cash can be made available either directly by the company or by arrangement with a finance house.

Although the employee may have to pay tax on the difference between your rate of interest and the market rate, it may still be of benefit to him because, in a world where interest rates tend to fluctuate from month to month, the Inland Revenue may impute a rate of interest lower than the actual market rate. Such loans will also be worth having, from the employee's point of view, if he would be unlikely to have been able to raise the money anywhere else.

A loans system may be of value to you as an employer:

(*a*) as an aid to employee retention;
(*b*) as a means of alleviating financial worry which might otherwise detract from job performance.

A loans policy needs to be carefully thought out, with adequate safeguards for the company, so that you do not end up making donations to lost causes or adding to the financial worries of the individual. In some instances, though, you may be able to help your employees purchase desired items at reduced rates, thereby avoiding the necessity for a loan.

15.6 Discounts, Preferential Rates and Allowances

(a) Discounts and Preferential Rates

In retailing, staff discount is an important benefit. It allows employees to purchase items of merchandise from their employers at reduced rates and is an expected addition to pay. In manufacturing industry, items produced by the company, be they chocolates or motor cars, can be offered to employees at preferential rates. In the retail travel industry, staff are encouraged, not just by their own employers but also by airlines, hoteliers and tour operators, to accept travel and accommodation either free or at preferential rates.

These are just three of the forms that this kind of benefit can take. Normally they do not involve the employer in cash outlay, but he does operate at a reduced profit margin on items sold to employees and the income tax position requires careful attention. There are three main reasons why employers feel that these are appropriate benefits to offer.

(i) Employees will, it is thought, feel an increased sense of identification with the company if they have used its products.

(ii) Your employees will give you a certain amount of free publicity if they are seen to be using your products themselves. They may also, as in the travel industry, be more effective in their jobs, having sampled the products they are selling.

(iii) In certain sectors this sort of benefit is expected as a right and is felt by employees to be as much a part of their job as their pay or working conditions. If you are operating in an industry where such practice is the norm, it will be difficult to compensate for the lack of the anticipated benefits.

(b) Allowances

Allowances fall into two broad categories.

(i) **Recompense for outlay or inconvenience.** Travelling allowances, dual residence allowances, shift allowances and allowances to cover tools and clothing necessary for the job fall into this category. The extent and generosity of the allowances will tend to depend both on what the company can afford and on the overall image of itself that it wishes to project. In some instances, money allocated to clothing allowances might be more tax efficient and effective if devoted to providing an appropriate company uniform.

In paying rail travel allowances some companies feel that members of management should travel first class, while other employees travel standard class on company business. In practice, it might be more sensible to look at the purpose of the journey, the distance travelled and the importance of arriving reasonably fresh, rather than using the traveller's position in the organisation hierarchy as the sole criterion. In addition, particularly in the case of shift or unsocial hours allowances, the premium must be viewed in relation to basic pay, to establish the true rewards of the job, in comparison with others in the organisation, to ensure recompense for inconvenience is adequate.

(ii) **Special allowances.** These may take the form of a subsidy for housing purposes, particularly if the job-holder is working abroad, or for education, either of the employee or of his children. The borderline between this type of allowance and our first group may tend to become blurred, especially where, as in the case of business clothing for example, it is difficult to establish how much outlay the employee is really involved in. The acid test is probably the way in which the employee views the allowance. Does he see it as rightful reimbursement or as a benefit which enhances his overall remuneration from the company?

This category of benefit is again broadly concerned with monetary rewards. There are, however, arguments for paying benefits in kind, rather than in cash.

15.7 Payments in Kind

We have discussed the possibility of making bonus payments in the form of shares rather than cash. There are many other alternatives to monetary reward, which can be used for their incentive value, as a mark of status and seniority, or as a means of helping employees to be more effective in their jobs. For whatever purpose they are primarily designed, payments in kind are even more likely to prove socially divisive than some of the other benefits we have been discussing. Any moves that you are making towards single status for all employees will need to take full account of the impact of the differences in status which these benefits imply.

(a) Company Cars

Almost all British companies provide cars for some of their executives. The proportion is higher than anywhere else in Europe. Company cars fall into two categories, both of which may broadly be regarded as benefits.

(i) Cars for business use. Sales representatives, for instance, are able to deal with more customers and carry more samples if they are provided with their own transport. They can also provide peripatetic publicity if you have your company name or logo painted on the side of the car or van. But if the sales person is allowed to use the vehicle for his own private mileage as well as on company business, he may count this as a very real benefit. It saves him the capital outlay and depreciation, service costs, road tax and insurance on a car of his own, and even if he is taxed on the benefit he will still normally find it a good deal less expensive than owning his own car. The company, too, can claim a proportion of the cost of the car against its tax bill, although cars which are used for private as well as business mileage may tend to deteriorate more quickly.

(ii) Cars as part of total remuneration. The chairman's Rolls Royce may or may not be designed purely with a view to helping him to be more effective in his job. Differential grades of car, from the humble saloon, through the sports car ranges, to the executive models, can be used to provide employees not only with a means of transport, but also with status and prestige. A few companies regard executive cars as so much a part of total remuneration that they will give them even to those executives who cannot drive. Some now provide more than one vehicle per executive. The extent to which the employee is taxed on the benefit will depend upon the amount of business mileage for which the car is used.

(b) Health Benefits

It is in the interests of both employer and employees that the latter are kept in good health. If they are not, they may be unfit to work or to work to their full potential. In addition, some health benefits are bestowed by companies according to status, presumably as a reflection of the individual's importance to the business. This, in turn, can bring health benefits into the total remuneration package expected by senior personnel. They take three forms.

(i) Free or reduced-rate membership of a private medical insurance scheme can be provided by the employer. This entitles the employee, and possibly his family, to receive medical attention privately, rather than under the National Health Service. It can mean faster treatment, in a private room, where an executive might be able to carry on some of his business activities from his hospital bed – something which would be impossible in a public ward. It may also enable the company or the employee to specify the timing of non-urgent treatment, thereby avoiding peak business periods. A further possible benefit may come from the peace of mind it provides.

We have already considered the tax situation in relation to medical insurance and established that, where such insurance is required, it is usually less expensive for the employer, rather than the employee, to purchase membership.

The main argument against medical insurance is that of social divisiveness. The expense may make it impossible to include all employees, but shop-floor workers are no more immune to pain and sickness than executives.

(ii) Regular medical checks can be arranged. Although for some jobs – for example, those involving contact with radioactive substances – there is a legal requirement for employees to receive medical supervision, for others regular checks may be an additional method of adding to peace of mind and of catching minor health problems before they develop into major ones.

(iii) A visit to a health farm is a benefit now being arranged by some companies for their senior executives. The executive spends a week or so resting and receiving revitalising treatment at an establishment, while the employer picks up a bill amounting to several thousand pounds. Although the companies concerned would claim that this is an important means of ensuring executive effectiveness, those lower down in the hierarchy may well view it as a divisive perk.

(c) Household Expense Items

Other benefits in kind can be provided through leasing arrangements, whereby you lease furniture, cars and other items for a fixed period and give your employees the use of them. At the end of the period the employee can purchase the item at a nominal rate, and may reduce his tax liability.

This kind of benefit needs to be explored carefully in relation to the tax implications, prevailing pay policy and executive preferences, if it is to be a useful part of total remuneration.

(d) Business Expense Accounts

It is debatable whether these should be classified as allowances, to reimburse the employee for expenses incurred on company business, or whether they really do amount to payments in kind. The employer may give the employee licence to use them as either, but how they are perceived by employees (and the tax inspector) will be the real test. The lavish business lunch with important clients may or may not be the employee's preference.

But expense accounts can be used to enhance both status and material rewards. The executive may be allowed to charge entertaining, for purposes in addition to that of purely business, to his account. He may be given a credit card with which to settle his bills, and the company may pay the credit card account without querying individual items. Some companies go so far as to instruct their executives to use their credit cards to draw cash from a bank at intervals, thereby putting money directly into their pockets. Almost half the companies participating in a recent survey of benefits made credit cards available to at least some of their employees, although many of them did restrict their use solely to company business expenses. Here again, though, the credit card and the expense account can degenerate into symbols of executive superiority if their use and their part in total remuneration are not thought out.

(e) Business and Educational Trips
Although these are not in themselves classifiable as benefits, the way in which some companies use them brings them into this category. A business trip can be turned into a benefit by allowing an executive to be accompanied by his or her spouse and scheduling plenty of time for relaxation and sightseeing.

(f) Voucher Schemes
These can be used for incentive purposes. The employee who achieves the highest sales figures or the best timekeeping record receives holiday vouchers or trading stamps, which he can spend as he wishes. They provide an alternative to a straight cash bonus and may add a special element. Those concerned with the marketing of such schemes claim that the chance to win a romantic holiday for two has higher incentive value than the cash equivalent, even though the winner may eventually settle for the money.

The part that any or all of the payments in kind that we have been discussing can play in total remuneration is a matter for individual company decision – in consultation with the Inland Revenue. Our final group of benefits is again non-monetary in nature, but perhaps of more universal application.

15.8 Time Off
To many employees time off is a highly prized benefit. Any opportunity to devote less time to their jobs, for the same reward, will be welcomed. For the employer it provides a means of reducing stress levels (see Unit 16.8) and improving the health, alertness and commitment of their employees – and increased costs.

Time off comes in a number of guises.

(a) Holiday Entitlements
During the twentieth century trade unions have worked for steadily increased entitlements. A common pattern now prevailing is for long-serving employees and more senior grades to receive between five and six weeks' holiday, with pay, and for other grades to have four to five weeks plus statutory holidays.

These holidays may have to be taken at prescribed periods, to coincide with the annual shutdown of the plant. Alternatively, there may be a degree of flexibility for the employee to negotiate his leave at a mutually convenient time. If this is the case, you will need to consider your policy on allocating time. Will it be done on a first come, first served basis, or should more senior employees be given priority? Whatever you decide, make sure all employees are aware of the policy and understand their entitlement and the procedure to be followed.

When considering the benefit to employees of granting additional holiday entitlement, you should weigh the advantages in terms of a more contented and refreshed workforce against the disruption and costs that you will incur. If each employee receives twenty-five days' paid leave each year, this will add 9.6 per cent per annum to your payroll costs. Each additional week will cost almost 2 per cent. Increasing holiday entitlements may also increase pressure for holiday bonuses, so that employees can afford to take a break.

(b) Sabbatical Leave
In higher education members of staff may qualify for a term, or even a year, off with pay every five years or so. This is usually granted for an express purpose, such as completing research or writing a book. It thus enables people to devote their full attention to something which the institution recognises as being of value, without the distraction of normal duties.

'When can I take my sabbatical?'

This practice is now being extended into industry and commerce, and being modified in the process. Senior executives may be allowed a three- or six-month break every few years, to rest and recuperate. (Although staff at all levels may be allowed to carry forward unused holiday entitlement from one year to the next and take a period of extended leave, perhaps to visit relatives in other parts of the world, this cannot properly be classified as a sabbatical.) It has been suggested that a year's sabbatical for longer-serving employees can help to reduce unemployment.

(c) Flexible Working Hours

Since its introduction to the UK in 1971, well over half a million employees have benefited from flexible working hours (FWH) or flexitime. Although there are several variations, the basic idea is that employees are permitted to decide for themselves what time they arrive for work in the morning and what time they leave in the evening. Provided that they are in attendance during core time, perhaps between 11 a.m. and 4 p.m., and provided that they work a specified number of hours during an accounting period of, say, one month, it is left to employees to determine their own daily working hours. If they work more or less than the required hours in the accounting period, some schemes allow them to carry over a credit or debit into the next accounting period. Some systems limit this to five or ten hours. Some also allow credits to be cleared, by prior arrangement, during core time, so that employees can take an extra day or half-day leave. For other systems, core time is sacrosanct.

Flexible working presupposes that you have some method of keeping track of people's attendance. This may be monitored manually but there is a growing industry for the manufacture of time recording equipment which enables employees to record their own hours. The time recording equipment most often used consists of small units which can be placed within the department, rather than in a daunting battery at the works entrance in the manner of the 'clocking-in' clock. Each employee has a personal coded key, which he slots in when he starts work and removes when he finishes. The units do not record actual times of arrival and departure, just number of time units worked.

So far, FWH has been used mainly among clerical and technical staff, in organisations such as the Civil Service, but its use among shop-floor workers is increasing. Although FWH will not reduce the total number of hours worked by employees, it does have several advantages as an employee benefit.

(i) It gives greater responsibility to employees to regulate their own times of attendance. It is therefore compatible with an open, participative, single-status approach.

(ii) It provides time for employees to attend to their personal business – visits to solicitors, dentists and so on – without disrupting their work.

(iii) It effectively abolishes bad timekeeping, if properly adhered to. Employees who are delayed on their way to work will not be expected until they arrive.

(iv) It allows employees to travel outside rush hours, whether before or after them. Particularly in large cities, this reduces the strain on employees, possibly lessens their journey time and incidentally reduces pressure on the roads and public transport system.

(v) It allows employees to control the pattern of their own lives, gearing their working arrangements round taking the children to school or getting home in time to dig the garden or cook a meal.

This seems quite an impressive list of advantages. In a survey among employers who had adopted FWH, most claimed even more specific benefits to the company. They believed that one-day absenteeism and labour turnover had been cut, recruitment and retention had been facilitated and the general industrial relations climate had been improved.

The only real difficulty lies in extending the system to employees whose jobs are regulated by the operating process or customer demands. You cannot run an assembly line, where one task depends on the completion of others further up the line, if half your operatives won't turn up until half-way through the shift. This does not entirely rule out FWH, if agreement can be reached in advance as to who will be in attendance to cover specific periods, but it does complicate the issue.

(d) The Shorter Working Week

Like holiday entitlements, the move towards an increase in leisure through a reduction in the working week has continued throughout this century. A thirty-nine-hour week is at present the norm for wage-earners, while salaried staff are more commonly contracted to work thirty-seven and a half or thirty-five hours per week. The pressure continues for a general reduction to thirty-five hours, without loss of financial reward. Many employers are opposed to the idea, as they foresee an increase in labour costs, without a corresponding increase in output.

One alternative, which gives greater flexibility to both parties, is the concept of **annual hours**. A total number of hours to be worked is agreed, for a year at a time. If the employee is needed for, say, forty-five hours per week for several weeks, he is not paid overtime. But when the workload is lighter he will enjoy paid time off. Such arrangements are particularly helpful where workloads fluctuate at different times of the year.

(e) Maternity Leave

Under the Trade Union Reform and Employment Rights Act **all** pregnant employees are entitled to fourteen weeks' basic maternity leave to give birth, starting in the eleventh week before the expected date of confinement. Those with more than two years' service can also take up to twenty-nine weeks' extended maternity leave from the date of the birth, making a maximum total of forty weeks – eleven before the birth and twenty-nine after – and more if they are sick when due to return.

The employee should notify her employer of her intention to take maternity leave. This should be done at least twenty-one days before the start of the basic leave period. Those eligible for extended leave must also declare their intention to return to work and notify their employer, in writing, at least three weeks before the date on which they intend to return. The employer must pay statutory maternity pay (see Unit 14.7) but can, of course, be more generous.

(f) Career Break Schemes
Unpaid absence from work for up to five years is allowed by some employers as part of a 'family-friendly' policy. Women who do not wish to return at the end of their maternity leave may exercise this option at a later date, returning to a job of equivalent status and conditions. In the meantime, they are kept in touch, – perhaps by attending training courses, receiving company information and maybe doing a few weeks' work each year.

(g) Sick Leave
Traditionally, salaried staff benefited from **occupational** sick pay, while wage-earners were thrown upon the state benefits system prior to the introduction of SSP (see Unit 14.7). In this field, too, more and more companies are now moving towards an extension of occupational sick pay entitlement to include all levels in the organisation.

Occupational sick pay entitlement may be formulated according to status and length of service. Full pay for the first six months and half pay for the next six months are common provisions for long-serving employees in the middle grades. Normally, payment is reduced by the amount which the employee receives in statutory sick pay. Absences of more than seven days should be accounted for by a doctor's statement.

Where a formal entitlement exists, there may be a temptation for employees to take one- and two-day periods of sick leave, even when they are not ill, because they see it as an entitlement. If the system is operated at management's discretion, on the other hand, this can lead to allegations of unfairness and is administratively more difficult, as a management decision must be made in each case.

Some three hundred million working days are lost each year in Britain through individual absence. This exceeds the number of days lost through strikes by a factor of several hundred.

(h) Study Leave
Some companies allow paid time off to those who are attending job-related courses not actually arranged by the company. This can take the form of half-day release for a period, or additional leave for field trips, revision or to sit examinations. Some companies also refund tuition costs, but occasionally this is made conditional upon examination success.

(i) Community Service Leave
This is a means of releasing employees to enable them to help others. A number of schemes have been launched in recent years, with a view to

providing particular expertise or just a pair of hands. ICI and IBM are among the large companies who have become involved in this sort of activity. You might consider releasing members of your accountancy staff to help with the books of a local charity, for instance. Or you could give paid time off to a member of your staff to take a party of handicapped children away on holiday. This aspect of social responsibility is something that we will be considering further in Unit 16.

(j) Miscellaneous Time Off
In Unit 14 we discussed the legal provisions regarding time off for trade union activities, maternity leave, to seek alternative employment in the case of redundancy and for ante-natal care, guarantee pay and pay in the event of medical suspension. In all of these areas, you are at liberty to exceed the minimum periods and amounts specified in the Act or the Code of Practice which relates to it. In addition, you may like to consider the possibility of giving time off for other reasons.

(i) **Compassionate leave** may be granted in the event of a family bereavement or severe domestic problems. This is not normally a prescribed entitlement, but may be granted at management's discretion, depending upon circumstances.

(ii) **Special leave** can be given to an employee who is getting married, either for the wedding day itself or for a few days immediately before and after it as well. Other special events, like christenings, could also qualify, as might a special leave period for someone who had been chosen to represent the county in a sporting activity.

(iii) **Paternity leave**, although not yet a statutory entitlement in the same way as maternity leave, is granted by some companies to permit a man to take time off when his wife has a baby. The length of time varies, but is usually counted in days rather than the months accorded for maternity leave.

(iv) **Shopping days**, although not common in the UK, are provided to employees in other parts of the world to enable them to keep abreast of their household responsibilities.

(v) **Casual leave**, which encompasses any other reason, is also an entitlement more common outside the UK, although some public sector organisations do allow additional days for the conduct of personal business.

While not exhaustive, the range of benefits, in cash and in kind, which we have discussed will serve to indicate that basic pay may only be the starting point in constructing a remuneration package. But over and above the remunerative devices we have considered in the last two units, there is another area in which the employer bestows benefits on his employees. This is employee welfare. But here, as we shall see, the motivation of the parties is rather different. Welfare provisions are made by an employer for his employees, not as part of the perennial wage–work bargain, but as one human being to another.

Questions

1. What considerations should an organisation bear in mind when designing an employee benefits package? Give reasons for your answer.
2. Examine the range of benefits currently applied in your own organisation. What purpose do they serve for (*a*) the organisation; (*b*) the recipients?
3. Discuss the implications of a rapid growth in (*a*) profit sharing; (*b*) share ownership schemes.

UNIT 16

Employee Welfare

16.1 Introduction

Apart from basic attention to the well-being of employees, welfare can also be taken to mean concern for the whole quality of working life. As such, it can encompass everything from job-enrichment programmes to flexible working hours, and from ergonomics to industrial democracy. We have discussed these aspects in other units and pointed out their contribution to employee motivation or increased effectiveness. Here we will concentrate on the more traditional manifestations of employer concern for employee well-being: eating and recreational facilities, medical facilities, welfare visiting and counselling. In the final section of the unit we will look at the role that the state plays in employee welfare, through the institutions of the welfare state, and the provisions of health and safety legislation. But first we will consider the place of welfare in modern employment practice.

16.2 Welfare and the Employer

To many people the word 'welfare' is synonymous with paternalistic do-gooding. In the early twentieth century some employers (prompted perhaps by a desire to forestall the growth of the trade unions, perhaps by more altruistic motives) began to pay rather more attention to the physical comfort of their employees than would have been thinkable during the early years of the industrial revolution. They engaged the services of middle-class ladies to dispense tea and sympathy to employees with personal problems and to place flowers on the tables in the area set aside for employees to eat their sandwiches in. Even these small gestures were regarded by many as sapping the initiative of the workers, and the extent to which an employer needs to concern himself with the welfare of his employees is still a subject for debate.

If welfare is not universally accepted as a management obligation, as we saw in the case of occupational pension schemes, the twin forces of law and trade union pressure serve to draw many of the things which a paternalistic employer might once have done of his own volition into employee rights.

(a) The Case against Welfare
(i) The existence of the Welfare State absolves employers from responsibility for the welfare of their employees.

(ii) If employees want welfare provisions, they can negotiate for them as employee benefits.

(iii) Employees have private lives of their own and do not wish to discuss these with their employer or feel tied to the social facilities which he provides.

(iv) Many welfare provisions, like canteens and sports and social clubs, are very capital intensive. It is a waste of money to provide them for the handful of employees who may use them.

(v) Where welfare facilities are provided, they are taken for granted. Where they are not, they are seldom missed.

(b) The Case for Welfare

(i) The Welfare State (see Unit 16.9), although theoretically available to all, is in practice only available to those who can take the time to find their way round it and use it for the resolution of their problems. By no means are all your employees likely to be completely aware of what it can provide or how it can help them. They may also be reluctant to absent themselves from work in order to find out. While the counselling aspect of employee welfare is not a substitute for all the facilities that the state can provide, it can be an on-the-spot means of airing problems and receiving advice on how to approach the state system. (The Welfare State itself is, in any case, under considerable strain. National economic considerations provide an argument for more welfare provisions to be made by the employer, to help relieve the cost burden on the state.)

(ii) Welfare provisions such as sports and social clubs increase the employee's involvement with the organisation. Playing in the company darts team can help the individual to identify more closely, if not with his employer, then at least with his fellow employees. This will be especially helpful if you employ people who may not have family or friends in the area, as in the case of off-shore oil exploration teams.

(iii) Dealing with problems before they become crises, and enhancing people's feeling of belonging, may help them to operate at optimum effectiveness. It will not make them more productive, but it will help to prevent them becoming less productive.

(iv) The basic dignity of human labour deserves recognition. Welfare facilities enable employees to feel that they are regarded as human beings, not just numbers on a clock card.

The deciding factors in this debate must be the extent to which you feel that employment is an interpersonal relationship, rather than a business contract, and the extent to which you consider that the general needs of your employees are met through the state and other agencies external to your organisation. (In some countries, for example Zambia, where the welfare state is less fully developed than in the UK, companies accept responsibility for employee housing, education, community activities and family medical care, as well as recreational facilities and other features more similar to the British concept of employee welfare.)

16.3 Eating and Recreational Facilities

You can provide food for your employees during working hours and/or facilities which employees can use during their leisure time.

(a) Canteens

A midday meal and other refreshments provided free or at a nominal charge to the employee can benefit both employer and employee in a number of ways.

(i) You can deduct the capital and running costs of the canteen as a business expense for tax purposes.

(ii) Employees can be given a shorter lunch break.

(iii) You are less likely to lose employees to local hostelries over the lunch break, with consequent adverse effects on performance in the afternoon.

(iv) Employees save money, not only because of any subsidy you provide towards the cost of a meal, but also because the additional cost of meals purchased outside would have to be met out of taxed income. A free meal to the value of one pound per day, for example, is equivalent to a pay rise of nearly £400 per annum for someone who pays tax at standard rate.

(v) A workforce which is properly fed is likely to be more effective and less prone to accidents and ill health than one which is left to fend for itself. If you are sited on a trading estate, some distance from shops and cafés, employees may not feel inclined to go out and search for food in inclement weather.

Clearly many of these advantages depend on the quality of food provided and the cost to employees. Marks & Spencer is among the leading employers who believe that high-quality meals at nominal prices are something to which employees are entitled during working hours. It encourages firms which supply its merchandise to follow its example.

On the debit side, we must weigh the costs of installing and maintaining a canteen. Cooking utensils, labour, crockery and food can average out at the equivalent of one month's extra pay for every employee, every year. On top of this, there is the opportunity cost of the space set aside for cooking and eating, which might otherwise have been devoted to production or other mainstream activities. You will also find yourself having to recruit and retain catering staff. This can create difficulties if you are not used to dealing with that particular section of the labour market. (You can circumvent this by contracting out the running of the canteen to a firm of specialist caterers, who will provide a full catering service, staffed by their own employees, on your premises.)

If you do offer eating facilities, you should also think carefully about the arguments for and against providing different eating areas for different categories of employee. The existence of separate dining rooms for directors, middle management and junior management, and of a staff restaurant and works canteen, all in the same building, is not unknown. It may be justified to a limited extent where confidential information is likely to be discussed at mealtimes, though we may query whether this is an aid to digestion. But it is a clear indication of what we may call company social stratification. In these days of increasing egalitarianism and participation, such rigid demarcation seems somewhat anachronistic.

(b) Recreational Facilities
In the years between the two world wars, a number of large employers developed extensive sports facilities for their employees. At that time, with far less competition from the mass media or public entertainment, and with more restricted travel-to-work patterns prescribing the areas in which employees lived, these provided a welcome focal point for employees to gather for sport and social activities.

Now, however, their value is less apparent, and some are rarely used. The large amounts of capital and space that they tie up are not always seen to be offset by increased employee involvement. But the provision of recreational facilities need not be so costly. A table-tennis table erected in the staff canteen or a dartboard in the corner of a rest area may be as much appreciated and more used than more elaborate facilities.

Where a sports and social club is already in existence, you might like to consider extending its membership to include other members of the local community, apart from just your employees. This should at least ensure that the premises are used, and at best will enhance your reputation as an employer. Alternatively, you might be able to use it for company conferences and training purposes.

16.4 Medical Facilities

In contrast with the position elsewhere in Europe, there is no general legal requirement for British employers to engage the services of professional medical staff. There is, though, under the Health and Safety (First Aid) Regulations 1981, an obligation on every employer to make adequate first-aid provision for employees. This means providing properly equipped first-aid boxes and travelling kits, and appointing at least one trained first aider for every fifty employees. Employees must be kept informed of the first-aid arrangements which affect them. You must keep records of all first-aid cases treated.

At present about a third of the employees in this country are covered by both medical and nursing facilities, but they are concentrated in only 2.5 per cent of companies. Another third of the workforce are covered only by first aiders.

The benefits of providing medical facilities at the workplace are:

(*a*) a healthy workforce, who can resolve minor health problems at work, with only minimum loss of productive time;
(*b*) on-the-spot treatment for industrial injuries, which may prevent them developing into worse problems;

'*I put that notice up. As company doctor
I consider this lot need more exercise.*'

(*c*) greater awareness of potential hazards in the workplace. The National Institute of Industrial Psychology reported some years ago that 75 per cent of accidents are likely to be notified to the management if there is a surgery to which they can be reported. If there is no surgery, the reporting rate may be as low as 5 per cent;

(*d*) specific medical action can save large amounts of absence. The Post Office once calculated that providing 'flu' vaccination for its employees saved it 120,000 working days which would otherwise have been lost through influenza.

Against all this must be weighed the cost of providing the services of professional medical staff, and the facilities and equipment that they will need. The borderlines between the jurisdiction of the company doctor and the general practitioner may also create friction, which can only be resolved by a careful definition of the responsibilities of the former.

16.5   Welfare Visiting

There are two main sets of circumstances in which you may wish to take your welfare activities outside the workplace.

(a) Sick Visiting

If your employees fall sick, you may feel it appropriate to show your concern by sending someone to visit them at home or in hospital. It is generally better that the visitor is already known to the employee, preferably his immediate boss.

Although the purpose of such visiting is to show people that you wish them well, this may be misinterpreted. Employees may suspect that they are being checked up on, to make sure they really are ill. If you are going to visit them it is therefore advisable to make the purpose of your visit unmistakably clear, in your manner as well as your words. And for every employee who thinks you are 'snooping', there will be another who is grateful for your company and interest.

(b) Funeral Attendance

If an employee dies, attendance at his funeral will at least show respect. Again the immediate boss is the most appropriate person, but, particularly for long-serving employees, a more senior member of management should also represent the company.

16.6 Employee Counselling

If an employee has domestic or job-related problems, the opportunity to discuss them with someone sympathetic may be all that is required to help him see how they can be resolved. If this is indeed the case, it is worth developing a sympathetic ear, the patience to listen and the tact to remain silent, while the sufferer diagnoses his own problem and the solution to it.

Unfortunately not all problems fall into this category, and it is important to know where to draw the line. There are two possibilities.

(*a*) If the problem is job-related, the skills of the coach are more appropriate than those of the counsellor. These were discussed in Unit 9.4.

(*b*) If the problem is a personal one, your best course of action may be to direct the employee towards an appropriate external service. Such services might be a solicitor, doctor, marriage guidance counsellor, the Department of Social Security or the local housing department. It is not normally advisable to attempt to dabble in any of these areas of expertise yourself: you could do more harm than good. If you have difficulty in working out where to send the employee for help, the Citizens Advice Bureau is a good starting point. It will, in any case, be considerably easier for you, who are not directly affected by the problem, to seek out someone who can help and put your employee in touch with them.

As with the other forms of welfare that we have mentioned, the early resolution of problems may help to prevent more serious difficulties developing. It can also help to build your relationship with your employees into one where trust and mutual concern have a rightful place.

16.7 Aid to Disadvantaged Groups

Although all employees have equal rights to receive or not to receive welfare from their employers, there are several sections of the population who have special needs. The extent to which you respond to these needs is not, in most cases, the subject of legislation. It is more a matter of individual conscience

which can be translated into company policy, usually to the ultimate benefit
of both company and employees.

(a) Disabled People

As we saw in Unit 3, the law regarding the employment of registered disabled
persons is under review. There are two main questions for the employer.

(i) How can you take positive action? If you have a range of jobs which
would be within the capabilities of the physically or mentally handicapped,
can you adapt your premises, entrances, stairs and lavatories to accommodate
them and provide them with a worthwhile occupation? Government grants
are available to help meet costs and the evidence is that such employees, properly placed, are hardworking, loyal and, depending upon the nature of their
disabilities, less likely to be distracted from their work than their able-bodied
colleagues.

(ii) How can you accommodate any of your current employees who become
disabled? Such accommodation might include physical adjustment of the
working environment, again with the help of a government grant, a change
in working hours or location, or retraining for another job. One particular
group which may need special thought are the victims of stress diseases. Few
companies so far make provision for this group, but the range of nervous
disorders and their causes and symptoms is wide, and there is no reason why
many sufferers should not be usefully retained in suitable jobs.

Circumstances will vary from company to company. It would obviously be
wrong to expose disabled people to risks which might affect them more than
others. But to dispense with someone's services because he is now disabled
and therefore unable to fulfil his original contract with you is to add financial
and emotional worries, at a time when the individual is already experiencing
major problems – and could be illegal.

(b) The Long-term Unemployed and Unemployed School-leavers

People who have been unemployed for more than a few months or who have
never worked since leaving school may pose particular problems for
employers. Because of this, there is a tendency to avoid employing them,
thereby perpetuating their difficulties.

There are dangers that people in this category may:

(i) accept a job in desperation and leave it as soon as something better
turns up;
(ii) not be particularly well adjusted to the discipline required, in relation
to things like timekeeping and other laid-down procedures.

Again, a policy decision to give preference to people in this group, where
possible, is required. Government subsidies and employment schemes may
provide an added inducement from time to time, but permanent employment
is only likely to be successful if special care is taken over selection and induc-

tion, to ensure that such people do not suffer further damage to their morale by being dismissed at the end of a trial period.

(c) Immigrants with Language Difficulties
We discussed the implications of the Race Relations Act in Units 3 and 7. The employment of recent immigrants does create particular needs, which can be met through training. The language barrier is a major stumbling block to integration, and can breed distrust and sometimes incite ridicule from colleagues. The provision of language training can help to remove this barrier and improve overall effectiveness through better communications. Cultural differences may still remain, and some would argue rightly so. But once you and your employees can understand each other, you are more likely to come to respect each other's points of view.

(d) Ex-offenders
People who have past convictions which are not 'spent' within the meaning of the Rehabilitation of Offenders Act 1974 often experience difficulty in finding employment. The probation and prison after-care services will help, but it is getting and keeping the first job which is the most difficult. On top of the adjustment problems that can affect people who have not worked for a living for some time, many employers are reluctant to consider employing people with a prison record. Sweeping generalisations are the ex-offenders' worst enemy. Will it really be tempting providence to employ an embezzler in a job where he has no access to money? Individual circumstances certainly merit careful consideration.

(e) Alcoholics, drug abusers and those who are HIV-positive
If one of your employees becomes an alcoholic or a drug abuser, or if someone with one of these problems seeks employment with you, your first reaction may be to dismiss him as unsuitable. Employees with a drink or drugs problem are notoriously unreliable: they can be a danger to themselves and others, and their effectiveness is generally reduced. Aids is still so little understood that many employees react negatively to the prospect of working alongside someone who has or may develop the disease.

But dismissal is not the only answer, any more than is well-intentioned chastisement. Indeed, as we shall see in Unit 21, you will need to go about it very carefully if you do decide to dismiss on these grounds. You can best help by persuading the employee concerned to take expert advice and pursue a course of treatment. Alcoholism and drug addiction are diseases and should be treated as such. The HIV virus may or may not develop into full-blown Aids. It may be helpful to draft a policy for dealing with each of these problems to protect the interests of all concerned.

(f) Employees about to Retire
Those who are about to retire and are therefore on the verge of acquiring considerably more leisure than they have been accustomed to may need help

in adjusting to this change. Many companies provide pre-retirement courses to assist employees to come to terms with and enjoy life after work. These may be staffed by in-house trainers, or it may be more cost-effective to sub-contract the work to a specialist provider such as Hogg Robinson Financial Services or use the open courses run by the Pre-Retirement Association. Advice on the use of leisure, financial matters and coping with bereavement are all appropriate items for inclusion.

Further help may be given by phasing out employment, reducing hours or days worked, so that the break will not be so abrupt. Alternatively, employees with particular expertise may be retained on a consultancy basis after retirement. This enables the organisation to continue to benefit from the employees' valuable experience, while the individuals concerned will avoid the shock that a complete break might induce. Post-retirement social activities can also help you to retain links with ex-employees.

(g) Mothers of Young Children

In addition to providing maternity leave and perhaps a career break scheme, there are other ways in which you can help. Many women are prevented from returning to work by the lack of anyone suitable to look after their children. If you have invested time and money in training them, or if you might find valuable new recruits from among this group, there is much to be said for trying to accommodate their needs. Shorter working hours and more flexible working arrangements are two possibilities. The establishment of a crèche system, where mothers can bring their young children to spend the day under trained supervision, is another possible line of approach. The latter is unlikely to be a viable proposition unless you have a number of mothers in this category working for you or can join forces with other local employers.

16.8 Stress Management

Job insecurity, understaffing, rapidly changing technology and working practices, ever-increasing management expectations and a host of other factors all conspire to make working a pretty stressful activity. Add to that the frustrations of commuting, even over relatively short distances, by road or rail. Mix in the divorce rate, the number of single-parent families and elderly dependants, negative equity and interest rate fluctuations. Throw in some workplace bullying and sexual harassment and it is not surprising that stress and stress-related illness are major problems for employer and employee alike.

Careful job design, employee empowerment and involvement in decision making, effective communications, adequate time off, well thought-through personnel policies and the provision of the sort of services discussed in this unit can go some way to help. But the employer who really wants to reduce stress levels will ensure that stress awareness counselling and programmes to help manage stress are available to all employees.

Early indications of stress include loss of appetite, fatigue, sleeplessness and irritability. By learning to recognise and deal with the causes of these, problems can be remedied before they develop further. Issues such as diet, lack of exercise, smoking or alcohol may need to be tackled.

Some Health Authorities have specialist units to provide information and education in the workplace – ranging from simple leaflets to exhibition panels to briefing sessions and courses. Offered free or at nominal cost these are a good way of sensitising people to the issues. You can go further, by offering training in relaxation techniques, dietary advice or health and fitness programmes to help employees increase their stress tolerance.

It is worth remembering, though, that the most insidious stress factors often come in human form. Harassment and bullying are not always easy to spot, especially as the victims are often too embarrassed to complain. Sexual harassment can include any conduct of a sexual nature which affects the dignity of men and women at work. It covers a range of things from explicit propositioning or physical contact to suggestive remarks. Make sure all your employees know what to do if it happens to them (see Unit 19.6).

Management style can be a major cause of stress. Training managers to coach, rather than to dictate, won't resolve the problems overnight. But by letting your people take more control of their own decisions and actions, you could be making a major contribution to their mental and physical well-being.

Not every heart attack or nervous breakdown your employees suffer will be your fault. But subjecting people to undue stress or failing to take appropriate steps to reduce its impact not only reduces effectiveness but may also lead to claims for compensation from those who suffer.

The first case of this type in the UK was *Walker* v. *Northumberland County Council* 1994, in which Mr Walker's employer was held liable for failing to provide a safe system of work for him after his first nervous breakdown. Promised assistance to help him cope with the pressure of his work did not materialise and he suffered a second breakdown as a result.

16.9   The State and Welfare

(a) Welfare Legislation
We have described welfare as something which is not part of the wage–work bargain and implied that it is a voluntary area. Although this is largely true, the Walker case may prove not to be an isolated example. There are, in any case, some statutory welfare requirements which most employers must observe. These include the provision of:

(i) hot and cold washing facilities, soap and towels;

(ii) sanitary accommodation: at least one lavatory for every twenty-five women and one for every twenty-five men;

(iii) drinking water;

(iv) accommodation for clothing not worn during working hours;

(v) sitting facilities, where workers can sit down without detriment to their work;

(vi) first-aid boxes or cupboards readily accessible to employees, the contents of which are prescribed (in addition, ambulance rooms and ambulances may be required for certain industrial processes, including chemicals, blast furnaces, sawmills and shipbuilding);

(vii) extractors to remove dust or fumes, where these are present in the atmosphere.

In addition, the Factories Act 1961 and the Offices, Shops and Railway Premises Act 1963, which originally laid down these standards, also stipulated standards of cleanliness, heating, lighting and ventilation, and working space. These are now incorporated in the Health and Safety Commission Approved Code of Practice (ACOP). Temperatures should be no less than 60.8°F (16°C) after the first hour of work and a comfortable temperature must be maintained – according to the Health & Safety Welfare Regulations 1992. In general there should be eleven cubic metres of space for each office employee.

Further developments in the legislative framework are likely in future, as a range of directives, recommendations and communications follows the implementation of the European Social Charter. These will cover issues ranging from social security for migrant workers to the establishment of maximum working hours, and from the development of childcare facilities to the provision of satisfactory working conditions for those under eighteen. The specific requirements of current Health and Safety regulations are discussed in Unit 17.4.

(b) The Welfare State
The concept of the Welfare State is underpinned by a desire to assist those suffering hardship and to improve living standards generally. Job-seekers' allowances, Income Support and the state pension scheme, the National Health Service and the range of educational, social and housing services provided by local authorities are part and parcel of this effort. Advice and help for the homeless, people with domestic problems or financial worries and for the sick, as well as education and care for the elderly and the handicapped are available, if not on request, then at least to those who are judged to be deserving cases. It is the extent and ease of access to these services which leads employers to question the need for them to shoulder this sort of more general welfare responsibility. As we have seen, however, at least one valuable contribution the employer can still make is to help his employees to find their way through to the appropriate service, without getting too tangled up in the bureaucracy which inevitably surrounds state services of this kind.

(c) Societal Responsibility
The responsibility of an employer towards his employees has been described as a series of concentric circles.

(i) **The innermost circle** includes adherence to statutory regulations, in relation to health, safety, welfare and employment generally.

(ii) **The next circle** is concerned with the kind of involvement which we discussed in Units 16.3 to 16.8: the voluntary welfare approach. It can also include other aspects of enlightened employment, designed to improve the quality of working life, perhaps through more participation and empowerment. Employers who exercise this second circle responsibility are, in some ways, doing voluntarily today what the law will insist upon tomorrow.

(iii) **The third (outer) circle** represents societal responsibilities. This can include giving employees the kind of community service leave which we mentioned in Unit 15.8. It also includes providing company finance to help resolve local problems or company facilities to help the development of the community generally. By becoming involved – through the education system, local sports and social activities, the Training and Enterprise Council, voluntary bodies and the local authority – in the general life of the community, you can not only ensure for yourself a continuing supply of eager new recruits, but also feel that you are contributing to the long-term good of the community. But it will also mean acting in a responsible way towards that community, despite difficult internal circumstances. When you are considering the possibility of redundancies, for example, you will need to consider not only the effects on the individuals concerned, but also the effect on the community at large (see Unit 20).

The extent to which you feel that you can accept this sort of societal responsibility – this concern for the quality of life in general – will depend to some extent upon the way in which you perceive the overall objectives of your business. If you believe that work is not an end in itself, but only a means to an end, community involvement is one means of serving the end of an improved quality of life, without detriment to the achievement of your other business objectives. The Body Shop provides one high profile example of this philosopy.

One area of concern for employee well-being which is not open to debate is the employer's obligation to safeguard his employees and prevent them from falling prey to industrial injuries or diseases. It is to this area of health and safety at work that we now turn.

Questions

1. Do employers still have a general responsibility for the welfare of their employees? Give reasons for your answer.
2. What are the arguments for and against the provision of (*a*) canteen facilities; (*b*) medical facilities; (*c*) counselling facilities; for employees?
3. What do you understand by the term 'societal responsibility'? How could an organisation set about fulfilling its responsibilities in this direction?

UNIT 17

Health and Safety

17.1 Introduction

In 1993-4 in Great Britain 379 employees were killed in accidents at work, and nearly 29,000 suffered major injuries. In addition, at least 135,000 were injured sufficiently seriously to have to take at least three days off work. While in some respects the situation has improved over the years (there were 452 deaths in 1992-3) there are now ten times as many asbestos-related deaths as in 1981.

Those who are injured may never fully recover their health and strength. They and their families, and the families of those who die, can never be adequately compensated for this loss. So the humanitarian implications of accidents at work provide an irrefutable argument for attention to health and safety in the workplace. On top of this, the lost time and sick pay, compensation payments and medical treatment, replacement labour and 'hidden' costs add up to a formidable financial total: some estimates suggest that about one per cent of the UK's gross national product is absorbed in paying for accidents.

If these considerations were not enough to persuade us, we also have a legal obligation to ensure, so far as is reasonably practicable, the health, safety and welfare of people at work.

We will start by considering why accidents happen, and how they can be prevented. Then we will examine the legal situation in more detail. We will use the word 'accident' to mean any unplanned and uncontrolled event which results in damage, whether through injury or disease, to an employee (although much of our discussion can also apply to accidents to plant, equipment and other materials).

17.2 Why Accidents Happen

There are two levels at which we can examine the reasons for accidents.

(a) Physical Causation Factors

According to the Royal Society for the Prevention of Accidents, accidents most frequently happen when people are handling and lifting goods and materials, are working with machinery, fall (from heights or on the same level), are hit by falling objects, bump into or step on objects, are using hand tools or come into contact with works transport. The factors which contribute to such accidents are:

(i) Environmental factors. The building itself may be unsafe. Floors may not be level; there may be protruding surfaces, rickety steps or dangerous openings. The machinery may be unsafe or badly maintained; lifting-tackle, for instance, may break and deposit its burden unexpectedly. Bad lighting can contribute to falls and collisions, while poor ventilation may lead to diseases and explosions. Untidy workplaces, faulty electrical connections, faulty hand tools and fire hazards can all play their part in contributing to accidents and injuries at work.

(ii) Work process factors. The way in which the work has to be done (the design of the job) may also create hazards. The cleaning or maintenance of machinery while it is in use, the lack of suitable seating, the need to lift or carry heavy objects, and processes which involve contact with dangerous substances or moving parts provide examples. Machines which require the operator to be of a certain height or have a certain hand or arm span may also constitute a danger if they are not adapted to suit different operator capacities.

But can we really blame inanimate objects or our physical surroundings for the misfortunes which befall us? Perhaps in order to find out what really causes accidents, we need to look a little deeper.

(b) Underlying Causation Factors

One American assurance assessor, H. W. Heinrich, has put forward the theory that accidents and the injuries which result from them are caused by the sequence of factors shown in Fig. 17.1.

Our ancestry and upbringing make us what we are. The faults that we develop are character weaknesses, like recklessness, nervousness, excitability, greed, ignorance, and so on. And it is because of these that we commit unsafe acts or allow dangerous situations to arise. We may stand under a lifting block without thinking about the dangers. We may remove the guard from a machine, inspired by the thought of an extra few pounds through the PBR system at the end of the week. But even more important, we may be placed in a job which we are not competent or trained to do, without adequate supervision, because the management is too lazy or too preoccupied with profit, or has some other human fault which deters it from giving due thought to such matters. So inanimate objects are not a danger in themselves. They are only dangerous because we make them so.

If we follow this argument through to its logical conclusion, we will lay all the blame for industrial accidents on managerial attitudes. And, in many ways, this is justified. Management controls the selection and training of employees and decides which work processes will be used in what sort of an environment. If it does not take due care over all these aspects, it is failing to safeguard the health and safety of employees.

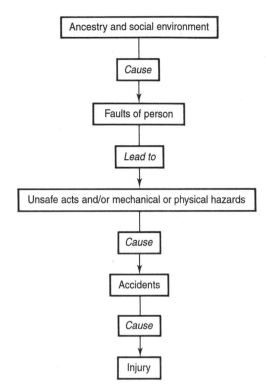

Fig. 17.1 The accident causation sequence

17.3   Preventing Accidents

We have identified two levels of accident causation and this may lead us to look for two levels of accident prevention. In fact, though, we are unlikely to rectify the physical causation factors if our underlying attitudes are wrong. The real key to accident prevention therefore lies in creating a climate of opinion, from top to bottom in the organisation, where the safe way of doing things is the right – indeed, the only – way to do them.

That this is not always the case at present is indicated by some research into attitudes towards wearing protective safety clothing. In the factories investigated, photographs of workers, fully attired in safety gear, were shown to both management and employees. The general tenor of the comments made by both was that the workers depicted in the photographs were slightly 'cissy' and not the kind of men that their management or employees held in high esteem.

So our first task is to change this sort of attitude.

(a) Creating Safety Consciousness

There are a number of techniques that can be used to try to persuade all levels, including management, that concern for safety makes sense. Few of them are likely to have much long-term effect, but they can be amalgamated quite effectively into a campaign, to produce a cumulative short-term effect.

(i) Posters. Visual reminders placed around the office or factory may serve to draw people's attention to the need to take care and wear safety clothes. They will, however, very soon become part of the furniture. It is doubtful whether employees will even see them after a few weeks, let alone register their message.

(ii) Films or videos. These have more specific impact than posters and can be more explicit and detailed in their message. But the fact that they must normally be shown away from the work environment may lessen their relevance. It may also be difficult to find one that depicts a set of circumstances to which your employees can readily relate.

(iii) Fear techniques. While both videos and posters can use shock tactics to frighten people into taking care, you can go further by showing people the actual consequences of accidents which have happened. These might include photographs of the scene immediately following an accident in their own workplace, a talk from someone who has actually suffered serious injury or a look at a collection of damaged tools and clothing, and pictures of those who have suffered injury. The immediate reaction to such tactics may be a resolve to take more care. In the longer term, people will forget.

(iv) Discipline. Laying down strict rules in relation to safe working practice and behaviour and punishing those who do not conform is regarded by some as the best way to teach people a lesson. In fact, there is evidence to show that, in the longer term, people's attitude to safety actually deteriorates where discipline is used. They become preoccupied, not with complying with the regulations, but with avoiding the detection of their non-compliance. If you do consider that discipline is necessary, you should adhere to the same procedure as for any other type of offence (see Unit 19). But you may gain more from a participative approach.

(v) Discussions. You may begin to get nearer to affecting the way people view the question of safety if you involve them in it, rather than bombarding them with propaganda about it. Discussions can be used to good effect in conjunction with other techniques, particularly videos. The emphasis should be on persuading individuals to air their own views and examine them critically.

(vi) Role play techniques. One of the more effective of the techniques we have listed so far, role play, can help to change attitudes towards safety, on a longer-term basis. The idea is to encourage one employee to think himself into the role of another. So you can arrange for an employee who is required to wear a safety harness to take the part of a supervisor and try to persuade another employee to wear one. In trying to convince his colleague, albeit in a training situation, he may well convince himself. The long-term effect of role play has been found to be greater than for any of the other techniques.

(vii) Coaching.   Individual or group coaching to raise awareness of hazards and danger points – and to enable employees to take responsibility for avoiding these – should produce the most long lasting change in behaviour.

Your aim must be to create the will to be safe. Only when this will to make safety a way of life is present can attacks on specific accident causation factors really succeed. Our next step is to analyse more closely the causes of the accidents which have happened in our own workplace, through a study of accident records and discussion with those involved. We can then move on to consider appropriate corrective action.

'I work in the office, so why should I need a safety helmet?'

(b) Making People Safe
Over and above a positive desire to be safe, individual workers must know how to operate safely.

(i) Newcomers.   All job training must revolve around the safe way of doing a job, not just the quickest or the easiest way.

(ii) Experienced workers. These people may have avoided serious accidents because they have become skilled in their bad habits. They need to be kept up to date, through regular coaching, formal training, briefing groups and other communication, with safe working practices. They must not be tempted to cast these safe practices aside by an incentive payment system which takes no account of safety standards.

(iii) Supervisors. First-line supervision forms a vital link in the safety chain. Supervisors must be trained to advise on safe working practice and to ensure that this is followed. They will also be involved in risk assessment (see Unit 17.4).

(iv) All employees. Everyone in the workplace needs to be made aware of the consequences of failing to adhere to laid-down safety procedures. These consequences include not only the danger of injury to themselves or others, but also the legal repercussions for themselves and the company if they are in breach of a relevant Act or regulation.

(c) Making the Job Safe

We have seen the kinds of hazards that can affect the work process. Machines which have to be cleaned or loaded while in motion may avoid lost production but increase danger. When examining the layout of an office, shop or factory, watch for the danger points: areas of congestion, cross-over points from one line to another, the siting of waste disposal points, and so on. When considering the operations necessary to get the job done, take into account the position that the operator will have to adopt, the loads he will be required to lift and the distances he will be expected to stretch. Wherever possible, tap the skills of an experienced organisation and methods analyst. But if the process is inherently dangerous, perhaps involving noxious fumes or high temperatures, consider the possibility of automating the work. This may mean that, in the short term, some employees lose their jobs, but it is surely preferable to risking employees losing their lives.

One technique which may assist you is known as **total loss control**. Pioneered at the Lukens steelworks in Pennsylvania, it is based on the premise that there is a significant relationship between property damage and personal injuries. If, therefore, you investigate all sources of loss, damage to plant and property, fire, security, health, hygiene, environmental pollution, and liability arising from defective products, as well as personal injuries, you will uncover the parts of the work process which are causing loss. You can then rectify them, perhaps before they cause serious personal injury.

(d) Making the Environment Safe

Regular maintenance checks, to ensure that the buildings, fixtures and equipment have not developed faults which might render them dangerous, should identify potential problems. More formalised procedures can also be invoked. **Safety sampling**, for example, is a process for counting the safety defects which can be spotted by trained observers in a given time, while systematically touring part of the workplace.

Action along these lines should ensure that all your operations are not only safe but legal.

17.4   Health and Safety and the Law

The health and safety of people at work has been the subject of legislation since the Health and Morals of Apprentices Act 1802. From that date onwards, a series of statutes emanated from Parliament. Acts were passed to regulate hours of work, working conditions and technical safety standards in factories, mines, agriculture, nuclear installations, the petroleum industry, offices, shops and railway premises, and off-shore operations. In addition, the Home Secretary was empowered to draw up special regulations for particular industrial activities.

By 1972 there were nine separate Acts of Parliament, more than five hundred sets of regulations and seven separate inspectorates to enforce them. That this situation had its shortcomings is borne out by the following points.

(*a*) The complexity of these arrangements made enforcement difficult, especially if more than one inspectorate was involved.

(*b*) The sanctions which could be applied by the inspectors involved prosecution and a fine on conviction, but there was no other method of persuasion.

(*c*) The safety standards imposed had regard mainly to technical and mechanical factors, rather than to the system of work or the part played by attitudes.

(*d*) Health and safety was seen as a management responsibility, and there was no scope for employee involvement.

The position in 1972 was clearly unsatisfactory both because of the complexity and superfluity of the law (many regulations referred to processes which were obsolete), and because of the high level of accidents which were occurring in spite of the legislation. In 1973 there were 1000 deaths and about 600,000 injuries at work. Lord Robens had been appointed to head a committee of inquiry and his report, published in 1972, paved the way for the single most important piece of health and safety legislation currently on the statute book.

(a) The Statutes

As a direct result of the Robens Report, the Health and Safety at Work Act became law in 1974. It was not designed to replace the other nine statutes or five hundred regulations; it was designed as a piece of enabling legislation, to introduce new penalties, a new enforcement agency and a broadening of the statutory responsibilities of employers and employees. It still requires other specific regulations and legal provisions to be observed.

The Management of Health and Safety at Work Regulations 1992, based on an EC Directive, and the 1994 Amendment to these specify the steps an employer must take to fulfil his basic duties under the Health and Safety at

Work Act. Some of the most widely applicable of the other current regulations are mentioned below.

The Health and Safety at Work Act 1974 had certain specified objectives:

(i) To secure the health, safety and welfare of persons at work.
(ii) To protect others from risks arising from work premises or activities.
(iii) To control the storage and use of dangerous substances.
(iv) To control the emission of noxious or offensive substances into the atmosphere.

In many ways it simply served to make the employee's common law rights, enforced through civil actions in the county and high courts, criminally enforceable. An employee injured as a result of the negligence of his employer has always been able to sue for compensation for the loss he has suffered. And theoretically, an employee who, although not actually injured, considered his employer to be using an unsafe system of work could apply for an injunction to order that the practice be discontinued.

But the Act and the later Management of Health and Safety at Work Regulations do specify a range of duties for both employer and employees which, as we shall see, can now be enforced through the criminal (magistrates' and Crown) courts.

(i) Employer's duties. The Act says: 'It shall be the duty of every employer to ensure, so far as is reasonably practicable, the health, safety and welfare at work, of all his employees.' It goes on to stipulate that attention be paid to plant, systems of work, the use, storage and movement of articles and substances, information, instruction, training and supervision, the working environment and the condition of the workplace and ways to and from it. (The Act also imposes duties in respect of those not actually employed by you but who use your premises or plant, are affected by what goes on there, or who use items which are designed, made or installed by you. The Chernobyl disaster in 1986, where a nuclear power station caught fire and sent a cloud of radiation all over Europe, was a devastating reminder that it is not only those **inside** the factory gates who need protection.)

Your duties might, therefore, seem clear enough. But what does 'so far as is reasonably practicable' really mean? Piecing together judicial interpretations of the term, five factors seem to emerge:

1. The likelihood of injury resulting from management action or inaction.
2. The likelihood of such injury proving serious.
3. The obviousness of the hazard.
4. The cost of putting it right.
5. The inherent risk factor. Some work (such as North Sea oil exploration) carries a risk of injury (through elements largely outside management control) higher than other jobs.

One judge (in *Edwards* v. *NCB* 1949) summed it up thus: 'Reasonably practicable is a narrower term than physically possible. A computation must be made ... in which the quantum of risk is placed on one scale, and the sacrifices involved in the measures necessary for averting the risk, whether in money, time or trouble, are placed in the other. And if it be shown that there is a great disproportion between them – the risk being insignificant in relation to the sacrifice – the defendants discharge the onus on them.'

Where there is actual risk of serious injury, however, claims of serious loss of production or financial hardship will not get you very far. Nor are you likely to succeed in an appeal if you are in breach of another relevant Act.

In addition, if you employ five or more people, you are required to issue a written statement of your **health and safety policy**. This should not only make clear your general determination to ensure the health and safety of your employees, but also specify who is responsible for carrying out the policy, what is to be done to make sure everyone is aware of his duties and responsibilities, and what other machinery (such as employees' safety representation and committees – see (ii) below) exists. There should be clear reference to safety rules and action to be taken in relation to the most common hazards.

The **Reporting of Injuries, Diseases and Dangerous Occurrences Regulations (1985)** – known as RIDDOR – state you have an obligation to report accidents which result in death or major injury. The Health and Safety Executive should be notified by telephone immediately after the accident and written confirmation (on form F2508) should be sent within seven days. The injuries which count as 'major' are laid down in the Regulations and include amputation of hand or foot, fractures of the skull, and loss of the sight of an eye. Accidents which cause more than three consecutive days' incapacity for work must also be reported on form F2508, within seven days. The Health and Safety Executive must also be informed of dangerous occurrences, such as the accidental ignition of explosives, and work-related diseases, like asbestosis. Full records of accidents and diseases must be kept at the workplace by a responsible person. These must be retained for at least three years.

Further sets of regulations add to your duties the requirement to assess and address the risks which are likely to arise from particular types of work. The **Control of Substances Hazardous to Health (COSHH) Regulations** came into effect in 1989. Employers must limit the use of hazardous substances and must train employees in their use and provide adequate safeguards where no safe substitute is available. The regulations have wide implications as they cover not only the chemicals used in industrial processes but also the correcting and cleaning fluids, aerosols and other preparations used in shops and offices.

The **Health and Safety (Display Screen Equipment) Regulations 1992** specify that employers must periodically assess, evaluate, eliminate or minimise the health and safety risks associated with work on display screens – whether electronic (e.g. personal computers) or non-electronic (e.g. microfiche readers).

Reflections, noise, ventilation, sitting position, working height and angle should all be examined. Those who use the equipment for long periods must be trained to be aware of and avoid the risks. They have the right to regular rest breaks and to be given a free eye test and, if necessary, corrective glasses on request. All work stations put into use since 1 January 1993 are covered and by the end of 1996 older workstations will also be included.

The **Manual Handling Operations Regulations 1992** require assessment of the risks associated with moving or supporting loads by hand or using 'bodily force'. The assessment must again be carried out by a trained person, taking into acount a range of relevant factors.

For those tasks where there is a risk of injury, the possibility of automating the task or eliminating it altogether should be pursued – so far as is reasonably practicable. Where loads **must** be moved, those involved must be properly trained to avoid the risk of injury.

The **Personal Protective Equipment at Work Regulations 1992** cover all equipment and clothing intended to protect the employee – from ear protectors, rubber gloves and safety shoes to anti-radiation suits and more sophisticated equipment. The employer has a duty not only to provide suitable equipment but to make sure it fits, train people in its use, make sure it is maintained in working order and provide accommodation for it when not in use.

Employees, including trainees and those on work experience schemes, must be made aware of the hazards against which the equipment is designed to protect them and trained in its use and maintenance.

The **EC 'Pregnant Workers' Directive** provides for additional protection for women who are pregnant, have recently given birth or are breast-feeding. Employers must assess the risks for these women separately and take whatever action is necessary – including a move to other duties or suspension on full pay if need be.

In each case, the regulations require that appropriate records – of assessments and training – are kept. As working practices evolve and more hazards emerge, yet more regulations are likely to follow.

(ii) Employees' duties. The Robens Report made the point that safety at work cannot be achieved without the active interest and support of employees. This is reflected in the 1974 Act in two main ways:

1. Independent trade unions which are recognised by the employer (see Unit 18) have the right to appoint safety representatives from among the employees. The functions of such representatives are laid down in the Safety Representatives and Safety Committees Regulations 1977. They include the investigation of potential hazards, investigations of complaints made by the employees they represent, making representations to the employer on matters arising out of such investigations, consulting with and receiving information from the inspectors of the Health and Safety Executive and attending the meetings of safety committees where the trade union has exercised its right to request that one be set up.

2. Employees have a duty to take reasonable care for their own and other people's safety, and to co-operate with their employers so far as is necessary to enable the latter to carry out their own obligations.

Employees shall not interfere with or misuse anything which is provided by their employer in the interests of health, safety or welfare.

The **Management of Health and Safety at Work Regulations 1992** go further and require them to make use of the equipment provided and use it in accordance with the training and instruction received.

The **Trade Union Reform and Employment Rights Act 1993** gives employees the right not to be dismissed for taking appropriate steps to protect themselves or others in circumstances of serious or imminent danger or for leaving a dangerous part of the workplace. Those performing health and safety duties designated by their employer, acting as safety representatives or members of a health and safety committee or bringing a reasonable health and safety concern to their employer's attention in the absence of a safety representative or committee are similarly protected.

In practice, the law seems to recognise two types of employee offence: 'horseplay' and deliberate disregard of safety requirements. The first was invoked, for example, in a case where two employees placed a colleague in a goods lift which collapsed, causing him to break his back. The second has been used where an employee was seen to be deliberately running his machine with the guard in a dangerous position.

(b) Complying with Statutory Duties

The Act itself spells out a number of things that employers must do in order to comply with their duties. They must:

(i) provide information, instruction, training and supervision;

(ii) issue a safety policy statement and advise employees of arrangements to implement it;

(iii) consult with trade union appointed safety representatives;

(iv) establish a safety committee where regulations require and representatives so request.

So one of the main ways in which you can set about complying with your statutory duties is through regular communication and training. All training must be done in working hours, be repeated periodically, and be adapted to take account of new or increased risks. The kind of technique which we discussed in Unit 17.3 will stand you in good stead here. Many employers feel that more dramatic action is necessary in order to compel employees at all levels to comply with the law. There have been instances of employers dismissing employees who refused to take appropriate safety precautions. As with any other dismissal, you do need to be certain that you have given due consideration to the employee's point of view, and have adhered to an appropriate procedure (see Unit 21).

In one case, *Mayhew* v. *Anderson (Stoke Newington) Ltd* 1977, a sewing machinist had suffered so many accidents to her eyes through needle breakage that the firm's insurance company threatened to withdraw insurance cover unless she wore goggles. So the company bought Mrs Mayhew a pair of goggles, priced 78p, which she refused to wear. She was warned that persistent refusal would lead to her dismissal. She persisted and was dismissed. When she appealed to an industrial tribunal, it found that she had been unfairly dismissed. She had never refused to wear suitable eye protection (custom-made goggles would have cost £35). She had merely found the particular goggles offered to her unsuitable. They were, she claimed, cheap and nasty, and they irritated her eyes. It was ruled that the company should have been more careful in investigating the reasons for Mrs Mayhew's refusal, and in finding suitable eye protection.

As a general rule, you should think first about job design, second about communication and training and third, as a last resort, about dismissal.

(c) Enforcement Agencies

The duties imposed by the Health and Safety at Work Act and the other extant Acts are enforced through the Health and Safety Executive. This is a three-person team, a director and two members, who now supervise the activities of the staffs of the various inspectorates which existed prior to 1974. The Health and Safety Inspectorate are the people with whom you are most likely to come into contact as it is their job to visit all kinds of industrial and commercial premises to ensure that they are complying with their legal obligations. Inspectors have authority to enter and examine premises, to remove items for subsequent investigation or to request that things be left undisturbed pending investigation. They can record and measure, question employees, and inspect your accident records and other relevant documents.

Inspectors have wide-ranging powers, but they are as concerned to improve industrial safety as they are to apprehend wrongdoers. They are a valuable source of information and guidance and you will almost certainly find it helpful to discuss safety queries with your local inspector, rather than waiting for him to spot your mistakes. The Employment Medical Advisory Service (EMAS) is another useful source of advice.

One other body of which we should take note is the Health and Safety Commission. This was set up in October 1974 and comprises a chairperson, three employee representatives, three employers' representatives and three further people who are appointed by other organisations, including local authorities. The Commission is an independent body, but must keep the Secretary of State for the Environment informed of its activities. It issues codes of safe working practice, prepares new regulations, and conducts general research and investigations into accidents and potential hazards.

(d) Penalties

Although the wide powers of inspectors to enter premises and conduct their investigation may themselves seem like a penalty, there are a number of specific courses of action that an inspector can take if he is not satisfied with your safety arrangements. They are laid out in Table 17.1.

These penalties can be invoked against the company as a whole or against an individual within it. Some directors and general managers, as well as safety

Table 17.1   Action taken against employers under the Health and Safety at Work Act 1974

Action	Grounds	Appeals	Effect of appeal
Improvement notice – to improve practice within given time limit	Legal contravention. No risk need be specified	To industrial tribunal within 21 days, then to High Court on point of law	Suspension of notice until appeal determined
Prohibition notice – to cease practice (immediate or deferred)	Risk of serious personal injury. No legal contravention need have taken place	As above	No suspension of notice unless tribunal so rules
Summary conviction – maximum fine £20,000 or six months imprisonment or both	Contravention of improvement or prohibition notice or court order or failure to fulfil obligations under Sections 2–6 of the Health and Safety at Work Act	Normal process of law	Modification of penalty
Conviction on indictment – unlimited fines and/or imprisonment for up to 2 years	Refusal to comply, grave or repeated breach of relevant Act	As above	As above

managers, have been prosecuted under the Act and some very substantial fines have been incurred. Separate charges of 'corporate manslaughter' may also be brought, and in one case this resulted in a three-year jail sentence for a director. For an individual manager to be prosecuted, it has to be shown that the breach occurred through his consent, connivance or neglect. And while some organisations seek to evade this responsibility by appointing a safety officer or manager, if he has not been carefully selected and trained, and is not given the appropriate degree of authority to enable him to perform his duties and fulfil his responsibilities, his employer cannot hide behind his errors of judgement. Responsibility will devolve upon whoever appointed him or obstructed him in the course of his duties.

Over and above the specific penalties for which the law provides, you might also like to think about the more general consequences of attracting the attention of the enforcing agents in unfavourable circumstances.

(i) Public inquiries. The Department of the Environment authorises the Health and Safety Commission to hold an inquiry wherever there is any 'accident, occurrence, situation, or other matter whatsoever' which the Commission thinks it necessary or expedient to investigate. Its findings may be made public, and you will have no redress against any statement made about you or your company.

(ii) Disclosure of information. The information required by the inspector may include important trade secrets. Although he is forbidden to divulge these secrets, except in so far as he needs to in order to do his job, they may have to come out at an inquiry or in a report.

(iii) Seizure of articles. Inspectors, as we have seen, have the authority to seize any article or substance which they consider to be a potential source of danger or serious personal injury and, if necessary, destroy it. This could be both costly and inconvenient.

(iv) Damages. Although the Act brings in no new civil liabilities, if any injury results from a breach of the Health and Safety at Work Act, the injured employee's complaint will automatically be actionable in a civil case.

(v) Public relations. Health and safety at work is a topical issue. Some companies pride themselves on their facilities and good accident records. Adverse publicity, whether through a public inquiry, a claim for damages or the observed practices of your employees, may damage your public image and thereby your company.

As we saw at the beginning of this unit, the general costs to the individual, the company and the country of a high accident rate will be considerable. Health and safety is also an area of concern to the trade union movement. Unions have an opportunity for involvement through representation and safety committees and a bad accident record may help their recruitment efforts, which you may not think desirable.

By giving legal backing to the appointment of safety representatives by recognised independent trade unions, rather than by all employees, the Labour Government of the 1970s pursued a conscious aim of institutionalising the relationship between employers and employed. It is to this area of the collective organisation of employees and their relationships with management that we will now turn.

Questions

1. Why do accidents happen?
2. How would you set about improving a bad accident record in an organisation?
3. Outline the main implications, for managers and employers, of the Health and Safety at Work Act and its attendant regulations. How would you set about ensuring that everyone in your organisation was able to comply with his statutory duties?

UNIT 18

Employee Relations

18.1 Introduction

So far we have tended to talk in terms of the relationship between you as an employer and your employees as individuals. But we must not lose sight of the role that trade unions can play in your relationship with employees collectively. In this unit we will examine the institutions and conventions of industrial relations (the collective aspect) before we move on to consider their implications for you and your employees and the way you regulate your relationship, in Unit 19.

The British industrial relations system was traditionally largely a voluntary one. The arrangements made between employer and employee were not closely prescribed by law, although we have seen certain exceptions to this (in the previous unit, for instance). Until quite recently, the involvement of the state was through the setting up of appropriate institutions, defining the legal standing of the parties in relation to the contract of employment and prescribing certain employee rights (some of which we have already discussed and others which will be dealt with in Unit 18.2). The last twenty years or so have seen the emergence of a rather more legalistic approach.

Two other significant features of the British industrial relations scene were highlighted by the Donovan Commission on industrial relations, which reported in 1968.

(a) The **formal** system of industrial relations comprises the overt process of negotiation and bargaining between employers and employees at a national level for each industry, the results of which are embodied in written agreements.

(b) The **informal** system consists of local arrangements arrived at by tacit agreement or through custom and practice, in the day-to-day dealings between employers and employed, at local or plant level.

Both of these aspects are important to the practical working of industrial relations. Both employers and employees may, from time to time, find that their national level decisions have been pre-empted at local level, or vice versa.

It is with the formal associations of employers on the one hand and employees on the other, and with the institutions established by the state to facilitate the relationship between the two, that we will now deal.

18.2 The Trade Unions

A trade union is defined by the Trade Union and Labour Relations (Consolidation) Act 1992 as an organisation which either:

(*a*) consists wholly or mainly of workers, of one or more descriptions, whose principal purposes include the regulation of relations between workers of that or those descriptions and employers or employers' associations; or
(*b*) consists of such organisations or their representatives.

The general mission of the trade unions has traditionally been seen as that of protecting the individual worker and improving his lot, through collective action. Although when Sydney and Beatrice Webb first described them in this vein in the 1920s they envisaged wage-earners, rather than salaried staff, as the workers in question, in the latter part of the twentieth century the concept must be widened to include all categories of employee: managerial, professional and technical, as well as wage-earning manual workers. It may also be necessary, now, to think in terms of trade unions as a vehicle for increasing employee participation in management decision-making on subjects which are not immediately related to the traditional wage–work bargain. Health and safety, occupational pension schemes and employee development are cases in point where long-term rather than short-term interests are at issue.

It would be a mistake to assume that all trade unions are identical in structure, membership, power, political affiliations or points of view. Quite clearly they are not. Their power depends not only on the size of their membership, but on the significance of those members to the smooth running of the organisations which employ them. Although the 'trade union movement' is a description often used, the interests of one union, perhaps representing managers and professional staff, may be at variance with the interests of a more general union.

(a) The Structure of Trade Unions

Although generalisations are dangerous, there are some basic similarities in structure which we can outline before moving on to consider the specific types of union.

(i) Trade unions are headed by a president or a general secretary and one or more executive committees. These are known as Principal Executive Committees (PECs) and are elected for a fixed term. A small, full-time headquarters staff give a range of advisory, legal, welfare and social services, and provide professional negotiators to take part in national-level negotiations with employers. Union policy is determined by delegates to the annual national conference which is held by each trade union. These delegates are elected by the membership through the branch structure (see below) and vote on issues of general importance, providing a framework within which the executive must act. Inevitably delegates will be swayed by the views aired by the executive in debate, as well as by those of the members that they seek to represent.

(ii) The next tier in the structure is generally the district or regional level, again with some full-time paid officers, but also comprising a committee of delegates from local branches. They help the branches by providing advice and can intervene in disputes between employers and union members, to ensure that union policy and practice are adhered to.

(iii) Next comes the local branch, which may simply consist of the union members at one place of work, as with the miners' lodges and the printers' chapels, or bring together the employees of a number of employers in the locality. Although a useful vehicle of union communication, and an opportunity for members to air their views, attendance at branch meetings is usually low, except when some vital issue is under discussion. Each branch usually has a voluntary part-time secretary and other officials, but it is made up of all the members of the union, rather than on a representational basis.

(iv) At the workplace level, the role of the shop steward is a key one. He is the daily point of contact for the membership and it is from him that most members get their information and opinions on union affairs. He is also their spokesman in day-to-day dealings with management and it is through him that they probably learn the outcome of negotiations with management. Not all unions refer to their part-time workplace representatives as a shop steward. The print unions, for instance, have 'fathers' or 'mothers' of the chapel; others refer simply to union 'reps', or to 'collectors' or 'collecting stewards'. This is an allusion to their role as collectors of the membership subscriptions which go to finance the union. This duty is now largely superseded by the system of **check off**, which means that employees authorise their employer to deduct the money at source and pay it over to the trade union on their behalf (see Unit 14.7).

This elected representative can be a very influential figure in company industrial relations. Certainly so far as the informal system of industrial relations is concerned, he is the lynchpin of management dealings with employees and it is from this, rather than his position in the union hierarchy, that the steward derives most of his power. Many managements in fact prefer to make local, domestic settlements with the stewards, rather than becoming involved in national negotiations.

Where there are a number of different unions operating within the same company or organisation, they may be linked by a stewards' committee. This discusses matters of common interest and tries to resolve conflicts of interest.

(b) Types of Trade Union

Although the changing pattern of industry and employment and mergers between unions have blurred some of the distinctions, there are four traditional types of trade union: craft unions, general unions, industrial unions and occupational or non-manual unions. Individual unions may join together as a federation, for example the Confederation of Shipbuilding and Engineering Unions. This enables bargaining to take place on an industry-wide basis. Some federations decide policy and take action on behalf of their member unions; others act purely in a consultative or co-ordinating manner.

(i) Craft unions. These consist of skilled workers who pursue the same craft. Multicraft unions, whose membership is still for skilled employees, but not exclusively those who have acquired their skills through the traditional apprenticeship route, are increasingly common. The Amalgamated Electrical and Engineering Union (AEEU) provides an example.

(ii) General unions. These bring together all categories of workers, across a range of industries. The Transport and General Workers Union (TGWU), for instance, organises almost all categories of employee working in overland transport and also extends into agriculture, quarrying, the manufacture of cement and bricks, power production, engineering and the metal trades, building, textiles, rubber, chemicals, food processing and other industries. It also has a special section, as do many of the general unions, for clerical and supervisory staff.

(iii) Industrial unions. These organise all the employees, whatever their craft, in a specific industry. This means that, in shipbuilding, for instance, all employees could belong to one union, instead of being split between craft (such as the boilermakers) unions and general unions. Although this is the pattern of trade unionism in some other countries (notably Germany), the federated structure and the multi-union plant are far more common features of the British scene. There are few truly industrial unions in this country, although 'enterprise unionism' where a union represents only the employees of a single employer is a further development.

(iv) Occupational or non-manual unions. These are concerned with organising technical, clerical, professional, supervisory and managerial staffs separately from other employees. Sometimes membership is drawn from a particular occupation, such as the Banking Industry and Finance Union (BIFU), or the National Association of Teachers in Further and Higher Education (Natfhe). They may also be constructed across occupations, more on the lines of a general union for salaried staff. The Managerial, Scientific and Finance Union (MSF) and the Association of Professional, Executive, Clerical and Computer Staff (APEX) provide examples. White-collar unionism, as it is sometimes called, is largely a phenomenon of the 1960s and 1970s. Pressures from beneath, in the form of the gains made by other unions for their wage-earning members, combined with pressure from above, in terms of reduced job security and a more distant relationship with top management, encourage salaried staff to deal with their employers on a collective rather than an individual basis.

The existence of these different types of union, with membership drawn from different sections of the workforce, each trying to achieve the best pay and conditions for its members, can create a complex situation for the employer. Despite the attractions of a 'divide and conquer' approach, fragmentation is usually more difficult to deal with than a single union to whom you have granted sole bargaining rights. Inter-union rivalry may be reflected both in arguments over pay differentials and in battles to recruit more members. The 1939 Bridlington Agreement and a further agreement reached at Croydon in 1969 attempted to regulate this sort of membership squabble by laying down principles for transfer arrangements and for organising groups of employees where another union already represented a majority of those employed. The Trade Union Reform and Employment Rights Act effectively abolished these rules and allows workers to join the union of their choice. Disputes between unions affiliated to the TUC (see Unit 18.3) must now be dealt with by the TUC disputes committee.

As union membership has declined and the benefits of co-operation between unions become self-evident, union mergers have become commonplace. The combination of the Union of Communication Workers (UCW) with the National Communication Union (NCU) to form the Communication Workers Union (CWU) is one of many examples.

Hostility and suspicion have characterised some employers' attitudes towards trade unions. The fact remains that they have in the past made a valuable contribution to the improvement of working conditions generally. They can also do much to reduce wasteful conflict by providing their own rules and procedures to which their membership must adhere.

The trade union movement was at its most powerful in Britain during the 1970s. Several factors served to lessen its influence during the 1980s. The worsening of unemployment meant a reduction in union membership as erstwhile members joined the dole queues. It also meant that many of those in employment were less ready to use the sanctions available to them (see (*e*) below) for fear that their employer would decide to close down altogether. The decline of the country's manufacturing base, the introduction of new technology and the trends towards part-time work and smaller, multi-skilled, service industry working units undermined the traditional strongholds of trade unionism. Government legislation to regulate the behaviour of trade union officials and their members may have compounded the process of decline. Union leaders are now required to ballot their members before calling them out on strike (see below). This has contributed to a dramatic decrease in the number of days lost through strike action – from 1,280 days per 1,000 employees in 1984 to thirty days per 1,000 in 1993. Even so, the unions are still a force to be reckoned with in many industries and have an important part to play in the future development of industrial relations.

(c) The Closed Shop or Union Membership Agreement

In some industries the possession of a union membership card was once as much an essential requirement in the selection process as the ability to do the job. The closed shop, as this insistence on union membership was called, is no longer permitted. As we saw in Unit 7.4, the Trade Union and Labour Relations (Consolidation) Act 1992 makes it illegal to employ or refuse to employ anyone on grounds of membership or non-membership of a trade union.

From the union point of view, there was much to recommend the closed shop. It strengthened its bargaining position vis-à-vis management and avoided the situation where some employees benefit from the improved terms and conditions of employment negotiated by the union, without having paid their subscription or contributed in any way.

From the employer's point of view, too, it had its advantages in terms of stability and a reduction in conflict between members and non-members. But the restrictive practices which frequently accompanied a closed shop were seen by many as an impediment to progress.

(d) The Rights of Trade Unions

An independent trade union is one which is neither under the domination or control of an employer, group of employers or employers' association, nor is likely to be deterred from taking action by the threat to withdraw any facilities provided by that employer. A union can apply to the Certification Officer, appointed by the Secretary of State for a certificate of independence. This grants the union and its members certain rights and privileges under the Trade Union and Labour Relations Act 1974 (TULRA), the Employment Acts 1980, 1982 and 1988, and the Trade Union Act 1984. These were brought together in the Trade Union and Labour Relations (Consolidation) Act 1992. They include:

(i) The right of employees to belong to the union, and to take part in its activities, and not to be dismissed or penalised for so doing.

(ii) The right to be consulted on impending redundancies (see Unit 20) or the planned transfer of the employer's undertaking.

(iii) The right to receive information from the employer to assist in the bargaining process. The sort of information which you might have to disclose includes payroll costs, structure and distribution; conditions of service; staffing information, such as numbers employed, labour turnover, absenteeism, overtime, staffing levels, planned changes in work methods; performance information (productivity indices, return on capital invested, sales and the state of the order book); and financial information (cost structures, gross and net profits, sources of earnings, assets and liabilities and allocation of profits). The ACAS Code of Practice on Disclosure of Information to Trade Unions for Collective Bargaining Purposes gives further guidance on what is required.

(iv) Members of a recognised independent trade union have the right to reasonable time off work to take part in union activities, while officials, such as shop stewards, branch officials and delegates to conferences must be given reasonable time off work, with pay, to carry out their duties or receive appropriate training. (There is guidance on these provisions in the ACAS Code of Practice for Time Off for Trade Union Duties and Activities.)

(v) The right to appoint safety representatives (see Unit 17.4).

(vi) Individual union members also have the right, under the Employment Act 1988, not to be unfairly treated by their own union. They must not be unjustifiably disciplined by the union – for refusing to take part in strike action, for example – and they can take legal action against their union if it calls for industrial action without a proper ballot (see below).

One point to note is that all except the first and last of these rights depend not only on the union being 'independent' but also on whether the employer recognises it for collective bargaining purposes – that is, whether he is prepared to negotiate with it on matters such as pay, conditions, allocation of work, discipline and termination of employment. Recognition can be formally expressed in a written agreement or implied by the fact that such negotiation takes place. The union's ability to recruit members and its negotiating strength will generally determine whether or not it is sensible to grant recognition. If most employees are members, the employer might be well advised to recognise the union – but does not have to.

(e) Trade Union Sanctions

As we have seen, trade unions derive their power from their membership. They can add weight to their point of view in their dealings with employers through invoking the sanctions available to them. Provided they act in accordance with the law they cannot be sued – they enjoy **immunity**.

(i) Where there is a trade dispute, **strikes** are the ultimate sanction or kind of **industrial action** which the trade union can invoke. A trade dispute is defined by TULRA as a dispute between employers and employees over any of the items listed below.

Disputes over:

(*a*) terms and conditions of employment, or the physical conditions in which any workers are required to work;

(*b*) engagement or non-engagement, termination or suspension of one or more workers;

(*c*) allocation of work between workers (demarcation disputes);

(*d*) matters of discipline;

(*e*) membership or non-membership of an independent trade union;

(*f*) facilities for officials of trade unions;

(*g*) machinery for negotiation or consultation and other procedures relating to any of the above.

Under the Trade Union Act 1984, any form of industrial action must have been approved in a secret ballot of the union members involved. The rules governing the conduct of ballots were extended by the Employment Act 1988 and there is a Code of Practice on Trade Union Ballots on Industrial Action. The ballot paper must draw employees' attention to the fact that they may be in breach of contract if they vote for industrial action. There must be no interference with voters, and all those likely to be directly involved in industrial action must be asked to vote. There must be a separate ballot for each workplace, and a majority at the workplace must vote in favour – on a properly drawn-up ballot paper – before industrial action can take place. This, rather than the traditional show of hands at a mass meeting, provides a safeguard for trade union democracy. If the vote is in favour of industrial action, the union must give the employer seven days' notice of the start of the action and let him know its nature and who will be involved.

The complete withdrawal of labour enables employees to show how, collectively, they have the power to interfere with a firm's production, and therefore profitability. The employer must weigh up the consequences of sitting it out, in terms of lost production and lost orders, against the consequences of conceding. The latter consequence may include not just the immediate cash cost of an increase in pay or a reduction in working hours, but also the longer-term precedent that will be set. This could mean that he will have to repeat the same sort of concessions again at a later date, or that the union will come to expect him to cave in at the threat of strike action.

The union will also need to think carefully about the consequences of strike action. Their members will be losing pay. They will therefore need to be financed out of a strike fund, or perhaps, as in the case of the miners' strike in 1984–5, with the assistance of public donations. Income Support is not payable to strikers through the Department of Social Security although their families or dependants may qualify for assistance.

(ii) When a strike has been called, the union members may engage in peaceful **picketing** to deter, by information and persuasion, other employees from entering the workplace and weakening the impact of the strike. It is only lawful if it is carried out by employees at or near their own place of work, although trade union officials may also stand on picket lines. The ACAS Code of Practice on Picketing suggests that no more than six pickets should stand at any entrance to a workplace. Those who engage in unlawful picketing are not committing a criminal offence, but those who suffer damage as a result of wrongs (torts) committed by the pickets can apply for an injunction to stop the action and may be awarded damages. Pickets who use threatening behaviour or cause criminal damage or injury are of course also guilty of breaches of the criminal law and may be prosecuted. During the 1984–5 miners' strike large numbers of individual pickets were prosecuted for their violent behaviour on picket lines often several thousand strong.

(iii) **Secondary action** occurs when attempts are made to persuade the employees of another employer, not involved in the dispute, to break their contract of employment. Lorry drivers whose own employers have a contract to deliver goods to the employer involved in the dispute may be approached and asked not to cross picket lines. Broader action designed to disrupt the supply of goods and services in furtherance of a trade dispute was outlawed in the Employment Act of 1990 and the Trade Union and Labour Relations (Consolidation) Act 1992. If a company associated with an employer in dispute takes over work from him, its employees may not lawfully refuse to deal with (**black**) that work. Nor is more general blacking of work from other companies still dealing with the employer in dispute lawful. Its victims may apply for an injunction to stop it.

(iv) A **work-to-rule** prohibits the working of overtime and means that employees must adhere strictly to laid-down procedures, manning levels, demarcation lines and job descriptions. In many industries, such as the railways, where considerable overtime is worked, the impact of a work-to-rule can be almost as disruptive as a complete stoppage. Where employees actually restrict their output and work slowly, this is known as a **go-slow.** (Following the introduction of a new grading system for National Health Service nurses in 1988, many nurses **worked to grade** by refusing to undertake any duties not specified for their grade, in protest at what they saw as the inequity of the system.)

(v) The **sit-in** was made famous by the workers at the Meriden Co-operative, where employees occupied the factory in 1973 and in 1975 began production as a government-backed co-operative after management had decided to transfer production away from the plant, with the loss of many jobs. A sit-in can also be used as a form of protest, most usually invoked where jobs are threatened, to persuade management to take another look at the situation.

Besides these overt signs of union discontent, there is a world of difference between a good industrial relations climate and a bad one. The first is built on mutual respect and trust and a willingness to resolve conflicts through the kind of procedures that we will be discussing in Unit 19. This minimises disruption and creates a situation where constructive solutions can be found. A bad industrial relations climate inhibits individual managers, making them either unnecessarily soft, because they fear union power, or unnecessarily harsh, because they feel they have to retain the upper hand.

18.3   The National Structure

Despite the differences between unions, substance is given to the concept of a trade union movement by the superstructure of trade unionism.

(a) The Trades Union Congress (TUC)

The collective voice of the British trade union movement is reflected through the Trades Union Congress (TUC), to which most of the larger trade unions are affiliated. Its structure is two-fold.

(i) **Full congress.** This is an annual meeting of about one thousand delegates, from all affiliated unions. During the first week in September they meet and elect the general council for the coming year, discuss the report of the retiring council, and debate resolutions, submitted either by individual unions or by the council, to determine TUC policy.

(ii) **General council.** This meets about once a month. Council members must be either full-time union officials or actually working at their trade. In fact the majority are general secretaries or presidents of unions. The monthly council meeting is normally concerned with dealing with the reports and recommendations of the various standing and *ad hoc* committees of the TUC. The former includes committees on incomes policy, economic issues, education, nationalised industries and international affairs. The committees are composed of members of the general council and, occasionally, co-opted experts.

The aims of the TUC are to promote the interests of its members, improve economic and social conditions, to help in extending membership of trade unions and to resolve disputes, both between unions and employers and between unions themselves. Although the council can intervene in disputes on its own initiative if deadlock is reached, it has no formal authority over the affiliated unions. Its resolutions are therefore not binding on trade unions, although in practice most unions bow to TUC policy on major issues.

At one time the council, and more specifically its general secretary, had a very important voice in national affairs. For historical and ideological reasons, this voice is always louder under a Labour government than under a Conservative one. During the 1970s the social contract (see Unit 14.8) and the acceptance of the twelve-month rule prescribing the interval between pay settlements seemed to mark a major step forward in government–trade union relations. The influence exerted by powerful unions at that time was thought by some to be excessive. Following the Conservative victory in 1979, a succession of steps were taken, in the Employment Acts of 1980, 1982 and 1988, and the Trade Union Act of 1984, to curb union power by regulating picketing and prescribing ballots for closed shops, strikes and picketing. As relations deteriorated, the regular formal and informal discussions between union leaders and government ministers which had become a feature of the Labour government's approach virtually ceased. The principle of tripartite (three-way) involvement, along with employers and independent representatives, which used to be reflected in the composition of a number of national bodies, such as the Manpower Services Commission, has been considerably weakened.

(b) Trades Councils

These are the local counterpart of the TUC. They are voluntary groupings of unions on a regional basis, normally without any full-time officials. They, too, meet monthly and their activities are concerned with representing their members' interests at a local level. They are also involved in promoting suitable educational, social and sports facilities. Although they have only one delegate to the TUC annual conference, they are able to influence it through a special conference which is held for them. Here they can pass resolutions which, although not binding on the TUC, can give a strong indication of the views of the rank and file members.

18.4   Employers' Associations

According to the Trade Union and Labour Relations (Consolidation) Act 1992, an employers' association is an organisation which either:

(*a*) consists wholly or mainly of employers or individual proprietors of one or more descriptions, whose principal purposes include the regulation of relations between employers of that description and workers or trade unions, or

(*b*) consists of such organisations or their representatives.

So an employers' association can be seen as the collective vehicle for the employers' point of view, in the same way as a trade union provides for the employees' point of view. They do not, however, deal exclusively with industrial relations. Some have become actively involved in training, especially the development of NVQs for their industry. Many also give assistance and advice on trade problems such as the standardisation of products or the development of collectively financed research into products or materials. Some employers' associations are basically defensive in their approach, trying to protect their members against trade union activity and government policies. Others are more aggressive in their stance, formulating joint action programmes to encourage progress.

Employers' associations, either individually or through a federated structure, form the other party in national negotiations over pay and conditions. They also help in the handling of disputes which cannot be resolved locally. Some seek to impose a uniform structure so that the terms and conditions offered by all members are in line with one another. Others merely try to influence members not to deviate too widely from the negotiated rates. Their membership, too, has declined recently.

Like trade unions, employers' associations normally have a headquarters staff of full-time officials, as well as local and possibly regional representation. Most operate through a number of standing committees comprised of representatives from member organisations. They are a valuable source of information and advice for many employers.

18.5   The Confederation of British Industry (CBI)

This is the employers' counterpart to the TUC, composed of employers' associations, trade associations and individual companies. It, too, has a committee structure, with a general purposes committee, which is broadly equivalent to the TUC's general council, and a series of standing committees. It also aims to provide a voice in government, putting forward the employers' point of view. The pronouncements of its Director General are frequently quoted in the press and are usually, although not always, at variance with those of the General Secretary of the TUC. It also seeks to establish a general consistency of approach between employers in dealing with industrial relations and other matters, but has no formal control over the actions of member associations.

Through the twin bodies of the TUC and the CBI, both employers and employees can put forward their points of view to the third party in the industrial relations scene: the state.

18.6   State Institutions

In Britain our basically voluntary system of industrial relations has a number of quasi-independent government bodies to help it operate smoothly.

(a) The Advisory Conciliation and Arbitration Service (ACAS)

ACAS was set up under the Employment Protection Act 1975. It was designed to assist in the smooth working of industrial relations through the extension of the traditional mechanisms of collective bargaining. Although set up by statute, it is an independent body and is not intended to interfere with existing procedures for negotiation and the resolution of disputes. What it will do is:

(i) intervene at the invitation of one or more of the parties to a dispute and, with the consent of all the parties, refer the dispute to arbitration (settlement by the decision of an independent person) which will be binding on both parties. The Central Arbitration Committee, which was set up in 1976, can provide arbitration;

(ii) fulfil the advisory part of its role through the issuing of codes of practice, for example on time off for trade union activities, disciplinary practice and procedures in employment, and the disclosure of information. It will also give advice to individual employers on matters ranging from recruitment, human resources planning and job evaluation, to procedure agreements and communications;

(iii) act as a conciliator and mediator, attempting to bring together the parties to a dispute. ACAS can mediate over claims for unfair dismissal, discrimination, failure to comply with the Equal Pay Act and similar matters. The normal procedure is for an ACAS conciliation officer to talk to both employer and employee(s) to help resolve the differences before the complaint goes further, perhaps to an industrial tribunal.

Many of the services of ACAS are available free of charge, and its regional structure means that advice is usually quite close at hand.

(b) Industrial Tribunals

These were first established under regulations to the Industrial Training Act 1964, to determine appeals against the training levy imposed on companies under that Act. The Lord Chancellor appoints a President of the Industrial Tribunals (England and Wales) who must be a barrister or solicitor of not less than seven years' standing. He holds office for five years. There is a regional structure, including a panel of chairpersons qualified similarly to the president, and tribunals sit in most major towns. Each industrial tribunal consists of three members: the legally qualified chairperson and two lay members drawn from the ranks of employers, trade unions and others.

The Trade Union Reform and Employment Rights Act 1993 specifies that if the contract of employment has been breached, the employer can be taken to an industrial tribunal, as can claims under any of the Acts listed below. The employee(s) must first fill in a form (IT1) which is obtainable at the offices of the Employment Service. A copy is sent to the employer who must respond in writing. Before the case is actually heard by a tribunal, the ACAS conciliation officer may, as we have seen, talk to both parties to attempt to procure a settlement.

Acts referable to industrial tribunals
(*a*) Race Relations Act 1976
(*b*) Sex Discrimination Act 1975 and 1986
(*c*) Equal Pay Act 1970
(*d*) Employment Protection Act 1975
(*e*) Employment Protection (Consolidation) Act 1978
(*f*) Health and Safety at Work Act 1974
(*g*) Employment Act 1980
(*h*) Employment Act 1982
(*i*) Employment Act 1988
(*j*) Employment Act 1990
(*k*) Wages Act 1986
(*l*) Disability Discrimination Act 1995

If you find yourself in a situation where an employee is bringing a case against you, the advice of the conciliation officer or a solicitor will probably be helpful. If the employee does have a case the financial consequences of proceeding to the tribunal could be quite considerable. These penalties are dealt with in our sections on law and aspects of employment. There are also the less tangible costs of time and adverse publicity to be taken into account. In many areas, it could be months before the case is actually heard, with the consequent worry and uncertainty adding to the stress for those involved.

So there may be something to be said for reaching a settlement privately before the case goes to the tribunal. To make certain this is the end of the matter, you will need either:

(i) to involve ACAS and have the details of the agreement recorded on form COT3. This makes it binding on both parties; or

(ii) to enter into a formal **compromise agreement**. Introduced by the Trade Union Reform and Employment Rights Act 1993, these allow for binding agreements to be made provided:

– they relate to a current complaint;
– the employee has obtained independent legal advice from a qualified lawyer;
– the agreement is in writing; and
– contains a declaration from the employee's lawyer that the necessary conditions have been met.

If the case does go forward, you are under no obligation to have legal representation and can defend the case yourself.

Tribunals are far less complex and splendid in their procedures and ceremony than courts of law and were designed as a means of allowing those who would be deterred by the pomp and expense of a court to obtain justice. In practice, though, because the law is complex, you could lose your case because you have failed to reveal all the relevant facts. Although the tribunal members will generally try, through careful questioning and by allowing you to make a written submission in advance, to help you avoid important omissions you will need to be very thorough in your preparation and ensure that you have all the facts at your disposal. Legal representation will, of course, add to your expenses considerably. But it may prove a good investment in the long run.

Each party at the tribunal generally meets his own expenses. If you lose, you will not have to pay your employee's costs. Either party, or the tribunal, may ask for a pre-hearing assessment of whether or not there is any substance in the case. If it is decided that there is not, and you proceed anyway, or if it is decided that you have acted frivolously, vexatiously or unreasonably in pursuing your case, you may be asked to pay the other party's costs.

Even if you do have legal representation, you will not be able to avoid all contact with the tribunal, as you will be required to give evidence. But the planning and conduct of the case will be in skilled hands. Alternatively, you may find that your employers' association can provide someone who will help you, in the same way as your employee may be receiving help from his trade union.

After an industrial tribunal has reached its decision on how the law applies to the facts of the case, it will be concerned to satisfy both parties that its decision is the right one. The report of the tribunal and the comments that it makes about the conduct of the parties in relation to the circumstances of the case can provide valuable lessons for the future. We will be looking at some tribunal findings in relation to unfair dismissal cases in Unit 21.

(c) Employment Appeal Tribunal (EAT)

This consists of judges and lay members from both sides of industry. The tribunal hears appeals on questions of law arising from the decisions made by industrial tribunals. Although you cannot dispute the facts of the case again before the EAT, the range, complexity and comparative newness of much employment law means that it is often not until a test case has gone before the EAT that any definitive interpretation of the law can be obtained. Even so, you can take an appeal still further, through the normal process of law, to the Court of Appeal and, ultimately, the House of Lords or to the European Court of Justice.

18.7 Collective Bargaining

The cornerstone of industrial relations is the **collective bargaining** process. The collective bargain is an agreement concerning pay and conditions, settled between trade union(s) on the one hand and employer or employers' association on the other. Each side has something to contribute: the employee provides his labour, the employer pays the reward. Their representatives therefore meet at intervals to negotiate the relationship between wages and work, the wage–work bargain. We will be looking at the actual process of negotiating in Unit 19. Here we need to differentiate between the two main categories of agreement which can be reached through the bargaining process and identify the alternative approaches to bargaining.

(a) Substantive Agreements
These lay down the terms and conditions of employment to be reflected in each employee's contract of employment. Pay rates, hours of work, holidays, pensions and retirement age, and sick pay arrangements provide examples. We have already dealt, in Units 14 and 15, with the sort of issues that may be raised here in relation to amounts of payment, methods of calculating it, and so on.

(b) Procedural Agreements
These set out the procedures which are to be adhered to in specific situations. We will consider two particular types, disciplinary and grievance procedures, in the next unit. Procedural agreements can cover the way in which any dispute is to be regulated, and the timing and method of approach to the making of substantive agreements. By providing a laid-down procedure to be followed (see Unit 19.7), the additional conflict that might be generated by uncertainty can be avoided. If there is machinery for achieving the desired result, a settlement is likely to be reached more quickly and more equitably than if there is not.

Whether the agreement to be reached is substantive or procedural in nature, there are two basic approaches to bargaining.

(c) Distributive Bargaining
This is based on the assumption that one party's gain will be the other's loss. So the annual wage round, for example, may be approached with a determination on the part of both employers and employees to minimise their losses and maximise their gains. Whatever the union wins in the way of additional pay or better conditions, the employer must pay for it. This underlying assumption will clearly affect the attitude of both parties, based as it is on the premise that there is bound to be a conflict of interest between them. The inevitability of a certain amount of conflict between employers and employees was propounded by Alan Fox, an eminent British industrial sociologist. Fox put forward the view that the organisation cannot be regarded as a single entity with a single set of purposes which both employer and employees will strive to attain. On the contrary, the industrial organisation is a plural society, containing different objectives and sets of interests which are bound to conflict with each other.

(d) Integrative Bargaining and Productivity Deals
In some circumstances both parties may be able to negotiate a gain, without a loss to the other. The productivity bargain provides an example of this. A productivity agreement was defined, by the National Board for Prices and Incomes, as a settlement in which workers agree to make changes in working

practice which themselves lead to more economical operation of a plant, a company or an industry. In return, an employer agrees to increase pay, to improve fringe benefits, to raise the workers' status, to increase their leisure or to make a combination of these improvements.

The first and most famous productivity deal was that concluded at the Esso oil refinery at Fawley in 1960. Prior to the agreement, a number of restrictive practices were keeping output down. Each craftsman, for instance, worked with a mate, even though his services were not usually required. Demarcation lines were drawn so that workers would not perform tasks which were part of someone else's job. The employees were also working excessive overtime, some 18 per cent of their total hours, which was proving very expensive for Esso. The company wanted to reduce this overtime to between 2 per cent and 6 per cent, introduce more flexible working agreements, and redeploy the 300 craftsmen's mates. In return, they offered the workers a 40 per cent wage increase, spread over two years, and a reduction in working hours from forty-two to forty. Within two years productivity had risen by about 50 per cent. The company were making more profit, and the employees were taking home more pay.

Since 1960, the productivity bargain has had a slightly chequered history. Its detractors claim that it is inflationary: it was far too easy, in times of pay restraint, for management to agree to a bogus productivity deal, merely to increase pay and thereby assist labour retention and minimise unrest. They also claim that it encourages employees to devise new restrictive practices so that they will, sooner or later, be able to negotiate again and secure their abolition.

On the other hand, a carefully thought out productivity bargain can, as did the initial Fawley agreement, have great benefits for both parties. And any method which increases pay through improved productivity and cost savings, rather than through higher prices to the consumer, must have its attractions. Another spin-off from productivity agreements, for better or worse, is the increased involvement that they tend to provide for the shop steward. As productivity deals are usually local in nature, there is more opportunity for the stewards to become involved than when negotiations are conducted at national level.

Although in productivity bargaining there is still an element of 'trade-off', in so far as it deviates from the traditional win–lose syndrome, it can be described as integrative. The interests of employers and employees may be different; but the interests of both can be served by the deal.

These are the main features of traditional collective bargaining. As a method of determining pay and conditions, it has its limitations.

(i) It may tend to fuel inflation, because in Britain we have created a climate where employees expect more every year: not just more in absolute terms but also, perhaps, more than last year's percentage increase. This is fine where there is a corresponding growth in the economy and the size of the profits to be shared out between the investors of capital and the investors of labour is getting bigger. When this is not the case, it can only be inflationary.

(ii) Leapfrogging may occur, through the absence of a universal settlement date. If company A awards a 3 per cent increase, its employees are quite happy until, two months later, company B awards 4 per cent. Then company A's employees start to demand 5 per cent, to keep themselves one step ahead. Suggestions have been made, by the CBI among others, that we should have just one annual settlement date, if not for the whole country, then at least for each industry. This is the concept of **synchropay**.

(iii) The power struggle which underlies the bargaining scene may prove counter-productive. There sometimes seems to be an implicit suggestion that might is right, and he who shouts loudest gets most.

(iv) The lack of information about the real position of the company, now and for the future, may lead the union side to press unrealistic demands, through a misreading of the situation. The disclosure of information prescribed by the Employment Protection Act goes some way towards reducing this risk.

(e) No-strike Agreements and Pendulum Arbitration

In traditional forms of collective bargaining, each side starts with a set of demands which are generally far in excess of what the other party is likely to accept. Negotiations become a complex ritual of claim and concession (see Unit 19.8). In the event of failure to agree, costly strikes or lock-outs may seem the only resort.

Pendulum arbitration provides an alternative and less confrontational approach. If negotiators fail to agree, the dispute is referred to an independent arbitrator (in the UK usually from ACAS). Both sides agree that the arbitrator's decision will be final and that he must accept one party's case in its entirety. This gives both sides a strong incentive to keep their bargaining positions fairly close together, reducing the chances of extravagant demands from either side. It also rules out the threat of strike action.

(f) Single Union and Partnership Agreements

No-strike agreements and pendulum arbitration are part of a new industrial relations scene emerging in the UK. In return for the freedom from industrial strife which they afford, employers are granting sole bargaining rights to unions, like the Amalgamated Electrical and Engineering Union (AEEU). Their leaders take the view that unions should work **with** management to create wealth in which all can share. They also believe in the equalisation of terms and conditions (Unit 14.6) for all employees.

In conjunction with employers like Nissan and Toyota, they are working towards a new kind of management–union relationship, in which training and employee development play an important role. The philosophy of continuous improvement and lifelong learning, rather than the confrontational ideology of the old unionism, encourage a joint search for new ways of working and new and more imaginative pay structures designed to reward skills and knowledge.

Each side surrenders some of its traditional sanctions. The threat of industrial action is sacrificed in exchange for agreements on job security or guaranteed employability – made possible as a result of enhanced learning.

18.8 Employee Involvement and Consultation

While collective bargaining remains the main vehicle for the development of terms and conditions of employment, employee involvement is increasingly becoming a central issue in industrial relations. The term itself is a wide one. It covers traditional processes of joint consultation (see below) and communication – meetings, briefing sessions, handbooks and the other methods discussed in Unit 13.6. Share option schemes and bonuses relating to company performance (Unit 15.3) which are designed to encourage employees' sense of involvement in the company's progress are also embraced. So too may be the kind of involvement in decisions about the way in which work is done that is implied by empowerment (Unit 13.5). Suggestion schemes and quality circles to encourage employees to put forward their ideas about how, for instance, quality can be improved, output increased, costs cut or safety enhanced, can also be considered aspects of employee involvement. In fact, 'employee involvement' includes anything which is designed

(*a*) to provide, systematically, information on matters of concern to employees;

(*b*) to elicit from employees, on a regular basis, information and opinions which can be taken into account in making decisions which may affect them;

(*c*) to encourage employees' commitment to company performance; or

(*d*) to enhance employees' awareness of the financial and economic factors affecting the performance of the company.

Interest in employee involvement has mounted in recent years. The Employment Act 1982 requires companies who employ more than 250 people to include a statement describing progress on employee involvement in their annual report.

Some of the practices which are now labelled as 'employee involvement' have been part of the British industrial relations scene for a long time. One example is the practice of formal consultation with employee representatives in a **joint consultative committee** (JCC).

The concept of joint consultation dates back to 1916, when the Whitley Committee recommended more employee involvement through consultation. Traditionally, JCCs have tended to get involved in the discussion of welfare issues, rather than the topics which form the subject for substantive bargaining. The quality of food in the canteen and the state of the washroom are held to be popular items for debate. They can, and do, also discuss more significant issues, and increasingly operate alongside established trade union machinery discussing such issues as pay, productivity and human resource levels.

There is no reason why joint consultation and collective bargaining cannot exist side by side. Indeed, whenever current legislation requires consultation with employees, as over health and safety or the notification of redundancies, it is with the recognised trade union that the employer is required to consult. Consultation, however, unlike negotiation, does not imply that both parties must agree on the outcome.

We have already discussed the importance of communicating with employees individually. Consultative machinery enables you to communicate with them, and they with you, collectively. Its effectiveness depends upon the use that you make of it. If you restrict your JCC's agenda to purely welfare matters, and then ignore your employees' point of view, do not be surprised if their representatives stop coming to meetings. If, however, you encourage them to contribute their views and air their grievances on a wide, but defined, range of subjects, and if you take conscious note of their views in arriving at your decisions, consultation can be reasonably effective. You may even find that you are making better decisions, as they will be based on a more accurate picture of what will and will not work.

You can go one stage further and consider the possibility of shared decision-making through some form of industrial democracy.

18.9 Industrial Democracy

The full embodiment of the concept of employee involvement is to be found in industrial democracy: government of employees, by employees, for employees. During the 1970s when the debate on the issue was at its height in the UK, two main options were considered.

(i) Employee representatives could be elected directly onto the main board of the company. The 1977 Bullock report suggested a $(2x+y)$ formula, $2x$ representing two equal groups of directors appointed by shareholders and directors appointed by employees, with the balance of power being held by outside independent directors (y), chosen by both sides. Only trade union members would be eligible to take up the employees' directorships.

(ii) A two-tier board, on the (former) West German coal and steel industry model, could be set up. Here a management board of full-time members conducts the day-to-day business of the company, but it is appointed by a supervisory board. This board normally comprises eleven members: five shareholder representatives, five employee representatives and one member who is independent of both. The employee representatives are nominated from the works council, the trade unions and independents. This supervisory board meets four or five times a year.

At the height of trade union power in the 1970s, such ideas seemed a logical next step in the UK. A number of organisations, including the British Steel Corporation and Harland and Wolff, actually appointed employee directors at that time. Now, the empowerment of **every** employee, rather than a seat in the boardroom for a few, is higher on many companies' agendas.

Creating employee directors is, in any case, not the only way of developing a more democratic approach.

(a) Works Councils

These take a number of different forms and have varying levels of power and influence. At one extreme they may be purely consultative and fulfil the functions of a JCC. At the other, they can carry considerable weight in the decision-making process. They usually consist of elected representatives and can be found in both unionised and non-unionised environments.

Britain has opted out of the European Social Protocol so the EU Directive which **requires** companies with employees in more than one Member State to set up European Works Councils does not apply to employees in the UK. Even so, British companies which have more than 1,000 employees elsewhere in the European Union with more than 150 in at least two different countries will have to set up a pan-European information and consultation system for them by September 1996. At least 300 companies are therefore likely to have to make arrangements for their non-British employees – and many will probably include those based here for the sake of completeness.

The Directive stipulates that unless there is already an agreed process in force companies must hold:

– an annual information and consultation meeting between employee (not necessarily trade union) representatives and central management
– consultation before major decisions affecting more than one Member State.

Some companies have already set up an international framework. United Biscuits, for example, has 20,000 employees in the UK, 6,000 in fourteen countries across Europe and 14,000 elsewhere in the world. They hold an annual meeting of representatives from every country – non-unionised as well as unionised. The representatives meet to discuss the issues they wish to raise with management – before the full consultative council meeting. At the council meeting itself senior management discuss the performance of the group, the direction of overall strategy and the broad commercial factors affecting the business.

This is neither consultation in the traditional sense nor full industrial democracy. It is an opportunity to encourage mutual trust and understanding as a basis for effective working relationships.

(b) Company Assemblies

Many more organisations have taken their traditional consultative structure and expanded it to provide a real chance for employees and/or their representatives to understand, question and influence what the business is trying to achieve and to embrace a new vision and set of values. From airlines to building societies, from car plants to electricity companies, employee rallies, conferences, workshops and other types of 'get-together' are taking place as part of the process of changing the culture of organisations. In Unit 19 we will explore just what that can mean.

Questions
1. Describe the principal types of trade union and give examples of each.
2. How can membership of a trade union assist employees?
3. Describe the structure and functions of (*a*) the TUC; (*b*) the CBI.
4. What are the functions of (*a*) ACAS; (*b*) industrial tribunals?
5. What do you understand by the terms (*a*) substantive agreement; (*b*) procedural agreement; (*c*) distributive bargaining; (*d*) integrative bargaining; (*e*) productivity deal; (*f*) pendulum arbitration; (*g*) partnership agreement?
6. What forms of employee involvement and/or participation would help **your** organisation? How might these work, and what would the benefits be?

UNIT 19

Regulating Employment

19.1 Introduction

We have examined the basic institutions and conventions of the industrial relations scene. We can now turn to see how, in practice, the employment of one group of people by another can be regulated to minimise wasteful conflict. This is done by two sorts of rules: the unwritten and the written. There are also three groups at work formulating these rules, sometimes together, sometimes in isolation from each other. These three groups are:

- (*a*) the government,
- (*b*) employees,
- (*c*) management/employers.

We have been looking at the way in which the government regulates conduct of and in employment, unit by unit, and we will continue to view specific pieces of legislation in relation to particular aspects of the employment process.

We have talked about formal employee organisations – trade unions – and will go on to consider their role in helping management to formulate and implement appropriate conflict-reducing procedures. We have not, as yet, dealt in any detail with the ways in which employees can organise themselves on an informal basis. We will do that now, before examining, in Units 19.3 and 19.4, the ways in which our third group, management and employers, can influence, both tacitly and overtly, the regulation of employment.

19.2 Work Group Norms

The possible existence of **work group norms**, or group-imposed standards of behaviour, was first discovered in the 1930s by Elton Mayo during an American research programme, the Hawthorne experiments. It was found that the workers being studied bonded together as a social group, and then sought to influence the behaviour of members of the group. An acceptable level of work output was determined by the group, and then anyone who tried to do more, or less, was labelled a 'rate buster' or a 'chiseller'. They would then have to bear the censure of the group. The existence of norms, which may be either prescriptive ('do help your mate') or proscriptive ('don't drink with the boss') saves discussion by the work group on the course of action that is to be taken in specific circumstances. Norms are believed to be enforced by the group in two ways.

(*a*) Externally, by education, surveillance, disciplinary and rewarding actions. Thus the individual group member feels that he must not step out of line, for fear of being ostracised by the group or of not being included in some group activity.

(*b*) Internally, perhaps as a result of external pressure where the individual eventually comes to believe that the way the group behaves is the right way to behave. He therefore conforms automatically.

If work group norms really do exist, they will be a powerful force in any workplace. They will control the behaviour of individuals so that no amount of management pleading will persuade them to deviate from the accepted level of output or type of behaviour. They will also colour your employees' perceptions of the work they do, how it should be done, and of the organisation as a whole.

There is, however, some evidence to show that work group norms may not be as binding upon the behaviour of individual group members as the Hawthorne experiments suggested. In 1946 Collins and Roy, who studied restriction of output and social cleavage in industry (*Applied Anthropology*, 1946, pp. 1–14) found a significant number of workers who were indifferent, or even hostile, to the social groupings they found in their jobs. In 1954 a study conducted by the University of Liverpool into dock working found that approximately half the longshoremen on the docks they studied had purposely avoided the social entanglements of work group membership. In the same year, Chris Argyris at Yale University studied groupings in an American bank. He found that employees who had a high degree of public contact – the cashiers – were less prone to forming their own social groupings than those with less opportunity for public contact.

Other factors may also influence the behaviour of the work group. In a study into the effect of group-working in coalmining, Trist and Bamforth of the Tavistock Institute found, in 1951, that the allocation and definition of roles and tasks, the organisation of work flow, the methods of control and the system of wage payments will all act as determinants of work group behaviour.

Whether or not we accept that particular norms of behaviour will bind all workers together, the fact remains that particular groups will tend to differ in their relations with management. Sayles, in his book *The Behaviour of Industrial Work Groups*, differentiates four types of work group.

(a) Apathetic
These groups are not likely to challenge management or union decisions. They tend to form where jobs are relatively low skilled and low paid or where each employee performs a separate operation. In such circumstances there is not

likely to be any concerted action by the members, because they have little in common with each other. The basic characteristics of such groups are:

(i) they have relatively few grievances;

(ii) they lack clearly defined or accepted leadership;

(iii) they tend to suffer from internal disunity and friction between the members;

(iv) they display evidence of suppressed discontent.

(b) Erratic

These are more likely to challenge management and become rapidly inflamed. Such groups tend to form where everyone has an identical or nearly identical task and a high degree of interaction with other members. Although commonly found on short assembly lines, their existence is more prevalent where the jobs are worker- rather than machine-controlled. Their basic characteristics are:

(i) easily inflamed but rapidly soothed;

(ii) inconsistent behaviour and application of pressure tactics towards management;

(iii) highly centralised work group leadership and active involvement in trade union organisation.

(c) Strategic

Work groups of this type are liable to challenge management and union decisions affecting the economic position of their members on a much more concerted and consistent basis than either of the first two groups. They tend to form where the jobs are not interdependent but are more highly skilled than in the case of apathetic groupings. The jobs concerned are often relatively important to both management and job-holders, and the latter seek to make them not only important jobs, but good jobs. In fact, they tend to be jobs which are at the top of the promotional ladder for the people performing them. Such groups are characterised by:

(i) continuous pressure on management;

(ii) well-planned and consistent grievance activity;

(iii) a high degree of unity within the group;

(iv) sustained union participation;

(v) a relatively good output record.

(d) Conservative

One step higher in terms of skill and occupational status, and consisting usually of individuals working on separate operations, the members of conservative work groups are self-assured and successful. They only act when some existing benefit is threatened or they find themselves left behind by some other group which has brought more pressure to bear on management. Their characteristics include:

(i) restrained pressure for highly specific objectives;
(ii) internal unity and self-assurance;
(iii) adherence to laid-down procedures for grievances and disputes.

This model of group behaviour stems from a time when management–worker relationships were essentially confrontational. When management is 'the enemy', group energy is directed against it. The workforce is more likely to behave as a 'gang' than a 'team'. It will adopt common patterns of behaviour but its energy is directed towards negative or destructive action rather than shared and constructive goals.

Of more relevance to those who want to build **teams** is some research, conducted by Dr Meredith Belbin at the Administrative Staff College, Henley, which suggests that the **composition** of a group is what really determines how it behaves and whether it succeeds as a team.

We each naturally adopt one or more roles when working with others. Some, the **plants**, are full of ideas – some of them quite unorthodox. Others, the **resource investigators**, can always track down the material, information or people needed for a particular task. **Shapers** make sure objectives and priorities are clear, **monitor-evaluators** are good at analysing problems and helping to evaluate ideas and **specialists** are single-minded and dedicated to the task. **Implementers** bring practical common sense, **team workers** do their best to support their colleagues, **co-ordinators** make sure each member is able to contribute to the full while **completers** see there are no loose ends.

Whether the 'team' is a permanent working group or a short-term working party or task force, an understanding of these roles and how to mix them is vital. A balanced team with clear goals, the right mix of technical competences and skills, responsibility for monitoring and measuring their own progress and the authority to root out the causes of errors and delays will develop quite a different norm. Their behaviour will be geared to enabling every member to do his best to get the job done well. Apathetic, erratic or strategic behaviours are far less likely.

19.3 Management Influence: Vision and Values

In any organisation employees will infer what is, and is not, appropriate behaviour. They will observe who gets singled out for praise – and guess why. They will observe who gets promoted – and guess why. They will observe who gets sacked – and guess why. They will observe how customers are treated, where costs are cut, how managers spend their time – and guess why.

Sometimes they will guess right. Sometimes they won't. Sometimes there **will** be a consistent thread binding all these actions together. Sometimes the pressure for short-term results, or even the whim of individual managers will be the real determinant.

To take the guesswork out of what is the right way to behave, the board of directors may publish a statement of the **values** which they believe should guide everyone's behaviour. Usually linked with the company **vision**, such

Table 19.1   Characteristics of visions and values

VISIONS should provide a statement of future direction which is:

- customer-focused
- owned by everyone in the business
- memorable and compelling
- concise
- easy to understand
- dynamic – not static
- realistic – not fanciful
- inspirational – yet credible
- capable of creating a 'warm glow' or 'feel good factor'

VALUES should be

- an unambiguous source of guidance on how to act
- based in the best of what the company is, and what it wants to be
- capable of – becoming second nature
            – being consistently and universally applied
            – uniting the whole business
- enabling – promoting positive, moral behaviour
- meaningful
- credible
- enduring
- worth fighting for

NEITHER must be allowed to become a strait-jacket or a set of inflexible dogma

BOTH must be demonstrated, not preached

---

statements can be a very powerful way of helping everyone understand how to act – without the need for a complex set of procedural guidelines or rule books (see Unit 19.4).

Table 19.1 summarises the characteristics of both visions and values, and Table 19.2 provides examples of each. These are for guidance only! The process of developing visions and values is, as Tom Peters suggested in his book *Thriving on Chaos*, a 'messy artistic process . . . and can't be prescribed'. Each organisation must find its own. Unless **your** chief executive is able to blend his or her own cherished beliefs with those of the senior team in a way that makes sense to everyone, the statements will be meaningless. Unless **every** member of the top team is prepared to be guided by them, and visibly so, they will be hollow.

Lip-service is worse than useless. If your values have implications for the way customers will be treated, every process in the business may need to be

Table 19.2 Examples of visions and values

VISIONS

DISNEYWORLD

'A place for families to find happiness and knowledge. It will be based on and dedicated to the ideals, dreams and facts that have created America. It will be filled with the accomplishments, joys and hopes of the world we live in and a source of inspiration to all the world.'

ROVER

'Internationally renowned for extraordinary customer satisfaction'

VALUES

DDI

- meeting customer needs
- teamwork
- empowerment
- quality of life for associates
- innovation
- constant improvement

overhauled to make sure it is capable of delivering the goods. If your values have implications for the way employees are treated, every aspect of your personnel policy, from recruitment, training and development to rewards, health and safety and discipline must be scrutinised and, if necessary, reformulated to reflect the appropriate values.

Clearly the vision and values should, wherever possible, permeate the whole organisation. But even if your colleagues seem reluctant to articulate theirs, there is nothing to stop you and your immediate team developing your own shared sense of the future and a framework of common values. Just try to ensure that these are compatible with what you know of the overall direction of the business.

Helping everyone to understand what the values imply is, in itself, a major communication and training task. Once everyone **does** understand, they can use their own best judgment to determine how to act. As long as it is consistent with the values and will help, in however small a way, to bring the vision a little closer to reality, they will **know** it is right.

19.4 Management Influence: the Company Rule Book

In a truly empowered organisation where the vision and values are crystal clear 'use your own best judgement at all times' may be the only rule you need. Nordstrom, a leading US retailer, operates on this principle.

To ensure fairness and consistency of treatment, most UK organisations do feel a need to be a little more formal. The Contracts of Employment Act 1972, the Employment Protection Act 1975 and the Trade Union Reform and Employment Rights Act 1993 require employers to provide written information about certain aspects of their disciplinary rules and procedures – usually embodied in a company handbook of some sort.

(a) Writing the Rules

The rules do not have to be written by management. If empowerment is your goal, ask your employees to draft them. One company which did this was amazed at the outcome. Not only was the resulting document clear and comprehensive, it also passed the scrutiny of an expert in employment law.

However you approach it, the starting point in devising the rules must again be the vision and values of the organisation. The framing of rules which are inconsistent with these will cause needless conflict and prove ineffective. If you are aiming for empowerment, numerous detailed rules, devised unilaterally and rigidly adhered to regardless of circumstances, will be inappropriate.

A checklist of some of the areas that might require specific regulation is given below.

Checklist for writing the rule book:

(1) attendance, frequency and hours;
(2) notification of absence;
(3) use of company property;
(4) rest periods;
(5) smoking and drugs;
(6) drinking alcohol;
(7) fraternisation, and sexual harassment;
(8) use of confidential company information;
(9) deception, dishonesty, fraud;
(10) fighting/disturbances;
(11) gambling and swearing;
(12) immoral conduct;
(13) sleeping on duty;
(14) unsafe practices, failure to comply with safety rules;
(15) complying with management instructions;
(16) meeting work standards.

But as the ACAS Code of Practice on Disciplinary Practice and Procedures in Employment points out: 'It is unlikely that any set of disciplinary rules can cover all the circumstances that may arise. Moreover, the rules required will vary according to the particular circumstances, such as the type of work, working conditions, size of establishment. When drawing up rules, the aim should be to specify clearly and concisely those necessary for the efficient and safe performance of work and for the maintenance of satisfactory relations within the work force and between employees and management. Rules should not be so general as to be meaningless.'

The precise content of each rule will be dictated by your organisation's specific policy – on issues such as alcohol, drugs, smoking. The whole area of relationships **between** employees, of the same or different status, should be comprehensively dealt with in a written *Equal Opportunities Policy*. This should set out:

- the organisation's commitment to avoid both direct and indirect discrimination on grounds of race, colour, nationality, sex, disability, pregnancy or marital status (see Unit 3.8);
- how the organisation seeks to avoid both types of discrimination: during recruitment, selection, training, career development and the termination of employment, and in disciplinary matters and dealing with grievances;
- the organisation's determination to reward all employees fairly in relation to objective criteria and without unfair discrimination;
- those types of behaviour between employees which may be construed as harassment (see Unit 16.8) and the action to be taken in such cases;
- the consequences for those found to be in breach of any aspect of the policy.

Both the Equal Opportunities Commission and the Commission for Racial Equality can provide detailed guidance on constructing such a policy. You may wish to extend it to include discrimination and harassment based on age, religion or sexual orientation.

(b) Publicising the Rules
It is not enough to specify what the rules are. You must also make sure that employees and managers are aware of them, understand them and are aware of the consequences of any breach of them.

To this end, you should ensure that every employee is given a personal copy of the rules on joining the organisation, and they should be explained during his induction period. You would be well-advised to ask each employee to sign to confirm that he has received and understood these rules. Amendments should be issued periodically.

(c) Enforcing the Rules
As we saw when we considered the specific question of safety at work, the fact that people know how something should be done does not mean that they will always do it that way. The same applies to this more general area of regulating employment.

(i) Employees. If employees do not feel that a rule is necessary, they will be less inclined to obey it than if they can clearly see its purpose. Smoking provides an example. If your employees know that there is a serious fire risk, as in a chemical plant, it is likely to be rather easier to persuade them not to smoke than if they are in an office, where the risk of fire is rather less obvious.

Employees will also be quick to spot deviations from the rules which go unchallenged and to build them into their normal work patterns. If the boss does not appear to mind if people come in ten minutes late in the morning, some employees may adjust their timekeeping accordingly.

(ii) Teams. Where the rules **do** have general support, breaches which make it harder for the team to achieve its goals may be dealt with by the work group itself. Absenteeism is a good example. In one manufacturing plant, the high level of one-day absences was disrupting work. Team members decided to set up their own signing-in procedure so they could tell straight away if they were shorthanded. Simply by drawing attention to the issue in this way they found attendance improved dramatically.

(iii) Managers. Where it does become necessary to enforce the rules, consistency must be the goal. This is not always easy. Rules require interpretation. The way in which individual managers choose to interpret them will depend upon a number of things: personality, the state of the labour market, production pressure, the industrial relations climate and the perceived gravity of the offence.

A manager who likes a quiet life, who knows that labour is scarce, production pressure great and the industrial relations climate volatile is not likely to dismiss someone or risk provoking a resignation or industrial action for the sake of what he sees as a minor offence. The consequences of doing so are likely to be worse for him than for the offender. There is also some evidence to show that managers tend to temper the penalty to suit the individual, rather than the offence. If you think that Joe will respond to a good talking-to, you will give him one. But perhaps the only language that Fred understands is a formal warning or suspension.

Although such flexibility of individual interpretation has its merits, in terms of employer–employee relations it has serious drawbacks. If different managers are interpreting the same rule in different ways, it might be that one would dismiss someone for an offence to which another has accorded a lesser penalty. An industrial tribunal would not look favourably on such a precedent, as we shall see in Unit 21.

One general principle which can be applied is Douglas McGregor's **'red-hot stove' rule**. This means that, as when you touch a red-hot stove you are burned immediately, whoever you are, and can see both cause and effect, so discipline should be uniformly and immediately applied, the penalties being the same for all, and the punishment clearly relating to the offence.

You will find it easier to comply with this principle if you ensure that serious offences and repetitions of more minor ones are governed by a disciplinary procedure. You will need to train managers in the use of such a procedure, and consider how employee or trade union representatives can be involved in its devising and implementation.

19.5 Disciplinary Procedures

Although disciplinary procedures are often thought of as a means of enforcing specific rules and regulations, they should also be followed where an employee's general standard of performance suggests that the necessity for remedial action should be drawn, formally, to his attention.

(a) Drawing up a Disciplinary Procedure

The ACAS Code of Practice on Disciplinary Practice and Procedures in Employment provides the best guide for the drawing up of a procedure. In order to comply with the code of practice (which does not have the force of law, but does constitute the kind of good employment practice for which an industrial tribunal would look when considering a claim for unfair dismissal), your disciplinary procedure should:

(i) Be set out in writing.

(ii) Identify the categories of employee to whom it applies.

(iii) Offer provision for matters to be dealt with quickly.

(iv) Indicate the disciplinary actions which may be taken: what categories of offence justify instant dismissal? If you wish to use the sanctions of a disciplinary transfer or suspension without pay, then these conditions must be written into each employee's contract of employment.

(v) Specify the level of management which has the authority to invoke particular penalties. It is unwise to allow the authority to dismiss to be distributed too widely or too far down the hierarchy: in the interests of justice and, as we have seen, of avoiding troublesome precedent. The code suggests that immediate superiors should not have the power to dismiss without reference to senior management.

(vi) Provide for individuals to be informed of complaints against them and to be given an opportunity to state their case before decisions are reached. This applies as much to initial verbal warnings at shop-floor level as it does to final formal warnings. If justice is to be done and, more important, be seen to be done, all the sides to the story must be considered at each stage.

(vii) Give individuals the right, when stating their case, to be accompanied by their union representative or a fellow employee of their choice. You will find that, at each stage, the level of trade union representation rises to match the level in the organisation hierarchy which is currently dealing with the issue. Thus you may start off with a supervisor and a shop steward, and end up with the general manager and his entourage, and a full-time trade union official and his.

(viii) Ensure that, except for gross misconduct, no employee is dismissed for a first breach of discipline. The things which constitute gross misconduct should be clearly specified, preferably in the rule book and contract of employment. Such offences commonly include theft, drunkenness and insubordination, but will depend on individual circumstances.

(ix) Ensure that disciplinary action is not taken until the case has been fully investigated. This will involve time for both management and employee to prepare their respective cases.

(x) Ensure that the individual is given an explanation for any penalty imposed.

(xi) Provide a right of appeal and specify the procedure to be followed.

(b) Implementing the Procedure

As the above points imply, the implementation of a procedure is a two-sided affair. The offender's immediate boss needs to investigate the offence and the circumstances surrounding it. The offender must be asked to give his side of the story. Other people – those higher up the hierarchy, the offender's colleagues or witnesses to the alleged offence – may need to be consulted. Only when it is established that a breach of discipline has indeed taken place (a rule has been broken) can you start to implement the procedure. The way in which you do this will depend upon the gravity of the offence.

(i) Minor offences. If Joe is five minutes late one morning, and his supervisor feels that the timekeeping rule must be strictly enforced, he should give Joe an oral warning. This means that, unless he has an explanation which his supervisor considers satisfactory, she will draw to Joe's attention the rule which specifies the time at which he should arrive for work. She will tell Joe the consequences of being late again, and advise him that this warning constitutes the first stage in the disciplinary procedure. A note should be kept of the date and circumstances of when the warning was administered.

(ii) Serious offences/repetition of minor offences. If Joe is late every morning for, say, a week, or if one day he turns up for work half-way through his shift, he should be issued with a formal written warning, this time perhaps by his manager. This, too, will spell out the nature of his offence, and the consequences of a repetition. Again he should be told that this is part of the formal disciplinary procedure, and you should be sure that any consequences you have specified are in line with those administered by other managers in similar circumstances, in case it is necessary to proceed further.

(iii) Further misconduct. If Joe persists in arriving a little late each day, or in going absent without prior permission, he should be issued with a final written warning. This should be given either by his own manager, or by someone more senior. It should specify the penalty which will be invoked if he does not mend his ways within a specified time-limit. The length of such a time-limit will vary according to the circumstances. In Joe's case, perhaps a few days, or a month at the most, would be appropriate. For other types of misconduct, or where it may be more difficult to produce an immediate change, a longer interval will be required. During this period, everything possible must be done to help him overcome his difficulties.

(iv) The final step. If, after the specified time lapse, Joe is still breaking the rules, the specified penalty must be invoked, by whoever has the authority to do so. Failure to do this will undermine the whole procedure. Such final sanctions can include dismissal, or if allowed for in the contract of employment suspension without pay for a stated period, or a transfer to another section. But a transfer, even for disciplinary reasons, could lead to a claim for constructive dismissal (see Unit 21) if it involves a downward revision of the employee's terms and conditions of employment. The penalty must be reasonable in all the circumstances, and the employee must have been given adequate opportunity throughout to put his side of the case and to remedy the problem. We will look at the sorts of action which an industrial tribunal will take into account in deciding what is reasonable in Unit 21.

Some organisations extend their procedure through one further stage, perhaps allowing for two oral warnings before the offender is issued with a written warning. The emphasis throughout must be on fairness. When you start to invoke the disciplinary procedure, you should always do so with a view to helping the individual overcome his shortcomings and become a satisfactory employee. Beware of the manager who says: 'He's got to go, but I'll have to go through all the procedure to get rid of him.'

(c) Special Cases

When dealing with disciplinary matters involving a trade union official, you would be well advised to discuss the matter with a senior union representative or a full-time official at an early stage.

You will also need to make special arrangements for those on shift work or in isolated locations, to whom the full procedure is not immediately available.

(d) Appeals Procedure

Although the employee will have had various chances to state his case, when a decision has actually been reached about the penalty to be applied, he must have a formal opportunity to appeal. The appeal should be dealt with speedily, and by members of management and the trade union of sufficient seniority to make a decision which will stick. In cases where no such decision is possible, it may be necessary, if all the parties agree, to involve an independent arbitrator.

(e) Keeping Records

Because an employee who is finally dismissed can claim that his dismissal was unfair, it is wise to keep detailed records not only of the nature of his misconduct or incompetence, but also of when, how and by whom each stage of the disciplinary procedure was applied. If an appeal is lodged, a record should be kept of that too, with particular reference to the outcome. These records should be kept confidential, but you need not keep them for ever. You can usefully apply the notion of a spent conviction (page 94) to internal transgressions.

19.6 Grievance Procedures

Where the organisation has cause to complain about the behaviour of an employee, the disciplinary procedure is used. Where an employee has cause to complain about the organisation, he requires a parallel mechanism. This helps to prevent minor disagreements sparking off major conflicts and can also improve employee retention. If they have a chance to air their problems and sort them out, employees are less likely to 'vote with their feet'.

Your grievance procedure should have the following features:

   (i) It should be in writing.
   (ii) It should specify to whom employees may take a grievance in the first

instance (normally their immediate boss), and that they have the right to be accompanied by a colleague or a trade union representative.

(iii) It should state where, in the event of the grievance remaining unresolved, an employee should then address his complaint. The grandfather figure of his boss's immediate superior can provide a second port of call before the grievance is finally taken before a director or senior manager or, in some instances, an ombudsman or a works council.

(iv) It should specify time limits within which the aggrieved employee can expect to be notified of the outcome of his complaint.

(v) All meetings to discuss the grievance should be properly minuted, and a record of proceedings sent to all the parties.

As in the case of the disciplinary procedure, the spirit in which you approach the implementation of the process is important. Action must be taken to search out the root causes of the problem – not just to deal with the symptoms.

The range of issues raised is likely to be wide – from complaints about work allocation to allegations of racial or sexual harassment (see Unit 16.8). The latter need particularly sensitive handling. If the complaint proves to be groundless, the alleged harasser may feel his or her reputation has been sullied and demand disciplinary action against the complainant. If it is upheld, the complainant will have the right to expect appropriate disciplinary action to be taken against the harasser – and may need protection from victimisation.

Then too, the harasser may be the victim's immediate boss. In any case, the victim may feel particularly embarrassed or humiliated by the behaviour. It is vital to make sure there is a well-publicised channel for dealing with these complaints, with right of access to specialist counsellors or more senior managers rather than the victim's immediate manager.

Ignoring employee grievances in the hope that they will go away is never a good idea. If the grievance is a serious one, like harassment, your failure to act could amount to a fundamental breach of the trust and confidence implied in the contract of employment. If the victim resigns, he or she could succeed in claiming to have been constructively dismissed (see Unit 21).

It is far better to take all the steps you can to raise awareness of what constitutes harassment and to educate your employees to deal with each other in a way which respects the dignity of every employee. A well thought out and communicated Equal Opportunities Policy (see Unit 19.4) should be your starting point.

19.7 Disputes Procedures

Disciplinary and grievance procedures are generally applied to individuals. You will also need some sort of procedure to take the heat out of group conflict. Your disputes procedure should follow these steps.

(i) Specify where all grievances raised by groups of employees or which affect more than one employee should first be taken – probably to the immediate superior, through a shop steward.

'Couldn't we settle this by some judicial process?'

(ii) Indicate the next point of appeal. This is usually the departmental manager, with perhaps a personnel manager and senior shop steward in attendance.

(iii) Specify further points of appeal. This may be the works manager, and then a wider conference at which senior members of management, preferably including a director, will sit down with the shop steward, senior shop steward and a full-time official of the union.

(iv) State that, if a mutually satisfactory agreement has not been reached during the previous internal stages, the matter will be referred to an outside body (probably ACAS) for conciliation and, if that fails, arbitration.

(v) Specify time limits within which the various stages of the procedure will be completed.

(vi) Provide for a record to be kept of all meetings in connection with the dispute.

(vii) Include a statement to the effect that no industrial action should be taken by employees before the procedure has been exhausted.

Although all three of the types of procedure that we have discussed will benefit from trade union involvement in devising them, no disputes procedure can operate without it.

Taken together, and properly implemented, these procedures will help you to regulate your relationship with your employees, individually and collectively. But their effective implementation does require certain skills of those concerned. Disciplinary and grievance procedures call for the exercise of interviewing skills by the managers involved. We have already discussed these in a selection and an appraisal context, and the basic principles will hold good here, too. Thorough preparation, a joint problem-solving approach and open questioning, and careful recording and follow-up are the key elements. A decision which has the commitment of both parties is, again, your prime aim.

Negotiating skills, such as those which will be required in a dispute or when bargaining, are something which we have not, as yet, considered.

19.8   Negotiating Skills

Wherever there is disagreement between management and union, you will need to seek a solution through negotiation, rather than confrontation, if you are to avoid disruption.

(a) Preparation
Your first task is to make sure that you are fully aware of the stages in any disputes or other procedures which may govern the proceedings. Then you must ensure that you know management's position on the points at issue. In some areas it will be possible to make concessions, in others you will need to stand firm because of the cost or the precedent which will be set by giving in.

(b) Strategy
Before going to the bargaining table, you will need to work out what you would like to aim for (your target or ideal settlement) and what you are likely to achieve (your realistic settlement). You should also be clear about the minimum in the way of a settlement that you are prepared to accept (your resistance point or fallback position).

(c) Tactics
The union side will also start with a target, and your aim as an employer will normally be to push them back to their fallback position. Your tactics can include regular adjournments to discuss developments, repeated probing to test what you are hearing from the other side, or endless repetition of your own position, to convince the other party. One vital thing is your degree of commitment. If you can clearly demonstrate your determination, the union is bound to take your arguments more seriously.

You may need to shift your position gradually, as new arguments are brought forward and the union's bargaining position emerges more clearly. Timing is also crucial. The conventions of the bargaining table are such that an early concession is taken as an opening bid, and you will find yourself pressed, if not to increase that offer, then to go further in other directions.

Compiling the agenda is important, too. Red herrings, or phoney concessions, can be introduced by one side or the other early on in the proceedings. For instance, you can demonstrate your reasonableness and commitment by agreeing to something of secondary importance, and then dig your heels in when it comes to the real issues: you have bent over backwards so far, so now it's their turn.

You can also look for signs of disagreement within the ranks of the other negotiating team, always assuming that your own party has worked out a united front, perhaps at a pre-negotiating meeting. Or you can concentrate on persuading the most influential member of the union team, in the hope that he will convince the others.

If all this strikes you as something of a ritual, you are right. It is, nevertheless, the traditional approach to formal industrial relations. Before you become involved in it personally, it will be essential to develop your own skills. A short course, where role-play exercises and possibly a real trade union negotiating team can be used, will be helpful, as will preliminary attendance at negotiations in the capacity of observer.

In these last two units we have considered how employee relations can be regulated and made to work, on both an individual and a collective basis. We will now turn to one of the most emotive issues in industrial relations: redundancy.

Questions

1. In what ways and by whom can the behaviour of groups of employees be regulated?
2. If you were asked to compile a set of rules and regulations for your organisation, how would you set about it?
3. Describe the stages in your organisation's grievance and disciplinary procedures. What contribution do you think they make towards reducing tension and potential conflict?
4. If you were nominated as a member of a management negotiating team to discuss pay and conditions with a recognised independent trade union, how would you prepare yourself for the task?

UNIT 20

Dismissing Redundant Employees

20.1 Introduction

A dismissal occurs:

(*a*) When an employer terminates a contract of employment for one of his employees, with or without notice. Termination without notice is known as **instant** or **summary dismissal**. If such dismissal takes place in breach of the terms of the contract of employment, this is **wrongful dismissal**;

(*b*) When an employer acts in breach of the contract of employment in such a way as to force the employee to terminate the contract. This is **forced resignation** or **constructive dismissal**;

(*c*) When an employee is employed under a contract for a fixed term and the term expires without being renewed under the same contract.

There are two basic causes of dismissal. Either the job has ceased to exist, so the services of the individual are no longer required, or the services of the individual are no longer required because, for some reason, those services are not satisfactory. In this unit we will be discussing the first cause. In Unit 21 we will consider the second.

We talked in Unit 2 about the importance of effective human resource planning. One of the consequences of failing to plan is that you may find, sooner or later, that you have too many employees for the continued prosperity of the organisation. The surplus is classified as redundant. Legally, redundancy occurs when an employer's requirement for *work* has come to an end or diminished. But because this redundant surplus consists of people – people who will be affected by your actions and are protected by legislation – you cannot simply discard them as you might an old piece of equipment which is no longer required.

Redundancy needs careful handling. But before we decide how this can best be done, we will consider the most common causes of redundancy, the costs of redundancy, and how redundancy can be averted.

20.2 Causes of Redundancy

In Unit 2.2 we listed a number of factors which will influence your demand for people. These included:

(*a*) Market fluctuations, affecting demand for your products.

(*b*) Changes in the availability of raw materials or components, affecting the amount that you can produce.

(*c*) Technological advances, affecting the way that the work is done.

(*d*) Government action, influencing product demand.

(*e*) Changes in the cost of labour relative to that of other resources.

There are also a number of specific occurrences which frequently lead to redundancy, which warrant more detailed consideration here.

(*f*) Changes of ownership – including mergers, takeovers and privatisation – frequently give rise to redundancies. In the case of mergers and takeovers, unnecessary duplication of functions will be a primary target. The new organisation is unlikely to need two finance directors, two personnel directors, two sales directors. Other functions – and their support staff – will be equally vulnerable. In the case of privatisation, the quest for a more cost-effective, leaner structure is likely to produce casualties.

(*g*) Rationalisation or cost-reduction programmes may be made necessary by any of the factors we have already listed. Alternatively, a falling return on investment or some other financial yardstick may prompt an organisation to try to reduce expenditure. And, if people constitute a significant part of your total budget, this is an obvious area in which to try to introduce cost savings. This can be done by amalgamating jobs, revising work methods or automating them, leaving some of your workforce surplus to requirements.

(*h*) Restructuring may be needed as a result of Business Process Re-engineering (see Unit 11) to make better, and more cost-effective, use of resources and to derive a more sensible and workable organisation structure. So, if you have one group of clerks sending out invoices and another group sending out statements, it may, in some circumstances, be an idea to combine the two. This can save duplication of effort, increase job satisfaction, reduce labour costs and improve customer service.

(*i*) De-layering, to remove whole levels of management and create a flatter, more empowered organisation, is a comparatively recent phenomenon. Whether driven by ideological reasons or purely on cost grounds, the result is the same. Middle managers are no longer secure.

(*j*) Relocation of premises can arise from a number of circumstances. High rents, poor accommodation, bad communications, staff shortages or even personal preference may determine that a new site is called for. But those who are unable to move with the organisation may be redundant, unless you can offer them reasonable alternative employment.

(*k*) Financial collapse or closure will mean that you have to declare all your workforce – not just a portion of it – redundant. Even if the company as a whole is viable, one factory, operating location or area of activity may have to close. In times of recession, local and national news bulletins are full of examples of such closures.

The evidence is that few, if any, sectors of employment can now offer long-term job security. The financial services sector, once regarded as one of the most secure, has shed 100,000 jobs in two years. A survey in 1994 revealed that 80 per cent of firms in the industry had declared redundancies in the recent past – as a result of restructuring, 'right-sizing' and 'down-sizing'. Half anticipated further redundancies in the next twelve months.

20.3   Costs of Redundancy

Redundancy involves costs in terms of time, cash, conflict and emotion. There are a number of parties concerned, and we will examine the implications of redundancy for each in turn.

(a) The Individual

Stephen Fink, in an article in the *Journal of Applied Behavioural Science* (vol. 7, no. 1, 1971), analysed four stages through which the human system passes as it adapts to crisis: shock, defensive retreat, acknowledgment, and adaptation and change. There is evidence that the victims of redundancy suffer several sorts of consequences.

(i) Psychological.   In a study of the stress to which people are subjected during and after redundancy, Kasl and Cobb looked at the effect on blood pressure, at monthly intervals, over a period of two years. Their findings are reported in *Psychosomatic Medicine*. In the period of anticipation of redundancy, blood pressure rises, and stays high for those who remain unemployed. Those who find jobs have a rapid reduction in blood pressure although it still remains higher than normal up to six months after they have been re-employed elsewhere. In an early study, Israeli, who investigated the outlook of the unemployed in Lancashire and Scotland in the 1930s and reported his findings in the *Journal of Applied Psychology* in 1935, found that the redundant who remained unemployed had expectations of failure in a variety of situations, not just at work. They tended to be confused and worried about the future, although calm about the past. Feelings of insecurity and loss of confidence are greatest for those to whom work has always been important intrinsically. In acute cases, the loss of purpose and the feeling of rejection engendered by redundancy can contribute to severe nervous disorders and even, some would argue, death. More recent studies, conducted during the recessions of the 1980s and 1990s, tend to confirm the gloomy picture.

(ii) Social.   Ours has traditionally been a society where people (especially men) are expected to work for a living for at least forty years. Those who find themselves out of work or even threatened with that prospect as a result of redundancy have their feelings of personal inadequacy fuelled by the unspoken censure of society. The fact that your neighbours are no more secure may not be much consolation.

(iii) Economic.   Although an employee with long service will receive some cash compensation from the organisation which declares him redundant, this

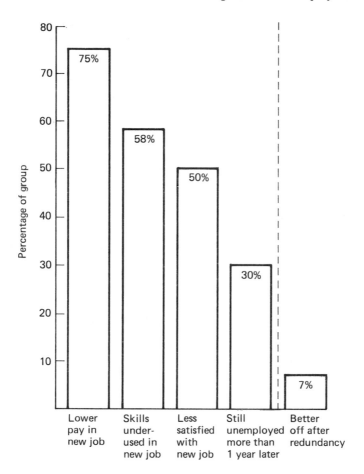

Fig 20.1

will not necessarily enable him to maintain his standard of living throughout a period of unemployment, the length of which he cannot predict. True, he can claim the Job Seeker's Allowance, or, later, Income Support, but these are almost bound to fall some way short of his previous total earnings. The economic problem of redundancy is more acute for some people than for others. It is related to the length of time for which they remain out of work following redundancy and to the level of employment which they subsequently find. Figure 20.1 gives an indication of the fate of a group of employees made redundant in south London some years ago. To the left-hand side of the dotted line we can see the adverse effects which the majority suffered. Especially worrying is the high proportion who were without work a year later. Statistics show that the longer a person has been unemployed, the longer he is likely to remain so. Young workers, those aged over fifty and the unskilled, who have faced a steadily falling demand for their labour, are particularly at risk. The higher the level of unemployment, the more likely it is that many of those who become unemployed will remain so for long periods. Although there are individuals for whom redundancy marked the beginning of a new and better way of life, these are the fortunate minority.

(b) The Company

Companies, too, go through a series of phases during redundancy. When management is confronted with the apparent inescapability of redundancy, it suffers shock. It will subsequently come to terms with the fact, acknowledge it, and begin to adapt to the new situation and plan for handling the redundancies and building for the future. The same sequence will be followed by the organisation as a whole. A period of defensive retreat may follow the shock phase, during which attempts will be made to persuade management that the redundancies are not necessary; or, failing that, to extract the best possible terms. Although the organisation will eventually adapt and learn to face the change, it may suffer in a number of ways in the process.

(i) **Loss of morale.**   Shock combined with uncertainty over the future can produce a sharp downturn in morale. This can be particularly acute before the redundancies are formally announced, when rumours are circulating freely. Even afterwards, **survivor syndrome** may mean that those who stay feel guilty at having survived and become demotivated and anxious, while the reallocation of work results in feelings of incompetence and stress.

(ii) **Employee reaction.**   We will consider the trade union view of redundancy shortly. Employee reaction during the defensive retreat phase can mean time lost through industrial action and disrupted production, while protracted meetings are held by employees to discuss their tactics.

(iii) **Loss of public confidence.**   We have seen that redundancy can happen for a number of reasons. It does not always mean that the company is on the verge of bankruptcy. It can, rather, be an indication that management is pruning, to strengthen its base in preparation for further growth. But your shareholders and other creditors – suppliers, for instance – may not see it like that. Your clients and customers, too, may start to look around for alternative sources of supply, in the fear that you will let them down.

(iv) **Time.**   Coping with employee reaction, complying with legislation, reassuring the public and counselling both leavers and stayers to help them adapt all take time. If redundancy is to be changed from a negative to a positive force for the future good of the organisation, you will also need to spend time redesigning the organisation structure to reflect changed objectives and making it work. This will mean time spent in discussions with managers, negotiations with unions, talks with individuals, general communications and a concerted effort to build and train a new team from the remnants of the old one. You will also lose time as, under the Employment Protection (Consolidation) Act 1978, redundant employees will have to be given reasonable time off, with pay, to look for alternative employment or to arrange retraining.

(v) Cash costs. Each of the foregoing costs to the company can be translated into financial terms. Over and above this, you will be obliged to make redundancy payments to all redundant employees between the ages of eighteen and sixty-five who have been with you for two years or more. The legal scale for these payments as specified by the Employment Protection (Consolidation) Act is given below.

Redundancy payments

$1\frac{1}{2}$ weeks' pay for each year of service between age 41 and age 64

1 week's pay for each year of service between age 22 and age 40

$\frac{1}{2}$ week's pay for each year of service between age 18 and age 21

There is an earnings limit under the Act, which is reviewed periodically. For 1995–6 this stands at £210 per week. You need also consider only the last twenty years of the employee's service, making the effective maximum payment under the Act £6,300 for 1995–6. In fact, individual redundancy payments may be much higher than this. This is because trade unions often negotiate far more generous redundancy arrangements than the legal minimum. It is common to waive the two-year service minimum, the twenty-year maximum, the earnings limit, or all three. The substitution of one month for one week in the wording of the above scale of redundancy payments also occurs.

Thus the cash costs of redundancy can mount up rapidly. In the past it was possible for employers to claim a rebate (from the state Redundancy Fund) to cover part of the cost of redundancy payments. This rebate has gradually been withdrawn, and employers must now meet the entire cost of redundancy payments from their own resources.

(c) The Unions

Large-scale redundancies among their members undermine the power of the trade unions. As we have seen, they also have unfortunate repercussions for the individuals concerned. Trade unions are therefore reluctant to accept redundancy and may agree to work-sharing or the forming of co-operatives, in order to sustain their members' right to work. TUC policy requires that all possible measures should be taken to avert redundancy, and that there should be close union consultation at all stages.

The long and crippling miners' strike of 1984 arose out of the refusal of the National Union of Mineworkers to accept the principle of the closure of 'uneconomic' pits – even though the (then) National Coal Board had promised that the only redundancies which would result would be volunteers who would receive very generous redundancy payments.

(d) The Country

Although industry which is overstaffed is unproductive and slows down the rate of economic growth, the dislocation and unemployment which can result from redundancy also has adverse effects on the national economy. Not all of those who are declared redundant will have skills which are obsolete; many could make a useful contribution to our economic prosperity. And a high level of unemployment costs the country dear, through social security payments, lost income tax and national insurance revenue, reduced spending power, and the effect on confidence among investors and the population at large.

20.4 Preventing Redundancies

The costs and problems of such enforced redundancy add up to a powerful argument for keeping it to a minimum. There are eight possible strategies which we will consider.

(a) Limits on Recruitment

This will enable you to reduce the overall size of the organisation, through natural wastage (labour turnover, retirements). Most trade unions will accept this as a valid way of dealing with overstaffing, but it has three drawbacks.

(i) Key positions may become vacant and cause serious difficulties through remaining unfilled.

(ii) The gradual rundown process will have an adverse effect on morale.

(iii) Reorganisation and rebuilding for the future will take much longer and will have to be done piecemeal.

(b) Dismissal of Temporary Employees

Those who are employed on a temporary basis, perhaps through an employment agency, may have a smaller stake in the company than most other employees. Make sure that such an approach does not have a disproportionate effect on one gender or the other, though, or you could find yourself facing a claim for indirect sex discrimination. Dismissing temporary employees will not solve your problem entirely, though, if most of your temporary staff are employed in one section and your overstaffing occurs in another.

(c) Dismissing those over Retirement Age

Although those over state retirement age may still have a valuable contribution to make, their long-term stake in the future of the company is also limited. Their dismissal has similar limitations to those mentioned in connection with temporary employees. It may also take more time to implement, if you have allowed these employees to become your sole source of expertise in particular fields.

(d) Early Retirement

If the rules of your occupational pension scheme allow it, you can offer people who are reaching the end of their working life the chance to retire early. Alternatively, you can reduce the retirement age across the board, although this will be expensive, in terms of both cash for improved benefits and lost expertise. Such methods will also take time to implement, as it can be just as brutal to cut off someone's working life and discard him in his sixties as it would be earlier. Pre-retirement counselling can help to ease the transition, and a voluntary approach will allow those who wish to remain to do so. If you do not have an occupational pension scheme, you cannot avail yourself of this method.

(e) Work Sharing

Reduction in overtime working is the first step in stretching out the available work in order to keep everyone employed. The next stage is to shorten working hours and introduce short-time working, perhaps by a transition to a four-day working week for a limited period. If the situation persists and you keep people on half-time for more than four weeks or on reduced hours for more than six weeks in any thirteen-week period, they will still be able to claim redundancy. Some employees who would otherwise face redundancy may be prepared to work on a part-time basis, but you cannot impose this unless their contracts specifically allow it.

(f) Transfer and Retraining

This may help where jobs are available in one section, while those in another are redundant. For an employee who recognises that his previous skill will no longer be required by any employer, training in a new skill will be vital. For others, the step into the unknown, either geographically or in terms of job skills, may be too daunting. If you do succeed in persuading them to try and retrain, do ensure that the new skills they acquire will be in long-term demand and bear in mind the need for a trial period (see below).

(g) Voluntary Redundancy

Where other measures are insufficient, the offer of redundancy terms to those who are prepared to volunteer to terminate their contracts sometimes produces a surprising number of willing employees. It is an expensive method, as the terms need to be attractive. It may also appeal to the people you most need to retain: those with initiative and marketable skills. But used with discretion, such a scheme can help to avoid much of the bitterness and negative impact of redundancy.

(h) More Effective Human Resource Planning

Although it is the last item on our list, more effective planning (see Unit 2) is perhaps the only real strategy for avoiding redundancies. It is too late to use it as a remedy when you find yourself in a crisis, but it is vital if you are to prevent yourself living from one crisis to the next, with no way out of the spiral.

Enforced redundancy is not inevitable. And, although some of the alternatives may, like short-time working and voluntary redundancy, be more expensive in cash terms, we have seen that this is not the only criterion. Where you need to be able to pick up the pieces and move forward, morale, employee reaction and the impressions of the world at large cannot be ignored.

20.5 Handling Redundancies

We have discussed the importance of having a laid-down procedure to regulate arrangements for dealing with potential problem areas and points of conflict. Redundancy is another such area. If procedures are worked out well before there is any need for them, agreement can be reached more calmly and rationally than might be possible when redundancies are imminent.

(a) Redundancy Procedure

Apart from detailing the steps that will be taken to avert redundancy, your procedure should:

(i) Allow for consultation with, and disclosure of information to, the relevant employees or their representatives, well in advance of the proposed date of the redundancy. (We will consider your legal obligations in this respect in the next section.)

(ii) Identify the methods which will be used to select those to be made redundant. 'Last in, first out' is customary in many organisations. Although this may force you to part with some of the very people that you have been recruiting to help the company through its present difficulties, it has its merits as a principle, particularly in view of the special problems to which older members of the workforce are prone after redundancy. Even where this principle is not adhered to, you should certainly not be using redundancy as an excuse to get rid of your trouble-makers or ineffective performers. The mechanism for doing that is, as we have seen, your disciplinary procedure.

(iii) Specify when and how individuals affected will be notified of their redundancy, and of the alternatives open to them. We will consider this in more detail below.

(iv) Specify to whom appeals may be made.

(v) Detail the method of calculation of redundancy payments, the procedure for paying them, and any special provision that will be made for those who leave before the completion of their notice period. The Employment Protection (Consolidation) Act 1978 or the terms of the employee's contract – whichever is more generous – regulates the amount of notice to which employees are entitled in redundancy, as with any other termination of employment. The employee does not have to work this notice if it is agreed that he shall be paid in lieu.

(vi) Specify whether any bonuses or other inducements will be offered to key personnel to encourage them to stay beyond the expiry of their official notice period, if required.

(vii) Outline arrangements for those affected by redundancy to take time off, with pay, to look for new employment.

(viii) State that employees who accept alternative employment within the organisation will do so on a trial basis. If either party is not satisfied within a specified period (the legal minimum is four weeks), the redundancy and the redundancy payments will stand. It is particularly important to avoid confusion over this, because technically it is jobs, not people, that are redundant.

If a job is subsequently filled by someone else, there is no redundancy. The alternative employment which the employee accepts cannot be classified as redundant, but the individual retains his redundancy rights by virtue of his tenure of his previous position.

Having devised a procedure, the first and most important thing to do is to stick to it. But, as we have seen, particular attention will need to be paid to the way in which we treat individuals and cope with the implications for the continued viability of the organisation.

(b) Dealing with Individuals

Because the costs of redundancy are not measured solely in cash terms, the most generous redundancy payment cannot solve all the individual's difficulties. A number of points need special thought:

(i) Notification of redundancy. This can be done in a number of ways, none of them perfect, but some more harmful than others. The most harmful is probably the terse note in the pay packet, perhaps enclosing pay in lieu of notice and the redundancy payment, telling the recipient not to come back next Monday morning. Informing people personally is more time-consuming, but reduces the initial shock phase slightly. One method is to address the whole work group, calling out the names of those who are to be made redundant. This at least relieves the uncertainty for those who are to remain. Alternatively, you can address the redundant group collectively, in the hope that each will gain comfort from knowing that he is not alone.

But if you are really concerned about how the fact of redundancy may affect people, you need to tell each employee individually. In so doing, you must reconcile the needs of each to talk about the problem with the need for those who have not yet been told to be put in the picture. Although you will have to advise people that their jobs are now redundant, you should try to avoid doing so until you have investigated alternatives and calculated redundancy pay. This way, you can give each one something positive to think about in the short term.

(ii) Retraining. This avoids the psychological, social and economic consequences of unemployment, even though the employee may take some time to adjust to the fact that his old job is no longer required.

(iii) Counselling. We have said that the individual should be told where he stands and what the alternatives are. Sensitive counselling at this stage will help him to identify the ways in which an apparently hopeless situation can be turned into something positive. Some companies go further than this, and arrange specialist career counselling through an outplacement agency and/or interviews with neighbouring employers. For those who would like to go into business on their own account, perhaps using their redundancy pay as part of their capital, courses can be arranged to help them broaden their knowledge and anticipate the difficulties of running a small business.

(iv) Additional financial assistance. For cases of special hardship, where the redundancy payment as calculated by the prescribed formula is small or non-existent, or where a long period of unemployment, perhaps due to disability or age, is likely to follow redundancy, you might consider making special provision. Some organisations make regular weekly payments to redundant employees, in addition to their lump sum redundancy pay, including, for a period, earnings supplements to those who find a new job with lower pay.

(c) Rebuilding the Company

(i) Morale. The way in which you deal with individuals and adhere to the spirit as well as the letter of your redundancy agreement will have an important bearing on morale. If people have been unjustly treated, lip service paid to union consultation and rumours allowed to circulate unchecked, your task after redundancy will be considerably harder than it need be. Increased employee involvement in management decision-making should mean that redundancies are not declared unless this really is the only sensible course of action. If all involved can be brought to recognise this, therein lies your best chance of building constructively for the future.

(ii) Adverse publicity. The reasons why redundancy is necessary should be made known, to avoid doubt and uncertainty. You should also try to avoid getting a reputation as a 'hire and fire' employer. If you regularly declare redundancies, and then have to recruit afresh a few months later, your image as an employer will suffer.

(iii) Reorganising. Effective communication and employee involvement are vital in dealing with redundancy. When it comes to rebuilding the organisation, the allocation of work, the shape and structure of the organisation, and future objectives can all be approached participatively. Here, as we have seen, lies your best chance of commitment. But commitment alone is not enough. People will need time to come to terms with changes, training to cope with new tasks, and help or individual counselling in accepting new patterns of behaviour and resolving the inevitable problems.

To overcome the feelings of guilt and dislocation felt by those **not** selected for redundancy, you need a clear strategy to deal with **survivor syndrome**. Anglia Railways, formed after the privatisation of Intercity, is one of a growing number of organisations to recognise this. To make sure employees understood that they were valued members of the new organisation and could share in its vision and values, it held a series of employee conferences. Each included a chance to voice the anger and uncertainty people still felt. One of the key suggestions to emerge was a request for counselling support to help them deal with changes. The company is also investing heavily in training and development and is working towards the National Standard for Investors in People (see Unit 10.7). The experience of other companies, such as the Birmingham Midshires Building Society, which have adopted similar strategies, is that motivation, commitment and productivity will be enhanced by the programme.

(d) Minimising the Cost to the Country

The best way of doing this might seem, at first sight, to be to avoid all redundancies. But we cannot afford to stand still. The real solution must lie in retraining and redeploying people, inside or outside the organisation, as quickly and effectively as possible. Although outplacement help is available, from the government Employment Service as well as private consultancies, British legislation is not really geared to this end.

20.6   Redundancy and the Law

The Acts which regulate the way in which you deal with individuals are the Employment Protection (Consolidation) Act 1978 and the Trade Union and Labour Relations (Consolidation) Act 1992, although some provisions are based on the Redundancy Payments Act 1965. The law requires that you select people for redundancy fairly and also implement the redundancy fairly otherwise they may have a case for unfair dismissal. You must also consult employees, notify the Employment Service and compensate those made redundant.

Current UK legislation does not fully reflect the EU Collective Redundancies Directive or the Acquired Rights Directive. It is currently being changed to include, among other things, a requirement to consult even in non-unionised workplaces (see below).

(a) Consultation

An employer who proposes to make employees redundant, and who recognises an independent trade union for that group of employees, whether or not the individuals involved actually belong to the union, must consult with the union as soon as possible. If you find yourself in this situation, you should disclose to the union:

(i) The reasons why employees are redundant.

(ii) The numbers and descriptions of the jobs concerned.

(iii) The total number of employees of that description that you employ in that location.

(iv) The method you propose to use for selecting the particular employees who may be dismissed.

(v) The method that you propose to use for carrying out the dismissals and the time span over which they will take effect.

(vi) How you propose to calculate any non-statutory redundancy payments.

If the trade union makes suggestions, about how to reduce the number affected or lessen the impact, you should consider these carefully. If you reject them, give your reasons.

All this should be contained in your normal redundancy procedure, but you should note the time limits imposed by the Act. Where you propose to declare more than a hundred redundancies in a ninety-day period, this consultation must take place at least ninety days before the first of the dismissals is due to take effect. If you are proposing to make more than ten people redundant within a thirty-day period, you must consult the union at least thirty days in advance.

If you fail to comply with these requirements, the union can complain to an industrial tribunal. You will then have to show that you did everything practicable in the circumstances to comply with the requirements, but that it was not feasible for you to comply more fully. If you cannot show this, the tribunal may make a **protective award**, entitling each employee affected to normal pay during a protected period. The length of this protected period will vary according to the extent of your failure to meet the statutory requirements, but will not exceed ninety days for a redundancy involving a hundred or more, thirty days for a redundancy of ten or more people within thirty days, and twenty-eight days in other cases.

In non-unionised firms, consultation with employees should still take place if twenty or more are to be made redundant.

(b) Notification

The time limits we have just specified also apply to the requirement to use form HR1 to notify the Secretary of State, through the Employment Service, of your intention to make ten or more people redundant. If there is a trade union involved, you must state which union it is and when your consultations with them began. Even if there is no trade union involved, you must still make notification. If you don't, you may incur a fine of up to £5,000.

(c) Compensation

As far as the individual is concerned, the main provision is for compensation, according to the scale of redundancy payments set out in Unit 20.3. You do not need to make these payments if you are able to offer the employee suitable alternative employment, which he can take up within four weeks of the ending of his original contract. If you make such an offer, you must give the employee a trial period of at least four weeks. If either of you then feels the work is not suitable, the employee may leave on the same terms as would have applied under the original redundancy. If the employee unreasonably refuses the offer of alternative employment he forfeits his right to redundancy payment. To be suitable, the alternative employment should not involve a significant reduction in status or conditions. Other criteria will depend on the circumstances. Your only other legal obligations are to provide reasonable time off with pay to look for alternative work (see Unit 14.7) and to provide a written statement for the employee showing how the redundancy payment has been calculated.

The Act does not apply universally. Crown servants and members of the armed forces are among those covered by other provisions.

British law places considerable emphasis on financial compensation. Some of its detractors claim that, so far from encouraging labour mobility as originally envisaged, it hampers it by making redundancy too expensive for employers to declare. Other accusations (for example, that it gives people the financial resources to survive without working) have now been largely discredited. The size or existence of a redundancy payment has no effect upon motivation to work, job choice or length of time unemployed. The real difficulty with the system is held to be that it allows both employers and the state to 'buy people off', rather than thinking more carefully about the root causes and long-term effects of redundancy. Consultation goes some way towards countering this, but full participation of employers, employees and the state is really what is required.

Questions
1. What does 'redundancy' mean? What are the main causes of redundancy?
2. What alternatives to enforced redundancy might be available to an organisation, and how might it make best use of them?
3. What are the true costs of redundancy? How can they be minimised?
4. If your organisation had no alternative to making 300 of its employees redundant, how would you advise the management to set about implementing the redundancies in a way which pays due regard to all the interested parties?

UNIT 21

Dismissing Unsatisfactory Employees

21.1 Introduction

This second group of dismissals is equally fraught with pitfalls for the unwary. Your conduct here, too, is prescribed in outline by legislation and circumscribed by the reactions of individuals and of groups. Because of this some people seem to think that you can no longer get rid of unsatisfactory employees. In fact you can. But you must make every effort to ensure that there is no way of helping the employee to become a satisfactory one before you do so, and you must also make sure that you have acted fairly by him in all the circumstances.

You can, of course, go ahead and dismiss him without regard to any of these factors, in the hope that your employee will not know or exercise his rights under the Employment Protection (Consolidation) Act 1978 or the Employment Acts 1980, 1982 and 1988. If he does not complain to an industrial tribunal and bring the penalties described in Unit 21.4 down upon you, there is no other legal retribution that you can incur (unless the dismissal is also wrongful, in which case you may be sued for breach of contract). But, as in the case of redundancy, you will have the reactions of the rest of your workforce and their representatives to contend with.

21.2 Grounds for Dismissal

Under the Employment Protection (Consolidation) Act only those employees who had been continuously employed for sixteen or more hours per week for two years or more (or between eight and sixteen hours for five years or more) had the right to complain to an industrial tribunal if they felt they had been unfairly dismissed.

In 1994 the House of Lords ruled, in the case of *R.* v. *Secretary of State for Employment ex parte Equal Opportunities Commission*, that the limitations on part-timers' rights to claim unfair dismissal were incompatible with the EC Equal Treatment Directive. Since most part-timers are women, they suffered disproportionately from the exclusion from protection. The Employment Protection (Part-Time Employees) Regulations 1995 have now removed the restrictions. The legality of the two-year qualifying period has also been called into question. The Court of Appeal held in *R.* v. *Secretary of State for Employment, ex parte Seymour-Smith and Perez*, 1995, that during the

'It's really simple – make one mistake and you're fired.'

period from 1985–91 the two-year rule was indirectly discriminatory to women. They tended to hold jobs for shorter periods than men – so a considerably smaller proportion of them could comply with the two-year service requirement. Further legislation is likely, but for practical purposes it would be safest to treat the advice in this section as applying to **all** employees, regardless of hours worked or length of service.

(a) Unfair Dismissal

There are a number of circumstances in which dismissal will be unfair.

(i) Dismissing an employee because he is, or proposes to become, a member of an independent trade union (see Unit 18.2).

(ii) Dismissing him for taking part, at an appropriate time, in the activities of an independent trade union.

(iii) Dismissing him for refusing to become or remain a member of any trade union or to join a closed shop.

(iv) Dismissing him through alleged redundancy, where it can be shown that the employee was selected for trade union reasons or that an agreed redundancy selection procedure was not followed.

(v) Dismissing her because she is pregnant.

(vi) Dismissing anyone on the grounds of race, marital status or sex.

(vii) Dismissing anyone for seeking to assert a statutory employment protection right.

(viii) Dismissing an employee for exercising his rights in connection with health and safety (see Unit 17.4).

(ix) In certain circumstances dismissing a shop worker for refusing to work on a Sunday.

(b) Fair Dismissal

Dismissal will generally be fair if you can show it was for one of the following reasons:

(i) Because the employee is incapable, after training, other assistance, and fair warning, of performing his duties to the required, clearly defined, standard.

(ii) Because the employee has committed gross misconduct, knowing the consequence of his action; or because he has been guilty of repeated misconduct in spite of warnings and opportunities to improve.

(iii) Because it would be illegal to continue to employ him.

(iv) Because he is genuinely redundant.

(v) Because of some other substantial reason – which could include personality conflicts among employees or setting up in a part-time business in competition with the employer.

If you are to dismiss employees fairly for incompetence (capability) or misconduct, it is vital that you both have and implement a disciplinary procedure as described in Unit 19.5.

The test which an industrial tribunal applies to unfair dismissal complaints is whether the dismissal was reasonable in the circumstances – that is, whether the punishment fits the crime. The size and resources of the organisation may also be taken into consideration, though – so what would be reasonable for a small organisation might not be so for a large one.

A brief review of some past cases will serve to illustrate the way in which a tribunal may regard particular sets of circumstances. Remember that tribunal findings can still be overturned by the Employment Appeal Tribunal (EAT) (see Unit 18.6) or a higher court, if you choose to pursue them that far.

21.3 Case Histories

(a) Gross Misconduct

The case of *Trust House Forte (Catering) Ltd* v. *Adonis* 1984 clearly demonstrates the importance of establishing, beyond doubt, the penalties for particular behaviour. Mr Adonis had been employed by Trust House Forte for eight years. At the time of his dismissal he was employed as a head waiter at one of its prestigious London restaurants although, due to staff shortages, he was also performing some of the duties of a wine waiter. He was dismissed, after a disciplinary hearing, five days after being suspended for being found smoking under a no-smoking sign, beside a wine chute.

The fact that Mr Adonis was actually standing beside a no-smoking sign might be thought sufficient indication that a no-smoking rule was in force. In addition, the company had, only a few months previously, placed a notice on the staff notice-board stating that 'anyone caught smoking in the no-smoking areas will be dismissed for gross misconduct'. But Mr Adonis's own written particulars of employment, which had recently been reissued, stated only that smoking was regarded as misconduct which might result in dismissal if it failed to improve after a warning. In the light of this, and of the fact that Mr Adonis had been allowed to continue working until the end of the evening before being suspended, the tribunal and the EAT both decided that his breach of the no-smoking rule did not constitute gross misconduct and his dismissal was therefore unfair.

(b) The Reasonable Employer

The tribunal and the EAT in *Trust House Forte (Catering) Ltd* v. *Adonis* 1984 also took the view that the company should have taken into account Mr Adonis's long service and good conduct before deciding to dismiss him. In failing to do so, it did not pass the test of the 'reasonable employer'. Other examples of employers disregarding employees' previously unblemished records abound. In the *Post Office* v. *Ramkissoon* 1993, Mr Ramkissoon was dismissed for falsifying a medical certificate and claiming sick pay to which he was not entitled. He had twenty-three years' service and no disciplinary record. The tribunal and the EAT took the view that no reasonable employer would have dismissed an employee in those circumstances.

A somewhat unusual facet of this aspect of the law is illustrated by the case of *Payne* v. *Spook Erection Ltd* 1984. The EAT held that it was unreasonable to dismiss Mr Payne, a foreman, for refusing to operate a system of merit appraisal which was arbitrary and contrary to good industrial relations practice. The scheme required Mr Payne to compile a weekly table of merit, ranking the endeavour of each of his twenty-five employees – in spite of the fact that he did not see every employee each week. The assessment was based purely on the foreman's personal view, rather than any objective measurement. Those who found themselves at the bottom of the ranking would be notified to that effect in a 'letter of registration'. Further registration would lead to a written warning and, ultimately, dismissal. Mr Payne who had reluctantly participated in an earlier version of the scheme refused to operate this system. He persisted in his refusal despite several meetings to attempt to persuade him to change his mind, and was eventually dismissed. Although the industrial tribunal felt the dismissal was fair, the EAT took the view that the appraisal scheme was 'obviously and intolerably unfair, wholly unacceptable as a matter of good industrial relations practice, striking at the principles of employment protection legislation' – so Mr Payne was fully justified in refusing to operate it, and it was unreasonable to dismiss him.

(c) Failure to Follow Agreed Procedure

In *Polkey* v. *A. E. Drayton Services Ltd* 1987, the House of Lords emphasised the need for employers to follow fair procedures when dismissing employees, whether on grounds of redundancy or for other potentially fair reasons. Failure to do so, as in this case, when the employer's procedure for handling redundancy was not followed, may make the dismissal unfair. Only if the employer can show that adhering to the procedure would have been pointless in the circumstances is he likely to win.

(d) Inflexible Rules

While it is vital that rules be clearly promulgated and the penalties for breaking them consistently applied, complete inflexibility may also lead to a finding of unfair dismissal – as in the case of *Ladbroke Racing Ltd* v. *Arnott and others* 1983. The company (turf accountants) had a strict rule against employees placing bets at work. Breach of the rule always led to dismissal. In this particular instance, however, the employees concerned were placing bets for two retirement pensioners and a relative, rather than for themselves, and thought that they had authority to place the bets. The employer was found to have focused too inflexibly on the no-betting rule, without considering the circumstances.

(e) Criminal Activity

The case of *Securicor Guarding* v. *R.* 1994 highlights some of the pitfalls associated with dismissal for alleged offences outside the workplace. A security guard was dismissed after being charged by police with sexual offences against children alleged to have occurred years earlier. He denied the offences.

Securicor took the view that its client would not want him on its premises, and dismissed him – in spite of the fact that its own disciplinary code would have allowed for him to be suspended or moved to an area where there was no risk. This, combined with the fact that Securicor had not actually asked the client for its views, led the EAT to find the dismissal unfair. A charge of a serious offence which is denied by the employee is not, of itself, sufficient grounds for dismissal.

In the case of *British Home Stores* v. *Burchell* 1978, the company had reasonable grounds for believing that its employee had committed a criminal act at work, that of stealing. Dismissal after investigation was therefore fair, even though actual guilt had not been proved.

Where the employee is given a custodial sentence, the contract of employment may be brought to an end through what is known as **frustration**. In *F. C. Shepherd and Co.* v. *Jerrom* 1986, Mr Jerrom, an apprentice plumber, was sentenced to six months youth custody for his involvement in a gang fight away from work. On his release he asked for his job back, was refused, and claimed unfair dismissal. Eventually the Court of Appeal ruled that imprisonment had made performance of the contract impossible or radically different. Even if Mr Jerrom went back, the loss of six months of his training would mean he was a much less valuable employee.

(f) Duty to Investigate

In the case of *FMO Ltd* v. *Sutheran* 1994 the employee had received a final written warning about attendance and unauthorised absence. She subsequently became involved in a serious shop-floor quarrel, instigated by another employee. This stopped production and looked likely to lead to physical violence. The woman was dismissed.

The EAT found that the existence of a final written warning did not absolve the employer from his duty to investigate the incident thoroughly. He should have suspended her while a full investigation and disciplinary hearing were held.

(g) Strike Action

In *Mariner and others* v. *Domestic and Industrial Polythene Ltd* 1977, four women went home from work when they found that the temperature in their workplace was only 53°F and that there was no fuel oil for central heating purposes on the premises. They told the forewoman that they would go home and return the following day. This they duly did. On arrival next day, they were handed a letter which read: 'In view of your strike action today, we are therefore dismissing you. Please find enclosed all wages due . . .' Although a tribunal has no jurisdiction to hear a claim for unfair dismissal if there is a strike and all the strikers are treated alike, in this case the tribunal found:

(i) since the date of the dismissal was the day when the employees returned to work, the employer would have acted unfairly even if there had been a strike;

(ii) the action of the women concerned was, in any case, insufficiently serious to be called a strike. They were simply trying to put pressure on their employer while protecting themselves against the cold, rather than instigating a 'deliberate withdrawal of labour in such circumstances as amount to a breach of a contract of employment'.

(h) Sickness

In *East Lindsey District Council* v. *Daubney* 1977, Mr Daubney had been dismissed on medical grounds. He had been ill and absent from work for considerable periods and, in June 1975, the council's personnel director asked Dr Haigh, the district community physician, to indicate whether he felt that Mr Daubney's health was such that he should be retired on grounds of permanent ill health. Dr Haigh asked Dr O'Hagan, of the Lincolnshire Area Health Authority, to examine him. As a result of Dr O'Hagan's report to him, Dr Haigh wrote to inform the personnel director that he felt that Mr Daubney was unfit and should be retired. No one discussed this with Mr Daubney. The first he knew of it was his letter of dismissal. The industrial tribunal held that this was unfair because:

(i) the council had failed to obtain sufficient information about the actual state of Mr Daubney's health;

(ii) it had dismissed him without giving him the right to contend against his dismissal, or to seek an independent medical opinion. The Employment Appeal Tribunal subsequently dismissed the first of these reasons, but upheld the second. They felt that employers could not really be expected to set themselves up as medical experts, but that, nevertheless, the decision to dismiss or not to dismiss was not a medical question but a question to be answered by the employers in the light of the available medical advice and sensitive discussion with the employee.

Particular care must be taken when dealing with those suffering from alcohol dependency. In *Strathclyde Regional Council* v. *Syme* 1994, the council dismissed Syme from his post as a school janitor for being repeatedly drunk while on duty. Mr Syme was in fact a manic depressive with a drink problem.

The tribunal, and later the EAT, took the view that a reasonable employer would have attempted to obtain independent medical advice before dismissing him. In such cases, too, the employer would normally be expected to discuss the matter with the employee before deciding whether rehabilitation is feasible.

(i) Pregnancy

The case of *Webb* v. *EMO Air Cargo UK Ltd* went all the way to the European Court of Justice in 1994. Ms Webb was dismissed from her job when she told her employers she was pregnant. The situation was complicated by the fact that she was employed to cover for another employee who was about to take maternity leave, although her contract was for an indefinite period.

The employer argued successfully in the UK courts that in the same situation they would have treated a man who was unavailable for work through sickness in the same way. They argued that Ms Webb was dismissed not because she was pregnant but because the pregnancy would have prevented her carrying out the job she was contracted to perform.

The European Court of Justice decided that there are no grounds for comparing a woman who is incapacitated by pregnancy with a man who is incapable of work for medical reasons. It invoked an earlier decision in which it had ruled that dismissal on account of pregnancy constitutes direct discrimination. It referred the case back to the UK courts to determine how much compensation Ms Webb should receive.

(j) Maternity

Employees on maternity leave still have the right not to be unfairly dismissed. In the case of *Philip Hodges and Co.* v. *Kell* 1994, Mrs Kell was employed as a legal secretary. When she gave notice of her intention to return after maternity leave, she was told that her position as secretary to Mr Hodges was redundant. Work had declined following the loss of a client and her employer claimed there was no suitable alternative employment available.

The industrial tribunal, and subsequently the EAT, took the view that Mrs Kell was not solely Hodges' secretary but also worked for other people. A new full-time legal secretary had been recruited some six weeks before, during Mrs Kell's maternity leave. The EAT held that the post should have been offered to Mrs Kell. The dismissal was unfair.

(k) Sexual Harassment

The case of *Dixon Stores Group Ltd* v. *Dwan and O'Byrne* 1994 shows just what a minefield this can be. The two managers had been dismissed by Dixons for what was described as 'a particularly lewd act' at the office Christmas party. Apparently such behaviour was traditional on these occasions and the two were encouraged by a divisional director.

The company had, apparently, been trying to change this culture and to prevent sexual harassment, but the two men had never been advised that this sort of conduct, which had previously been tolerated, could now lead to dismissal. Despite the fact that a full investigation had taken place and a proper procedure followed, the EAT still found that the company's failure to communicate its changed attitude to harassment made the dismissal unfair.

(l) Constructive Dismissal

Where an employee resigns as a result of a breach of the contract of employment by the employer, he may claim that he has been **constructively dismissed**.

In *Lucas Service UK Ltd* v. *Cary* 1984, an employee who resigned at the end of an informal performance appraisal interview was found to have been constructively dismissed because the company had failed to follow the established disciplinary procedure for poor performers. Mr Cary was a sales representative whose sales were falling short of his target. Normal practice in this situation was to begin with an informal discussion and then, if matters did not improve, to invoke the disciplinary procedure – including allowing the employee to be represented by a friend or trade union official. (Adherence to the disciplinary procedure is a fundamental right established by the contract of employment.) In Mr Cary's case, however, there was no preliminary informal discussion, no formal hearing and no representation. Instead, Mr Cary was summoned at short notice without being told that he would be required to answer criticisms of his sales performance, and as the meeting went on, it assumed the character of a disciplinary interview. He resigned and claimed that the company's failure to follow the normal procedure was a breach of the contract of employment and that he had been constructively dismissed. The tribunal and the EAT upheld his claim. The test which was applied, and which was first enunciated in *Western Excavating EEC Ltd* v. *Sharp* 1976 in the Court of Appeal, was whether the employer had breached the terms and conditions of Mr Cary's contract of employment to such an extent as to justify Mr Cary's own repudiation of that contract.

The cases that we have quoted can do no more than give a brief glimpse of the kind of issues that weigh with tribunals in applying the legislation. If you would like to learn more about tribunals and how they operate, you can attend one locally. You can keep up to date with their findings on some of the more significant cases through reading various industrial relations periodicals, like the *Industrial Relations Review and Report*.

We have deliberately focused on dismissals which were found to be unfair. But remember, of the 42,757 cases initiated in 1993–4, nearly 13,000 were withdrawn and over 15,000 were settled by ACAS. Fewer than 6,000 actually succeeded. If your company has devised and implements a clear disciplinary procedure, following the ACAS code that we discussed in Unit 19, there should be no need for you to join the ranks of losing employers.

21.4   Penalties for Unfair Dismissal

An employee who feels that he has been unfairly or constructively dismissed may, as we have seen, complain to an industrial tribunal, within a set time-limit usually three months. The procedure is as we described in Unit 18.6. The remedies for unfair dismissal fall into two categories.

(a) Reinstatement or Re-engagement

If the employee so wishes, the tribunal can order that the employer takes him back into his employment. This can be by means of reinstatement in his original job, or re-engagement on terms and conditions of employment broadly similar to those which he previously enjoyed. The employer cannot argue that this is impracticable simply because he has engaged someone else to replace the dismissed employee, unless he can show that he had no alternative.

(b) Compensation

If an employer has been ordered to re-engage or reinstate someone and fails to do so, he will have to pay compensation, as detailed below. In addition, he will be required to pay an **additional award** of not less than thirteen weeks' pay and not more than twenty-six weeks', with a maximum (for 1995–6) of £210 per week. In cases where the original dismissal was on the grounds of race or sex discrimination, these amounts are doubled.

If the dismissed employee does not wish to be reinstated or re-engaged, or it would be impracticable, the tribunal can order that he is compensated for the fact of his dismissal. This compensation falls under two headings:

(i) **Basic award.**   This is related to length of employment, and is calculated on the same basis as a redundancy payment. So the effective maximum (for 1995–6) is £6,300. In cases where the dismissed employee also receives redundancy pay, this is deducted from the basic award.

(ii) **Compensatory award.**   This takes account of the actual loss suffered by the dismissed employee, attributable to the dismissal. The length of time for which he remains unemployed and such things as injury to health caused by the stress of the dismissal are taken into consideration. The maximum (for 1995–6) which a tribunal can award under this heading is £11,300.

If the employee is held by the tribunal to have contributed to his own dismissal, his compensation may be reduced to take account of this.

Those who have been dismissed on trade union related grounds are treated differently and may receive a **special award**, with (for 1995–6) a minimum of £2,770. Where reinstatement/re-engagement has been requested by the employee but not ordered by the tribunal, the minimum is one week's pay × 104 or £13,775, whichever is greater. The maximum is £27,500. Where it has been ordered, but the employer does not comply, the special award will be at least one week's pay × 156 or £20,600, whichever is greater. There is no upper limit in those cases.

21.5 Other Consequences

As we have seen, you may or may not have to answer a complaint before an industrial tribunal if you dismiss an employee. And you may or may not be daunted by the financial implications of conducting your case. But, if the dismissed employee is a member of a trade union, a dismissal which is felt by a person's workmates to be unfair could lead to industrial action. And the balance of industrial relations is occasionally so precarious, and the underlying power struggle so important, that a union may take up a case even if its members are aware that the dismissal was probably justified.

There is one other point to watch if you are involved in dismissing an employee. Although it does not affect the fairness or otherwise of your decision to dismiss, the employee is entitled, if he has more than two years' continuous service, to request a written statement of the reasons for his dismissal. If he does ask you for this or says anything which could be construed as asking for it ('Can you put it in writing?'), you must comply with his request within fourteen days. If you don't, a tribunal will order you to pay two weeks' wages as compensation. (Women dismissed during pregnancy or basic maternity leave must automatically be given such a statement.)

In the case of *Horsley Smith and Sherry Ltd* v. *Dutton* 1977, the EAT elaborated on what is required in such a written statement. 'The document must be of such a kind that the employee, or anyone to whom he may wish to show it, can know from reading the document itself, why he has been dismissed . . . there is no objection to its referring to other documents as well, provided that the document that the employee receives at least contains a simple statement of the essential reason for dismissal.' It is clear, from other cases, that the statement cannot be too simple. Just to say that the employee was dismissed on grounds of misconduct or of incapacity, for instance, is too vague. You need to spell out what he did wrong or where he fell short.

This statement can be used as evidence at a tribunal hearing, so it is never a good idea to falsify the information on it, even with the intention of helping the dismissed employee in his application for other jobs or state benefit, where he may be asked to show the statement. This may seem harsh, as the dismissed employee risks the same sort of emotional and other consequences as others during a period of unemployment. And even if his dismissal was perfectly fair and justified, he probably needs all the help he can get. But a mis-statement of the facts is likely to create more difficulties than it resolves.

Questions
1. On what grounds can an organisation fairly dismiss an employee?
2. Take three cases of unfair dismissal from recent tribunal findings. Where did the employers' faults lie in each case?
3. Describe the steps that you would take to ensure that all dismissals from your organisation could be upheld as fair by an industrial tribunal.

UNIT 22

Monitoring Employment

22.1   Introduction

We have now considered the main aspects of the employment process. The essential elements in what we have discussed might seem to be empowerment and a belief in the potential of human beings. But underpinning both of these is the need for a hard core of information. This is vital if we are to keep track of employees, individually and collectively, and to monitor the health of the organisation. Careful comparison of data, from one year to the next, between departments, between companies and against predictions, can help us to highlight ineffective personnel policies or procedures and enable us to make the most effective use of our resources.

22.2   Compiling Statistics

(a) Staffing Levels

You can count the number of people employed in particular categories or on particular types of work and use the figures for comparison and for employee utilisation studies. If some of those you employ work part-time, the equivalent number of **full-time employees** (FTEs) will be more helpful. Calculate this by totalling all the hours worked and dividing by the standard number of hours for a full-time employee. You can also identify **key staffing ratios**, such as direct:indirect labour, by using the formula:

$$\frac{\text{Number of employees or FTEs engaged in production}}{\text{Total number of employees or FTEs}} \times 100 = \begin{array}{l}\text{STAFFING} \\ \text{RATIO}\end{array}$$

(b) Productivity Indices

You can calculate these in terms of numbers of units or value of units produced in a given period. The formulae are:

$$\frac{\text{Total output in period}}{\text{Number of FTEs available}} = \text{units per FTE per period} \quad \begin{array}{l}\text{(OUTPUT} \\ \text{RATIO)}\end{array}$$

$$\frac{\text{Total value of output in period}}{\text{Number of FTEs available}} = \text{£ per FTE per period} \quad \begin{array}{l}\text{(VALUE OF} \\ \text{OUTPUT RATIO)}\end{array}$$

Another significant ratio, to help you judge whether you are reaching an adequate level of output from employees, can be arrived at by using the kind of value-added formulae we discussed in Unit 15.

(c) Current Staff Costs

We talked in Unit 1 about the component parts of the total payroll cost, but it is sometimes the relative figure which is important. A per capita figure can be arrived at using the formula:

$$\frac{\text{Annual payroll cost}}{\text{Average number employed in year}} = \text{AVERAGE PER CAPITA COST}$$

This will give you a more manageable statistic than simply totalling salaries, overtime, fringe benefits, administration costs and so on as raw figures. You can compare this figure with your output value figure, to see what sort of a return each employee is bringing you.

Other significant costing ratios will include the ratios of overtime to basic pay, of fringe benefits to total payroll and as a proportion of salary costs.

(d) Future Staff Costs

These can be arrived at by adjusting your present per capita cost to take account of likely levels of pay settlement, changes in benefits and government action in the field of national insurance, and then multiplying by your projected future number of employees. You can also identify changes in the other costing ratios that will result, provided that you can anticipate changes to the top line of the ratios as well as the bottom.

(e) Recruitment Costs

Again, a per capita figure for particular categories of employee will provide a useful yardstick. The component parts of this cost were discussed in Unit 1.3. You should use the formula:

$$\frac{\text{Total recruitment costs for category/department}}{\text{Total recruited for category/department}} = \frac{\text{PER CAPITA COST}}{\text{OF RECRUITMENT}}$$

This can also be refined to examine particular parts of the recruitment process, such as advertising costs.

(f) Training Costs

These too are more manageable on a per capita basis, divided either among all employees or only among those who actually received training during the period under review. You can also consider training costs in relation to value added, or as a proportion of payroll costs.

(g) Absence Rates

The basic formula here is:

$$\frac{\text{Number of employee hours lost in period}}{\text{Total possible employee hours in period}} \times 100 = \text{ABSENCE RATE}$$

You can refine this further, to highlight the proportion of certificated absence, the proportion of prolonged absence or the proportion of absence without explanation. You can also calculate an incidence rate (the average number of days lost per employee per year):

$$\frac{\text{Total days lost in period}}{\text{Total employees in period}} = \text{ABSENCE INCIDENCE RATE}$$

The mean duration of absences can be arrived at by:

$$\frac{\text{Number of employee hours lost in period}}{\text{Number of separate absences in period}} = \text{MEAN ABSENCE DURATION}$$

If a number of employees seem prone to absence for a particular complaint, you can calculate the hours lost through this cause as a percentage of all time lost.

(h) Accident Rates

The formulae are:

$$\frac{\text{Number of accidents in period}}{\text{Average number of employees in period}} \times 1,000 = \begin{array}{l}\text{ACCIDENT INCIDENCE}\\ \text{per 1,000 employees}\end{array}$$

$$\frac{\text{Number of accidents in period}}{\text{Number of employee hours worked in period}} \times 100,000 = \begin{array}{l}\text{ACCIDENT}\\ \text{FREQUENCY}\end{array}$$

$$\frac{\text{Number of employee hours lost in period}}{\text{Number of employee hours worked in period}} \times 100,000$$
$$= \text{ACCIDENT SEVERITY/LOST TIME INDEX}$$

$$\frac{\text{Number of employee hours lost through accidents in period}}{\text{Number of lost time accidents}}$$
$$= \text{MEAN ACCIDENT DURATION}$$

(The figure of 100,000 is used in calculating frequency and severity as this represents the total number of hours in an average working life.) Accident rates can also be studied further, to examine the incidence of accidents through particular causes, or of particular types of injury, and to distinguish between **lost time** (those which prevent the employee from continuing at work) and more minor accidents.

(i) Dispute and Grievance Rates

The number of hours lost through industrial disputes and other employee relations problems can be calculated in the same way as hours lost through other absences. The mean duration of stoppages can be arrived at by:

$$\frac{\text{Number of hours lost through stoppages in period}}{\text{Number of stoppages in period}}$$

$$= \text{MEAN DISPUTE AND GRIEVANCE DURATION}$$

The number of working days lost through such causes can be averaged out over the number of employees. Costs, rather than time, can be brought into the picture by examining the costs of stoppages in relation to payroll costs. You can also view your disputes and grievances in a more positive light, and register the proportion of them that are settled at each stage in the relevant procedure.

These formulae, together with the stability and labour turnover indices that we discussed in Unit 1 and the skills inventories and succession plans which we considered in Units 2.3 and 11.5 respectively, should help you to monitor and control employee costs and employee numbers. The basic principles are clear and can be applied over a much wider range to tell you almost anything you need to know about your employees. The results of your investigations and calculations can be presented as graphs and histograms, to highlight trends and problem areas graphically. But a word of warning in using your statistics. As with any statistical data, you must ensure that you are comparing like with like. This means that you must take account of external variables, and that you cannot compare the results of a calculation obtained using one formula with the results of a calculation obtained by using a different formula.

22.3 Data Protection

Calculating such statistics is obviously much quicker if it is computerised. There are special rules regarding the computerised personal information on which such statistics may be based. These are contained in the Data Protection Act 1984.

If you wish to keep personal data on a computer you must register with the Data Protection Registrar and give him details including what sort of data you wish to store and to what uses it will be put. 'Data subjects', that is the people whose details you wish to store, have a right to inspect the information kept about them. Information which is intended only for payroll purposes or where individuals are not separately identified is exempted.

Any data stored about employees must conform to a set of Data Protection Principles. These include:

(i) the data should have been obtained legally;

(ii) it should only be held for the purpose(s) you have specified;

(iii) it should not be used or disclosed in a manner incompatible with the specified purpose(s);

(iv) you will only hold enough data to achieve the specified purpose(s) and won't hold it for longer than is necessary;

(v) you will keep the information accurate and up to date;

(vi) you will take appropriate security measures to safeguard it;

(vii) you will tell employees that you hold the data and how they can get access to it.

22.4   And Finally

In managing people, as in every other sphere of management, measurement is vital. Yet it is not always necessary for this to be done **by** management. Some of the measures suggested here will be at least as relevant to your team as they are to you. Secrecy, in measurement as in other matters, breeds suspicion and fear and kills all sense of empowerment.

Encourage your people to keep track of the information that helps them to improve what they do and how they do it. Give them the tools to do it visibly and intelligibly. They **may** need PCs or other technological aids. It is quite likely, though, that they will be able to plot the trends and monitor progress on wallcharts and clipboards for all to see.

Once you are all in the habit of regularly reviewing current reality in relation to your goals, you will find it that much easier to see how best to move forward.

Questions

1. Select six formulae which would help you to monitor the effectiveness of your organisation's personnel policies and procedures.
2. Explain why you have chosen these formulae and how you would use them.

Suggested Further Reading

Assessment Centres
Woodruffe, Charles: *Assessment Centres, Identifying and Developing Competence*. Institute of Personnel and Development (London, 2nd edn, 1994).

Coaching
Whitmore, John: *Coaching for Performance*. Nicholas Brealey Publishing Ltd (London, 1992).

Communications
Blakstad, Michael and Cooper, Aldwyn: *The Communicating Organisation*. Institute of Personnel and Development (London, 1995).

Competences
Weightman, Jane: *Competencies in Action*. Institute of Personnel and Development (London, 1994).

Contracts of Employment
Aikin, Olga: *Contracts*. Institute of Personnel and Development (London, 1992).

Counselling
Megranahan, Michael: *Counselling, A practical guide for employers*. Institute of Personnel and Development (London, 1989).

Discipline
James, Philip and Lewis, David: *Discipline*. Institute of Personnel and Development (London, 1992).

Discrimination
Clarke, Linda: *Discrimination*. Institute of Personnel and Development (London, 1994).

Employment Law
Croner's Reference Book for Employers. (Available from Croner Publications, London Road, Kingston on Thames, Surrey KT2 6SR.)
Lewis, David: *Essentials of Employment Law.* Institute of Personnel and Development (London, 4th edn, 1994).

General Management
Peters, Tom: *Liberation Management.* Macmillan (London, 1992).
Semler, Ricardo: *Maverick.* Century (London, 1993).

Health and Safety
Heinrich, H. W.: *Industrial Accident Prevention: a Scientific Approach.* McGraw-Hill (Maidenhead, 1980). (O.P.)
Hitchcock, Teresa: *Health and Safety.* Institute of Personnel and Development (London, 1995).

Human Resource Planning
Bramham, John: *Human Resource Planning.* Institute of Personnel and Development (London, 2nd edn, 1994).

Industrial Tribunals
Greenhalgh, Roger: *Industrial Tribunals.* Institute of Personnel and Development (London, 2nd edn, 1995).

Interviewing
Hackett, Penny: *The Selection Interview.* Institute of Personnel and Development (London, 1995).
Hackett, Penny: *Interview Skills Training: Practice Packs for Trainers.* Institute of Personnel and Development (London, 3rd edn, 1991).

Monitoring Employment
Bee, Roland and Frances: *Management Information Systems and Statistics.* Institute of Personnel and Development (London, 1990).

Motivation
Handy, Charles: *Understanding Organisations.* Penguin (Harmondsworth, 3rd edn, 1986).
Herzberg, F.: *Work and the Nature of Man.* Crosby Lockwood (St Albans, 1975). (O.P.)
Robertson, Ivan, Smith, Mike and Cooper, Dominic: *Motivation: Strategies, theory and practice.* Institute of Personnel and Development (London, 1992).

Negotiating
Fowler, Alan: *Negotiation: Skills and Strategies.* Institute of Personnel and Development (London, 1990).

Pay

Armstrong, Michael and Balon, Angela: *The Job Evaluation Handbook*. Institute of Personnel and Development (London, 1992).

Cannell, Michael and Wood, Stephen: *Incentive Pay: Impact and Evolution*. Institute of Personnel and Development (London, 1992).

Cross, Michael and Cannell, Michael (eds): *Skills-based Pay, a guide for practitioners*. Institute of Personnel and Development, Issues Series.

Incomes Data Services: *Pay and Benefits*. A European Management Guide available from the Institute of Personnel and Development (London, 1992).

Palmer, Steve (ed): *Determining Pay: A guide to the issues*. Institute of Personnel and Development (London, 1990).

Performance Appraisal

Fletcher, Clive: *Appraisal: Routes to Improved Performance*. Institute of Personnel and Development (London, 1993).

Performance Management

Neale, Frances (ed): *The Handbook of Performance Management*. Institute of Personnel and Development (London, 1992).

Walters, Mike: *Performance Management*. Institute of Personnel and Development (London, 1995).

Recruitment and Selection

Courtis, John: *Recruitment Advertising, Right First Time*. Institute of Personnel and Development (London, 1994).

Hackett, Penny: *Choosing the Players*. Institute of Personnel and Development (London, 1994).

Herriot, Peter: *Recruitment in the 90s*. Institute of Personnel and Development (London, 1989).

Redundancy

Fowler, Alan: *Redundancy*. Institute of Personnel and Development (London, 1993).

Stress

Cranwell-Ward, Jane: *Managing Stress*. Pan (London, 1987).

Teams

Belbin, R. Meredith: *Management Teams: Why They Succeed or Fail*. Butterworth Heinemann (1981).

Hardingham, Alison and Royal, Jenny: *Pulling Together: Teamwork in Practice*. Institute of Personnel and Development (London, 1994).

Testing

Toplis, John, Dulewicz, Victor and Fletcher, Clive: *Psychological Testing, a Manager's Guide*. Institute of Personnel and Development (London, 2nd edn, 1991).

Total Quality Management

Price, Frank: *Right First Time. Using quality control for profit*. Gower (Aldershot, 1984).

Wheatley, Malcolm: *Understanding Just in Time in a Week*. British Institute of Management/Hodder & Stoughton (Sevenoaks, 1992).

Trade Unions

Farnham, David: *Employee Relations*. Institute of Personnel and Development (London, 1992).

Pope, Colin and Ellis, Peter: *Working with the Unions*. Institute of Personnel and Development (London, 1995).

Training and Development

Harrison, Rosemary: *Employee Development*. Institute of Personnel and Development (London, 1992).

Reid, Margaret Ann and Barrington, Harry: *Training Interventions*. Institute of Personnel and Development (London, 4th edn, 1994).

Index

Note. Numbers in **bold** type indicate a figure on the page.